To Kathryn and Daniel,

candida vita mea

CONTENTS

THE EDITION AND TRANSLATION 64/65

FOREWORD

   The modern interpretation of the musical Middle Ages hinges upon our knowledge of the theoretical works that have survived. Were all the treatises now before us and were we able to read them with accuracy, our understanding would be very greatly increased. Alas, relatively few documents have survived perfectly, and (the truth be known) not all of us have the ability to read them with great accuracy. What a happy event it is then, that a major treatise long known to the community of medievalists is now presented in a critical Latin edition that includes a careful translation with complete scholarly apparatus and an insightful introductory essay.
   It is a source of great pleasure for me to introduce this remarkable work. My good friend and colleague Jeremy Yudkin has selected one of the most important medieval music treatises for study and translation. The treatise is actually a didactic poem accompanied by a prose commentary with interlinear glosses. Modelled after the treatise of Johannnes de Garlandia, it discusses the great notational issues of the thirteenth-century *musica mensurabilis* and offers new and precise details surrounding the performance of discant, copula, organum, hocket, and motet. The many musical examples add to the clarity of the presentation, a welcome event in the environment of medieval texts, where clarity seems always to be at a premium. This work is destined to be influential in arousing, sustaining, and to a certain extent satisfying our interest and curiosity about that artistically important and generative period during which the later course of Western music was determined.

Thomas Binkley
Early Music Institute
Indiana University School of Music

ACKNOWLEDGEMENTS

It is heartening in this era of hard realities and straitened circumstances to find out how much support can be garnered for a specialized project of this scope and magnitude. It could not even have been undertaken without a generous grant from the National Endowment for the Humanities, an organization funded by the United States government and supported by the advice and professional judgment of countless scholars throughout the country. The Endowment provided me with a Fellowship which allowed me to devote an entire academic year to the initial preparation of the edition, including a sojourn in Munich to study the manuscript at first hand.

In Munich I was the recipient of the generosity and learning of the members of the staff of the Bayerische Staatsbibliothek, especially Dr. Hermann Hauke of the Handschriftenabteilung of that magnificent library. It was a privilege to become, for those few weeks, his close colleague.

From the very beginning Michel Huglo has been an enthusiastic supporter, knowledgeable interlocutor, and occasional mealtime companion. He sent me the facsimile of a chant I could not locate and copies of two lengthy and highly pertinent articles long before their submission for publication, in addition to a stream of correspondence on matters ranging from codicology to Bavarian monastic orders.

The complex work on the introductory essay was helped by consultation with a number of scholars, most particularly Eleonore Stump of the Virginia Polytechnic Institute, Craig Wright of Yale University, John Baldwin of the Johns Hopkins University, and Jan Ziolkowski of Harvard University. With all of these I had lengthy and enlightening conversations and fruitful correspondence. I thank them sincerely for their time and their generosity.

During this latter phase of the work I was a member of the Society of Fellows of Boston University. I am grateful to the other members of the Society for their stimulating contributions to our meetings and to the university for the honor of this appointment.

Two graduate assistants, Alice Garrett and Teresa Neff, helped me at various stages with philological and bibliographical problems: locating rare dictionaries, filling in order forms, tracking down manuscript sigla, and reminding me to return books on time. I am grateful to them both.

Members of the staff at the Indiana University Press have toiled long and hard to present the complex elements of this book in the clearest and most useful format. I am particularly grateful to Natalie Wrubel, the music editor, and to Marita Link, who transformed awkwardly formatted floppy disks into clean, clear pages. Her work was partially supported by a grant from the Graduate School of Boston University.

Every single one of the nearly two hundred musical examples was painstakingly drawn (several times) into the computer by Andrew Hughes. As if this were not enough, he also wrote and ran the program that would allow me to compile the unusually complex and detailed Index Verborum. It will take me a while to repay his generosity in bottles of beer.

Thomas Binkley is editor of this remarkable series. Over the last ten years we have collaborated on a number of very disparate projects. I look forward to more of the same kinds of unique challenges and rewards that every interaction with him brings.

My parents, Milly and John Yudkin, have not only been unfailingly supportive in the best tradition of parents, but have provided direct, specific, and knowledgeable assistance at every stage of the work.

My wife, Kathryn, has tolerated the intensity and duration of this project with understanding and enthusiasm; and my son Daniel arrived during its initial stages. It is to them both that this book is dedicated.

INTRODUCTION

The musical treatise by the author known for many years as the Anonymous of St. Emmeram (from the recent provenance of the manuscript) is a central document of thirteenth-century music theory. It is not only one of the few detailed discussions of the music of the Notre Dame school to have survived, but is also one of the longest and most comprehensive musical treatises of the middle ages to have been written up to its time. The work comprises approximately fifty thousand words, while the treatises of Johannes de Garlandia, Lambertus, and Anonymous IV contain about five thousand, eight thousand, and twenty-two thousand words respectively. Even the monumental *De Institutione Musica* of Boethius stands at approximately thirty-five thousand words.

But it is not only in sheer length that the treatise is remarkable. For it is written in a style unlike that of any other important musical treatise, though it is a style which captures the essence of a long tradition of medieval thought and exegesis. The work is cast as a prose commentary upon a didactic poem written in leonine hexameters. The poem is complex, epigrammatic, and dense. The commentary, by contrast, is leisurely, detailed, rich, and expansive. A further level of elucidation is provided by interlinear glosses. These provide synonyms or explanations for single words or phrases within the poem, or brief additional comments upon a line or two of the verse.

The standard model for this kind of work was of course provided by biblical exegesis, in which the words of scripture are given a commentary, usually exceeding the original in length by several times; and interlinear glosses translate, suggest synonyms for, or otherwise elucidate individual words or phrases.[1] That this became the common

---

[1] The canonical example was the twelfth-century biblical *Glossa Ordinaria*, consisting of the collected commentaries of the Fathers of the Church. In the thirteenth century the Bolognese *Glossa Ordinaria* on the law became the standard summary of all legal commentators up to that time. See John Baldwin, *Masters, Princes, and Merchants: The Social Views of Peter the Chanter and His Circle*, 2 vols. (Princeton, 1970), especially vol. 1, pp. 29, 48, and 91-92; and Giulio Silano, "Glossators," in *Dictionary of the Middle Ages*, vol. 5 (New York, 1985), pp. 565-568.

form for scholarly work is shown by thousands of manuscripts from Augustine to Aquinas and beyond. It was used by both Jewish and Christian commentators since the early middle ages, and in both Jewish and Christian scholarship the commentary of important sages became crystallized itself into the basis for further commentary. It was a form of learning which spread outwards from biblical exegesis to pervade all scholarly disciplines,[2] which fostered the profound and far-reaching concept of *auctoritas,* and which ultimately affected university teaching for many hundreds of years. Lecture notes from the late fifteenth century still display the time-honored format: *littera, commentum,* and *glossae.* The original text *(littera)* is written in heavy script in the center of the page. In fine writing (often produced with the back of the quill) the glosses appear above many of the words and between the lines of the original. Surrounding the text, and sometimes spilling into the margins, is the copious commentary. Heading each section of commentary, underlined or in heavy script, are the opening few words or *incipit* of the text to be discussed.[3]

The pervasiveness of this technique would lead us to believe that the present treatise is the product of at least two men: the author of the original didactic poem (the *auctoritas*), and the commentator. In fact, as will be shown, the format is deceptive. Both *littera* and *commentum* are by the same author. The form is indeed a deliberately fictive one, in which the tension is exploited between expectation and fulfillment, supposedly divergent or interactive points of view are appropriated by a single source, and the reconciliation of doctrines (the central aim of Scholasticism) becomes unexpectedly easy. The result is a particularly rich and textured whole, a façade that reflects the design of its interior.[4]

The author makes plain his clever scheme at the outset:

> Immo utens consilio magistrorum quorum vestigia sum
> secutus, prosae venerabilis practicam partim et theoricam

---

[2]Examples of glossed manuscripts abound. Some spectacular items include New York, Columbia University, X 88 Ar 512, a Latin Aristotle from Paris of c. 1300 glossed by several different hands; Paris, Bibliothèque Nationale, lat. 8422, a glossed *Doctrinale* of Alexander of Villedieu from 1276; and the commentary of Rhabanus Maurus on a curious cruciform poem concerning the cherubim and seraphim reproduced in *Patrologia Latina,* vol. CVII, pp. 163-166. I am grateful to Michel Huglo, Marie-Thérèse d'Alverny, and Joseph Dyer respectively for drawing my attention to these items.

[3]The way the technique of glossing affected the layout and design of manuscripts in the twelfth and thirteenth centuries has been discussed by Malcolm Parkes in his essay "The Influence of the Concepts of *Ordinatio* and *Compilatio* on the Development of the Book," in *Medieval Learning and Literature: Essays Presented to Richard William Hunt* (Oxford, 1976). Several useful plates illustrate the varieties and development of glossed texts.

[4]Cf. Erwin Panofsky, *Gothic Architecture and Scholasticism* (Latrobe, Pennsylvania, 1951; reprint, New York, 1957).

> sub quadam capitulorum serie divisionis sententia
> declarata, prout ingenioli mei paupertas exigit, propono
> metrice compilare, quia carmen metrice compilatum ad
> retinenda levius mentes excitat auditorum;
> unde quidam:
> *Metra iuvant animos, comprendunt plurima paucis,*
> *Pristina* etc.
>
> (Prologus 64,23 - 66,2)

> (Rather, using the judgement of the teachers in whose
> footsteps I have followed, I propose to put together in
> verse the theory and in part the practice of the revered
> prose work in a certain sequence of chapters and with the
> meaning of the method of division stated, as the poverty
> of my feeble intellect allows; because a poem put
> together in verse more easily stimulates the minds of
> those who are hearing it to remember; whence it is that
> someone said:
> "Verse meters help minds, for then they understand very
> many new things in few words," etc.)

The interior quotation is a proverb that reflects the view of generations of schoolteachers and theorists from Classical times to the thirteenth century (and indeed until our own day):[5] verse is a mnemonic device.

The use of verse for didactic purposes came strongly into vogue in the twelfth and thirteenth centuries.[6] Grammar, law, medicine, theology,

---

[5]Generations of British schoolboys learned their Latin grammar (not to mention their morality) from the "memorial lines" of *Kennedy's Latin Primer*. For example:

> To Nouns that cannot be declined
> The Neuter Gender is assigned:
> Examples *fas* and *nefas* give
> And the Verb-Noun Infinitive:
> *Est summum nefas fallere:*
> Deceit is gross impiety.

(*Kennedy's Revised Latin Primer* [London, 1962], p. 221.)

[6]Two little-known examples of versified music treatises from a somewhat later period are contained in Erfurt, Wissenschaftliche Bibliothek der Stadt, Ca 8° 94, folios 70v-71, and Rome, Biblioteca Apostolica Vaticana, Regin. lat. 1146, folios 47-48. The former begins with the leonine hexameter:

> Ars discantandi datur hic et dulcisonandi . . .

the latter:

> Discantare volens normas istas bene seques.

These treatises are listed in the "Verzeichnis der Handschriften und Texte" of Klaus-Jürgen Sachs, *Der Contrapunctus im 14. und 15. Jahrhundert: Untersuchungen zum Terminus, zur Lehre und zu den Quellen,* Beihefte zum Archiv für Musikwissenschaft XIII (Wiesbaden, 1974).

sermons, and even the Bible were rendered in verse.[7]   There were
treatises which gave directions and provided exercises and examples for
would-be versifiers -- treatises such as the *Ars Versificatoria* of
Matthew of Vendôme,[8] Gervase of Melkley's *Ars Versificaria*,[9] or Geoffrey
of Vinsauf's *Poetria Nova*.[10]   Some of these *artes poeticae* were
themselves written in verse, and Matthew's treatise also provides the
opportunity for a polemic against the poet and *glossator* Arnulf of
Orleans.[11]

    Amongst the most famous didactic treatises in verse were the
Doctrinale of Alexander of Villedieu,[12] an account of the morphology and
syntax of the Latin language, and its counterpart, the *Graecismus* of

---

[7] See R. R. Bolgar, *The Classical Heritage and Its Beneficiaries*
(Cambridge, 1954), pp. 208-211; and Jan Ziolkowski, *Alan of Lille's
Grammar of Sex: The Meaning of Grammar to a Twelfth-Century
Intellectual*, Speculum Anniversary Monographs X (Cambridge,
Massachusetts, 1985), pp. 71-72.   Ziolkowski writes that in the twelfth
century "versification was a habit that bordered on a mania." (*op. cit.*,
p. 71)

[8] Edition: Edmond Faral, *Les arts poétiques du XIIe et du XIIIe
siècle* (Paris, 1924; reprint, 1971).   Translation: Roger Parr, *Matthew
of Vendôme: Ars Versificatoria (The Art of the Versemaker)*, Mediaeval
Philosophical Texts in Translation XXII (Milwaukee, 1981).

[9] Edition: Hans-Jürgen Grabner, "Ars Poetica," in *Forschungen zur
Romanischen Philologie* XVII (Münster, 1965).

[10] Edition: Edmond Faral, *Les arts poétiques*.   Translation:
Margaret Nims, *Poetria Nova of Geoffrey of Vinsauf* (Toronto, 1967).

[11] See Parr, *Matthew of Vendôme*, pp. 8-13.

[12] The *Doctrinale* is made up of two thousand six hundred and
forty-five lines, filled with examples of numbers, genders, cases,
declensions, tenses, conjugations, meters, accents, and figures of
speech.   The standard critical edition is Dietrich Reichling, *Das
Doctrinale des Alexander de Villa-Dei*, Monumenta Germaniae Paedagogica,
Schulordnungen, Schulbücher und pädagogische Miscellaneen XII (Berlin,
1893).
    The following couplet may exemplify the procedure:
        Pluralem numerum retinent *aes* atque *metallum;*
        raro per reliqua dabitur plurale *metalla*.
                        (ll. 395-396)
The verse grammar remained in use in France until the late sixteenth
century.   (See R. R. Bolgar, *The Classical Heritage*, p. 209.)
    Distinct echoes of the *Doctrinale* may be heard in the present music
treatise.   Cf. *Doctrinale* ll. 19, 22, 253-4, 309, 411, 530, 787, 841-2,
845, 857, 1080, 1150-1151, 1160, 1171, 1237-1238, 1365-1368, 1374-1377,
1555-1556, 1602, 1793, 2192, 2282, 2321, 2330-2331, 2528, 2550, and the
devout *explicit* (2642-2645).

Evrard of Béthune.[13] Both of these became immensely popular, appearing in hundreds of manuscripts from the thirteenth to the fifteenth centuries, and continuing even into a printed existence.[14] The *Doctrinale* is written in hexameters, the *Graecismus* in a mixture of metrical schemes, but both depend heavily upon the type of rhyming hexameter verses which were known as leonines.[15]

Our author has also written a verse treatise in leonine hexameters, but the novelty of his didactic method (supplying both the "inner" verse text and the layers of commentary) is disguised by a double appeal to authority. His *magistri,* his teachers, judge verse to be the most efficient vehicle for learning,[16] and so he writes in verse. But the content is based upon *auctoritas,* upon the "venerable" prose work of none other than Johannes de Garlandia, the author of the most influential treatise on the styles and notational and rhythmic systems of the new

---

[13] Ed. Johann Wrobel, Corpus grammaticorum medii aevi, vol. 1 (Breslau, 1887). The *Graecismus* is in twenty-seven chapters, treating such subjects as nouns, pronouns, figures of speech, interjections and the like. It is approximately contemporary with the Doctrinale (c. 1200).

[14] See Reichling, *Das Doctrinale,* pp. clxix-cccix; and R. R. Bolgar, *The Classical Heritage,* p. 420.

[15] Discussions of *leonitas* may be found in Ernst Robert Curtius, *European Literature and the Latin Middle Ages,* trans. Willard Trask, Bollingen Series XXXVI (New York, 1953), p. 151; Dag Norberg, *Introduction à l'étude de la versification latine médiévale,* Acta Universitatis Stockholmiensis, Studia Latina Stockholmiensia V (Uppsala, 1958), pp. 39-40, 65-66; and Paul Klopsch, *Einführung in die mittellateinische Verslehre* (Darmstadt, 1972), pp. 76-77 (where a wonderful example of a Virgilian hexameter transformed into a leonine is given). Eponymous contenders for the origin of the name for this form of verse have ranged from the Parisian canon Leonius (Jean Lebeuf, *Histoire de la ville et de tout le diocèse de Paris,* [Paris, 1755-58; reprint 1883]; to the mid-twelfth century poet Leo (Charles Du Cange [ed.], *Glossarium Mediae et Infimae Latinitatis,* 7 vols. [Paris, 1840-50], *s. v. Leonini*); to the fifth-century Pope Leo the Great (Curtius, *European Literature and the Latin Middle Ages,* trans. Trask, p. 151). The term appears to have come into general use in the early eleventh century. (See Carl Erdmann, "Leonitas: Zur mittelalterlichen Lehre von Kursus, Rhythmus und Reim," in 'Corona Quernea': *Festgabe Karl Strecker zum 80. Geburtstage dargebracht* [Leipzig, 1941], pp. 15ff. [cited in Norberg, *Introduction,* p. 39, fn. 6].)

[16] This was a common belief: see Eberhard of Béthune, *Graecismus* (ed. Wrobel, p. ix); Leoninus, *Hystorie Sacre,* lines 1-8 (quoted in Craig Wright, "Leoninus, Poet and Musician," *Journal of the American Musicological Society* XXXIX [1986]: 18); and the proverb quoted in the the present treatise (*Prologus* 66, 1-2). (Throughout this book references are to chapter, page, and line number of the Latin edition: *Prologus, Cap.V,* etc. -- or of the English translation: Prologue, Chap.V, etc.)

polyphony.[17] "Venerabilis" is a word that implies both longevity and respect, as its cognate does in English, and it is used rarely in our treatise, and then only in connection with Garlandia or the author's immediate teacher, about whom more will be said later.

The treatise also incorporates elements of the *quaestio,* that form of investigation through argumentation which was a popular tool of the Scholastic system.[18] The *quaestio* is recognized by its formulaic elements: *Quaeritur utrum* ("The question is whether"), *videtur quod* ("it seems that"), *sed contra* ("but on the other hand"), *respondemus dicentes* ("we answer, saying"), *ad primum* ("to the first argument"), *ad secundum* ("to the second argument"), and *sciendum est* ("it should be known that"). Much thirteenth-century scholarly writing is informed by the *quaestio* method, including that masterpiece of theology, the *Summa Theologica* of Thomas Aquinas, which was produced in Paris in the 1270s.

Similar in technique to the *quaestio,* the formal classroom genre of the *disputatio* involved the marshalling of arguments on both sides of the question, and the ultimate reconciliation of the case.[19] The *disputatio* was strongly influenced by the infiltration of dialectic into university disciplines in the twelfth and thirteenth centuries and the obsession with, resistance to, and final triumph of Aristotelianism in Paris.[20] Our music treatise reflects the use of the *disputatio* genre in its argumentation over several controversial issues, especially those concerning the notation and interpretation of ligatures.

However the most immediate impetus for the composition of the treatise was provided by the appearance of the work of Lambertus, with whom our author disagrees in several theoretical respects, and against whom the treatise is directed as a thinly-disguised diatribe. Even without his being named, Lambertus may easily be discovered as the target of attack, for the objectionable doctrines are discussed in full, sometimes even quoted, and may be traced to the Lambertus treatise, which also survives.[21] But Lambertus is in fact named, once in the poem and

---

[17]Another music theorist, possibly also from the later thirteenth century, who may have written a treatise with commentary based on Garlandia's work was Roger Caperon. See James Haar, "Roger Caperon and Ramos de Pareia," *Acta Musicologica* XLI (1969): 26-36. Similar in content to Caperon's treatise, but written in verse with a commentary, is the *Flores Musice* of Hugo von Reutlingen (*art. cit.,* fn. 15).

[18]See John Baldwin, *Masters, Princes, and Merchants,* vol. 1, pp. 13, 96-97; and Anders Piltz, *The World of Medieval Learning,* trans. David Jones (Totowa, 1981), pp. 87-89, 186-188.

[19]See Baldwin, *Masters, Princes, and Merchants,* vol. 1, pp. 96-101.

[20]See my paper, "The Influence of Aristotle on French University Music Texts," which is to appear in the proceedings of the conference "Musical Theory and Its Sources: Antiquity and the Middle Ages," held at the University of Notre Dame, Indiana, April 30 - May 2, 1987.

[21]See Charles de Coussemaker, *Scriptorum de musica medii aevi nova series* I (Paris, 1864), pp. 251-280. Gilbert Reaney is engaged upon the production of a new edition of the treatise.

once in the prose commentary,[22] so that there may remain no doubt or
ambiguity as to the identity of the offender. The opening words of the
present treatise are a deliberate imitation in Latin of the beginning of
the *Tractatus* of Lambertus (and indeed both may have served as a model
for Franco):[23]

Lambertus	*Anon. 1279*
Quoniam circa artem	Quoniam prosam artis
musicam necessaria	musicae mensurabilis ab
quedam ad utilitatem	excellentibus in arte
cantantium tractare	musicis compilatam, quam
proponimus, necesse	etiam clericorum universi-
est . . .	tas . . .
(P *1*, 1)[24]	(*Prologus* 64, 1-3)

The work of Lambertus served as the most important forerunner for the
treatise of Franco, for Lambertus established the primacy of the perfect
long, the significance of individual ligature shapes, and the precise
indication of the length of rests, all of which are fundamental to the
new Franconian mensural doctrine. In accordance with his insistence upon
the triple long as perfect and with the newer motet repertory of the
time, Lambertus posited a system of nine rhythmic modes instead of the
usual six, beginning with the standard Mode 5 (all perfect longs), and
adding three modes which incorporated the new semibreve length. In the
context of thirteenth-century developments, therefore, Lambertus may be
seen as an innovator of considerable (and, so far, insufficiently
appreciated)[25] significance, and he is cited approvingly in the *Speculum
Musicae* of Jacques de Liège (c. 1300).[26]

It is in his attacks upon Lambertus that the author of the present
treatise, ostensibly a traditionalist and preserver of the past, is at

---

[22]See *Prologus* 74, 3:

Arte nova rapti Lamberti nunc ita capti.

and *Cap.Iii* 148, 3-4:

Unde magister Lambertus de tali figura dicit . . .

[23]See the *loci paralleli* to this passage. The "Quoniam" opening was
a favorite device of thirteenth-century arts treatises. See the table of
incipits in Palémon Glorieux, *La Faculté des arts et ses maîtres au xiiie
siècle,* Etudes de philosophie médiévale LIX (Paris, 1971), especially pp.
539-542.

[24]All citations and quotations from Lambertus are according to the
new edition by Gilbert Reaney and André Gilles.

[25]See, however, Wolf Frobenius, "Zur Datierung von Francos Ars
Cantus Mensurabilis," *Archiv für Musikwissenschaft* XXVII (1970): 122-127;
and Rebecca Baltzer, "Lambertus," in *The New Grove Dictionary of Music
and Musicians,* vol. 10, (London, 1980), pp. 400-401.

[26]*See Jacobi Leodiensis Speculum Musicae,* ed. Roger Bragard, Corpus
Scriptorum de Musica III ([n. p.], 1973), Book VII: Chapter I, 5 (p. 5),
Chapter 5, 8 (p. 12), Chapter 11, 5 (p. 26).

his most colorful, for he indulges in both vitriolic invective and learned allusion. In a brilliant display of *expositio*[27] he refers to the famous Classical myth of Io, alternately comparing Lambertus to Argus, the watchman, and Mercury, the winged messenger. At other times Lambertus is opposed by clear and tenacious argument and refutation, or vilified as a wilful and destructive pillager of the past.

In one respect our author is in fact indebted to Lambertus, for already in the earlier treatise verses are used to enliven the prose text, as in the following couplet (expressing a central doctrine):

> Ante vero longam, tria tempora longa fatetur,
> Si brevis addatur, duo tempora longa meretur.
> > (ed. Reaney/Gilles IV 5, 4)

> (Before a long, a long expresses three units of
> time.
> If a breve is added, the long deserves two units.)

These are end-rhymed hexameters *(versus caudati)*, not leonines,[28] though on occasion even a leonine verse makes an appearance:[29]

> Solo recta brevis moderatur tempore quevis.
> > (ed. Reaney/Gilles IV 7, 2)

> (Each correct breve is governed by a single unit of time.)

In its complex form, therefore, the present treatise is quite unique amongst medieval treatises on music, for it is a *prosimetrum* in the tradition of *The Consolation of Philosophy*,[30] a closely-reasoned

---

[27] *Prologus* 74, 14-40.

[28] For a brief survey of the various verse forms in use in Latin in the later middle ages, see Dag Norberg, *Introduction à l'étude de la versification,* pp. 64-86.

[29] There are many verses in the treatise which are not printed as such in the Coussemaker edition. See Gordon Anderson, "Magister Lambertus and Nine Rhythmic Modes," *Acta Musicologica* XLV (1973): 57-73; and the new edition by Gilles and Reaney.

[30] Amongst the encyclopedists, Martianus Capella, in his *De Nuptiis Philologiae et Mercurii,* one of the most widely read schoolbooks in the later middle ages, made flamboyant use of a mixture of prose and verse. Book IX, "De Musica," begins with 28 verses in elegiac couplets and ends with a complex autobiographical poem (unfortunately textually corrupt in the manuscript tradition). Included in the book are also a dazzling prothalamium and the Classically-inspired response of Harmony, with its varying metre and two-line refrain.

Other important *prosimetra* were the *Cosmographia* of Bernard Silvestris and Alan of Lille's *De Planctu Naturae.* See Jan Ziolkowski, *Alan of Lille's Grammar of Sex,* p.9.

diatribe, a fictive commentary,[31] a series of *quaestiones,* and a
reaffirmation of *auctoritas.* It is all of this, of course, and much
more, for it also contains a wealth of information upon the notation,
aesthetics, and performance practice of one of the greatest bodies of
music in the history of Western culture.

FORM AND STRUCTURE OF THE TREATISE

The treatise begins with a Prologue which recalls Lambertus in its
phraseology and takes him to task anonymously for departing from the
precepts of the established authority in the field of *musica
mensurabilis,* Johannes de Garlandia (also unnamed, but quoted copiously
throughout the treatise). Several paragraphs are then devoted to the
requisite definitions of music, compiled from various sources, including
Boethius, Cassiodorus, Martianus Capella, and Isidore of Seville. Of
these only Isidore is named as well as quoted.

The following section introduces a technique found as an
organizational device throughout the treatise: The verses which make up
the first part of the poem are discussed by *incipit,* and a rationale is
given for their arrangement. Systematization was a hallmark of the
Aristotelian influence that had fully pervaded scholarly writing by the
last quarter of the thirteenth century, and its clearest exposition is
given in the *De Divisione* of Boethius.[32] A model of organization, and
borrowing from Aristotle's *Categoriae,* this book discusses the division
of a whole into parts; the arrangement of matter by genus, species,
differentia, proprium, and accident; and the division and categorization
of signifying terms.[33] The music treatise of 1279 is thoroughly
orthodox in its systematic discussion of its contents and in its
scholastic rationalizations for its own arrangement.

Boethius had written that the science of division is "maximus usus

---

[31] The separation of the writer from the written work, either for
self-justification or as a literary conceit, is not unknown in the
twelfth and thirteenth centuries. John of Salisbury is suspected of
having himself written the *Institutio Trajani* and then citing it as an
authority, and Gerald of Wales is himself probably the "quidam sapiens"
who is referred to at several points. (Giles Constable, *per litteram.*)

[32] See Lorenzo Pozzi, *Trattato sulla divisione* (Padua, 1969).

[33] Alexander of Hales, the English *doctor irrefragabilis* who was
master of theology at Paris, wrote in his *Summa Theologiae:*
  . . . apprehensio veritatis secundum humanam
  rationem explicatur per divisiones, definitiones,
  et ratiocinationes.
  (. . . the understanding of truth according to
  human reason is gained by means of divisions,
  definitions, and thought processes.)
(ed. Klumper, *Tractatus introductorius, Questio* i, *art.* I, *cap.* 4, *ad
secundum;* quoted in Parkes, "The Influence," p. 119.)

facillimaque doctrina,"[34] and the author of our music treatise echoes this sentiment with an additional practical rationale (a rationale first stated at the outset of the treatise for the advantages of poetry over prose):

> Since indeed a division of the subject matter is helpful for the fuller clarity of what follows and for a stronger memory on the part of the listeners, for that reason let us divide . . .
>
> (Prologue 67, 53-69, 1)

The listing and explanation of the incipits of the first part of the poem are followed by an additional rationalization, which carries both Aristotelian and Augustinian theological overtones:

> And thus the meaning and method of division of the leonine verses is clear in general, and in this way it is divided into single portions, since a division is not sufficient or perfect unless it arrives at and leads to things that are indivisible.
>
> (Prologue 69, 48-51)

Although the Scholastic process of division and subdivision was an important forerunner of modern methods of analysis, it does not conform in every respect to modern modes of thought or to our expectations of arrangement and classification. The author considers the arrangement of his poem by sections, and each section is analyzed (and its arrangement justified) in advance by preliminary discussion and analysis. The part of the poem that falls within each chapter of the treatise is considered by section, and each section is analyzed by verse-group, each group comprising from one or two to six or eight lines of the hexameters.

The Prologue, for example, contains forty-five lines of the poem. The analysis divides these into groups, which comprise from two to eight lines each. But the groups are not discussed in the order in which they appear, rather they are analyzed by a continual process of division and subdivision, until each one of the groups has been mentioned, its content summarized, and its order of appearance justified. The author starts by separating out the groups that are the furthest apart and continues the segmentation from the end towards the beginning, each time classifying out the last group. The process does not immediately appear patent to the modern reader, especially to one who does not yet have the order of the poem fixed in his mind. However there is a clear and reasonable logic to the process, which, once learned, makes comprehension of the treatise and the rationale of its contents far clearer.

The system is best demonstrated by means of a chart. Here each line of verse is represented by a horizontal line, and the incipits mentioned in the analysis are given in their correct position. Each group is marked by an upper-case letter. Diagram I displays in visual form the analytical method used, proceeding in order of the discussion in the treatise. A brief glance up the right hand branches of Diagram I will demonstrate the strict logic of the system.

---

[34]*Trattato*, p. 107.

A   Music

B   If you would like to know*

C   If it is with measure

D   Let divine virtue

E   Through verses

        ——— (Argus)

F   The leonine treatise*

G   Let them displease*

H   Jealous one*

I   O prose*

J   Learn first*

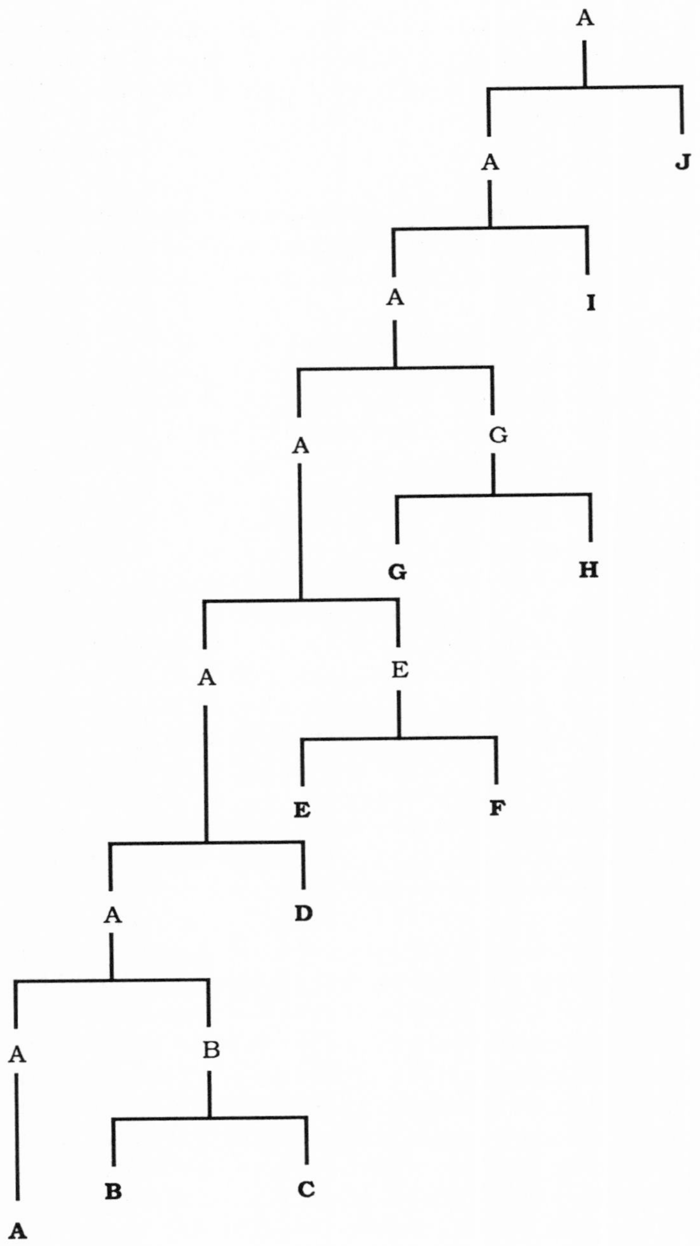

DIAGRAM I

This logical basis, however, does not prevent the author from utilizing considerable variety of treatment. The asterisks in the chart indicate those verse-groups which are preceded by *commentum,* a section of commentary in prose, headed by the incipit of the group to which it refers. Most, but not all, of the groups are preceded by such commentary, and in the case of one group that is not provided with a commentary (**E**), it is *followed* by a lengthy exposition on one of the images contained in an inner line. This is the Argus and Io reference, with which the author has such witty fun.

Towards the end of the Prologue there are two other brief analyses of this kind. The first explains the order and content of the main chapter divisions of the treatise as a whole. The second is a further, more detailed analysis of the last group (**J**) in the previous discussion. Diagram II will serve to clarify the method.

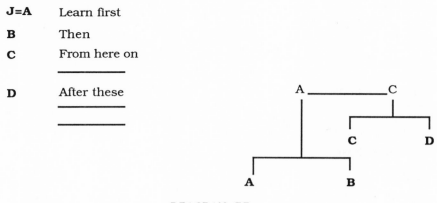

J=A	Learn first
B	Then
C	From here on
D	After these

DIAGRAM II

The Prologue is relatively short and because of its prefatory nature is in some ways not completely representative of the main body of the treatise. Nevertheless the same method is used to explain and rationalize throughout the treatise. One further example may stand for the whole. Chapter Two is one of the longest chapters in the treatise. The chapter contains one hundred and eleven lines of the poem, organized into four large sections. As can readily be seen from the diagram of this chapter (Diagram III), the treatment of the material is characterized by the same combination of rigidity and flexibility that has been alluded to above. The third section is not analyzed in advance in the text, but the other three are. Most of the verse-groups are preceded by commentary, and many of those which are not (as well as some of those which are) contain lines which are commented upon anyway. No group of more than six lines occurs in the text without being preceded by commentary in prose.

An important aspect of this passion for division is rationalization, as has been mentioned before. The author has to justify his arrangement, not just present it. Readers are therefore provided with a fascinating array of justifications for the chosen order of the material. Examples of both the practical and the sententious-theological type are given above. Other practical appeals which show the influence of contemporary Logic abound:

De musica mensurata

Section 1

A   Music is the true measuring*
      ——

B   The reader states*

C   Thus recites the prose

D   If it is the first*

Section 2

D   If it is the first*

E1   Three precepts*

E2   Perceive those

F   The pause*

G   The order*

H   As I learned once*

I   The third which follows*

J   The fourth species

K   The fifth species*

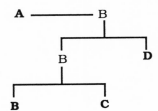

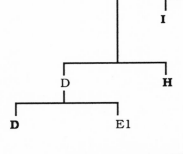

Section 3

L   Say that the sixth*

Section 4

M   To any mode*

N   You may give semibreves

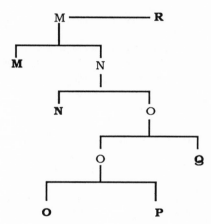

O   If the mode*

P   Look and see*

Q   Thus the breve*

R   Let the pause hold*

DIAGRAM III

> And because an introduction serves fore-knowledge, and a
> tract practical knowledge, therefore the introduction
> comes first, because everyone should arm himself with
> knowledge about future things before suddenly dealing
> with them in practice.
>
> (Prologue 69, 3-6)

> And because one should first touch on what is dealt with
> before dividing it . . .
>
> (Prologue 69, 13-14)

Some rationalizations are pedagogical:

> But just as in each science one should first put the
> smallest unit, for example the letter in grammar and the
> term in dialectic, so in measurable music one should
> first put the form, which represents the orthography of
> music.
>
> (Prologue 83, 34-37)

Others are philosophical:

> And if they concede that there is arrangement in some
> things, it is necessary to concede that it is in all
> things; as Boethius says elsewhere: "Nothing can be
> without order and retain its nature."
>
> (Prologue 81, 49-52)

But they appear throughout the treatise, embedded in its very
fabric, and reflecting the thorough absorption of the Scholastic method
into all disciplines of late thirteenth-century scholarly writing.

The treatise as a whole, however, is modelled upon that of Johannes
de Garlandia.[35] This indebtedness to *auctoritas* may be seen not only in
the reiteration of precepts or doctrine, but in the shape and design of
the entire work. Johannes de Garlandia had outlined the form of his
little book at the outset:

> Sciendum est ergo, quod ipsius organi generaliter accepti
> tres sunt species, scilicet discantus, copula et organum,
> de quibus dicendum est per ordinem.
>
> (ed. Reimer I, 3)

> (It should be known therefore that of organum in its
> generic sense there are three species, that is to say
> discant, copula, and organum, about which we should speak
> in order.)

This overall design is faithfully carried out: eleven chapters are

---

[35]Erich Reimer discusses some aspects of this dependency. See
Reimer, *Johannes de Garlandia: De mensurabili Musica: Kritische Edition
mit Kommentar und Interpretation der Notationslehre*, 2 vols., Beihefte
zum Archiv für Musikwissenschaft X-XI (Wiesbaden, 1972), especially vol.
1, pp. 29-30.

devoted to aspects of the new species -- discant -- and its attendant technicalities, while the final two chapters discuss copula and organum respectively.[36] It is not generally recognized how closely the music treatises of the later thirteenth century are based upon this design, both in its general outline and in its specific details. Even those treatises which deliberately break with the Garlandian notational and conceptual tradition follow similar organizational plans and borrow much terminology and phraseology from Garlandia. Lambertus writes:

> Primo igitur sciendum est quod tria tantummodo sunt
> genera per quae tota mensurabilis musica discurrit,
> scilicet discantus, hoketus et organum.
> > (ed. Gilles/Reaney IV, *2,* 1)

> (First therefore it should be known that there are only
> three genera which the whole of measurable music
> traverses, and they are discant, hocket, and organum.)

This form is followed up through the second topic, hocket, but the treatise appears to break off abruptly before the treatment of organum.[37]

Even Franco deals with the species of *musica mensurabilis* in the same order. For him (as for the Anonymous of 1279) hocket and copula are parts of discant. But his treatise follows the same general outline as that of Garlandia: Prologue, definitions, modes, single notes, ligatures, plicas, rests, concords, discords, copula, hocket, organum.

Those theorists who most closely adhere to the format of Garlandia's treatise are the Anonymous of 1279 and Anonymous IV -- the former one who had set himself the task "prosae venerabilis famam in statum pristinum

---

[36]The arrangement of scholarly material into chapters is itself a reflection of the new orderly view of intellectual endeavors. Vincent of Beauvais, the thirteenth-century Dominican theologian, discusses the arrangement of his *Speculum Maius:*

> Ut huius operis partes singulae lectori facilius
> elucescant, ipsum totum opus per libros, et libros
> per capitula distinguere volui.

> (So that the individual parts of this work might
> be clearer to the reader, I have decided to separate
> the whole work into books, and the books into chapters.)

(*Speculum Maius, apologia, cap. II,* quoted in Parkes, "The Influence," p. 133.)

Of the five main music treatises of the thirteenth century -- Garlandia, Lambertus, Anon. 1279, Franco, and Anon. IV -- only the Anonymous of 1279 and Anonymous IV explicitly divide their work into chapters.

[37]Professor Reaney informs me that for the mensural portion of Lambertus the manuscript tradition is dependent upon a single source -- Paris, Bibliothèque Nationale, lat. 11266. It is possible, therefore, that this source is defective.

revocare" ("of bringing back the reputation of the highly regarded prose
treatise to its former state"), the latter attempting to explain the
glories of Parisian polyphony to his English compatriots. Anonymous IV
does not announce the tripartite plan at the beginning of his book, but
it clearly informs his conscious design.

The deliberate formation of both treatises upon the Garlandian model
is best demonstrated by a chart (see Diagram IV),[38] which reflects the
structure as well as the content of all three treatises in schematic
form. Differences in length as well as in density and detail of
treatment are thus minimized, while overall parallels emerge. New
material is indicated in italics. Chapter numeration is based upon the
latest editions[39] (including this one).

The dependency of both later treatises upon their model is thus made
quite clear. The question as to the exact dating of all three treatises
will be taken up later; it is not important in this context, as there is
no doubt that the treatise of Johannes de Garlandia preceded the other
two by some years, and there appears to be no evidence that Anonymous IV
knew the treatise of 1279.

LITERARY STYLE

Compared with other music treatises of the thirteenth century, the
present work is strikingly rich in style, linguistic quality, and
literary allusion. The author makes reference to many of the Classical
authors whose works were read in educated circles at the time, including
Ovid, Horace, and Cato the Elder; he quotes or paraphrases late Latin
authors such as Boethius (and from works other than the *De Musica*) as
well as the encyclopedists Capella, Cassiodorus, and Isidore; and he is
familiar with a broad range of more recent material, including some
popular proverbs or maxims and at least one well-known sequence by Adam
of St. Victor. Of contemporary treatises on music, he was obviously
intimately acquainted with the works of Johannes de Garlandia and
Lambertus (quite possibly having copies of these treatises in front of
him as he wrote), and he knew (directly or indirectly) the writings on
music of earlier theorists such as Johannes Afflighemensis, Boethius, and
Guido. None of this indicates a range of reading greater than one might

---

[38]An earlier version of this chart was distributed as an
accompaniment to my paper "*Imitatio* and Originality in Thirteenth-
Century Music Theory," presented at the forty-ninth annual meeting of the
American Musicological Society, Louisville, Kentucky, October 27-30,
1983.

[39]Reimer, *Johannes de Garlandia*; Fritz Reckow, *Der Musiktraktat des
Anonymus 4*, Beihefte zum Archiv für Musikwissenschaft IV-V (Wiesbaden,
1967). One might quibble with some of the chapter divisions in the
Reimer edition of Garlandia's treatise. While most of them are based
upon the explicit broaching of a new topic ("Sequitur de . . . "), some
appear arbitrary (VI and XII, for example). This does not affect the
presentation of the material in the chart, however.

Garlandia (c. 1260)	Anon. St. Emmeram (1279)	Anonymous IV (c. 1285)

I.   Prologus
     Species
     Modi
	Prologus
	   Genera
		I. Prologus
		
		     Modi
		     Fractio modorum

II. De repraesentatione
     figurarum
	I. Formae et proprietates
	     figurarum
	  i) figurae simplices
	 ii) figurae compositae
	    de semibrevibus
		II. Puncta materialia:
		
		    (figurae simplices
		     et ligatae)

III. Proprietas, perfectio		
IV. Figurae modorum		

V. Modi imperfecti	II. De modis:
	     modi
	     hoqueti
	     motetti	

VI. Ligatio		
VII. Pausationes	III. De pausis et	III. De pausationibus
VIII. Figurae pausationum	figuris pausationum	(figuris pausationum)
IX. Consonantiae	IV. De consonantiis:	IV.i) De concordantiis

X. Concordantiae,
    discordantiae
	(concordantiae et
	     discordantie)
		ii) *Exempla*
		     concordantiarum

XI. Discantus	V. De discantu i) discantus	iii) De discantu

		V. *De triplicibus et*
		    quadruplicibus et
		    copula

XII. Copula	ii) copula	
		VI. *Magnus Liber*
XIII. Organum per se	VI. Organum speciale	VII. Organum purum

DIAGRAM IV

expect or that is surprisingly wide for the period and the milieu.[40] What
is to be noted is only that these readings are clearly reflected in the
expansive and textured style of the writing, which is not generally the
case with the other music treatises of the time.

The extent to which the author is dependent upon his sources and the
deliberate use to which he puts them varies widely, and this diversity of
approach may be seen in the broad spectrum of ways in which the sources
appear in the context of his own writing. Other authors may be directly
quoted with an attribution ("As Boethius says . . . "), or without an
attribution ("As it is said elsewhere . . . "). Johannes de Garlandia
never appears by name, and yet several passages from his treatise are
given verbatim. Lambertus is also often quoted directly, though usually
under the cover of "Someone has written . . . ." Quotations are often
deliberately adapted, such as when passages from Garlandia are expanded
to cover music for three voices.

A common occurrence is paraphrase, in which a rule or general
statement summarizes or rephrases the content of another writer's work.
There is usually some sign to indicate the dependency: "The rule is
generally found, in which . . . " or "It is said that . . . "

But by far the most frequent form of borrowing occurs unannounced and
with no sign. This is the incorporation into the text of terms, phrases,
sometimes whole sentences from other writers in the technique of
imitatio. Again the original may appear whole or in adapted form, and
its meaning may be imported unchanged or undergo subtle transformation as
a result of its new context.

The format of the treatise as poem and commentary also allows for a
richness and diversity of literary treatment that is most unusual.
Firstly a few words about the verse itself: leonine hexameters were not
uncommon in didactic writing at this time, as has been noted above;
however the difficulties of writing Latin verse, and rhyming Latin verse
at that, to expound a specialized subject such as music should not be
underestimated. Technical terms and vocabulary need to be fitted into a
line that demands six dactylic or spondaic feet and a pair of words that
rhyme. This is no easy task, and the obscurity of some of the words, as
well as the obliqueness of many of the verse "explanations" that occur in
this treatise may be readily understood if this is borne in mind. Indeed
it is instructive to read a portion, or all, of the poem by itself,
skipping the glosses and commentary, in order to gain a clearer picture
of the multi-faceted nature of the work as a whole.

It is clear, even if the author had not immediately admitted the
source of his *littera,* that often the poem is designed to stimulate, or
provide the opportunity for, a prose explanation. The author
deliberately exploits the fictive nature of his overall design to weave a
subtle play of meaning between poem and commentary. The glosses too are
used not only to explain, or provide synonyms for, words in the hexameter
verse, but for a variety of purposes, which are stimulated by the
identity of *actor* and *glossator*. The glossator is here in a privileged

---

[40] A comprehensive survey of readings in the medieval schools is
given by Günter Glauche, *Schullektüre im Mittelalter: Entstehung und
Wandlungen des Lektürekanons bis 1200 nach den Quellen dargestellt,*
Münchener Beiträge zur Mediävistik und Renaissance-Forschung V (Munich,
1970).

position. He may not only illuminate or clarify, but may, and often
does, also rephrase, contradict, or interpret -- secure in the certainty
of his superior knowledge. Conversely, of course, the author of the poem
is given a freedom of expression and a release from the demands of
absolute clarity of exposition -- a flexibility of *inventio* in his verse
-- knowing that there will be future opportunity for clarification. This
interplay within the treatise is one of its most particular features, one
that sets the work quite apart from contemporary writings on music.

   With this sketch of the overall design of the treatise in mind, it
will be useful to examine a little more closely the individual styles of
the three main layers of compositional activity -- the poem, the glosses,
and the commentary -- as they stand separately within the work.

THE POEM

   The innermost layer of writing is of course represented by the poem
itself, the implied original text, or *littera*.[41] Made up of over four
hundred hexameter verses, the poem is abstruse, witty, tortuous,
sometimes simplistic, often unclear. Rare words are used for their
metrical or rhyming value, at least one *hapax legomenon* appears,[42] and
syntax is stretched to the limit. The result is a virtuoso performance,
however -- an achievement which might only begin to be appreciated by a
modern reader who spends an hour or two attempting to explain by means of
a sonnet the procedure for balancing the air-fuel mixture in a pair of
two-barrel carburetors. Consider, for example, the following line,
which occurs during the discussion of multiple-note ligatures. The prose
commentary takes two paragraphs to deal with the problems of ligatures of
seven, eight, nine, and ten notes. The poem, in a brilliant display, and
utilizing various forms of the Latin numerals (especially the quite rare
distributive adjective), dismisses all four of these curiosities in a
single line:

   Octo septenae praesint denisque novenae.

   (Let the eight, the seven, and the ninefold precede the tenfold.)

   Sometimes even the author despairs of his task, as when he is faced
with the prospect of discussing a technical term which he simply cannot
fit into the metre of his verse. "Semiditonus" is a term which is
ungainly and awkward even in prose; in verse it is an impossibility. The
solution is as captivating as it is clever: the part is made to stand
for the whole, and the line itself is an admission of the limitations of
the verse in which it is written:

   Ditonus, et semi, volo ditonus ob metra demi.

---

   [41]The author himself refers to it, almost interchangeably, as
littera or *textus*.

   [42]Not strictly speaking a *hapax legomenon,* the word "brios" occurs
twice in the treatise, but a thorough search turned up no other
occurrences in any other work, and the *Mittellateinisches Wörterbuch*
(Munich, 1967-), the only one of all Classical and medieval Latin
dictionaries to define the word, indicates this treatise as its source.

([**Then come**] **the ditone, and the semi-, for I wish
"ditone" to be removed because of the meter.**)

Some of the lines are models of clarity and concision, as well as of
limpid rhythmic scansion, as, for example, the following, which describes
the architecture of the sixth rhythmic mode:

Dic speciem sextam rectis brevibus fore textam.

(**Say that the sixth species is woven from correct breves.**)

Others are obscure, dense, and difficult.

Most of the lines stand syntactically by themselves, but occasional
enjambement enlivens the flow of the verse. The first half of each line,
up to the caesura, may be made up of two spondees:

Binas perfectas . . .

or two dactyls:

Voceque composita . . .

or a combination of the two:

Lexque figurarum . . .

Plodding *versus spondaici* (lines made up exclusively of spondees,
except for the obligatory dactyl in the fifth foot) are rare:

Est sub mensura discantus, subque figura.

There is evidence of no artistic reason for their appearance, which seems
to be dictated only by the exigencies of subject-matter and verse.

The commonest form places a dactyl before the fifth foot, and may or
may not include an additional dactyl in the first half of the verse. The
line which does not is a particularly attractive combination, with its
weighty opening and speedier, lilting conclusion:

Haec si perfectae sint proprietate refectae.

Provisions against the use of a monosyllable at the end of a line:[43]

Nunc ibi prolixe, cito nunc, scemate vix e

---

[43]Rarer amidst the *gravitas* of Classical verse, the final
monosyllable could achieve considerable effect. Horace, in his *Ars
Poetica*, satirized the new epic style in both the form and content of
his famous line:

Parturiunt montes, nascetur ridiculus mus.
(ed. James Kirkland [Boston, 1901], line 139).

or immediately preceding the caesura:[44]

> **Huic duo tempora das si tractum bis ita tradas.**

are usually observed. Again the violation is usually for practical rather than for artistic reasons. (It would not be easy to find another rhyme for **prolixe**.) Other liberties involve irregular scansion or accentuation of individual words within the metre. In the following line both **media** and **nunc** require unorthodox readings. Indeed the first **nunc** has to be long, the second short:

> **Parte manent prima, media nunc, nunc et imma.**

The standard rhyme scheme for leonines requires a two-syllable rhyme between the word that precedes the caesura and the word that ends the line:[45]

> **Pausaque sit *tanta* fertur paenultima *quanta*.**

Either one of the words may be longer than two syllables (**imperf*ectas*/ l*ectas*, Instrument*orum*/sonorum**) or, very occasionally, shorter (**ign*ote*/ doceo *te***).

The fact that the first rhyme word comprises the end of the second and the beginning of the third foot of the line, whereas the second rhyme word forms the whole of the sixth foot, makes for a flexible and shifting accentuation of the words, which is a feature of medieval leonines. In the following line the rhyme word before the caesura (**dare**) is accented short-long, whereas the final word (**care**) is long-long:

> **Ex hinc iura dare specierum sex volo care.**

Indeed whenever there is a dactyl in the second foot, this accentual

---

[44]In its less restrictive form the rule counselled against monosyllabic prepositions in this position.

[45]One late annotated manuscript of Eberhard the German's thirteenth-century *Laborintus* (Munich, Bayerische Staatsbibliothek, Clm 11348) defines the form as follows:

> Leonini dicuntur versus in quibus sextus pes per similitudinem vocalium et consonantium consonantiae respondet ultimae sillabae secundi pedis et primae tertii.

> (Leonines are verses in which the sixth foot corresponds to the last syllable of the second foot and the first syllable of the third foot by means of a similarity of sound in the vowels and consonants.)

This definition is reproduced in Wilhelm Meyer, "Radewins Gedicht über Theophilus und die Arten der gereimten Hexameter," in *Gesammelte Abhandlungen zur mittellateinischen Rythmik* I (Berlin, 1905), p. 83.

shift will occur. It is particularly effective when both of the rhyme
words have the same form, but are distinguished by their accentuation:[46]

   Quamlibet inde metas, si vis hinc ordine metas.

The first **metas** is accented short-long, the second long-long.
   Again, in the following line, the noun **notas** at the caesura (short-
long) is distinguished from the verb **notas** at the end (long-long):

   Atque figura, notas tria dant simul hoc tibi notas.

In extremis the author will resort to vowel rhyme alone (**tegma/
antesuprema**), or to single-syllable rhyme (**duplex/simplex, binae/ternae,
trium/solum**), but none of the lines are without rhyme. In six
instances[47] there are pairs of lines which use crossed rhymes, a pattern
in which the word before the caesura in line A rhymes with the end word
of line B, and the word at the end of line A rhymes with the word before
the caesura of line B. The opening lines of the poem are of this kind:

   **Musica di*catur* cantandi iure soph*ia*,
   Et brevis esse v*ia*, qua cantus lege patr*atur*.**

Three of these occurrences are at the beginning of the (verse sections of
the) Prologue, Chapter One, and Chapter Two, leading one to suspect that
it might have been the author's original intention to begin all of the
chapters in this way.
   The three other pairs of crossed rhymes all involve rhetorical
figures, and this may be an additional meaning of the reference in the
Prologue to the "eloquence marked with a cross"[48] which the author
promises to employ during the course of his book.[49]
   In the language of the poetry paronomasia (pun) is a favorite device.
Though sparingly used, it is encouraged by the requirement of two
rhyming words to make up the leonines. In the following line the author
plays with two meanings (there are others) of the word **versus**. In the
first instance the form is the accusative plural of the fourth
declension noun that signifies a line of poetry. In the second it is the
nominative singular of the past participle of the verb "verto" -- to
turn.

   Huius per versus stilus hic meus est modo versus.

   (This pen of mine is now turned to write verses about this.)

---

[46]See the discussion on paronomasia below.

[47]*Prologus* 70, 4-5; *Prologus* 74, 7-12; *Cap*.Ii 88, 39 - 90, 1;
Cap.II 188, 28-33; *Cap*.II 192, 19-21; *Cap*.VI 288, 18-19.

[48]Prologue 77, 9. As mentioned below in the description of the
codex, occasional vertical crosses also occur drawn in ink in the margins
of the manuscript.

[49]Meyer ("Radewins Gedicht," p. 84) cites the term *cruciferi* for
this rhyme scheme.

Other puns involve plays on **frustra**, an adverb meaning "in vain," and also the plural of "frustrum" (= piece, or part); **metas**, the second person present subjunctive of the third conjugation verb "meto" and the accusative plural of the feminine noun "meta" (this occurs more than once); and the use within the same verse of **pausas** as a verb and **pausas** as a noun.

Word-play, however, is often less explicit and may depend upon derivation or ambiguity. At one point the author describes the sorry state of the original prose treatise (Garlandia's) which he has decided to defend. Addressing it directly, in an already established conceit, he describes it as "fusa." The word derives from the verb "fundo" -- to pour out -- and means "extended," "diffuse," or by extension, and perhaps better here, "sprawling." The gloss explains the word as "confusa" -- confused -- a deliberately oblique interpretation, justified only by the direct derivation of the word from the same root: "con-fundo" -- to pour or mix together.

The verse is enriched with imagery and figures of speech, including simile and metaphor, apostrophe, alliteration, chiasmus, and zeugma. In a charming simile the author compares his verses to chicks, which hide under the wings of the mother hen, as his verses hide beneath the protection of their guardian, the treatise of Garlandia. At other times Garlandia's treatise is compared to an orchard or forest.[50] Mode is a chain which binds notes together. The sign which marks the place for a breath or a break between modes is like a zero: it has no significance in itself, yet it provides added meaning to its surroundings.[51]

THE GLOSSES

Moving outwards from the kernel of the book, the second layer of compositional activity is represented by the glosses. These are written in the manuscript in a small hand above the lines of verse. The majority of the glosses involve single word explanations or synonyms for words of the poem. For example, over the word *nunc* in one verse appears the gloss: "id est, quandoque." The word *nunc* can mean either "now" or "sometimes," and the gloss shows that it is the latter meaning that is required in this case. In another instance the word **brevis** is glossed: "sive modus." Thus the noun that is implied but missing in the verse is supplied by the gloss.

Both *id est* ("that is . . .") and *sive* ("or . . .") are used as introductory formulas in the glosses. The former has explanatory value, the latter precedes words that are to be interpolated. Occasionally *pro* ("instead of . . .") introduces exact or near synonyms.

Single word glosses also serve very often to elucidate the syntax of the verse, making clear which part of speech is intended by an unusual word, or what role it is designed to play in the structure of the sentence. Sometimes almost every word in a line is glossed, with five

---

[50] It is possible that this image was motivated by Lambertus, who uses both *arbor* ("tree") and *vinea* ("vineyard") in comparisons.

[51] The word *cifra* ("cipher") came into Latin usage from the Arabic *sifr* in the mid-twelfth century. See Ziolkowski, "Alan of Lille's Grammar of Sex," p. 8, fn. 22.

out of eight, or seven out of nine, of the words appearing with glosses above them in the manuscript.[52]

Occasionally an ironic interplay between verse and gloss counteracts the reader's expectations, and the gloss is used to turn the original meaning of the poem on its head. In the Prologue one of the poetic lines begins:

Displiceant nulli . . .

(**Let [my verses] displease no-one . . .**)

and this is glossed with the following phrase:

id est, displicendo noceant alicui super hoc invidenti

(that is, by displeasing let them hurt anyone who is envious about this)

At other times the author makes use of the gloss to provide additional information which is not strictly necessary for an understanding of the poem, but which elaborates and enriches the material. Often these glosses take the form of a whole phrase. In the second chapter, over the word **tenor** in a discussion of the fifth mode, the gloss reads: "id est, primus cantus, qui aliis esse dicitur fundamentum" ("that is, the first melody, which is said to be a foundation to the others").

Often, if a verse is particularly vague or abstruse, the gloss gives a clear and unequivocal reading of the entire line. These interpretations are usually preceded by the words "Quasi diceret," which can best be translated as "He means to say, . . ." or "Put in another way, ..." Here the collaboration between author and glossator is at its most patent. In a discussion of the length of longs, the poem sums up the precepts with the rather vague statement:

Regula fit talis quocumque modo generalis.

(**Such a rule is general to any mode.**)

The gloss provides the crucial doctrine in the clear and straightforward language of a "rule":

Quasi diceret: ubicumque longa ante longam reperitur, prior tria tempora continebit.

(He means to say that whenever a long is found before a long, the first will contain three units of time.)

This shows an expansion of the gloss from phrase to entire sentence as well as from explanatory clarification to central precept. In these instances it would not be an exaggeration to say that the verse is contrived as an elaboration on the gloss.

---

[52] See, for example, *Cap*.II 190, 37 and *Cap*.III 246, 1.

For these glosses the length of the sentence is limited physically by the layout of the manuscript, for even in its smaller hand and with pervasive use of abbreviation the gloss cannot take up more space than the length of the verse line over which it is written. The author overcomes this limitation in certain instances, however, by allowing the glosses to run on from one line to another. Very often this occurs in the same pedagogical situation discussed above: a situation in which the instructional material may best be expressed in the form of "rules." In these cases the nature of the glosses very closely approaches that of the commentary, and a merging of the styles becomes apparent.

THE COMMENTARY

The commentary itself, the outside layer of the work, takes up the bulk of the book. It is written in prose and is outwardly designed as a section-by-section elaboration of the material presented in oblique form in the poem. Each prose passage (there are some exceptions, such as the opening of the Prologue) is headed by an *incipit* which ties it to a section of the poem.[53] The passage then discusses in detail, often with musical examples, the material contained within that section. This discussion is expansive, closely reasoned, and thorough. Sometimes the author is not content even with this amount of exposition, and the verses are followed by additional analysis. It is in the prose commentary that the fullest presentation of the musico-theoretical content of the treatise appears.

The prose commentary, however, contains more than commentary. It is by means of the prose that the author engages in the most colorful vilifications of Lambertus as well as the densest and most carefully argued refutations of his proposals. The prose passages go far beyond their poetic stimulus in the detail and depth of their subject-matter. Several pages (a thousand words) may be devoted to the discussion of concepts covered in four lines of verse.

Generally the prose maintains the fiction of separate authorship by introducing each passage after its incipit with the words: "Hic recitat actor . . ." ("Here the author explains . . ."), or "Hic vult actor ostendere . . ." ("Here the author wishes to show . . ."). Sometimes the mask slips, and the first person singular, or the authorial plural, appears. Later in this essay, in the discussion on authorship of the treatise, an important possessive adjective ("noster") is considered.

The style of the prose writing is elaborate but lucid, with a single train of thought often carried through a lengthy series of final, conditional, and concessive clauses, adjectival and adverbial phrases, within balanced complex sentences. Amongst the figures of speech, alliteration is favored:

> . . . quae inter ceteras cum *proprietate positas* dicitur
> optinere *dominii dignitatem* . . .

> . . . cum *proprietate propria protrahi* videretur . . .

---

[53] It should be noted that the heading does not always quote from the *beginning* of the line to which it refers. See my discussion of the edition below.

A clever antithesis occurs in the discussion of the division of a long note into semibreves. Since by means of the division a larger number results, the author writes in a gloss: "id est, per divisionem multiplico" ("that is, I multiply by division").

Sometimes in the leisurely flow of the prose a pithy Latin phrase worthy of Tacitus makes an appearance:

> . . . nihil in se superflui, nihil in se continet diminuti.
>
> (. . . it contains in itself nothing superfluous, nothing diminished.)

On one occasion a high-flown rhetorical passage competes in intensity with the quotation from Isidore with which it is juxtaposed. Indulging in apostrophe, hyperbole, *cursus velox,* and a rich mixture of metaphors, this passage displays a tendency to *purpuratio* which is otherwise successfully suppressed:

> Attendas igitur, mi dilecte, tu qui tantae dulcedinis ac
> modulationis cupis aquas potabiles exaurire, ut ea quae
> secuntur aure vigili uringinis suscipias, cordis
> armariolo pacifice reponendo, ne quod a paucis cognitum
> et honorifice reservatum est provulgatum communiter iam
> vilescat.
>
> (*Cap.*II 224, 22-26)

> (You should pay attention therefore, my beloved, you who
> desire to drain the thirst-quenching waters of so much
> sweetness and sound, so that you may take up those things
> which follow with the alert ear of desire, and put them
> peacefully in the book-case of your heart, lest something
> that is understood by few and honorably reserved should
> be widely promulgated and now become worthless.)

In a somewhat self-conscious, but nevertheless witty, linguistic conceit, the author often reflects in the choice of his vocabulary the subject-matter which he is about to broach. Near the beginning of the third chapter he discusses the division of rests into different types, and the passage is full of various forms of the verb "dividere." When considering the number of spaces that the notational sign for a rest will contain, the verb "continere" appears three times within a' single sentence.

Finally, the prose commentary borrows stylistically from both of the other compositional layers represented in the treatise. There are occasions when quotations within the prose reveal themselves as scanning or rhyming poetry. The glossing technique too is taken over into passages of the prose, and it is here that the author seems most to delight in the intellectual challenge of his design. The most notable example of this overt display occurs towards the very end of the treatise[54] when four completely different interpretations are offered for a single relative pronoun.

---

[54]*Cap.*VI 288, 23-27.

THEORETICAL CONTENT

It has been demonstrated above how the treatise is modelled in its overall design upon that of Johannes de Garlandia. Here the theoretical content of each chapter will be summarized in more detail, and the place of the treatise as a whole in the development of contemporary theory is briefly discussed.

The Prologue announces the scope as well as the format of the treatise at the outset. It is to be a defense of Garlandia's work, which, although held in high regard, has come under attack. Garlandia's precepts will be put into verse. Music is defined according to tradition, but the treatise will deal only with *musica mensurabilis,* which may be divided into three genera: discant, copula, and organum. The contents of the six chapters are announced in advance.

Chapter One is divided into two parts. Part One deals with the notation of single notes, Part Two with the notation of ligatures. Part One presents the notation of three single notes: the long, the breve, and the semibreve. The correct notation of plicas for longs and breves is demonstrated; as for the semibreve, a plica may only occur in the case of the larger semibreve. Both the pitch and duration of plicas are discussed. Longs, breves, and semibreves are of two types: larger and smaller. It is quite wrong to call these perfect and imperfect, as Lambertus does. Indeed it is the smaller breve and the smaller long which should be called perfect. A double long is notated as, and has the duration of, twice a larger long. The rhythmic modes in which all of these single notes occur are listed. Part One ends by anticipating the discussion of ligatures in Part Two: ligatures of from two to ten notes are analyzed as to whether they ascend or descend and as to the written form of their beginning and end. The key concepts of propriety and perfection are introduced, though they are not yet defined or explained.

In Part Two of the first chapter propriety and perfection are examined at length, and the general rule is given that all ligatures with propriety and perfection which contain more than three notes are reducible to the *ternaria* with propriety and perfection. (This rule appears also in Garlandia, Anonymous VII, and Anonymous IV.) Ligatures of this kind with from four to ten notes are discussed, and examples of all but the last two are given. Ligatures without propriety are discussed, and incorrect notational procedures for them dismissed. The *quaternaria* of this kind cannot be reduced to the *ternaria* mentioned above. Details are given about the notation and duration of ligatures with opposite propriety. Chapter One, Part Two, continues with precepts regarding perfection -- the ending of ligatures -- and the notation of plicas. Perfect ligatures are discussed first, then plicas, then imperfect ligatures, and examples given of all of these.

Chapter Two concerns the rhythmic modes. These are divided into authentic (Modes 1, 3, and 5) and plagal (Modes 2, 4, and 6), as well as perfect and imperfect. The modes are analyzed as to composition, notation, and order of ligatures, and each is then discussed in turn. Some of them are called *ultra mensuram.* Lambertus is taken to task for changing the number and order of the modes. The proper combinations of modes in polyphonic music are discussed, as is the theory of equipollence. In this context hockets serve to clarify both topics, and

several examples are given. The chapter ends with a discussion of motets and the introduction of the concept of "long" and "short" modes.

Chapter Three deals with rests. Definitions are given, followed by a discussion of notation. The system of Lambertus is critized for its irrationality.

Chapter Four discusses consonances and dissonances. The latter should be avoided.

Chapter Five is in two parts. Part One discusses discant in general, Part Two discusses copula, which is considered a species of discant. *Musica ficta* is briefly considered under Part One. In Part Two copula is defined and examples of it cited.

Chapter Six is about *organum speciale*. It is the preeminent genus of music. Its performance is discussed. The treatise ends with the traditional request for a benevolent hearing, a prayer, and the dated *explicit*.

The treatise purports only to convey the precepts of Johannes de Garlandia regarding *musica mensurabilis*. Of course it does this in far more detail than Garlandia ever achieved, and it goes considerably beyond this modest aim. For the treatise rationalizes, argues, and explains these precepts in great depth and with penetrating intelligence and logic. It expands Garlandia's theory in precisely those areas which had become the mark of advances in thirteenth-century music: semibreves, hockets, motets, and three- and four-part writing. It also disagrees with the *auctoritas* on occasion. Garlandia had given the *divisio sillabarum* as one of the possible types of rest. Our author states forthrightly:

> Quidam dicebant divisionem sillabarum poni in numero
> pausationum; quod non est ponere, quia nihil soni
> importat.
>
> (*Cap*.III 256, 29-30)

> (Some people said that the division of the syllables
> should be placed in the category of the pauses, but this
> is not to place it at all because it conveys no sound.)

The formula "Quidam dicebant" ("Some people said") is usually reserved for Lambertus. Indeed, as has been mentioned above, it was the aberrations of Lambertus that provided the main stimulus for the composition of the treatise in the first place.

The main topics on which Lambertus had violated tradition were the primacy of the perfect long (indeed even the use of the word "perfect" for this note) and the number of rhythmic modes. And on these topics our author is particularly virulent, insisting upon a return to the established view. But he takes Lambertus to task in other areas as well: the notation of the breve plica, the notation of the *quinaria*, the notation of the ascending *binaria*, the notation of the ascending *ternaria*, the notation of the *ternaria* with opposite propriety, the order and duration of the semibreves in a *binaria* with opposite propriety, the equipollence of semibreves in a *binaria* with opposite propriety to a breve of two *tempora*, the notation of rests, and the definition of the ditone and the semiditone.

In most of these instances the offending doctrine is given, preceded by the formula "Quidam dicunt" ("Some people say") or "Quidam asserunt"

("Some people assert"), and although no attribution is made, the words may often be traced to Lambertus' treatise.[55] In only one case (apart from the Prologue) is Lambertus mentioned by name, and that is when he is quoted on the order and duration of semibreves in a *binaria* with opposite propriety (see *Cap*.Iii 148, 3-5).

The unusual form of the treatise and its posture as defender of tradition tend to disguise the new and unusual aspects of its pedagogy and contents. In Chapters Two and Three, for example, the author presents fascinating evidence as to why he considers the theory of hockets and rests crucial to the understanding of *musica mensurabilis* as a whole. In Chapter Two he extends the concept of authentic and plagal from the melodic modes to the rhythmic modes. He also introduces the use of the terms "perfect" and "imperfect," "long" and "short" to classes within the modal system. Throughout the treatise he formulates previously held doctrines into invariable rules. He suggests the practice of analyzing polyphony from the rhythmic mode of its tenor, much as fifteenth-century theorists did in terms of melodic modal analysis; and he combines the concepts of "proprietas" and "perfectio" with the rhythmic modal system, thus throwing increased light on both.

In some ways the author's overt conservatism is as important as his disguised innovations. For he retains the traditional view of organum as a separate species of polyphony, and thus gives us valuable insights into its method and style of performance.[56] In preserving the distinctiveness of organum, he also maintains a special view of copula, and cites examples of its use in actual compositions from the Notre Dame repertoire, which can be thus traced and analyzed.[57] He does not hesitate to borrow precepts or definitions from Lambertus when he considers them useful, while at the same time rejecting those terms and ideas which he finds illogical or without merit.

In time, perhaps, this treatise, with both its forward-looking and its conservative tendencies, will come to be seen as an important representative of that fertile period between Johannes de Garlandia and Franco of Cologne -- fertile both in the production of musical compositions and in the formulation of musical theory.[58]

---

[55]See above, pp. 7-9.

[56]See Jeremy Yudkin, "The Rhythm of Organum Purum," *The Journal of Musicology* II (1983): 355-376.

[57]See Jeremy Yudkin, "The Anonymous of St. Emmeram and Anonymous IV on the *Copula*," *The Musical Quarterly* LXX (1984): 1-22.

[58]Some aspects of the notational procedures of this period have been discussed in Fritz Reckow, "Proprietas und Perfectio; zur Geschichte des Rhythmus, seiner Aufzeichnung und Terminologie im 13. Jahrhundert," *Acta Musicologica* XXXIX (1967): 115-143; and Gordon Anderson, "The Notation of the Bamberg and Las Huelgas Manuscripts," *Musica Disciplina* XXXII (1978): 19-67.

DATING OF THE TREATISE

In the final three verses of the poem that represents the core of this treatise a date is given: the Feast of St. Clement (November 23), 1279. This date has been generally accepted as the correct date for the completion of the composition of the treatise itself; indeed Sowa incorporated the year into the title of his edition.[59] More recently, and quite properly, the significance of this date has been called into question.[60] Might it not refer to the *copying* of the treatise, rather than to its composition?

Here it will be suggested that the date does indeed refer to the completion of the composition of the treatise, and that the accepted interpretation may continue to stand. The argument is based upon observations regarding the content and layout of the treatise, as well as upon the results of research conducted into questions of authorship and audience.

The first of these concerns the format of the treatise itself, especially the last few lines. As has been discussed above, the treatise is designed to look like a commentary upon an original poem. In fact, as we have seen, both poem and commentary are by the same author. In the sole surviving manuscript of the treatise, the poem is written in a large, bold hand in the center of the page, with the spaces between the lines filled in by the glosses; and sections of the poem alternate on the page with a lengthy prose commentary in a considerably smaller hand.[61]

The last three lines of the poem, with the date encoded into verse (no easy task), run as follows:

> **Anno millesimoque ducentesimo quoque nono**
> **Post decies septem, cartam prosae fore neptem**
> **Decrevi festo Clementis carmine praesto.**
>
> (*Cap*.VI 288, 35-37)

> (In the twelve hundred and ninth year
> After seventy, I have decided that these pages
>   should serve as a granddaughter to the prose
> On the feast of Clement with this poem.)

The demands of the metre and the rhyme account for the curious formulation of the date (indeed it was miscalculated by seventy years by the eighteenth-century abbot of St. Emmeram and cataloguer of its

---

[59] Heinrich Sowa, *Ein anonymer glossierter Mensuraltraktat 1279*, Königsberger Studien zur Musikwissenschaft IX (Kassel, 1930).

[60] Michel Huglo, "De Francon de Cologne à Jacques de Liège," *Revue belge de musicologie* XXXIV (1980): 48.

[61] See the description of the codex below and the facsimile on p. 2.

library),[62] but there are other aspects of importance in these few lines. The first is the use of the first person singular ("Decrevi," -- "I have decided"), a form in which the author indulges not infrequently in the course both of the poem and the commentary, despite his supposed disappearance behind the façade of separate authorship. It is the author who is speaking here, not the scribe. Secondly, it has been his announced intention all along to provide a helpmeet for the prose treatise (Garlandia's) by means of a poetic one (his own). The Prologue presents this announcement at the outset (though in less metaphorical terms than here) and also in the first person.[63] Finally, the lines are written in the same bold hand that confirms their existence as a part of the interior poem itself. The actual manuscript ends with an additional couplet appended after these lines in the smaller hand that has been reserved for gloss and commentary:

> Sit decus huic musae praesens velut ore Medusae
> Hostes contrivit, sic scriba suos ubi vivit.
> Amen.
>
> > (*Cap*.VI 288, 39-41)

> (May there be present glory to this Muse, and as with the
> > face of Medusa
> He destroyed his enemies, so may the scribe destroy his
> > where he lives.
> Amen.)

Here is the voice of the scribe. Not to be outdone, he has added his own comment at the end of the work, in the manner of those many monks who, over the centuries, celebrated a job well done, and the end of a tiring day, with their "Bibemus atque vivemus" or "Laus Deo" formulas. Prompted by the militant nature of much of the text, he writes a prayer for the confounding of his own enemies; stimulated by the learned verse he has spent so many days transcribing, he writes his prayer in leonines.

As will be shown below, the results of research into authorship of the treatise confirm this evidence from the work itself. We may thus retain the traditional date with some confidence.[64]

---

[62] See [Johann Baptist Kraus,] *Bibliotheca principalis ecclesiae et monasterii ord. S. Benedicti ad S. Emmeramum Epis. et Martyr*, 4 vols. (Regensburg, 1748), in which the date of the treatise is listed as "M.CCIX" (*op. cit.*, vol. 2, p. 135).

[63] See Prologue 65, 27-33.

[64] The date of this treatise clearly has repercussions for the dating of many of the other important music treatises of the thirteenth century. The evidence is summarized in Jeremy Yudkin, "Notre Dame Theory: A Study of Terminology, Including a New Translation of the Music Treatise of Anonymous IV," (Ph. D. dissertation, Stanford University, 1982), pp. 232-238. Briefly, my conclusions were as follows: Johannes de Garlandia, c. 1260; Lambertus, c. 1260-1279; Anonymous of 1279, 1279; Franco of Cologne, c. 1280; Anonymous IV, after 1280; Hieronymus of Moravia, 1280-1304.

AUTHORSHIP, AMBIENCE, AND AUDIENCE

There are several ways of approaching the problem of authorship of the treatise. One is by assumption: The author writes in defence of Johannes de Garlandia, who was a teacher at the University of Paris around the middle of the thirteenth century.[65] He attacks Lambertus, who may also have been French.[66] Therefore he was a Parisian music theorist.

Even this version has less currency than the following: The manuscript comes from St. Emmeram. The author has always been referred to as "The Anonymous of St. Emmeram." Therefore he was a Bavarian music theorist.

Here the following evidence will be examined: Terminology and vocabulary of the treatise; allusions to Garlandia and Lambertus; intended audience; musical examples; references to the author and his teacher.

TERMINOLOGY AND VOCABULARY OF THE TREATISE

The treatise is saturated with terminology borrowed from the disciplines of the university Trivium and incorporates a large number of Aristotelian terms and concepts.[67] Most particularly it uses words and ideas from logic, philosophy, and significative grammar,[68] subjects of particular importance in the curriculum of the University of Paris, which had by the second half of the thirteenth century become thoroughly overtaken by the "new" Aristotle and stood as the primary center for the study of dialectic and theology in Europe. The principal modes of thought and argument in the treatise are Scholastic. The ordering of material, the rationalization of principles, the division of the subject matter -- all reflect the aims and influences of Scholasticism. The Scholastic synthesis was not confined to Paris, but its focal point in the thirteenth century was the university where Bonaventure, Albertus Magnus, and Thomas Aquinas were *magistri*.

ALLUSIONS TO GARLANDIA AND LAMBERTUS

At the very beginning of our treatise the author declares his

---

[65] See Erich Reimer, *Johannes de Garlandia*, vol. 1, pp. 1-17. I have suggested a revised view of the date of Garlandia's treatise. See fn. 64.

[66] See Rebecca Baltzer, "Lambertus," *The New Grove*, vol. 10, pp. 400-401.

[67] See above, p. 7 and fn. 20.

[68] A single instance may stand for many:
> Sicut autem in unaquaque scientia est ponere primum et minimum, utputa in grammatica litteram, in dyalectica terminum, sic et in ista musica mensurabili . . .
> (Prologus 82, 29-31)

> (But just as in each science one should first put the smallest unit, for example the letter in grammar, and the term in dialectic, so in measurable music . . .)

intention to defend the prose work "on the art of measurable music," which had been so highly regarded by the *universitas clericorum*.[69] Garlandia's little book became the most widely influential treatise on the polyphony of Notre Dame, and his association with Paris is not in doubt.[70] As early as 1210 the new center of learning in Paris had begun to be known as an *universitas*, a "guild" or "corporation" of teachers and students.[71]

There is an allusion amongst the glosses of the treatise to the possible identity of Lambertus. In Chapter Two on the modes one pair of verses reads:

> **Sic recitat prosa studio multiplice rosa,**
> **Quae male lactavit hunc illam qui laceravit.**
> > (*Cap*.II 190, 43 - 192, 1)

> **(Thus recites the prose, worn by much hard work,**
> **Which has unfortunately suckled him who has mutilated it.)**

---

[69]See *Prologus* 64, 1-4. Other references to Garlandia's work in the present treatise are: *Prologus* 64, 24; *Prologus* 72, 25; *Prologus* 72-74, *passim*; *Prologus* 76, 33; *Prologus* 76, 39; *Prologus* 78, 3; *Prologus* 78-80, *passim*; *Cap*.Ii 100, 5; *Cap*.Ii 112, 34; *Cap*.Ii 116,7; *Cap*.Iii 142, 44; *Cap*.Iii 158, 37-38; *Cap*.II 200, 12-13; *Cap*.II 208, 1; *Cap*.II 216, 23ff.; *Cap*.III 246, 9; *Cap*.III 248, 44; *Cap*.IV 258, 25; *Cap*.IV 264, 19-24; *Cap*.IV 266, 37-40; *Cap*.V 270, 18-19; *Cap*.V 272, 15-19.

[70]See Reimer, *Johannes de Garlandia*, vol. 1, pp. 1-17; and Rebecca Baltzer, "Johannes de Garlandia," *The New Grove*, vol. 9, pp. 662-664. Neither of these studies, however, makes mention of the several Parisian documents which may include a reference to this Johannes. They are as follows: Molinier, *Obituaires*, vol. 1, part 1, pp. 200, 218; vol. 2, p. 168; Glorieux, *Aux origines*, vol. 2, p. 540; Guérard, *Cartulaire*, vol. 1, pp. 150, 159, 160, vol. 2, p. 64, vol. 3, pp. 144, 165, 167, vol. 4, p. 186. The identification of the Parisian music theorist has been complicated by the theory that he might have been the English John of Garland. This been shown to be implausible (see Rudolf Rasch, *Iohannes de Garlandia en de Ontwikkeling van de voor-Franconische Notatie*, Musicological Studies, vol. 20 [Brooklyn, 1969]; and Reimer, *loc. cit.*). A thorough search of contemporary documents shows that the problem is even more thorny than has so far appeared, for the following reasons: 1) There are several variant spellings of the last name; Garlandia, Gallandia, Garrendia, Guallandia, and Garlanda being the most common. 2) These may refer to at least two very well known places: a) a street in Paris on the left bank called the rue Garlande; b) a town in the commune of Réau, Seine-et-Marne, arrondissement of Melun, in the canton of Brie-Comte-Robert. Therefore 3) A knight Johannes who is the *dominus* of Tournan in the same area as b) above may also appear as Johannes de Garlandia. 4) Some of the entries are clearly from the early fourteenth century.

[71]See *Chartularium Universitatis Parisiensis*, ed. Denifle and Chatelain, 4 vols. (Paris, 1891; reprint 1964), vol. 1, p. ix; and Anders Piltz, *The World of Medieval Learning*, p. 129.

   This lurid and colorful metaphor is heavily glossed, but no further
meaning is given for **lactavit** ("**suckled**").   It is possible that Johannes
de Garlandia taught Lambertus directly.   Alternatively what is meant is
only that Lambertus was nourished by Garlandia's treatise.   However the
word **hunc** ("**him**") has the explanation *sive clericum vel magistrum* ("the
cleric or teacher").   Lambertus too may have been a teacher at the
University of Paris.   The only prose passage from the treatise which
mentions his name describes him as "magister Lambertus."[72]

   Amongst all the official documents that have been examined concerning
university, cathedral, and court affairs in Paris during the thirteenth
century, only one mentions a figure who is a plausible candidate for this
magister and music theorist.   This document (See Appendix II, Document
1), recorded by the judicial officer of the ecclesiastical court
("officialis"), registers a change in the will of a Parisian *magister*
Lambertus who was dean of the cathedral at Soignies.   Soignies is near
Brussels, about two hundred kilometers north-north-west of Paris.   He is
described as "sick in body, but healthy in mind," and the decision was
witnessed by clerks who were sent from Paris to his bedside.   Lambertus
bequeaths small legacies to his housekeeper and chaplain, his household
effects to his nieces and nephews, and the remainder of his estate,
including some books, to the "poor scholars and masters" of Paris.
Robert de Sorbon (who was chaplain to King Louis IX and the famous
benefactor of the University) is named as his executor.   The document is
dated April 8, 1270.

   If this is the Lambertus who wrote on music and whom the Anonymous of
1279 attacks (and the identification seems plausible, since he is the
only known thirteenth-century person of that name who is also a *magister*
of Paris; his affection for the university is manifest; and the date
falls within the requisite period[73]) then we may now know the identity of
one of the principal theorists of the thirteenth century and at least a
terminus ante quem for the writing of the Lambertus treatise.[74]

---

[72]*Cap.*Iii 148, 3.

[73]See fn. 64.

[74]There is another Lambertus, a canon of the collegiate church of
St. Cloud, mentioned in connection with an earlier transaction in June of
1264, but the lack of the title *magister* suggests that this is not the
same man (although it is possible that he received his *licentia docendi*
after this date).   See Paris, Archives Nationales, S 6213, no. 13; Paris,
Bibliothèque Nationale, lat. 16069, fol. 96c-97a; and Palémon Glorieux,
Aux Origines de la Sorbonne, 2 vols., Etudes de philosophie médiévale LIV
(Paris, 1965), vol. 2, *Le Cartulaire*, no. 236 (pp. 266-267).   The volumes
of the early nineteenth-century published collection of obituaries from
the province of Sens contain a large number of references to men with the
name Lambertus or variations thereof ("Lantbertus," etc.); however these
have all been eliminated from consideration either by reason of their
date or because of the lack of the title *magister*.   A single exception
records the anniversary of a magister Lambertus, a canon of Troyes, in
the obituary list of the Hôtel-Dieu of Provins.   No year is given.   See
Auguste Molinier (ed.), *Obituaires de la province de Sens*, Recueil des
historiens de la France, Obituaires, 4 vols. (Paris, 1902-1923), vol. 1,

INTENDED AUDIENCE

There are several references throughout the treatise to the intended audience for the work. These take two forms: descriptions of the work itself, and addresses to the reader. For the work itself the terms used are *volumen, liber, libellus, compendia,* and *introductio.* The latter two particularly are terms in common use in the medieval university setting for schoolbooks for university students.

Often in the treatise, either in the prose or in the verse, the reader is addressed directly. Sometimes this is in the most general rhetorical form: "care" ("O dear one"), for example, or by means of the second person singular imperative: "nota" ("note that"), "cerne" ("perceive"), etc.[75] But on two occasions[76] a far more specific form of address is used. These gloss the general imperatives with the direct vocative: "O cantor vel lector" ("O cantor or reader"), and "O lector vel cantor" ("O reader or cantor").[77] The intended audience may include not only university students, but professional singers in local churches as well.[78]

MUSICAL EXAMPLES

Apart from the numerous instances throughout the treatise in which notational procedures are illustrated by means of ligatures or single notes, there are several compositions which are cited or of which a small portion is given as a musical example. These are listed together with their sources in Appendix III.

Amongst these compositions there are polyphonic chant settings, conductus, motets, and hockets. The polyphonic chant settings and conductus may be traced to the surviving manuscripts of the repertoire of the Cathedral of Notre Dame in Paris. Several of the motets have French dupla or tripla, and most of the motets, both French and Latin, can be

---

part 2, p. 937. A Lambertus, *sigillifer* for the court, makes an appearance in the printed cartularies of the Cathedral of Notre Dame in a document of 1263. He is not described as *magister.* See M. Guérard (ed.), *Cartulaire de l'église Notre-Dame de Paris,* 4 vols., Collection des cartulaires de France IV-VII, *Collection de documents inédits sur l'histoire de France,* series 1 (Paris, 1850), vol. 2, p. 9. Finally the anniversary notice (without year) of a "Lambertus subdiaconus" in the obituary list of the cathedral should be mentioned. (Molinier, *Obituaires,* vol. 1, p. 101.) At this rank the "magister" is sometimes omitted. Cf. Appendix II, Document 12.

[75] This device is common also in Anonymous IV. See Reckow, *Der Musiktraktat,* vol. 1; and Jeremy Yudkin, *The Music Treatise of Anonymous IV: A New Translation,* Musicological Studies and Documents XLI (Neuhausen-Stuttgart, 1985).

[76] *Cap.*II 200, 5 and *Cap.*II 202, 10.

[77] The *vel* in these cases is probably not adversative but separative.

[78] Although the position of *cantor* was a high-ranking one amongst the dignitaries of a cathedral, the word appears in music treatises also as a general term for a trained singer.

found in the Montpellier Codex, which is almost certainly of Parisian provenance.[79] Some of the notational characteristics of the examples and the choice of quotations from the middle of pieces suggest that the author may even have been directly familiar with this manuscript.[80]

REFERENCES TO THE AUTHOR AND HIS TEACHER

So far the bulk of the evidence suggests that the anonymous author of the treatise of 1279 lived and worked in Paris, and that he was connected with the university.[81] That he was also knowledgeable about practical music-making is indicated by his familiarity with contemporary musical compositions -- with details of their sound, their effect, and their method of performance, as well as with their notation.

In the very last chapter of the book, a gloss reveals a further hint as to the identity of our author. The chapter concerns *organum speciale*, that species of polyphony for which the author reserves his greatest enthusiasm. It is the "consummation" of his "little work;" it "surpasses . . . all types of melodies with the delightful sweetness of its musical sound." The verse portion of the chapter begins with the line:

> **Nobis organica specialis vox fit amica.**
> > (*Cap*.VI 284, 1)

> **(To us the special organal voice is a friend.)**

The word **Nobis** ("**To us**") is provided with the gloss *cantoribus* ("cantors"). Perhaps the author too was a professional singer.

There is only one name mentioned in the treatise apart from that of Lambertus and the several Classical or late Classical authors whose works are quoted in the course of the work. The name appears in Chapter Two in the following context:

> Unde venerabilis magister noster Henricus de
> Daubuef ait versu:
> *Tot sunt cantores et cantus fabulatores,*
> *Quod cantus mores deserit atque fores.*
> > (*Cap*.II 218, 5-9)

---

[79] See *Manuscripts of Polyphonic Music: 11th - Early 14th Century* (ed. Gilbert Reaney), Répertoire international des sources musicales B/IV/1 (Munich, 1966), p. 273; Robert Branner, *Manuscript Painting in Paris During the Reign of Saint Louis: A Study of Styles* (Berkeley, 1977); Ernest Sanders, "Sources, MS, V, 2: Early Motet," in *The New Grove*, vol. 17, p. 656; and Ellen Beer, "Parisian Book Illustrations at the Time of Louis IX (King and Saint) in the Last Quarter of the 13th Century," *Zur Kunstgeschichte* XLIV (1981): 62-91.

[80] See, for example, *Cum gaudio* in Appendix III. This is an extract from the middle of the *motetus* part of a Latin motet. The words and music appear at the very top of a column in the Montpellier Codex.

[81] In the Prologue the author describes his method as like that of "masters of the liberal arts" (*more artificum*). See Prologue 69, 52-53.

> (And so our revered master [teacher] Henricus de
> Daubuef says in verse:
> "There are so many cantors and makers of melody,
> That melody abandons its customs and hearth.")

The couplet is in the form of verses known as *unisoni*[82] from the single rhyme, and presents a common type of *sententia* (see the note to the translation.) The name of the author's teacher is of course a piece of evidence of considerable value. Unfortunately a thorough search of all documents, published and unpublished, relating to both the University and the Cathedral of Paris throughout the thirteenth century revealed no Henricus de Daubuef.

The search, however, did provide an excellent candidate for the person of Magister Henricus. In the immense index of the *Chartularium Universitatis Parisiensis*,[83] under "P" for "Parisiensis Ecclesia" and within the subheading "Canonici," is listed a "Henr. Tuebuef." It seems likely that this is the right man, for there exist a fair number of documents that mention his name; his dates correspond to the period under consideration (the second half of the thirteenth century); and his sphere of activity encompassed both the University and the Cathedral.[84]

The University of Paris and the Cathedral of Notre Dame were closely connected. The university was a direct descendant of the cathedral school; from the beginning the right to teach (*licentia docendi*) was granted by the chancellor of Notre Dame; and the lecture-halls and schoolrooms of the university were situated on the Ile de la Cité around the cathedral, eventually spilling over to the left bank of the river, just across the "petit pont" from Notre Dame.

The *licentia docendi* was not distributed wholesale. It was earned by at least two years of teaching and study after the first degree, and its bestowal was marked by special ceremonies.[85] If Henricus Tuebuef is known as a "magister," then he was indeed licensed to teach at the University. Apart from the quotation from the present treatise given above, two of the other documents which mention his name refer to him as "magister."

Henricus, however, was also a member of the cathedral chapter, and the glimpses that have survived of his life and career are mostly from

---

[82] See Meyer, "Radewins Gedicht," p. 84; and Norberg, *Introduction*, pp. 67-68, fn. 3. Meyer has also located the term *leonini et caudati simul*, since the form incorporates both middle- and end-rhyme.

[83] Ed. Denifle and Chatelain, 4 vols. (Paris, 1891-99; reprint 1964).

[84] There is no other Henricus with a last name of Dauboeuf, Dubeuf, or anything remotely similar to the spelling given in the manuscript. There are several instances of the generic "Henricus," but these cannot help us. Only one other Tuebuef appears -- a Raymundus, who is listed in Document 3 of Appendix II, together with Henricus.

[85] See Hastings Rashdall, *The Universities of Europe in the Middle Ages* (ed. Powicke and Emden, 3 vols. [Oxford, 1936]), vol. 1, pp. 278-290, 456-465; and Piltz, *The World*, p. 127.

cathedral records. All of the original documents referred to below are
transcribed in Appendix II.

The first mention of Henricus occurs in a statute of January 1249
(Document 2), which lays out the taxes to be paid by members of the
chapter on the houses they occupied within the cathedral close. On the
house of Henricus Tuebuef a tax is imposed of one hundred *solidi*. That
he did not live in a very imposing house at that time may be deduced from
the fact that this figure represents the lowest assessment in the
statute. The succentor of the cathedral was assessed nearly twice this
amount; the dean two and a half times.

In April 1249 Henricus appears as one of the executors of the will of
Guillelmus, bishop of Paris.[86] (See Document 3.) Here Henricus is
listed, together with Raymundus Tuebuef, as both a *magister* and a canon
of the cathedral. Nothing more is known of Raymundus, who may have been
a relative.

Later in the same year, on the thirteenth of September 1249,
Henricus acted as one of the witnesses to the paying of homage by the
knight Ansellus of Tournan to the new bishop, Galterus.[87] Document 4
records the ceremony, which took place at St. Victor. Here Henricus is
simply "canon of Paris."

No further mention of Henricus is extant until twelve years later,
when, on the thirtieth of December 1261, he is appointed by the chapter
as *praepositus,* "provost" or administrator, of Rosetum. (See Document
5.) Rosetum is the Latin name for the town of Rozay-en-Brie, about fifty
kilometres east-south-east of Paris. Evidently the cathedral chapter had
land holdings there, and Henricus had risen to a position of administrative responsibility for the area.

On the eighteenth of February 1264, he appears as a representative of
the chapter in a dispute between the chapter and a certain Johannes de
Atrio of Rozay. (See Document 6.) He is also given the title *dominus,* a
general term of honor and respect, one which indicates the possession of
considerable social stature.

On the first of March 1269, Henricus was officially reconfirmed as
provost of Rozay-en-Brie. Document 7 is a letter spelling out the length
and conditions of his tenure. He was to hold the post for six years,
during which time he would undertake, out of the income from the area,
the repair of the chapter house at Rozay. The dean and chapter of Notre
Dame confirm the appointment.

All was not always peaceful between the administration and the local
inhabitants of Rozay-en-Brie. In February of 1272 a hearing was held in
the presence of Cardinal Ancherus, archdeacon of the cathedral. (See
Document 8.) Several representatives of the town (including a clothing
supplier ["forbitor"], a middleman in produce ["regratarius"], and
Johannes de Atrio, whose presence was noted above) appeared before the
cardinal in order to lodge a complaint against the chapter. Two men had
been apprehended in Rozay -- one for theft, the other for breaking the
night curfew -- but had escaped from the jail. The townsfolk blamed the
chapter, and its provost, Henricus Tuebuef, *dominus* and canon of the

---

[86]Guillelmus III Arvernus, bishop from 1228 to 1248.

[87]Galterus II de Castro Theodorici (Château-Thierry) was bishop of
Paris only from June to September 1249.

chapter, for breach of responsibility. As a result of this complaint the chapter appointed its dean and archdeacon to look into the matter and determine precisely who owned the jail and who was responsible for its administration. The townspeople agreed to abide by their findings.

The first occasion on which Henricus is given the adjective *venerabilis* is in a document dated the thirteenth of April 1278. A man had been caught poaching in one of the woods owned by the cathedral and excommunicated as a result. He was now to be handed over to the jurisdiction of two "venerable" canons of Paris, a certain Gervasius de Clinocampo and Henricus Tuebuef. (See Document 9.) Henricus' term of office as provost of Rozay, if it had run for the requisite period, would have expired in 1275.

On the fourth of April 1279, Henricus officially donated to the cathedral chapter a substantial amount of property he had acquired a year earlier in the area of Sucy-en-Brie. (See Document 10.) Sucy-en-Brie is just twenty kilometres outside Paris in the same direction as Rozay. (The extent of cathedral holdings in and around Paris in the middle ages may be hinted at even today by a large wooded area next to Sucy which is still called the Bois Notre-Dame.)

Henricus Tuebuef was only human, however. Four years later, on the nineteenth of March 1283, he was fined by the chapter for striking a servant. (See Document 11.)

By the year 1286 Henricus must have been feeling his age. On the twenty-sixth of March of that year, the chapter granted to Henricus Tuebuef the right to be buried within the cathedral upon his death. (See Document 12). This was a right granted to certain members of the chapter as a mark of honor in their old age.

One of the last official proceedings in which Henricus took part dates from the ninth of April 1286. (See Document 13.) This concerned a far more serious matter than the minor disputes and transactions documented so far. And the litigants were, on the one side, the cathedral chapter, and on the other, the University of Paris.

A student of the university had been murdered right in front of the cathedral, on the "parvis" or courtyard. Three clerics from the choir of the cathedral had been implicated in the crime, and the university had therefore requested the cathedral chapter to render judgement in the case. In what must be regarded as a move of great wisdom and tact, and "being kindly disposed to the aforementioned request, and desiring to fulfill the true love and affection which we bear towards the said university," the cathedral chapter appointed three men who were *magistri* from amongst the canons of the cathedral to discover the "full truth" of the matter. One of the *magistri* is Henricus Tuebuef. All three are described as being "skilled in both ecclesiastical and civil law." Sworn confessions are taken from the accused, and depositions from witnesses are studied; as a result of which the three clerks, found guilty of "excesses" but not of homicide, are removed from their posts in the choir and banished from the city and diocese of Paris for a period of three years.

It is not known in precisely which year Henricus Tuebuef died. An obituary notice dated June 11, but with no year given (Document 14), records his death and states his rank as subdeacon -- not a particularly high-ranking ecclesiastical order (indeed he was not even a priest), but yet one step above an ordinary canon.

It is not unusual for the year of death to be missing from

obituaries. These usually list the names in calendar order, starting
with January the first and continuing throughout the year, since it was
only the day of the year that needed to be known for memorial purposes.
Even the exact day may vary somewhat in the records.[88] Two other
obituary notices give slightly different dates for the anniversary of
Henricus. One, contained in an obituary list from St. Victor, (Document
15) gives May 27. This document also mentions a bequest from Henricus of
the sum of twenty *livres* to the Abbey.[89] The other (Document 16)
designates June 9. Neither gives the year of death.

One last mention of Henricus Tuebuef occurs in a fourteenth-century
obituary list from the Hôtel-Dieu of Provins (Document 17). This records
the anniversary date -- December 12 -- of a certain Robertus de Urcheyo,
described as a *clericus* of the late Henricus Tuebuef.

From all of these records we are able to piece together a sketch of
the life of this man, one which may be representative of a large number
of otherwise unremarkable people involved in the administrative affairs
of the mid-thirteenth century. His known activities cover a span of
nearly forty years. In 1249 he is already listed as a canon and
magister. He might by then have been in his mid-twenties, and his date
of birth could therefore be placed at about 1225. By 1261 he is acting
as provost for the cathedral chapter and by 1264 he is described with the
honorific *dominus*. In 1269 he is officially reappointed to the post of
provost and represents the cathedral in local disputes within his area of
responsibility until 1275. In the late 1270s he starts to be known as
venerabilis (he would by then have been in his fifties) and is entrusted
with legal cases. He has become sufficiently wealthy to acquire some
property outside Paris,[90] which he gives to the chapter. He is still
active in 1286, when he investigates a murder charge on behalf of the
university. However in that same year preparations are made for the
disposition of his grave after his death. He may have died in about 1290
at the age of sixty-five or seventy, leaving a sizeable bequest to the
Abbey of St. Victor.

Henricus Tuebuef (c. 1225-1290), *magister, dominus,* canon, provost,
and subdeacon of the Cathedral of Notre Dame, is probably the "Henricus
Daubuef" whose name is given as the teacher of the author of our
treatise. He would have been fifty-five or sixty years old in 1279, old

---

[88]For other examples, see Craig Wright, "Leoninus," fn. 34.

[89]The importance of the Abbey of St. Victor and its connection with
Notre Dame, as well as the affection and esteem in which the Abbey was
held by members of the cathedral clergy, are sensitively sketched in
Margot Fassler, "Who Was Adam of St. Victor? The Evidence of the
Sequence Manuscripts," *Journal of the American Musicological Society*
XXXVII (1984): 233-269; and Wright, "Leoninus," pp. 15-16. The
obituaries of several notables from the cathedral were celebrated at St.
Victor, and the ceremony recorded in my Document 3 took place there. The
fullest account of the great monastery (unfortunately now destroyed)
remains Fourier Bonnard, *Histoire de l'abbaye royale et de l'ordre des
chanoines réguliers de St. Victor de Paris,* 2 vols. (Paris, 1904-1908).

[90]The canons of the cathedral were secular clergy and were therefore
allowed to own property.

enough by thirteenth-century standards to be known as "venerabilis," as indeed he is called in the single mention of him in the treatise, and as he is listed in almost exactly contemporaneous administrative documents.

Apart from its importance in suggesting a link between the music theory of the thirteenth century and the cathedral of Paris -- a link we have always assumed but not been able to demonstrate -- this investigation tends to confirm the internal evidence about the date of the treatise analyzed above. The treatise may be considered reliable when it records its date of completion as 1279.

About the author himself there are far fewer clues. Yet the investigations presented above may be summarized as follows: The Scholastic clothing of the treatise, its bookish references, its learned structure -- all these point to a man of university training and influence. Johannes de Garlandia was a *magister* at the University of Paris. Lambertus was also a *magister* at the same university.[91] The treatise is described in terms of a university text. Its audience is comprised both of *lectores* and *cantores*. Its musical examples are from the repertory of Notre-Dame polyphony and Parisian motets. The author's teacher was both a *magister* and a canon of Notre Dame, who seems to have spent his whole career (from c. 1250-1290) in and around Paris.

All of these facts point to the following hypothesis: The author of the 1279 treatise on *musica mensurabilis* was a university teacher, living and working at Paris, possibly also with connections to the cathedral, and he may himself have been a singer, either at Notre Dame or at another local church. At the end of his impressive and remarkable book he writes that the work was completed "**floribus aevi,** id est in ferventi flosculo iuventutis vel aetatis virilis" ("**in the flower of my age,** that is, in the shining flower of youth or manhood"). In 1279, therefore, he may have been twenty-five or thirty years old,[92] which would place his date of birth at about 1250. Details of his life and career are almost certainly contained amongst the records and documents of the Cathedral of Notre Dame and the University of Paris of the late thirteenth century. All we need is his name.

---

[91] It is beginning to appear more and more likely that Franco too composed his *Ars cantus mensurabilis* in Paris. Its construction is directly in the tradition of Garlandia, Lambertus, and the present treatise; it adopts and modifies much of Lambertus' theory; it imitates the opening of the present work; a French term appears in the text (ed. Reaney/Gilles IV, 15); and one of the manuscripts of the treatise (Milan, Biblioteca Ambrosiana, D5) describes Franco as "magister Franco parisiensis." See Andrew Hughes, "Franco of Cologne," in *The New Grove*, vol. 6, pp. 794-797; and Michel Huglo, "Recherches sur la personne et l'oeuvre de Francon," (forthcoming paper, generously provided by the author).

[92] That he was of the next generation after that of Johannes de Garlandia is suggested by the frequent references to *primi actores* ("the first authors") and *nos posteri* ("we, the next ones") throughout the work.

DESCRIPTION AND HISTORY OF THE MANUSCRIPT

DESCRIPTION OF THE CODEX
     The treatise on mensural music in the form of verse and commentary is
bound into a codex now held by the Handschriftenabteilung of the
Bayerische Staatsbibliothek in Munich. The codex is identified by its
current shelf number in that library: Clm (= *Codex latinus monachensis*)
14523. It contains several important writings on music as well as
treatises on the Zodiac and *computus*.[93] As far as can be determined,

---

     [93]References to aspects of the codex other than the mensural music
treatise include: August Eduard Anspach, *Las Etimologías en la tradición
manuscrita medieval* (León, 1966); Günter Bernt, *Das lateinische Epigramm
in Übergang von der Spätantike zum frühen Mittelalter*, Münchener
Beiträge zur Mediävistik und Renaissance-Forschung, vol. 2 (Munich,
1968); Bernhard Bischoff, *Literarisches und künstlerisches Leben in St.
Emmeram (Regensburg) während des frühen und hohen Mittelalters*, Studien
and Mitteilungen zur Geschichte des Benediktiner-Ordens und seiner
Zweige, vol. 51 (Munich, 1933); idem, *Mittelalterliche Studien:
Ausgewählte Aufsätze zur Schriftkunde und Literaturgeschichte*, 3 vols.
(Stuttgart, 1966-81); idem, *Die südostdeutschen Schreibschulen und
Bibliotheken in der Karolingerzeit*, 2 vols.: *Die Bayrischen Diözesen*
(Leipzig, 1940 [Reprint Wiesbaden, 1960]), *Die vorwiegend
Österreichischen Diözesen* (Wiesbaden, 1980); Edward Buhle, *Die
musikalischen Instrumente in den Miniaturen des frühen Mittelalters: Ein
Beitrag zur Geschichte der Musikinstrumente*, vol. 1: *Die Blasinstrumente*
(Leipzig, 1903); Michel Huglo, *Les tonaires: Inventaire, analyse,
comparaison*, Publications de la Société française de musicologie III, 2
(Paris, 1971); Elisabeth Klemm, *Die romanischen Handschriften der
Bayerischen Staatsbibliothek: Katalog der illuminierte Handschriften der
Bayerischen Staatsbibliotek in München*, 4 vols. (Wiesbaden, 1980-);
Raymund Kottje, "Klosterbibliotheken und monastische Kultur in der
zweiten Hälfte des 11. Jahrhunderts," *Zeitschrift für Kirchengeschichte*
LXXX (1969): 145-162; Bernhard Lambert, O.S.B., *Bibliotheca Hieronymiana
manuscripta: La tradition manuscrite des oeuvres de St. Jérôme*, 7 vols.,
Instrumenta Patristica IV, 1a-4b (Steenbrugge, 1964-72); Michael Masi,
"Manuscripts containing the 'De Musica' of Boethius," *Manuscripta* XV
(1971): 89-95; *Musik in Bayern*, 2 vols. (Tutzing, 1972); Otto Pächt,
Illuminated Manuscripts in the Bodleian Library Oxford, 3 vols.: *German,
Dutch, Flemish, French and Spanish Schools* (Oxford, 1966), *Italian School*
(Oxford, 1970), *British, Irish and Icelandic Schools* (Oxford, 1973);
Reinhold Schlötterer, "Münchener Musikhandschriften," in *Die Musik in
Geschichte und Gegenwart*, vol. 9 (Kassel, 1961); Hans Schmid, *Die
musiktheoretischen Handschriften der Benediktiner-Abtei Tegernsee: Ein
Beitrag zur Erfassung und Sichtung der musiktheoretischen
Hinterlassenschaft des Mittelalters*, diss. Ludwigs-Maximilians-
Universität (Munich, 1951); Tilman Seebass, *Musikdarstellung und
Psalterillustration im früheren Mittelalter: Studien ausgehend von einer
Ikonologie der Handschrift Paris Bibliothéque nationale fonds latin
1118*, 2 vols. (Bern, 1973); Hugo Steger, *Philologia musica:
Sprachzeichen, Bild und Sache im literarisch-musikalischen Leben des*

the mensural music treatise survives uniquely in this codex.

The codex measures 23 x 16.5 cm. and is bound in boards with leather back and corners.[94] The binding is from the nineteenth century. On the spine are four labels: Two read "Cod. Lat. 14523" and "Cim. 397," and are from the time of the binding. Of the other two the first carries the words "Scriptores de Musica alia Sec. X XII & XIII," and the last has the shelf number "F XXVI." These two labels are from the eighteenth century. The foliation, [2] + 159 + [2], includes, inside the binding on each end, one paper leaf and an older parchment folio from a service-book in fourteenth- or fifteenth-century *textura formata*. Both parchment binding folios carry traces of glue from an earlier binding process, and the front paper leaf is inscribed with the number 810 in lead point with the characteristic eighteenth-century style supine 8. On the outside edges of folios 2, 49, 53, 118, 126, and 134, small white tags have been glued to mark major divisions within the codex (*libellus* I, *libellus* II, the Boethius treatise, *libellus* III, Guido, and *libellus* IV.)

The codex is made up throughout of quaternios with the following exceptions: Folio 49-55 is a ternio with a single added folio in the middle. Folio 59 is an added (partial) folio. Folio 73 is an added strip. Folio 90 consists of two added strips. Between folios 101 and 102 is an added strip (unnumbered in the foliation). Folio 111 is a single folio added to a ternio (107-113). Folio 114-117 is a binio. Folio 126-133 is a ternio (whose central bifolio is of smaller size, each folio measuring 19.8 x 14.5 cm.) with two added single folios.

Folio 20 has a tear of 4.5 cm. repaired by sewing. The skin of the quaternio 65-72 is very thin. The parchment of folios 118-133 is grey and poorly prepared.

The codex is made up of four *libelli*[95] of different date and provenance bound into a single collection. The contents and arrangement of each *libellus* are as follows:

Libellus I (Folios 1-48)

Mittelalters: Lire, Harfe, Rotte und Fidel, Münstersche Mittelalter-Schriften, vol. 2 (Munich, 1971); Georg Swarzenski, *Die Regensburger Buchmalerei des X. und XI. Jahrhunderts: Studien zur Geschichte der deutschen Malerei des frühen Mittelalters*, Denkmäler der süddeutschen Malerei des frühen Mittelalters, vol. 1 (Stuttgart, 1969); Otto Ursprung, *Die katholische Kirchenmusik*, Handbuch der Musikwissenschaft, Lieferung 74, vol. 9 (Potsdam, [1931]); Wilhelm Wattenbach, *Deutchlands Geschichtsquellen im Mittelalter: Die Zeit der Sachsen und Salier*, 3 vols. (Darmstadt, 1967-71); Reinhard Wiesend, *Die Notierungen der Musikbeispiele in den Münchner Guido-Handschriften*, Magister-Prüfung Ludwigs-Maximilians-Universität (Munich, 1971).

[94]I would like to express here my appreciation to Michel Huglo for his generosity in providing for me while still in early proofs the pages relating to the description of Clm 14523 from RISM B/III/3, now published as *The Theory of Music: Manuscripts from the Carolingian Era up to c. 1500 in the Federal Republic of Germany* (Munich, 1986).

[95]For the concept and description of the *libellus*, see Michel Huglo, "Les 'libelli' de tropes et les premiers tropaires-prosaires," in *"Pax et Sapientia": In Memoriam Gordon A. Anderson* (Stockholm, 1986), pp. 13-22.

Fol. 1:   Walafrid Strabo, *Versus de quatuor divisionibus zodiaci.*

Fol. 2-48v: Rhabanus Maurus, *De compoto.*

Libellus II (Folios 49-117)
   Fol. 49:   "Musica Boetii, Musica Sancti Hieronimi, Dardanideque assit principio."
   Fol. 49v-50v: Pseudo-Jerome, "Incipit epistola . . . Explicit epistola Sancti Hieronymi de carminibus."
   Fol. 50v-51:   Isidore of Seville, "Item Isidorus in tertio libro . . . et sonum faciunt. Finit."
   Fol. 51-52:   Illustrations of musical instruments in yellow and red: "Organum, psalterium, cythara, bunibulum, cimbalum . . . " etc.
   Fol. 52v-117:   Boethius, *De musica.* "Omnium quidem perceptio sensuum . . . ut in diatonicis generibus nusquam." With diagrams of the Greek scales, divisions of the octave, musical intervals etc., in red.
   Fol. 117v: "Kolikophanes, id est incepta vocis compositio."

Libellus III (Folios 118-133)
   Fol. 118-125v: Guido d'Arezzo, *Micrologus.* "In nomine summae et individuae Trinitatis incipit Mikrologus . . . Explicit Mikrologus, id est brevis sermo in musica, editus a domino Guidone, peritissimo musico et venerabili monacho, directus ad Teobaldum Retianae civitatis episcopum."
   Fol. 125v-127:   Guido d'Arezzo, *Regulae rhythmicae.* "O venerande amice Dei Benedicte . . . variant loca cuius idipsum." Example of the four tetrachords in Dasian notation.
   Fol. 127-133v: Guido d'Arezzo, *De ignoto cantu, Prologus antiphonarii, Regulae tonorum* etc. "Ita igitur disponuntur voces . . . Beatus es et bene." Several musical examples in neumatic, verbal, and letter notation, including polyphonic examples.

Libellus IV (Folios 134-159)
   Fol. 134-159:   Anon., *De musica mensurata.* "Quoniam prosam artis musicae mensurabilis . . . Hostes contrivit, sic scriba suos ubi vivit. Amen." In the form of verses with commentary. Musical examples in square notation.

As well as the continuous foliation numbers throughout the codex, each *libellus* bears its own number on the top right-hand corner of the first folio. *Libellus* I is marked xvi, *libellus* II xxxix, *libellus* III lxxv, and *libellus* IV lxxiiii. The first three *libelli* are written in various forms of Caroline miniscule. Libellus I (with various hands) dates from the first half of the tenth century, *libellus* II from the second half of the ninth century, *libellus* III from the mid-eleventh century. The form and layout of the fourth *libellus* suggest a French

provenance, but do not permit a closer dating than the second half of the thirteenth century.[96]

DETAILED DESCRIPTION OF LIBELLUS IV

The fourth *libellus* of the codex is devoted entirely to the treatise on mensural music. The text of this treatise covers 51 folios in a very small *littera textualis* that fills from 45 to 62 lines per side.[97] The hexameters are written in a markedly larger form of the same script.

The first gathering is a quaternio (folio 134-141). The second gathering is a binio (folio 142-145). The third gathering is a quaternio (folio 146-153). The fourth gathering was originally a quaternio, but the final folio was cut off as being unnecessary, and very little of the penultimate folio (folio [160]) remains. The verso of folio 159 and recto of folio [160] were ruled with 5-line (occasionally 6-line) staves in red, but contain no music. The verso of folio 159 also carries the early nineteenth-century stamp of the Königliche Hofbibliothek (later the Bayerische Staatsbibliothek) of Munich, "Bibliotheca Regia Monacensis," as does the verso of the final parchment binding folio.

Gathering 1 (Folio 134-141)

The writing area of the first gathering was prepared by two sets of prick marks at the upper and lower portion of each folio, 6-8 cm. apart, designating the left margin, the position of the verse initials, the second letter of the verses, and the right margin.[98] Single (occasionally double or triple) prick marks in the outer margin of each folio designate the position of the first and last lines. The scribe (Scribe A) favors "above first line" practice. The area thus designated is marked out in barely visible dry point or occasionally in extremely fine lead point. The intended writing area is 15.4-14.7 x 9.2 cm. The writing sometimes encroaches upon the margins, especially for the musical examples or at a line ending before a set of verses. Often the scribe ignores the intended area in favor of beginning slightly to the left and continuing to the right of the boundaries. Once, this seems to be the result of a desire to cover the same area on the verso as is covered on the recto (folio 137), but there is no such apparent rationale on folio 138, where the left margin stands 3 millimeters to the left of the intended line. Folio 138v blocks out the corresponding area. The number of lines per side ranges from 48 to 55.

The initials that mark off main sections of the text are in red. All of the verse initials are rubricated (as is the second letter of

---

[96] For this ascription and the other dates given here I am indebted to Dr. Günter Glauche of the Handschriftenabteilung of the Bayerische Staatsbibliothek. Mark Everist and Patricia Stirnemann were kind enough to examine facsimiles of *libellus* IV and reached similar conclusions.

[97] Throughout this description the number of lines per side includes spaces left for the insertion of interlinear glosses even if these were not filled in.

[98] Many of the lower prick marks have been trimmed or are very near the bottom of the folio.

"Quoniam"), and red paragraph marks delineate sections. (Paragraph marks
are lacking on folios 136 and 136v, and folios 139v and 140.) The
openings at folios 136v-137 and 140v-141 were closed too soon after the
rubricator's work, allowing the red ink to stain the opposing folios.
Occasional guides to the rubricator (two d's on folio 136, v and d on
folio 140) may still be seen in the left margins. A miniature three-line
staff in red has been drawn for the musical example "Omnes" on folio 139.

The ink of this gathering is very dark brown-black, wearing to dark
brown in places. The verses and musical examples are consistently darker
than the glosses and commentary. Occasional crosses are drawn in the
left margin in an informal hand in light ink. The verses have been
numbered by fives in modern lead point, usually in the left margin,
sometimes in both the left and the right margins. This continues
throughout the manuscript. The main script is very small, the body of
each letter occupying a minimum of one and a maximum of two square
millimeters. The letters of the verses occupy from two (i) to nine (m)
square millimeters.

Folios 134 and 141v (the outer folios) are notably worn, with some
fading of the text, possibly indicating a temporary independent existence
for this gathering.

Gathering 2 (Folios 142-145)

The second gathering is written in a slightly larger and more formal
hand (Scribe B) in light-brown or olive ink on a different grade of
parchment from that of the other gatherings. There are fewer lines per
side (between 45 and 48), with the exception of folio 144v, which
contains 52 lines. (One line for glosses is empty.) Scribe B also
begins "above top line."

The smaller number of lines per side is partly the result of the more
formal and larger script, but also of the fact that individual lines are
ruled, in dry point or in very fine ink, for every line of text. The
outer and inner prick marks required for this have been trimmed, but
where the individual ruled lines are clearly visible (for example on
folio 143v, whose parchment is particularly white) the distance between
the lines can be accurately measured. They stand at 3 millimeters apart.
(The distance for Scribe A is approximately 2.5 millimeters.) The triple
left margin is retained for text, verse initials, and second letters of
verses. The right hand margin is far more carefully adhered to, giving a
more rectangular, neater appearance to each side. Abbreviations are less
frequently used. Cancellations are indicated by underdotting in this
gathering, in the others almost always by striking through the offending
word. The intended writing area is 16.1-15.5 x 9.3-8.9 cm.

Paragraph marks are in red (apparently by the same rubricator as that
of the other gatherings). Verse initials are rubricated except for two
verses that intrude on the lower margin of folio 142. On folios 144v
and 145, the rubricator has used red ink to go over the underlining of
some verse incipits and the vertical lines used for demarcation of
musical examples. The text ends in the middle of folio 145v.

Gathering 3 (Folios 146-153)

The third gathering is distinguished by a clearly visible series of
prick marks running down the outside margin of each folio, spaced
alternately 3 and 3.5 millimeters apart, and 1.2 cm. from the outside
edge of the folio. The intended writing area is 15.9-15.2 x 9.2 cm. The

hand is that of Scribe A and the number of lines per side is from 49 to
62, with the second half of the gathering exhibiting the greater
compression, having many sides of 58 lines of text. The first side
begins in the middle of a sentence.

Paragraph marks continue in red, as do the initial letters of sections. Verse initials are rubricated. On folio 151v one paragraph mark
has been finely outlined in red but not filled in. Guide letters may be
seen on folio 150v on the prick line (s), and also on 151v (e -- though
the rubricator has written A -- and d). Some underlinings of verse
incipits have been gone over either wholly or partially in red, and
miniature three, four, and five line staves are ruled in red for the
musical examples.

For the polyphonic musical examples on folios 153 and 153v space was
left in the text, flourishing and musical text were written first in
black, red staff lines were ruled next, and clefs and notes were added
last in black. In these instances close cooperation was needed between
scribe and rubricator, if indeed they were not the same person.
Occasional fine marginal crosses reappear in this gathering.

Gathering 4 (Folio 154-159)
The fourth gathering has the same pattern of pricking as the first
gathering, with an additional two pairs of prick marks on the outside
margin of each folio. An additional single prick mark runs through all
the folios of this gathering on the outside margin. This mark must have
been made at the time of binding, as it continues into the parchment
binding folio and the final end paper. The intended writing area is
16.1-15.9 x 9.2 cm. There are from 53 to 60 lines per side.

The gathering exhibits the same compressed hand and ink color as
gatherings 1 and 3, and the pattern and style of rubrication is also the
same. Paragraph marks and rubrication of verse initials are lacking in
the opening 156v and 157, despite the fact that staves have been ruled in
red for the example of the musical intervals on folio 156v. Whoever drew
the red staves also rather whimsically filled in the u of *unisonus,* and
the d's of *dyapason, dyapente, dyatessaron,* and *ditonus* with little red
blobs. Guide letters are visible for many of the red initials. A single
lightly drawn cross is visible in the margin of folio 155.

On the first part of the penultimate side (folio 158v) the ink for
the interlinear glosses is light brown. These may have been written by
Scribe A or by a different hand. On the last part of this side the
interlinear glosses have been added by another hand, which may be that of
Scribe B. The script is marked by the same tall ascenders (particularly
on l and h, with their pointed serifs) and ink of the same olive color as
those of the second gathering. The last side (folio 159) has been
prepared with spaces between the verses for interlinear glosses, but
these were not written. The final pair of verses on the last side
intrude into the lower margin.

Summary
The manuscript is primarily the work of two scribes. Scribe A is
responsible for gatherings 1, 3, and 4, while the whole of gathering 2,
as well as certain corrections, additions, and marginalia (and possibly
the interlinear glosses on the second half of folio 158v) were written by
Scribe B. A small number of other corrections and marginal expansions
may be the work of one or even two other hands. There is a certain

amount of overlap in textual material between the end of the second
gathering and the beginning of the third.

Paragraph marks, initial letters, and other rubrication appear to
have been done at one time and after the inclusion of the second
gathering into the whole, with the exception of red staves, which must
have been ruled during the preparation of the text. Paragraph marks are
used to delineate the beginnings of commentary sections and the
beginnings of verse groups, except as noted, and except for the places
where these already begin with a red initial. The only verse group that
is divided internally is the second group (folio 134v-135).

The square notation of the musical examples is of French origin.[99]

On paleographical evidence and on the basis of the layout of the text
and the style of the hands the manuscript may be assigned a French
provenance and a date of production in the second half of the thirteenth
century.

HISTORY OF THE CODEX AND OF THE MANUSCRIPT

As described above, the codex in which the mensural music treatise is
contained carries a contents label and three different shelf numbers. Of
these three numbers the current one is the number Clm 14523 of the
Bayerische Staatsbibliothek.[100] Two earlier shelf numbers are also still
visible on the spine. Until 1974 the codex belonged to a separate group
of particularly valuable holdings of the library (the "Cimelien"), and
had its own number in that group: Cim. 397.[101] In 1974 this group was
integrated into the main collection. The final number, F XXVI, is the
original shelf location mark from the Benedictine Abbey of St. Emmeram
in Regensburg.[102]

---

[99] According to Michel Huglo, square notation was not used in Bavaria
at this time, except by the Dominican and Cistercian orders and the
Augustinians of Schäftlarn. In Germany as a whole square notation was
confined to certain specific locations and orders: the Benedictine Abbey
at Einsiedeln, and the Carthusians, Dominicans, Cistercians, and
Premonstratians. (See Walther Lipphardt, "Notation," in *Die Musik in
Geschichte und Gegenwart,* vol. 9 [Kassel, 1961], p. 1625.)

[100] The numbering of the Latin manuscripts in the Staatsbibliothek is
alphabetical by place of origin, starting at Clm 2501 for Abensberg, 2531
for Aldersbach, etc. Regensburg begins at 13001. Regensburg, St.
Emmeram, runs from 14000 (the famous and sumptuous ninth-century gospel
book known as the *Codex aureus*) to 15028.

[101] For many years items from this special collection were on exhibit
in the "Cimelien-Saal" of the library. For a concise history of the
Staatsbibliothek and the formation of its collections, see Irmgard
Bezzel, *Bayerische Staatsbibliothek München: Bibliotheksführer:
Geschichte und Bestände* (Munich, 1967).

[102] The magnificent eighteenth-century library of St. Emmeram, with
frescoes by Cosmas Damian Asam, still displays its Roman-numeral shelf
marks above each book-case. Since 1812 the monastery and its adjacent
buildings have belonged to the princes of Thurn and Taxis, who now make
their residence at St. Emmeram. The imposing Romanesque abbey church,

The current manuscript holdings of the Munich library are best
described in the nineteenth-century printed catalogue.[103] Indeed this
catalogue, with additions and emendations, is still used as the most
reliable means of access to the collection. Clm 14523 is listed in
Volume 4, Part 2,[104] of this series as follows:

> 14523 (Em. F 26) membr. in 4°. s. X. XII. XIII. 159 fol.
> f. 1 s. X Walafridi Strabi versus de IV divisionibus etc.
> edidit Dümmler in Anzeiger für Kunde d. d. Vorzeit 1875 n. 6.
> f. 2 Hrabanus Maurus de computo.
> f. 49 s. X. Hieronymi de carminibus epistola ad Dardanum.
> Migne 30 p. 213.
> f. 50 Excerpta ex Isidori Etymologiis III, cap. 19 - 21 cum
> pictis figuris instrumentorum music., quas Gerbert Musica
> Sacra II tab. 23 - 25 edidit. f. 52 Boetius de musica.
> f. 118 s. XII. Guidonis Aretini 'mikrologus id est brevis
> sermo in musica.'
> f. 125 Eiusdem versus de musicae explanatione. f. 128 Aliae
> Guidonis de ignoto cantu directa. f. 132 Regulae tonorum
> secundum Guidonem.
> f. 134 s. XIII Poema de arte musica 'Musica dicatur
> cantandi iure sophia' cum commentario.

The codex came to Munich together with a large number of other
volumes[105] in 1811 or 1812 as a result of the annexation of Regensburg by
Bavaria and the secularization of the St. Emmeram monastery. Although
most of the monasteries in Southern Germany were secularized in 1802-3,
St. Emmeram was given at that time, together with the city and bishopric
(later archbishopric) of Regensburg, to the Prince Carl Theodor Anton
Maria von Dalberg as compensation for lands and titles lost in Constance

---

the largest from the period in the whole of Southern Germany, is now the
church of the parish.

[103]*Catalogus codicum manu scriptorum Bibliothecae Regiae Monacensis*
(Munich, 1856-). From this catalogue it is possible to reconstruct the
organization of the library at St. Emmeram before the removal of the
books to Munich. In the section "F" were also Persius, Horace, Villa-
Dei, Cicero, Lucan, Alcuin, Jerome, Sallust, Porphyry, Petrus Hispanus,
Raymond Lull, Rhabanus Maurus, Aristotle, Seneca, Boethius, the Venerable
Bede, and Hermannus Contractus.

[104]*Catalogus codicum latinorum Bibliothecae Regiae Monacensis*, vol.
2, part 2 (Munich, 1876 [Reprint, Wiesbaden, 1968]).

[105]Over one thousand were brought from St. Emmeram alone. The major
portion of the influx, however, occurred in 1802 and 1803. In the former
year approximately thirty thousand books and manuscripts came to Munich;
in the latter about two hundred thousand. (See Bezzel, *Bayerische
Staatsbibliothek München*.)

and Mainz.[106] Dalberg kept the monastery functioning until 1810, when Regensburg passed to Bavaria, and secularization of the remaining monastic establishments was completed.[107] The rich collection at the St. Emmeram library was sealed until the following year when transfer to Munich could be arranged. These events are recalled in handwritten notes by Johann Andreas Schmeller, *custos* of the Munich library from 1829-52:

> Regensb. St. Emmeram. Den 13t. X[ber]. 1811 wurde Custos
> Joh. Bapt. Bernhart beauftragt sich zu ubernahme u'.
> resp. Aussuchung der Emm. u'. der übrig. Biblioth. nach
> Regensb. zu begeben.[108]

Particular care had been taken to obtain the *Codex aureus* even earlier than this, for apparently others were expressing an interest:

> Der berühmte Emmeramte Codex Evang. den 29[t]. April 1811
> zur K. Hofbiblioth. eingekommen. Der verstorbene Herzog
> Carl v. Wurttemberg habe 40000 dafür gebot. gehabt, sagt
> der Hofkommissar Bar. v. Weichs in seinem Bericht
> darüber.[109]

The mensural music manuscript appears to have been in the library at St. Emmeram for a long time, and it is possible to trace back its existence there through various catalogue entries made over the centuries.

Shortly before the removal of the monastery's holdings to Munich, one of the monks at St. Emmeram, Colomann Sanftl, compiled a catalogue of the manuscripts in his charge arranged by subject matter.[110] This hand-written catalogue is in four large folio volumes, running to nearly two thousand four hundred pages, and was completed in 1809, one year before the secularization of the monastary. It is now also in the possession of the Staatsbibliothek in Munich.[111] In the third volume of

---

[106]For more on the career of Dalberg -- Bishop of Constance, Elector and Archbishop of Mainz, and Archchancellor of the German Reich -- see *Neue deutsche Biographie*, vol. 3 (Berlin, 1957).

[107]See Josef Hemmerle, *Die Benediktinerklöster in Bayern*, Germania Benedictina, vol. 2 (Augsburg, 1970), pp. 241-2.

[108]These notes are the possession of the Handschriftenabteilung of the Bayerische Staatsbibliothek. Sincere thanks are due to Dr. Hermann Hauke for drawing them to my attention.

[109]*loc. cit.*

[110]"Catalogus veterum codicum manuscriptorum ad S. Emmeram Ratisbonae." Sanftl did not confine himself merely to listing the manuscripts, but often copied out lengthy passages from them, or made comments about their content.

[111]Munich, Bayerische Staatsbibliothek, Cbm C. 14. Cl-4.

this catalogue, in the section devoted to "Philosophia, Mathesis, Medecina, et Musica," pp. 1764-5, Sanftl lists the codex and its contents beginning at folio 52 (the Boethius *De Musica*). About the "Tractatus de Arte Musica, versibus hexametris scriptus, cum Commentario. Seculi XIII." he writes (in not entirely faultless Latin): "Notae musicae in hoc opusculo occurrentes, formam quod attinet, ab hodiernis in cantu chorali usitatis haud dissentiunt." ("The musical notes which occur in this little work, as to the form which they have, do not differ from the ones we use today in the chant.")

The codex makes two appearances in eighteenth-century catalogues. The first is in a partial alphabetical listing of the contents of the St. Emmeram library drawn up in 1769.[112] Under the heading *De Musica*, the codex is described as follows:

> Item *Strabi versus de circulo. Rhabanus de Computo. Hieronymi Epistola de Carminibus. Micrologus,* id est *Brevis Sermo in Musicam. Widdo* (=Guido) *ad Teutaldum Episcopum.* etc. Codex in folio minori divers. secul. membran.[113]

The numbers given include the St. Emmeram shelf location mark, F XXVI, and the number 810. This, it transpires, is the number in a slightly earlier printed catalogue from the eighteenth century.[114] This catalogue gives the contents of the codex in more detail:

> Versus Strabi, fragmenta: de 4. divisionibus Zodiaci.
> De Circulo, de terminis quadragesimalibus.
> Rhabanus de Compoto. Capitula 96. membr. saec. 9.
> Hieronymi Epistol. de Carminibus.
> Tractatus de Musica. saec. 9.
> Micrologus, id est, brevis sermo in Musica.
> Widdo ad Teutaldum Episcopum. saec. 13.
> Tractatus Metricus de Musica cum notis. M.CCIX.(*sic*)[115]

---

[112] "Catalogus manuscriptorum bibliothecae monasterii S. Emmerami," Munich, Bayerische Staatsbibliothek, Cbm. Cat. 13. This list was drawn up by Roman Zirngibl, historian, monk at St. Emmeram until its dissolution, and later author of several books on aspects of Bavarian history. (See *Allgemeine deutsche Biographie* [Leipzig, 1875-1912].)

[113] Cbm. Cat. 13, folio 60v.

[114] [Johann Baptist Kraus,] *Bibliotheca principalis ecclesiae et monasterii ord. S. Benedicti ad S. Emmeramum Epis. et Martyr,* 4 vols. (Regensburg, 1748). Kraus served as abbot of St. Emmeram from 1742 until his death in 1762. He achieved a certain amount of notoriety for his virulently anti-Protestant tracts, published anonymously at the monastery. (See *Allgemeine deutsche Biographie, and Hemmerle, Die Benediktinerklöster in Bayern,* pp. 241 and 243.)

[115] *op. cit.,* vol. 2, pp. 134-5. Kraus miscalculated the final verse *explicit* of the text by seventy years.

The codex is assigned the number 810 in the section on philosophy, medicine, the four mathematical arts, and the other arts. The shelf location mark F 26 has been written in ink in the margin of the book.

There seems to be no mention of the codex during the seventeenth century, for it does not appear in the very brief list of holdings at St. Emmeram from 1610,[116] although a later hand has added "et cetera" after the final entry.

In 1595 Maximilian I, Duke (later also Elector) of Bavaria, ordered all of the monasteries under his jurisdiction to prepare catalogues of their holdings. These are extant, and are contained in a manuscript codex in the Staatsbibliothek.[117] The catalogue from St. Emmeram runs from folio 158 to 174v of this manuscript, and entry No. 277 lists at least the major portion of our codex:

> Rabanus de computo. Hieronymus de carminibus. Boetius
> quoque de Musica, et de eadem re Guido Monachus ad
> Teudaldum Episcopum, ante 400. ann. in 8.

It is possible that the last *libellus* (the mensural music treatise) is to be understood in this listing, or that it had not yet been bound into the codex and is cited in another listing (No. 294 on folio 172) as "Musicus libellus."

A previous trace of the treatise alone, separately from the other members of the codex, appears in the catalogue of St. Emmeram compiled by Dionysius Menger in 1500-1501.[118] The entry (on folio 44v)[119] is quite specific:

> Item musica cum commento et textu, et incipit commentum
> Quoniam prosam artis etc., sed textus incipit Musica
> dicatur cantandi iure sophia etc., et sunt 4 quaterni
> parvissimae scripturae text pleter [=blätter?].

This describes our treatise exactly.

Two other entries in this catalogue may refer to *libelli* now bound into the Codex 14523. An entry immediately following the one above designates:

---

[116]"Annotatio manuscriptorum librorum Bibliothecae Monasterii S. Emmerami Ratisbonae." Munich, Bayerische Staatsbibliothek, Cbm. Cat. 3, folios 54-61v.

[117]Munich, Bayerische Staatsbibliothek, Cbm. C. 1.

[118]"Registrum sive Inventarium librorum bibliothecae monasterii Sancti Emmerammi episcopi et martyris." Munich, Bayerische Staatsbibliothek, Clm 14675. This catalogue has been edited by Christine Ineichen-Eder in *Mittelalterliche Bibliothekskataloge Deutschlands und der Schweiz IV, 2: Bistümer Passau und Regensburg* (Munich, 1977), pp. 185-385.

[119]Ineichen-Eder, p. 270.

Item alia musica Mikrologus, id est brevis sermo in
musica, et incipit Divini timoris etc., et sunt duo
quaterni et est Gwidonis.

This might be *libellus* III of our codex, containing the Micrologus
and other writings of Guido in two quaternios, although the *incipit* is
different.[120]

There is less doubt about an earlier entry[121] in the same catalogue:

Item musica Boetii et sunt libri V, sed in ultimo libro
desunt 12 capitula, et incipit epistola sancti Ieronimi
in eandem Cogor a te ut tibi Dardane. Sed liber incipit
Omnium quidem perceptio sensuum etc., cum suis figuris,
et sunt 9 quaterni in bona parva scriptura.

which, with some minor differences,[122] describes the section now forming
libellus II of our codex.

That the treatise may have been at the monastery considerably earlier
can be inferred from an entry in a manuscript of 1347:[123]

Item Alexander. Item Statius Achilleidos. Item opus
super primam partem Prisciani minoris. Item Oratius
epistolarum. Item opus super Boetium de disciplina
scolarium. Item opus super algorismum. Item Ovidius de
remediis. Item *scriptum de musica mensurata*. Omnes in
uno volumine.
(My italics.)

From this bare mention it is not possible to be certain that this is
our treatise. Yet the fact that its form as commentary and verse is not
mentioned in the entry should not be counted against this inference,

---

[120] In Clm 14523 the third *libellus* begins "In nomine summae et
individuae Trinitatis incipit Mikrologus . . ." (in majuscules) followed
by some leonine hexameters before a new *incipit* and the majuscules
"Divini timoris . . ."

[121] Folio 43. (Cf. Ineichen-Eder, p. 267.)

[122] See my description above.

[123] Munich, Bayerische Staatsbibliothek, Clm 14397. Folios 14-19v
contain the St. Emmeram catalogue: "Liberia ecclesiae sancti Emmerammi
Ratisbonensis." This catalogue has also been edited by Ineichen-Eder
(*op. cit.*, pp. 154-161). The entry appears on folio 19 of the manuscript
under "28.. pulpitum. Libri artium." The catalogue is cited in Gustav
Becker, *Catalogi bibliothecarum antiqui* (Bonn, 1885), p. 291; and Max
Piendl, "Fontes monasterii S. Emmerami Ratisbonensis: Bau- und
kunstgeschichtliche Quellen," in *Quellen und Forschungen zur Geschichte
des ehemaligen Reichstiftes St. Emmeram in Regensburg*, Thurn und
Taxis-Studien I (1961): 79.

since the outside folio of the *libellus* is a single uniform rectangle of
script containing no verses in larger letters or interlinear glosses to
catch the eye of the cataloguer. Also no other entry in this list
invokes details of the make-up of the manuscripts or the size of the
writing. The middle words of the very first line of our text are indeed
"musicae mensurabilis."

There remains, however, the question of how a French music treatise
might have come to a Benedictine abbey in south-eastern Germany in the
first half of the fourteenth century.

Connections between Paris and Regensburg were not unknown in the
thirteenth century. Albertus Magnus served as Bishop of Regensburg from
1260-1262,[124] and later abbots of St. Emmeram are known to have spent
time in the papal court at Avignon.[125] One of the most influential and
scholarly abbots in the history of the monastery was Albert von
Schmidmühlen, Abbot of St. Emmeram from 1324 to 1358.[126] Albert had
studied in Paris before he came to St. Emmeram, and was steeped in French
learning and culture.[127] He travelled to Paris once more (in 1327 or
1328) during his abbacy, and took the opportunity on this visit to
acquire several books and manuscripts for his monastery.[128] The account

---

[124]This was before the abbey had finally gained exemption from
control of the local bishop. See Hemmerle, *Die Benediktinerklöster in
Bayern*, pp. 238-40.

[125]Hemmerle, *Die Benediktinerklöster in Bayern*, pp. 239-40.

[126]It was Albert who had the 1347 catalogue compiled and who, the
previous year, had had a new library built for the monastery's collection
of manuscripts. See Munich, Bayerische Staatsbibliothek, Clm 14397,
folio 14:

Anno Domini M.CCC.46 constructa est haec liberia per
venerabilem patrem dominum Albertum abbatem monasterii
huius. Anno vero Domini M.CCC.47 inventi et conscripti
sunt libri inferius annotati in praedicta liberia. Erant
250 volumina in 32 pulpitis.

(In the year of our Lord 1346 this library was constructed
by the revered lord father Albert, abbot of this monastery.
And in the year of our Lord 1347 the books noted below were
gathered and catalogued in the aforesaid library. There
were 250 volumes in 32 bookshelves.)

[127]See Bernhard Bischoff, "Studien zur Geschichte des Klosters St.
Emmeram im Spätmittelalter (1324-1525)," in *Mittelalterliche Studien:
Ausgewählte Aufsätze zur Schriftkunde und Literaturgeschichte*, vol. 2
(Stuttgart, 1967), pp. 115-119.

[128]Some of the manuscripts that Albert von Schmidmühlen might have
obtained in Paris are beginning to be identified. In his article on Clm
28212 in the new volume of the Staatsbibliothek manuscript catalogue,
Hermann Hauke suggests that Clm 14067 might have been brought to St.
Emmeram by Albert. (See Hermann Hauke, *Katalog der lateinischen*

book of St. Emmeram for the year 1327-28, which is in the collection of the Bavarian State Archives,[129] contains the following entry:

> Pro vectura librorum ac aliarum rerum manuscriptarum
> de Parisiis Ratisbonam vii solidi x denarii.
>
> (For the transportation of books and other manuscript
> items from Paris to Regensburg: 7 solidi and 10
> denarii.)

Perhaps the "scriptum de musica mensurata" was a part of this transaction.

SUMMARY

The manuscript of the anonymous mensural music treatise was prepared in the latter half of the thirteenth century, probably in Paris. It was acquired by the Benedictine abbey of St. Emmeram at Regensburg before the middle of the fourteenth century, where it remained for several centuries. Certainly by the eighteenth century and possibly considerably earlier it was bound into a codex with three other *libelli* relating to music. At St. Emmeram the codex bore the shelf location mark F XXVI. Following the dissolution of the monastery the codex was brought in 1811 or 1812 to the Königliche Hofbibliothek (now the Bayerische Staats-bibliothek) in Munich, where it was rebound. Until 1974 it was treated as part of a special collection known as the "Cimelien," and its number in that collection was 397. Its current catalogue number is Codex latinus monachensis 14523 in the Handschriftenabteilung of the Bayerische Staatsbibliothek in Munich.

EDITORIAL METHOD

In 1930 appeared the only previously published version of this treatise, edited by Heinrich Sowa.[130] Sowa's work is inconsistent. Many of his readings of the cramped and heavily abbreviated manuscript text are accurate, but in many cases they are quite misleading. The brilliant and colorful passage on the Io myth discussed above is quite obscured in Sowa's text, as he reads *illo* and *illum* for *Io*. Some repetitive passages are omitted entirely; others have become unsyntactical. Occasional verses of the poem will not scan, and his introduction suggests that he might have misunderstood the form of the treatise as a whole. One pair of verses, placed in the manuscript at the lower margin, are inserted into the wrong location in the text. Some of the main chapter divisions are incorrectly placed, and subdivisions of two chapters are not in the

---

Handschriften der Bayerischen Staatsbibliothek München: Clm 28111-28254, Catalogus codicum manu scriptorum Bibliothecae Monacensis IV, 7 [Wiesbaden, 1986], p. 173.)

[129]Munich, Haupt-Staats-Archiv, Reg. St. Emmeram, Lit. 19 1/2.

[130]See fn. 59.

original. Several of the musical examples have been inaccurately
transcribed. Nonetheless his work has provided a useful means of access
to this important treatise for nearly sixty years.

Editorial principles are partly a matter of fashion. Since
Altertumswissenschaft was begun, editions followed eighteenth- and
nineteenth-century Continental practice in orthography, punctuation, and
regularization of syntax. Medieval studies imitated the model of the
Classicists, and tried to make medieval works appear as though they were
written in Classical Latin. Rather than representing a literary style of
their own, the productions of the middle ages were believed to be
inferior in quality -- a tarnished, baser metal than the "golden" or
"silver" masterpieces of the early Empire. This view may still
occasionally be found amongst critics of published editions of medieval
writings. Fashion is changing, however. Some literary series are now
presenting critical editions of works from the middle ages in versions as
close as possible to the originals, with all their inconsistencies of
spelling, irregularities of syntax, vernacularized grammar, and period
structure far from a Classical purity.

Ideally, this edition would have followed this practice in its
entirety. Musicology, however, is by no means on the cutting edge of
literary or scholarly fashion, and to insist upon the *nouvelle vague*
would in some ways have been counterproductive. One of the things we are
beginning to learn about medieval music theory is the strength of the
Classical tradition of *imitatio*. The abundance of *loci paralleli* in the
present edition is a vivid indication of the interdependency of the
treatises of the time. It is only by building a collection of critical
editions of the works of musical theory from the period that we shall
begin to understand the strength of this interdependency. The works with
which the present treatise is most closely connected are the *De
mensurabili musica* of Johannes de Garlandia and the music treatise of
Anonymous IV, which have appeared in the series *Beihefte zum Archiv für
Musikwissenschaft*,[131] and the *De musica* of Lambertus and the *Ars cantus
mensurabilis* of Franco, edited in the series *Corpus Scriptorum de
Musica*.[132] This edition follows in broad outline the practices adopted
in those publications,[133] so that comparison is facilitated, and the
relationship between all of these works may appear at its most evident.

---

[131]Reimer, *Johannes de Garlandia;* and Reckow, *Der Musiktraktat.*

[132]Gilbert Reaney and André Gilles (eds.), *Franconis de Colonia Ars
Cantus Mensurabilis,* Corpus Scriptorum de Musica XVIII ([n. p.], 1974).
The Lambertus treatise will appear in the same series.

[133]These are summarized in *General Rules for the Editions of Corpus
Scriptorum de Musica* (Rome, 1950); and Karl-Werner Gümpel, *Die
Musiktraktate Conrads von Zabern,* Akademie der Wissenschaften und der
Literatur, Abhandlungen der Geistes- und Sozialwissenschaftlichen
Klasse, 1956 No. 4 (Wiesbaden, 1956). I have supplemented these sources
with James Willis, *Latin Textual Criticism,* Illinois Studies in Language
and Literature LXI (Urbana, 1972); and Martin West, *Textual Criticism and
Editorial Technique Applicable to Greek and Latin Texts* (Stuttgart,
1973).

MAIN TEXT

Within the main text the orthography of the original has been maintained, including inconsistent or aberrant spelling, such as the random appearance of single or double consonants in such words as *appello* or *opositio*. (In some cases, however, the distinction is crucial, as in *consumo/consummo*; and here the scribe has been careful.) Classical usage is followed in the appearance of *ae* for *e*, *ti* for *ci*, *i* for *j*, *qu* for *c*, and *v* for the consonantal *u*. The rules of assimilation have been followed in the expansion of abbreviations, which has been accomplished silently. *Circom-* is written *circum-*, and *-cumque* appears for *-comque*. Numbers are spelled out in full. Punctuation is according to grammatical rather than rhetorical considerations *(dicimus, quod. . . ; dicimus. . . esse; dicimus: . . .)*, and layout and indentation are designed to facilitate comprehension of the design of the original. (When an *incipit* which heads a section of commentary is not from the beginning of a verse, ellipsis points are used.) Editorial additions to the text are enclosed within angle brackets < >. Cancellations are indicated in the *apparatus criticus*. Titles and quotations which are announced by the author are printed in italics. Slight adaptations, expansions, or grammatical variants in these quotations have not been drawn attention to, since these may all be discovered by comparison with the originals in the *loci paralleli*. The interior poem is bold, as indeed it is in the original manuscript. Incipits are also bold, for visual consistency, although underlining is used in the manuscript. Glosses are tied by numbers to the words or phrases to which they refer. They appear after the line, though the manuscript has them above each line, so as to approximate more closely the intent and meaning of the original. Verses which appear within the prose commentary are indented, so that the form of the quotation is made visible. Manuscript foliation is recorded in parentheses.

The overlap of material between the end of the second gathering of the manuscript and the beginning of the third is presented in Appendix 1. Editorial procedure follows that for the main text.

APPARATUS CRITICUS

Since there is only one known manuscript version of the treatise, the *apparatus criticus* is able to convey a considerable amount of detail. It is used to indicate every aspect of the original state of the text, including scribal errors, corrections, deletions, or additions; to record manuscript idiosyncrasies (marginalia, for example); and to provide the alternative readings given in the Sowa edition (Sowa's orthography has been maintained in these cases). The *apparatus* is tied to the main text by line reference, and each entry is separated by several spaces. Italics are used for editorial comments, text is in Roman (bold for the verse). Double square brackets indicate scribal deletions.

PARALLEL READINGS

The collection of parallel readings (pp. 291-325) provides a sizeable body of passages from other authors whose content, phrasing, or exact wording runs parallel to (or in some cases at right angles to) the passage indicated in the present work. Anteriority is not implied: some of the parallel readings are from Franco (probably later) and Anonymous IV (certainly later). But by means of this and other such collections a clearer view of the complex interrelationships between treatises of music

theory may begin to emerge, as well as a precise demonstration of the concepts of *compilatio, imitatio,* and *inventio* in technical writing procedures in the later middle ages. In order to facilitate these possibilities the parallel readings are given in chronological order according to the following plan :

> Biblia Sacra
> Classical authors (Horace, Ovid, Cato etc.)
> Capella
> Boethius (*Arithmetic, Music, Geometry, Consolation*)
> Cassiodorus
> Isidore of Seville
> Guido of Arezzo
> Johannes Afflighemensis
> Proverbs, hymns, etc.
> Johannes de Garlandia
> Anonymous VII
> Lambertus
> Elias Salamon
> Franco
> Anonymous IV
> Anonymous II

Careful perusal of these readings in conjunction with the passage indicated in the present treatise will stimulate some questions. Why, for example, are some passages based closely on Anonymous VII but not found in Garlandia? Is Anonymous II as late as we think? How well did Lambertus know the treatise of Franco?

The *loci paralleli* are also used to provide complete or accurate rendition of quotations which appear in partial, adapted, or garbled form in the main text. Although the unusual form of the treatise results in the twofold appearance of many doctrines (once in the commentary, once in the verse), parallel readings are listed only once, at the first appearance of the passage which most nearly reflects the phraseology of the extract. Reference to the main text is by page and line numbers.

The readings given have not been re-edited. Wherever possible the most recent and reliable edition has been used for each author, and the orthography, punctuation, and sectionalization of that edition retained. Very occasionally, when an error is patent, a *sic* is inserted into the text in square brackets.

METHOD OF THE TRANSLATION

The difficulties in attempting to translate a technical text of this length and complexity are considerable. In the first place the central portion of the treatise is written in rhyming metrical verse which can in no way be reproduced in English. The language is often abstruse and recondite, involving unusual vocabulary, unexpected turns of phrase, and circuitous modes of expression.

Secondly, the glosses are, on the other hand, deliberately economical, terse, and epigrammatic. A clear distinction needed to be made between those glosses which supply missing nouns or adjectives

(*sive*), and those which are explanatory (*id est*). It was not always immediately obvious to which word or phrase of the verse each gloss referred.

Finally, the prose commentary, though clear and of unassailable logic, is not written as we would write it today. It does not proceed according to modern views of order and presentation; it is argumentative, often presenting both sides of the case,[134] and exhaustive in its argumentation; and it manipulates terminology in a subtle and fluid way. In some instances problems are caused by the multiplicity of possible meanings of a single word; in others the difficulty proceeds from the fine distinctions represented by different terms which have no parallel in English (*punctus, nota, notula, vox, figura, actus, sonus, cantus, melos, melodia, modulatio*).

I have attempted to keep track of all of the occurrences of every term which appears in the treatise. This was made possible by the "Search" command of the computer on which the edition and translation were assembled. Strict control was therefore maintained on the equivalents used, and considerable consistency could be achieved. Language, however, is a flexible device, capable of subtle shifts and great finesse of signification. Where it seemed to me that the author was not being consistent, therefore, I have not tried to be. If two Latin words are similar in meaning, two related English words are used. Often it seemed that the author was attempting to maintain a distinction (*littera/textus; vox/figura; pausa/pausatio*), which only collapsed in later pages. Cognates are of course often misleading, but in medieval Latin an adjective derived from a substantive carries more of the meaning of its derivation than its cognate does today. *Regularis* means something like "regular," but it still carries a strong overtone of "according to the rules," from the noun *regula* ("rule"). The existence of glosses to many of the words in the verse helped to clarify meanings, especially when words were rare or obliquely used. On the other hand many of the glosses seem redundant or tautologous.

In the cases where a single word carried many meanings, I have tried to be sensitive to the various possibilities in each context. The word *ars*, as used in this work, means 1) the art of music in general, 2) the music treatise of Johannes de Garlandia, 3) the present treatise, 4) established, traditional music theory, and 5) theory as opposed to practice (*usus*). These meanings shade into one another, but there is no single English word that would serve in all cases.

Notes to the translation, indicated by an asterisk, are sparingly used to provide immediate, essential commentary on the text, to explain allusions and trace citations, and to give cross-references for the fairly frequent reiterations and self-quotations which appear in the work. (Throughout this book -- in the notes to the translation, in the footnotes to this essay, and in Appendix III -- references are by chapter, page, and line number; if to the edition, then in Latin: *Cap*.III 8, 14 -- if to the translation, then in English: Chap.III 8, 14.) Announced quotations, either from other authors or from the treatise itself, are enclosed in quotation marks (italics in the Latin text), as are titles and names of compositions.

The translation is designed to be as accurate as possible. As a

----

[134]See the discussion on *disputatio* above.

result it is not always particularly elegant. The facing-page format
allows every reader to compare the English immediately with the
established Latin text, so that alternative interpretations may be made.
Page breaks in the translation correspond as closely as possible to those
of the edition.

APPENDICES, BIBLIOGRAPHY, AND INDEX

As mentioned above, Appendix I is used to record the material that is
duplicated by the overlap between the second and third gathering of the
manuscript. This has been edited in accordance with the main text.
Appendix II presents in full all of the original documents regarding
Lambertus and Henricus Tuebuef whose contents have been summarized in the
preceding essay. These documents have not been edited, apart from some
punctuation and capitalization and the expansion of abbreviations. The
relevant names are printed in bold characters. Appendix III lists all
the compositions that are quoted or cited in the course of the treatise.
They are listed in alphabetical order, and for each piece page and line
reference to the edition are given, as well as a brief extract from the
context in which it appears. All possible manuscript sources have been
traced for each composition.
The Bibliography is divided into three categories: manuscripts;
medieval and classical sources; and modern studies and reference works.
In the first section I have not included those manuscripts which are
pertinent only to the appendices. Medieval authors appear under their
first names. Reference works are listed by title.
The Index includes both words and names. All important terms are
given, and the form used is the nominative singular for a noun, the
infinitive for a verb. References are to page and line number of the
edition.

THE EDITION AND TRANSLATION

\<Prologus\>

(fol. 134) Quoniam prosam artis musicae mensurabilis ab
excellentibus in arte musicis compilatam, quam etiam clericorum
universitas ibi studens in meliorem huius scientiae summulam
dignumduxerat exaltare, quidam in suis artibus de novo compositis
reprehendere praesumpserunt, ipsam prosam cum modorum serie prorsus per
singula fere capitula destruendo, figuris saepius protractiones varias
apponentes, ipsasque, quas perfectas dicimus, dispendiosis rationibus
asserunt imperfectas, prout inferius locis debitis ostendetur. Quorum
reprehentionem nec non et variationem in pluribus figurarum tanquam
10   factum credimus puerile.

Antecessores nostri, musicae mensurabilis inventores, figuras artis
sub quibusdam protractionibus se ipsas repraesentantibus distributas
prout sibi placuit nec irrationabiliter sub quadam modorum serie
statuerunt, indeque artem conficientes approbabilem reliquerunt ad
introductionem et commodum posterorum. Cum autem factum sapientis
commendabile nec non in fornace studii totiens expurgatum vulgariter et
expertum a nullo reprehendi debeat condemnando, nisi redarguentis
correptio possit etiam lucidissimis rationibus probabiliter declarari,
prout in Cathonis proverbio continetur, cum dicitur:
20   *Alterius dictum vel factum* etc.,
alibi:
        Si non intendes reprehensor etc.

Inde est quare reprehentionem talium quamvis non approbem, non
condemno, ne praesumptionis vitio possim mordacius accusari. Immo utens
consilio magistrorum quorum vestigia sum secutus, prosae venerabilis
practicam partim et theoricam sub quadam capitulorum serie divisionis
sententia declarata, prout ingenioli mei paupertas exigit, propono
metrice compilare, quia carmen metrice compilatum ad retinenda levius
mentes excitat auditorum; unde quidam:

----

9 figurarum *in marg.*   10 puerile [[eo quod]] antecessores *cod.*

Prologue

(fol. 134) Some people* in their recently composed treatises have
dared to censure the prose work* on the art of measurable music, which
was compiled by musicians who are outstanding in the art, and which even
the university of clerics studying from it has thought worthy to elevate
as the best summary of this science.* And those people are destroying
that prose work which has a precise sequence of modes in almost every
single chapter; and they often designate different kinds of notation for
the figures, and assert with prejudicial arguments that those figures
which we say are perfect are imperfect, as will be shown below in the
requisite places. And we believe their censure and also their
diversification of the figures in many ways to be a childish thing.

Our forebears, who invented measurable music, established, as seemed
best to them and in a rational manner according to a certain sequence of
modes, the figures of the art arranged under certain systems of notation
that represent them. And then, putting together a worthy treatise, they
left it as a profitable introduction for future generations. But the
commendable deed of a wise man, one that has been vindicated and tried
out so many times and in such a widespread manner in the furnace of
study, should not be censured or condemned by anyone, unless the reproof
of him who is refuting it can be stated convincingly and with the
clearest reasons. As it says in Cato's proverb:

> "Never carp . . ." etc.,*

or elsewhere:

> "If the censurer . . ." etc.*

That is why, although I do not approve of the censure of such people,
I do not condemn it, lest I be accused even more sharply of the vice of
presumption. Rather, using the judgement of the teachers in whose
footsteps I have followed, I propose to put together in verse the theory
and in part the practice of the respected prose work in a certain
sequence of chapters and with the meaning of the method of division
stated, as the poverty of my feeble intellect allows; because a poem put
together in verse more easily stimulates the minds of those who are
hearing it to remember. Whence it is that someone said:

----

*(Notes to the translation appear on pp. 326-337.)

> *Metra iuvant animos, comprendunt plurima paucis,*
> *Pristina* etc.

Sed quia praesens tractatus est de expositione musicae, ideoque in primis descriptiones ipsius continuo videamus.

Musica sic describitur a quibusdam: Musica est varietas vocum concors, et haec siquidem dividitur in tres partes, scilicet mondanam, humanam et instrumentalem. Mondana musica consistit in concordia complexionis quatuor elementorum ac temporum ac corporum superiorum, quae aliter dicitur aurea cathena vel modulus triplicis armoniae, scilicet

10 dyapason, dyapente, dyatessaron. Humana consistit in homine, et haec dicitur concordia quatuor humorum et coniunctio corporis et animae. Instrumentalis consistit in musicis instrumentis, et haec siquidem dividitur in tres partes, scilicet rismicam, melicam et metricam. Rismica consistit in rimis sub quadam proportione tam soni quam numeri constitutis. Melica consistit in melodiis vocum seu cantuum dulciter resonantium, ut in ecclesiis et cantilenis mundanis seu notis sive naturalibus seu artificialibus instrumentis compositis et creatis; et de tali sumus quoad musicam mensurabilem in sussequentibus tractaturi. Metrica consistit in metris melicis variis scematibus purpuratis, sicut

20 patet in metro heroyco, iambico, elegyaco, Ysidoro atestante.

Item sic describitur: musica est varias vocum distantias simphoniasque proportionaliter diiudicans, vel musica quo ad nos et magistros nostros est verasciter canendi scientia et facilis via ad perfectionem canendi, vel musica est scientia de numero relato ad sonum vel de numero est sonorum. Et dicitur a *moys*, quod est aqua, et *icos*, scientia, quasi scientia inventa iuxta aquas, secundum quod dicitur Graecos in mari musicam invenisse, vel quia nulla melodia naturalibus instrumentis formata absque humore possit ullatenus generari; vel dicitur a *moys*, aqua, et *sicox*, ventus, ut quidam asserunt, dicentes, quod ex

30 resultatione venti et aquae inventa fuit musica a quibusdam Graecis, et hoc in quodam saxo convaco in mari longe posito, in quo Syrenes esse putabantur. In ipso autem erant quaedam foramina, per quae ventus et aqua ibant et revertebantur, indeque fiebant melodae, quibus nostra musica primo dicitur reperiri.

Ista siquidem musica sic describitur ab Ysidoro: *Musica est peritia modulationis sono cantuque consistens, et dicta per derivationem a Musis. Musae autem dictae sunt ab 'apotumasion,' quod est acquirere, eo quod per eas, ut antiqui voluerunt, vis carminum et vocis modulatio acquireretur;* subiunxitque post: *Moyses dicit repertorem musicae artis*

40 *fuisse Tubal, qui fuit de stirppe Caym ante diluvium. Graeci vero Pithagoram dicunt huius artis invenisse primordia ex malleorum sonitu et cordarum extensione percussa.*

De ipsavis inventione seu commendatione sarcinam relinquimus philosophis inde tractantibus exponendam, ne prolixitas recitandi aures audentium impediat aut perturbet.

Quia vero prodest divisio ad evidentiam sussequentium pleniorem et ad memoriam audientium firmiorem, ideoque in primis praeambulam partem

----

15 seu *super* se *cod.*   16 notis [[et d]] sive *cod.*   20 ysidore *pro* Ysidoro *cod.*   27 [[nulla]] *cod.*   28 nullatenus *cod.*   32 quaedam *om. Sowa*   37 musis [[eo quod]] musae *cod.*   39 quereretur *pro* acquireretur *Sowa*   47 audientium [[pleniorem vel]] firmiorem *cod.*

"Verse meters help minds, for then they understand
Very many new things in few words," etc.*

But because the present tract is about the exposition of music, let us first therefore immediately look at descriptions of it.

Music is described as follows by certain people: Music is the concordant diversity of voices and it is divided into three parts, that is to say music of the universe, music of man, and instrumental music.* Music of the universe consists in the concord of the combination of the four elements and units of time and higher bodies; which otherwise is called the golden series or the measure of threefold harmony, that is to say the octave, the fifth, and the fourth. Music of man consists in humanity and this is called the concord of the four humors and the conjunction of the body and the soul. Instrumental music consists in musical instruments and this is divided into three parts, that is to say the rhythmical, the lyrical, and the metrical. The rhythmical consists in rhythms arranged under a certain proportion both of sound and of number. The lyrical consists in the musical sounds of sounding notes or melodies sweetly sounding, for example in churches and in secular tunes composed and created either with written-down notes or on natural or artificial instruments; and it is with this, in its form as measurable music, that we are about to deal in the following chapters. The metrical consists in lyrical meters embellished with various patterns, as can be seen in the heroic meter, or the iambic or elegiac, as Isidore confirms.

It is also described thus: Music is something that proportionally distinguishes harmonious sounds and the various degrees of separation between sounding notes. Or, according to us and our teachers, music is the science of singing truly and the easy route to perfection in singing. Or, music is the science of number as it relates to sound or about the number of sounds.* And it is so called from *moys,* which is water, and *icos,* a science -- that is, a science discovered by the side of the waters; according to the saying that the Greeks discovered music in the sea, or because no musical sound formed with natural instruments can be generated without liquid. Or it is named from *moys,* water, and *sicox,* wind,* as some assert, saying that music was discovered by certain Greeks from the reverberation of wind and water in a certain hollow rock situated a long way off at sea, in which the Sirens were thought to be. However there were some holes in the rock, through which the wind and the water came and went, and thus musical sounds arose, from which our music is first said to have been discovered.

Indeed music is described thus by Isidore: "Music is the skill of producing musical sounds consisting of sound and melody, and it is named by derivation from the Muses. The Muses are named from *apotumasion,* which means to acquire, because it was through them, as the ancients liked to believe, that the power of poetry and the ability to produce musical sounds with the voice might be acquired." And he added: "Moses says that the discoverer of the art of music was Tubal, who was from the lineage of Cain before the flood. The Greeks however say that Pythagoras discovered the first beginnings of this art from the sound of hammers and the striking of stretched strings."*

We leave the burden of expounding upon the discovery or praise of music to the philosophers who deal with the subject, lest the verbosity of the explanation burden or disturb the ears of our listeners.

Since indeed a division of the subject matter is helpful for the fuller clarity of what follows and for a stronger memory on the part of

huius operis in duas partes prout decet dividamus, in prohemium videlicet
et tractatum. Et quia prohemium deservit providentiae, tractatus vero
operationi, ideo prohemium antecedit, quia quisque debet sibi prius de
futuris providere quam improvise super hiis operari.

Ideo patet ordo partis praeambulae ad sequentem: prima pars incipit
Musica dicatur etc., secunda ubi dicit **Ecce tibi formas** etc. Haec
secunda remanet indivisa, sed prior in duas dividitur, in quarum prima
describit actor musicam, de qua est in sussequentibus tractaturus, in
secunda illud dividit (fol. 134v) de quo agit. Et quia prius est de quo
10 agitur tangere quam dividere, ideo patet ordo: prima pars **Musica** etc.,
secunda **Disce prius** etc. Item prius prima in duas: in prima tangit
materiam de qua debet agere, in secunda quoddam apponit incidens ad hoc,
ut per illud alliciat auditores. Prima pars incipit **Musica** etc.,
secunda **Prosa quid exponam** etc. Item prior in duas: in prima tangit
materiam suam, in secunda ostendit librum suum debere recipi duplici
ratione. Prima incipit **Musica** etc., secunda **Displiceant nulli** etc. Haec
secunda in duas: in prima ostendit librum suum ratione duplici
appetendum, in secunda ad invidos sermonem suum dirigit ipsos prout decet
blaphemando. Et quia prius est pronuntiare aliquid recitando quam
20 improvise super hoc invidos reprobare, ideo patet ordo: prima pars
incipit **Displiceant nulli** etc., secunda **Invide mutesce** etc. Istae partes
remanent indivisae, sed pars principalior in duas dividitur, in quarum
prima describit musicam, in secunda ostendit se practicam illius metrice
compilare. Prima pars incipit **Musica** etc., secunda **Per metra nunc inquam**
etc. Haec secunda in duas: in prima ostendit se practicam huius musicae
metrice compilare partim et theoricam, in secunda innuit, quibus
coloribus sui libri seriem purpurabit. Prima incipit **Per metra** etc.,
secunda **Esse leonina** etc. Istae partes remanent indivisae, sed prius
prima in duas dividitur: in prima describit musicam, in secunda invocat
30 divinum auxilium. Prima incipit **Musica** etc., secunda **Virtus divina** etc.
Item prima in duas: in prima descriptionem ipsius musicae declarat, in
secunda ipsam in duas species dividit sive partes. Prima pars incipit
Musica etc., secunda **Si sapias artes** etc. Haec secunda in duas: in
prima parte dividit musicam, in secunda ostendit, de qua parte musicae
sit solummodo tractaturus. Prima pars incipit **Si sapias artes** etc.,
secunda **Si cum mensura** etc.

Et sic patet in generali sententia et divisio leoninis, et ita per
membra singula dividitur, quoniam divisio non est sufficiens nec perfecta
quousque ad indivisibilia veniat et ducatur.

40   Et nota quod actor more artificum tria facit: primo proponit,
secundo invocat, tertio narrat. Proponit igitur ubi dicit **Musica** etc.,

----

12 decet *pro* debet *Sowa*   16 prima pars *Sowa*   27 prima pars *Sowa*
29 invocavit *pro* invocat *Sowa*   30 prima pars *Sowa*   35-36 **Si sapias
artes** et **Si cum mensura** *sine sublinea in cod.*   41 **Musica** *sine sublinea
in cod.*

listeners, for that reason let us at first divide the prefatory part of this work into two parts as is proper, namely, the introduction and the tract. And because an introduction serves fore-knowledge, and a tract practical knowledge, therefore the introduction comes first, because everyone should arm himself with knowledge about future things before suddenly dealing with them in practice.

So the order of the prefatory part to what follows is clear. The first part begins **Music may be said**, etc., the second where it says **Look, now I shall give you the forms**, etc. This second part remains undivided, but the first is divided into two; in the first of which the author describes music, which he is about to discuss in the following chapters; and in the second he divides up the subject (fol. 134v) with which he deals. And because one should first touch on what is dealt with before dividing it, the order is clear. The first part begins **Music**, etc., the second **Learn first**, etc. Also the first of these is divided into two parts. In the first he touches upon the material with which he should deal, in the second he adds something incidental to that, so that he can attract the listeners. The first part begins **Music**, etc., the second **O prose, I shall expound**, etc. Also the first part is divided into two. In the first he touches upon his material, in the second he shows that his book ought to be received for two reasons. The first part begins **Music**, etc., the second **Let them displease no-one**, etc. This second part is divided into two. In the first he shows that his book should be sought for two reasons, in the second he directs his speech to those who are envious, reviling them as is proper. And because one should first announce something by explaining it before suddenly reproaching the envious about it, the order is clear. The first part begins **Let them displease no-one**, etc., the second **Jealous one, be quiet**, etc. These parts remain undivided, but the more important part is divided into two, in the first of which he will describe music, in the second he shows that he will discuss the practice of music in verse. The first part begins **Music**, etc., the second **Through verses now I say**, etc. This second part is divided into two. In the first he shows that he will discuss in verse the theory of music and in part also the practice; in the second he suggests with what rhetorical devices he will embellish the sequence of his book. The first part begins **Through verses**, etc., the second **The leonine treatise**, etc. These parts remain undivided, but the first is divided into two. In the first he describes music, in the second he invokes divine aid. The first part begins **Music**, etc., the second **Let divine virtue**, etc. Also the first is divided into two. In the first he states the description of music, in the second he divides it into two species or parts. The first part begins **Music**, etc., the second **If you would like to know the arts**, etc. This second part is divided into two. In the first part he divides music, in the second he shows which part of music is the only one with which he will deal. The first part begins **If you would like to know the arts**, etc., the second **If it is with measure**, etc.

And thus the meaning and method of division of the leonine verses is clear in general, and in this way it is divided into single portions, since a division is not sufficient or perfect unless it arrives at and leads to things that are indivisible.

And note that the author, in the manner of masters of the liberal arts, does three things: First he proposes, second he invokes, third he narrates. He proposes therefore when he says **Music**, etc., he invokes

invocat cum dicit **Virtus divina** etc., narrat ubi dicit **Disce** etc.

    Quasi vellet dicere musica est verasciter canendi scientia:
        Musica dicatur cantandi iure sophia,
        Et brevis[1] esse via,[2] qua cantus lege patratur.[3]
        1 dicatur
        2 id est, facilis via ad perfectionem canendi
        3 id est, efficitur
    Juxta id, quod alibi dicitur:
        Nulla salus est in domo,
        Nisi cruce munit homo etc.
        Sinit cruce signata metra primula crux quia lata.
    et alibi:
        Hoc animo senti, dat praemia nulla ferenti
        Crux vestimenti, nisi sit prius insita menti.
        Praemia dat grata prius alta mente locata.

    Si sapias artes etc. Visa superius descriptione musicae, hic accedit
actor ad divisiones eiusdem, dicens, quod ista musica in duas partes
dividitur principales, scilicet in immensurabilem et mensurabilem. Et
nota, quod immensurabilis est illa, ubi non sunt longae vel breves vel
aliqua quantitas temporum sub certo numero distributa. Mensurabilis est
illa, in qua sua quantitas temporum reperitur. De prima non proponimus
in praesenti, de secunda autem sumus in sussequentibus tractaturi.
    Cuius mensurabilis musicae tria sunt genera, scilicet discantus,
copula et organum. Et est aliud organum, quod idem est quod musica
mensurabilis, et, prout ita sumitur, est genus generale ad tria genera
supradicta, de quibus per ordinem locis debitis sussequetur. Quidam loco
copulae hoquetorum manierem posuerunt, quorum opinionem acquiescere satis
potest. Sed nos antecessorum semitam imitamur atque de hoquetorum
generibus in fine capituli sex modorum doctrinam tradimus generalem, per
libri seriem de necessariis et utilibus mentionem prout decet facientes,
dubia et oscura et sophisticis rationibus verissimilia subticendo.
    Littera patet.

        Si sapias[1] artes,[2] dat binas musica partes.[3]
        1 O cantor
        2 sive liberales
        3 quoniam aut est mensurabilis aut immensurabilis
    Hic accedit actor ad divisionem partium, dicens, quod una est
immensurabilis:
        Est sine mensura, de qua non sit modo cura.

----

1 etc. *post* **divina** *add. Sowa*   22-23 mensurabilis est illa est illa *cod.*
22 *Crux in marg.*   23 nisi *pro* non *cod.*

when he says **Let divine virtue,** etc., he narrates when he says **Learn first,** etc.

> He would like to say, as it were, that music is the science of singing truly:
>> **Music may be said to be the wisdom of singing rightly,**
>> **And the road[2] to be short,[1] by which melody is accomplished[3]**
>> **correctly.**
>> 1 it may be said
>> 2 that is, an easy road to the perfection of singing
>> 3 that is, achieved
> According to that which is said elsewhere:
>> "There is no safety at home, unless a man
>> Furnishes himself with a cross," etc.*
>> **The first cross, because it is broad, allows verse marked with a**
>> **cross.**
> And elsewhere:
>> "Feel this in your soul: The cross gives no rewards
>> To him who carries it on his clothing,
>> Unless it is first inculcated in his mind."*
>> **It gives pleasing rewards when it is first established in the**
>> **noble mind.**

If you would like to know the arts, etc. Since the description of music has been seen above, here the author broaches its divisions, saying that music is divided into two principal parts, that is to say into unmeasurable and measurable. And note that unmeasurable music is that in which there are no longs or breves or any quantity of units of time distributed in a fixed number. Measurable music is that in which a quantity of units of time is found. We do not propose to deal with the former at the present time, but we are about to deal with the latter in the following chapters.

There are three genera of measurable music, that is to say discant, copula, and organum. And there is another organum, which is the same as measurable music, and, as it is used in that way, is a general genus to the three genera mentioned above, which are taken up in order in the appropriate places. Some have put the category of hockets in place of the copula,* and it could be enough to accede to these people's view. But we imitate the path of our forebears and give a general doctrine about the genera of hockets at the end of the chapter on the six modes, making mention as is proper throughout the sequence of the book of necessary and useful things, and keeping quiet about those things that are dubious and obscure and very much like sophistical reasonings.

Here is the text:

> **If you would like to know[1] the arts,[2] music provides two parts.[3]**
> 1 O cantor
> 2 the liberal arts
> 3 since it is either measurable or unmeasurable

Here the author broaches the division of the parts, saying that one is unmeasurable:

> **There is one without measure, and it is not of concern now.**

Ecce dicit, quod si sit mensurabilis, de illa parte solummodo est
agendum:

> **Si cum mensura, sit curam ponere cura,**
> **Nam tibi pro posse reserabo, si queo nosse.**[1]

1 id est, secundum ingenioli mei paupertatem et sic devitat
arrogantiam

> **Huius**[1] **per versus stilus**[2] **hic meus est modo versus.**[3]

1 sive musicae mensurabilis

2 id est, mea materia vel ingenium

10   3 id est, conversus

> **Virtus**[1] **divina carmen**[2] **regat absque ruina,**[3]

1 id est, favor et miseratio summi dei

2 id est, praesens scriptum

3 id est, corruptione

(fol. 135) **Ut queat**[1] **ad**[2] **finem**[3] **verum comprendere finem.**[4]

1 id est, possit

2 prousque sive

3 id est, consummationem operis

4 id est, actionem

20   **Ne**[1] **in scriptori**[2] **fiat doctrina**[3] **pudori,**[4]

1 ne pro quod et non

2 id est, compositori

3 id est, introductio

4 id est, reprehentioni

> **Metrifico**[1] **prosam nonquam michi laudo perosam,**[2]

1 id est, metrice expono

2 id est, quam nonquam habui odio

> **Cuius**[1] **enim metra**[2] **fugiant**[3] **aenigmata**[4] **taetra.**[5]

1 sive prosae

30   2 mea sive

3 id est, evittent

4 id est, locutiones dubias vel fractas

5 id est, oscura

Per hoc innuit actor dubia et oscura fugere et utilia singula
recitare:

> **Per metra nunc inquam communia fusca relinquam,**
> **Practica**[1] **tractando,**[2] **quia prosae cetera**[3] **mando,**

1 id est, usitata et approbata

2 id est, recitando

40   3 id est, dubia et oscura

> **Quam**[1] **qui despiciunt**[2] **errantes,**[3] **ut puto, fiunt.**

1 sive prosam

2 id est, despicere intendunt

3 id est, non sane intelligentes

----

12 vel *pro* et *Sowa*   18 consumationem *pro* consummationem *Sowa*
44 intellegentes *pro* intelligentes *Sowa*

Now he says that if it is measurable, he should deal only with that part:

> If it is with measure, let it be of concern,
> For I shall unlock it for you to the best of my ability, if I
> have the knowledge.[1]

1 that is, according to the poverty of my feeble intellect, and thus he avoids arrogance

> This pen[2] of mine is now turned[3] to write verses about this.[1]

1 measurable music
2 that is, my talent or intellect
3 that is, directed

> Let divine virtue[1] rule the poet[2] and do so without ruin,[3]

1 that is, the favor and compassion of the supreme God
2 that is, the present writing
3 that is, injury

> (fol. 135) So that it may[1] at[2] the end[3] understand the true
> ending.[4]

1 that is, it may be able
2 all the way to
3 that is, the consummation of the work
4 that is, the plot

> Lest[1] in the writer[2] there exist the instruction[3] to shame,[4]

1 lest instead of because let there not
2 that is, the composer
3 that is, the introduction
4 that is, censure

> I versify[1] the prose which I praise as never hateful to me,[2]

1 that is, I expound in verse
2 that is, which I never hated

> And let the verses[2] flee from[3] its[1] odious[5] riddles.[4]

1 those of the prose work
2 mine
3 that is, let them avoid
4 that is, dubious or broken expressions
5 that is, obscure

In this way the author suggests that he will avoid dubious and obscure things and explain those that are simple and useful:

> Through verses now I say that I shall leave behind things that
> are common and unclear,
> Dealing with[2] practical things,[1] because I leave the rest[3] to the
> prose.

1 that is, usual and approved things
2 that is, explaining
3 that is, dubious and obscure things

> And those who disdain[2] it[1] are in error,[3] I think.

1 the prose work
2 that is, intend to disdain
3 that is, not understanding clearly

Quidam nuper composuit quandam artem, in qua prosam de qua loquimur
corrumpebat:
   Arte nova rapti Lamberti nunc ita capti.
   Qui[1] sunt more pari, poterunt Argo simulari.[2]
   1 id est, qui artem illam approbant alteram condemnando
   2 id est, similes fieri
   Prosam[1] damnando nonquam me iudice sontem.
   1 subaudi, de qua loqui intendimus; haec, dico, licet alicubi
   sit oscura:
10   Per hoc innuit actor iste illud nonquam vituperandum esse, quod
   alimentum scientiae administrat:
   Nimis ego, fontem non reprobo depreciando.

   Argo etc. Nota est fabula de Argo, qui fuit deceptus a Mercurio per
cantus calamorum noviter inventorum. Per Argum igitur in praesenti
possumus intelligere quemlibet sophisticum hominem et versutum, qui
praecepto Iunonis Io redegit in servitutem, per eius oculos sophisticas
rationes. Per Io in servitutem redactam possumus intelligere prosam de
qua loquimur, quae per tales sophisticas rationes dignitate postposita
20   succubuit servituti. Per Mercurium siquidem, qui Argum interfecit Io a
servitute misera liberando, intelligimus quemlibet sapientem prosae
venerabilis famam in statum pristinum revocantem.
   Et nota, quod sicut mediantibus tribus devicit Argum Mercurius,
scilicet virga caducea, talaribus et calamis, sic mediantibus tribus
prosam de qua loquimur a tali servitute proponimus revocare, scilicet
tribus coloribus rethoricis, quibus utimur in hoc libro, sicut immediate
declarabitur et per textum.
   Alia potest esse expositio. Per Argum possumus intelligere
quemlibet sapientem, per eius oculos lucidas rationes, per Mercurium
30   siquidem maliciosum hominem et versutum, qui versutia sua et sophisticis
rationibus saepius introductis sapientem vel eius operationem
fraudulenter reprobat et concludit. Quae etiam sophisticae rationes
perceptae ad ultimum et discussae a discretis in ea facultate clericis
tanquam frivolae reputantur. Inde est quare antecessorum scripta in
fornace studii per diuturnitatem temporis elimata totiens et experta
sequimur, blaphemantes reprehentionem aliquorum noviter exaltatam, per
quam prosa commendabilis a pluribus impedita turpiter minoratur,
cupientesque ipsius famam in statum pristinum revocare, ne ars per
capita sita tenet plurium varie lacerata, tanquam nugatoria vel incerta
40   utilitati omnium videatur.
   Cum omnis ars una et eadem esse debeat apud omnes, ideoque ipsam
dedimus metrice compilatam, quia in metro compendiose loquimur et aperte,
nam in metro rationes sophisticae sopiuntur; insuper metrice compilata
memoriali cellulae levius quam prosaice commendantur, et impressa leviter
ad memoriam citius reducuntur, etiam metra favorabilius quam prosa
mentes excitant auditorum.

----

2 corrumpebant *cod., corr. Sowa*   16 intellegere *pro* intelligere *Sowa*
17 illo *pro* Io *Sowa*   18 illum *pro* Io *Sowa*   servitute *cod.*   redactum
pro redactam *Sowa*   intellegere *pro* intelligere *Sowa*   20 illo *pro* Io
Sowa   21 intellegimus *pro* intelligimus *Sowa*   28 intellegere *pro*
intelligere *Sowa*   39 capito sitatet *pro* capita sita tenet *cod.*
45 citius [[commendant]] reducuntur *cod.*

Someone has recently composed a certain treatise, in which he injured the prose work about which we are speaking:

Infatuated with his new treatise, Lambertus is now caught.
Those[1] who have the same views can copy[2] Argus.

1 that is, those who approved of that treatise and condemned the other

2 that is, become similar to

Never in my judgement could anyone condemn the prose[1] as guilty.

1 understand: about which we intend to speak; this one indeed, although in places it may be obscure

In this way this author suggests that that which provides nourishment for the science should never be disparaged:

Not at all do I reject or undervalue our fountain source.

Argus, etc. The story of Argus is well known.* He was deceived by Mercury through the melodies of newly discovered pipes. Argus therefore we can interpret at the present time as any sophistical and cunning man, who by the order of Juno reduced Io to slavery; and his eyes we can interpret as sophistical reasonings. Io reduced to slavery we can interpret as the prose work about which we are speaking, which because of such sophistical reasonings has lost its dignity and succumbed to slavery. And Mercury, who killed Argus, freeing Io from wretched slavery, we interpret as any wise man bringing the reputation of a worthy prose work back into its former state.

And note that just as Mercury conquered Argus with the help of three things, that is to say his messenger's staff, his winged sandals, and his pipes, thus we propose to bring the prose work about which we are speaking back from a similar slavery with the help of three things, that is to say with three rhetorical devices which we use in this book, as will be immediately stated by means of the text.

There can be a different explanation. Argus we can interpret as any wise man, his eyes as clear reasonings, and Mercury as a malicious and cunning man, who, through his cunning and sophistical reasonings which he often uses, deceitfully condemns and restrains the wise man or his work. And these sophistical reasonings, perceived at last and examined by clerics who are discerning in that capacity, are judged to be worthless. That is why we follow the writings of our forebears, which have been polished so many times in the furnace of daily study, and revile the recently praised censure of some, through which the prose work that has been found commendable by many is shamefully hindered and threatened. And we desire to bring its reputation back into its former state, lest the treatise, wasted and mangled in different ways in the minds of many, seem of trifling or uncertain usefulness to all.

Since every treatise should be one and the same to everyone, we have given it composed in verse, because we speak briefly and openly in verse, for in verse sophistical reasonings are laid to rest. And also things composed in verse are received more easily in the store-house of memory than things composed in prose, and since they are impressed easily on the memory they are more quickly recalled. Also verses arouse the minds of the listeners more favorably than prose.

Esse leonina etc. Hic vult actor ostendere, quibus coloribus
rethoricis proponit sui libri seriem purpurare, dicens, quod solummodo
tria ornatuum genera per libri seriem ordinabit. Et hoc primo in
commemoratione summae et individuae trinitatis, scilicet leoninitatem pro
maiori parte, eo quod levior, gratiosior, aptior et commodior omnibus
aliis coloribus perhibetur; consonantiam, quia affinitatem habet cum
leoninitate; nunc cruce signatum eloquium, et praecipue in primo sui
libri, quia inter (fol. 135v) signa cetera signum crucis reverentiae et
virtutis optinet dignitatem.

10   Item tribus, quia summa perfectio consistit in tribus, scilicet
longitudine, latitudine et profunditate. Et ipse apetit librum suum
perfectioni, quamquam non plane deduceret, cum in humanis inventoribus
nihil ex omni parte sit perfectum. Item tribus, ad instar caelestis
armoniae, quae in tribus consonantiis consistit, ex quibus caelestis
musica modulatur, sicut superius est expressum; ad cuius similitudinem
nostra musica primo dicitur reperiri. Vel tribus, ad hoc ut textus
conveniat glosulae supradictae; vel tribus, eo quod voces ex quibus ista
musica depingitur et formatur sunt in forma solummodo tripartitae,
quoniam omnes tales aut sunt longae vel breves vel semibreves.

20
    Hic ostendit actor, quibus coloribus sua proponit carmina purpurare:
    Esse leonina petit ars metra parte supina.[1]
    1 id est, maiori
Ecce dicit, quod quandoque reponuntur consonantiae propter
affinitatem leonitatis:
    Hic metra qui finxit nunc consonantia pinxit,
    Nunc cruce[1] signata quia crux est laude beata.
    1 isto colore quandoque utitur actor iste et praecipue in primo
    sui libri, quia crux est prae signis ceteris commendanda

30
    Displiceant nulli etc. Hic ostendit actor librum suum ratione
duplici apetendum. Una siquidem est, quia procedit secundum sententiam
sapientum prosae cuiusdam commendabilis dogmata recitando metrice. Alia
est, quia cruce signato eloquio quo utitur praemunitus credit securius
invidorum insidias evitare.
    . . . sunt quasi pulli. Methaphora sumpta est ad exemplum,
quemadmodum gallina pullos suos sub alis congregat, ad hoc ut ibi tutius
lateant et melius nutriantur, sic actor carmina sua sub protectione
prosae credit latitare.

40
    Displiceant[1] nulli, mea carmina sunt quasi pulli,[2]
    1 id est, displicendo noceant alicui super hoc invidenti
    2 metaphora est

----

2 proposuit *pro* proponit *cod.*   5 commodior *scripsi,* communior *Sowa*
8 inter si signa *cod.*   12 deducere *pro* deduceret *cod.*   24 consonantia
pro consonantiae *Sowa*   34 sapientium *pro* sapientum *Sowa*   quo *add.*
super scriptum   36 etc. *post* **pulli** *Sowa*   metaphora *pro* methaphora
Sowa

The leonine treatise, etc. Here the author wishes to show with which rhetorical devices he proposes to embellish the sequence of his book, saying that he will arrange only three genera of ornament through the sequence of the book. And this is first of all in commemoration of the supreme and indivisible Trinity; and the three genera are: the use of leonine verse for the most part, because it is thought to be easier, more pleasing, more appropriate, and more fitting than all the other devices; verbal consonance, because it has an affinity with leonine hexameters; and eloquence marked with a cross,* and especially in the first chapter of his book, because among (fol. 135v) the other signs the sign of the cross connotes the dignity of reverence and virtue.

Also three genera are used because the highest perfection consists in three things, that is to say in length, breadth, and depth. And he strives after perfection for his book, although he might not entirely achieve it, since in human creators nothing is completely perfect. Also three things in imitation of celestial harmony, which consists in three consonances, out of which celestial music is produced in sound, as has been said above. And our music is first said to have been discovered in imitation of this. Or three things so that the text may agree with the gloss given above; or three things because the sounding notes by which music is represented and formed are in form only of three kinds, since they are all either longs or breves or semibreves.

Here the author shows with which rhetorical devices he proposes to embellish his poems:
> **The leonine treatise seeks verses in its extended[1] part.**
> 1 that is, greater

And here he says that consonances are sometimes put in on account of the leonine relationship:
> **He who contrived the verses sometimes painted consonances**
> **Marked with a cross,[1] because the cross is blessed with praise.**
> 1 this author sometimes uses this rhetorical device and especially in the first chapter of his book, because the cross is to be recommended above the other signs

Let them displease no-one, etc. Here the author shows that his book should be sought after for two reasons. One is that it proceeds according to the opinion of the wise men of a certain worthy prose work, explaining its doctrines in verse. Another is that, furnished in advance with the use of a cross to mark its eloquence, it seeks to avoid more securely the ambushes of the envious.

. . . are like chicks. The metaphor is taken as an example. Just as the hen gathers her chicks under her wings so that they can hide there more safely and be fed better, so the author believes that he can hide his poems under the protection of the prose work.

> **Let them displease[1] no-one, my poems are like chicks,[2]**
> 1 that is, by displeasing let them hurt anyone who is envious about this
> 2 this is a metaphor

> **Tutius absque malis[1] matris[2] latitando sub alis,[3]**
> 1 id est, absque insidiis invidorum
> 2 id est, prosae exponendae
> 3 id est, sub deffensionibus

Ecce subiungit aliam rationem, quare sua carmina dicit securius
provulganda:

> **Postea vexillo sanctae crucis illa sigillo.**

Invide mutesce etc. Hic convertit actor sermonem suum ad invidum vel
10 invidos, dicens, quod eorum enormitas nonquam cessans benignorum semper
successibus ac probatis operibus contristatur. Actor, dico, considerans,
praenoscens aliquos invidos non solummodo opus suum sed etiam meliorum
livoris stimulo deridentes, ideoque tales reprobans et postponens, ad
ipsos sermonem suum dirigit, illos prout decet blaphemando, dicens se
nullatenus eorum invidiam dubitare immo etiam postponere, iuxta
sententiam Ovidii sic dicentis: **Quod volet impugnet** etc.

> **Invide[1] mutesce,[2] livoris labe[3] tepesce.[4]**
> 1 id est, improbe vel proterve
20 2 id est, silentium habe
> 3 id est, infamia
> 4 id est, refrenate vel dilabere
> **Sub serie[1] quadam numerorum[2] carmina[3] tradam.[4]**
> 1 id est, ordinatione sententiae
> 2 id est, metrorum
> 3 sive praesentia
> 4 id est, disponam
> **Quis[1] nisi tu cedas,[2] favet ordo,[3] ne metra laedas.[4]**
> 1 id est, quibus metris
30 2 id est, locum des vel faveas
> 3 id est, dispositio sententiae ordinatae vel divisae
> 4 id est, corrumpas

Prosa quid exponam etc. In fine sui prologi vult actor ostendere,
qua de causa hoc opus susceperit describendum, dicens in primis se
frustra huius operis expositionem aggredi, cum a quibusdam turpiter
reprobetur. Quod cum videat iniuste et absque causa rationabili
redargui et postponi, super hoc condolendo, reprehensores tales
redarguit et blaphemat, ne quod actum est et a sapientibus exprobatum
40 ruinam vituperii patiatur. Indeque prosae compatiens exponendae ad ipsam
tanquam ad rem rationalem sermonem suum dirigit, sibi consulens bona
fide, ne de cetero tales iniurias patiatur. Sed utens consilio meliorum
famam sibi iniuste sustractam cupiat in statum pristinum revocare. In
cuius rei opinione consistens, actor iste quicquid utile in prosa
cognovit, compilavitque metrice ad usum et commodum posterorum;

----

16 dicetis *pro* dicentis *cod.*   *Quod volet impugnet cod.*   28 **tu** *add.*
super scriptum   38 proponi *pro* postponi *Sowa*   reprenhensores *pro*
reprehensores *Sowa*   39 reprobatum *pro* exprobatum *Sowa*   43 iniuste *in
marg.*   45 -que *addi.*

Hiding more safely and without harm[1] under the wings[3] of their mother.[2]
1 that is, without the ambushes of the envious
2 that is, of the prose work that is to be expounded
3 that is, under the defenses
Here he adds another reason why he says that his poems should be promulgated more safely:
Also they have the seal and banner of the holy cross.

Jealous one, be quiet, etc. Here the author turns his speech to the envious man or men, saying that in their evil behavior, which never ceases, they are always made resentful by the successful and proven works of those who have good intentions. The thoughtful author, therefore, anticipating that some envious people, inspired by malice, will mock not only his work but also the work of better men, and chiding such people on that account, and disregarding them, he directs his speech to others, reviling those men as is proper, saying that he has no doubt of their envy and that he certainly disregards it, according to the maxim of Ovid, who says: "Let whoever wishes attack," etc.*

Jealous one,[1] be quiet,[2] cool off[4] the sickness[3] of your malice.
1 that is, wicked or shameless one
2 that is, be silent
3 that is, the disgrace
4 that is, restrain or disperse
In a certain sequence[1] of numbers[2] I shall deliver[4] my poems.[3]
1 that is, arrangement of meaning
2 that is, verses
3 the present ones
4 that is, I shall distribute
And unless you yield[2] to them,[1] the order[3] protects them, so that you do not harm[4] the verses.
1 that is, to the verses
2 that is, you give them a place or favor them
3 that is, the disposition of the meaning as it is arranged or divided
4 that is, injure

O prose, I shall expound, etc. At the end of his prologue the author wishes to show why he has taken up the task of explaining this work, saying at the outset that he has undertaken the exposition of this work in vain, since it is shamefully condemned by certain people. And since he sees it refuted and rejected unjustly and without reasonable cause, feeling sorry on this account, he refutes and reviles those censurers, lest what has been done and approved by wise men risk the ruin of disparagement. And so, making an agreement to expound the prose work, it is to it, as to a rational thing, that he turns his speech, advising himself in good faith not to risk such wrongs otherwise. But, using the advice of better men, he desires to bring its reputation, which has been unjustly damaged, back to its former state. And holding this view, the author has recognized something useful in the prose work and has compiled it in verse for the use and advantage of posterity. And he has

specialiter coadiungens modum inveniendi organum et motellos similiter et
hoquetos, postea dans doctrinam, qualiter unus modus potest in alium
transmutari.

> **Prosa[1] quid exponam[2] tibi deposuere coronam.[3]**
> 1 de qua loqui intendo sive
> 2 id est, cur metrice recitabo
> 3 id est, privilegium
> **Quidam vesani[1] sunt canone teste prophani.[2]**
> 1 id est, elationis animo furibundi
> 2 id est, excommunicandi de procul et phanum
> **Fusa[1] iaces[2] pateris famae, nec honore frueris.**
> 1 id est, confusa
> 2 O prosa, et hoc est, quia nemo tibi manum porrigit ad vitricem
> (fol. 136) **Condoleo[1] misere damnique[2] tui piget haere.[3]**
> 1 id est, miseriae tuae compatior
> 2 id est, tui vituperii
> 3 id est, adhaerere proprie
> **Iudicio[1] cleri laudo[2] pete[3] kiura tueri.**
> 1 id est, communi sententia sapientum
> 2 id est, consulo
> 3 tu, dico, requirens pristinam libertatem
> **Tolle moram[1] propera, pete Romam damna[2] severa.[3]**
> 1 id est, noli amplius moram facere
> 2 id est, calculum iudicii seu libram
> 3 id est, crudelia
> **Posce reformari,[1] cur fers[2] ita depreciari?[3]**
> 1 id est, in statum pristinum revocari
> 2 id est, pateris
> 3 in tanto vituperio colloquari
> **Consulo[1] sic repetoque statum[2] nunc dogmate[3] spreto.**
> 1 id est, in consilio tibi laudo
> 2 id est, materiam supradictam
> 3 sive eorum qui te vilipendunt

Disce prius etc. Finito prologo sive prohemio huius opusculi,
ideoque actor in hoc loco sui libri vult seriem declarare, quod est
contra quosdam penitus ignorantes, dicentes de talibus non oportere
quaerere vel facere mentionem, de quibus ait prius in minori. Si autem
in quibusdam ordinationem concedant esse, necesse est eam et in omnibus
concedere, et alibi dicit Boethius: *Nihil est, quod non retineat ordinem
servetque naturam.* Ex hiis igitur actoritatibus supradictis plenarie

----

11 excogitandum *pro* excommunicandi *Sowa*   18 proprie *scripsi,* propera
cod., propria *Sowa*   20 sententie *cod.*   sapientium *pro* sapientum *Sowa*
39 minore *pro* minori *Sowa*   42 auctoritatibus *pro* actoritatibus *Sowa*

specifically added the method of creating organum and also motets and hockets, afterwards giving the principle by which one mode can be changed into another.

> **O prose,**[1] **I shall expound**[2] **to you why they have removed your crown.**[3]
>
> 1 about which I intend to speak
> 2 that is, I shall explain the reason in verse
> 3 that is, privilege
>
> **Certain people are mad**[1] **and, as the law witnesses, profane.**[2]
>
> 1 that is, raging in their souls with pride
> 2 that is, they should be excommunicated far from their sanctuary
>
> **Diffused**[1] **you lie,**[2] **and suffer in your reputation, nor do you enjoy honor.**
>
> 1 that is, confused
> 2 O prose; and that is because no-one stretches out their hand to you as to a stepchild
>
> (fol. 136) **I grieve with you,**[1] **wretched one, and am troubled to be close to**[3] **your injury.**[2]
>
> 1 that is, I symathize with your wretchedness
> 2 that is, your disparagement
> 3 that is, properly, be associated with
>
> **I recommend**[2] **that you seek**[3] **the rights of protection by the judgement**[1] **of the clergy.**
>
> 1 that is, in the common opinion of wise men
> 2 that is, I advise
> 3 I mean you, seeking again your former freedom
>
> **Hurry and remove delay,**[1] **seek at Rome severe**[3] **punishments.**[2]
>
> 1 that is, do not make any more delay
> 2 that is, the reckoning or weighing of judgement
> 3 that is, cruel
>
> **Demand to be reformed;**[1] **why do you bear**[2] **to be thus undervalued?**[3]
>
> 1 that is, to be brought back into your former state
> 2 that is, tolerate
> 3 discussed with such disparagement
>
> **I advise**[1] **thus, and I seek again your state**[2] **and spurn the doctrine.**[3]
>
> 1 that is, I recommend in advice to you
> 2 that is, the above-mentioned material
> 3 of those who despise you

Learn first, etc. Since the prologue or introduction to this little work is finished, the author wishes in this place to state the sequence of his book, which is against the view of certain people who are completely ignorant, who say that one ought not to concern oneself or make mention of such things; and he says first that these people are in the minority. And if they concede that arrangement exists in some things, it is necessary to concede that it exists in all things; as Boethius says elsewhere: "Nothing can be without order and retain its nature."* And so from these authorities mentioned above it is fully confirmed that nothing can be perfectly and sufficiently fulfilled without any arrangement. And that is the reason why the author at the

confirmatur, nihil ordinatione postposita satis perfectius adimpleri;
hinc est igitur, quare actor in primis vult ordinem disserere sui libri,
ne ignoranter peccasse super hoc arguatur, dicens, quod per sex capitula
sui operis materiam terminabit.

    In primo igitur capitulo docet actor figurarum formas,
repraesentationes proprietatesque pariter et effectus. Et illud in duo
membra dividitur, eo quod duae sunt species figurarum, quoniam omnes
tales aut sunt simplices aut compositae, ut patebit. Ideoque in primo
membro agit de simplicibus, et illud incipit **Ecce tibi formas** etc., in
secundo de compositis, et illud ibi **Disce ligatarum** etc. In secundo
enim capitulo modorum species manifestat, et illud incipit ibi **Est
mensura modus** etc. In tertio de figuris pausationum et naturis pariter
dat doctrinam, et illud incipit ibi **Hic dabo pausarum** etc. In quarto de
consonantiis huius artis dissonantias evitando, et illud incipit ibi **Sunt
bene qui pangunt** etc. In quinto de discantu, et illud in duo membra
dividitur, in quorum primo agit actor simpliciter de discantu, in secundo
specialiter de copula, quae est membrum ipsius discantus, nec ab eo
differt nisi solummodo in figmento; primum igitur incipit **Unit discantus**
etc., secundum ibi **Copula cantores** etc. In sexto et ultimo de organo
speciali, quod omne genus cantuum superat dulcedine melodiae, et illud
incipit **Nobis organica** etc. Et sic patet in universo libri ordinatio
supradicta.

    Cum autem divisio leoninum sententiam et ordinationum notitiam
delucidet et ostendat, propterea istam praesentem leoninis particulam
breviter in duas partes dividamus, in quarum prima promittit actor
orthographiam ostendere huius artis tam per effectus notitiam quam per
formam; in secunda promittit ostendere, qualiter per sex species
ordinatae ad perfectionem cantuum operentur.

    Sicut autem in unaquaque scientia est ponere primum et minimum,
utputa in gramatica litteram, in dyaletica terminum, sic et in ista
musica mensurabili formam, quae orthographiam musicae repraesentat;
ideoque patet ordinatio partis praeambulae ad sequentem: prima pars
igitur incipit **Disce prius iure** etc., secunda **Ex hinc iura dare** etc.
Prius prima remanet indivisa, sed secunda in duas dividitur, in quarum
prima promittit actor se de modis facere mentionem subiungendo
pausationum genera, per quae modorum species distinguntur; in secunda
promittit se cantuum genera declarare sub modorum serie contentorum. Et
quia prius est continens quam contentum, eo quod contenti continens
esse dicitur fundamentum, ideo patet ordo. Prima pars incipit **Ex hinc
iura dare** etc., secunda pars ibi **Postea discantus** etc. Istae partes
remanent indivisae, sed pars principalior in duas dividitur. In prima
promittit figurarum formas ostendere, in secunda repraesentationem
cuiusque et effectum. Prima incipit **Disce prius iure** etc., secunda
Postea pandetur etc. Et sic patet sententia et divisio leoninis.

- - - - - - - - - -

1 proposita *pro* postposita *Sowa*   2 gratie *pro* igitur *Sowa*   11 **Est**
sine sublinea   18 figmentando *pro* figmento *Sowa*   19 etc. *om. Sowa*
30 grammatica *pro* gramatica *Sowa*   dialectica *pro* dyaletica *Sowa*
37 modorum serie species *Sowa*   39 **Ex** *sine* sublinea in cod.
43 cuiuslibet *pro* cuiusque *Sowa*   44 I[[ndeque]] *pro* **Postea** *cod.*

outset wants to lay out the order of his book, lest he be accused of having transgressed ignorantly in this regard. And so he says that he will complete the material of his work in the course of six chapters.*

In the first chapter therefore the author teaches the forms of notational figures, as well as the ways of representing them, their properties and effects. And that chapter is divided into two portions, because there are two species of figures, since all of them are either single or composite, as will be made clear. And so in the first portion he deals with single figures, and that begins **Look, now I shall give you the forms,** etc., and in the second with composite figures, and that begins **Learn about the ligatures,** etc. In the second chapter he displays the species of the modes, and that begins **Mode is the true measuring,** etc. In the third chapter he deals with the notational figures for pauses and their natures and he also gives the principle about them, and that begins **Here I shall give the species of the pauses,** etc. In the fourth chapter he deals with the consonances of this art, avoiding the dissonances, and that begins **There are certainly those who compose,** etc. In the fifth chapter he deals with discant, and that is divided into two portions, in the first of which the author deals simply with discant, in the second specifically with copula, which is a portion of discant, and does not differ from it except only in its representation. So the first part begins **Discant unites,** etc., the second **Copula makes cantors,** etc. In the sixth and last chapter he deals with special organum, which surpasses every genus of melody in the sweetness of its musical sound, and that begins **To us the special organal voice,** etc. And thus the above-mentioned arrangement of the book is clear throughout.

But since division clarifies and shows the meaning of the leonine verses and the concept of the arrangements, therefore we shall divide this present fragment of the leonine verse briefly into two parts, in the first of which the author promises to show the orthography of this art both through the concept of its effect and through its form; and in the second he promises to show how these are arranged in six species and work to the perfection of the melodies.

But just as in each science one should first put the smallest unit, for example the letter in grammar and the term in dialectic, so in measurable music one should first put the form, which represents the orthography of music. So the arrangement of the prefatory part to what follows is clear. The first part therefore begins **Learn first by law,** etc., the second **From here on I wish to give the laws,** etc. The first part remains undivided, but the second is divided into two, in the first of which the author promises that he will make mention of the modes, adding to that the genera of rests by means of which the species of modes are distinguished. In the second he promises that he will state the genera of melodies in the sequence of the modes that are contained in them. And because first comes that which contains before that which is contained -- because that which contains is said to be the foundation of that which is contained -- therefore the order is clear. The first part begins **From here on I wish to give the laws,** etc., the second part **After these the discant,** etc. Those parts remain undivided, but the principal part is divided into two. In the first he promises to show the forms of the figures, in the second the representation and effect of each one. The first begins **Learn first by law,** etc., the second **Then will be laid out,** etc. And thus the meaning and division of the leonine verses are clear.

Disce[1] prius iure[2] formas[3] cuiusque figurae.[4]
1 O cantor vel lector
2 id est, ratione
3 id est, protractiones
4 id est, tam simplicis quam compositae
Postea pandetur[1] quaevis nota[2] quanta[3] locetur.
1 id est, deinde declarabitur
2 id est, tam simplex quam composita
3 quo ad effectum sive

10 (fol. 136v) Ex hinc[1] iura[2] dare specierum sex volo care.[3]
1 id est, postea
2 id est, documentales regulas vel differentias huius artis
3 id est, O dilecte mi
Hiis[1] quoque subpangas pausas[2] quis[3] scemata[4] iungas.
1 sive speciebus supradictis
2 id est, pausarum differentias seu formas
3 id est, quibus pausis
4 id est, consonantias
Postea discantus[1] hinc copula vult dare cantus.

20 1 vult dare cantus et hinc ex altera parte copula vult similiter suos dare
Organicum[1] cantum specialem subiungo tantum.
1 sive ad differentiam organi generalis, quod est genus ad tria genera supradicta
Ordine praedicto[1] dabo[2] carmina, quae tibi dicto.[3]
1 id est, praemonstrato
2 id est, declarabo
3 id est, dictare vel recitare intendo

----

19 **Post** [[haec]] *pro* **Postea** *cod.*   20-21 copulam vult suo se dare *Sowa,* copula vult similiter suo se [?] dare *pro* copula vult similiter suos dare *cod.*   23 *inter* organi *et* generalis *ras.*   25 **preterito** *pro* **praedicto** *Sowa*

Learn[1] first by law[2] the forms[3] of each figure.[4]
1 O cantor or reader
2 that is, by reason
3 that is, the notations
4 that is, both the single and the composite

Then will be laid out[1] each written-down note[2] and how[3] it is placed.
1 that is, then will be stated
2 that is, both the single and the composite
3 as to its effect

(fol. 136v) From here on[1] I wish to give the laws[2] of the six species, dear one.[3]
1 that is, afterwards
2 that is, the exemplary rules or distinctions of this art
3 that is, O my beloved

From these[1] you may also determine the rests[2] to which[3] you may join the patterns.[4]
1 the above-mentioned species
2 that is, the distinctions or forms of the rests
3 that is, to which rests
4 that is, the consonances

After these the discant[1] and then the copula wishes to give melodies.
1 it wishes to give melodies and then on the other hand the copula similarly wishes to give its melodies

I add only the special organal[1] melody.
1 distinguished from general organum which is a genus according to the three genera mentioned above

In the order mentioned above[1] I shall give[2] the poems which I express[3] to you.
1 that is, pointed out beforehand
2 that is, I shall state
3 that is, I intend to express or explain

\<Capitulum primum\>

<Pars prima>

Ecce tibi formas etc. Finito prologo et assignato superius ordine
huius libri, actor in hoc loco principaliorem partem sui libri, tractatum
videlicet, agreditur et assignat, in quo de figuris universis et singulis
faciet mentionem. Et est notandum, quod non inmerito istud capitulum
prae ceteris debuit ordinari, quoniam sunt tres generalissimae species, e
quibus omne genus cantuum efficitur et habetur, scilicet figura, tempus
et mensura. Cum ergo figura sit causa et principium omnis cantus, quae
etiam sub certa diminutione temporis seu temporum mensurata compositionis
huius artis fons esse dicitur et origo, sicut supra patuit in illa
glosula: *sicut autem in unaquaque scientia est ponere primum et minimum*
etc.; ideoque in primis volumus ostendere formas et proprietates omnium
figurarum ac etiam quot tempora quaelibet earum pro sua parte in se
contineat et observet. Unde primum videndum est, quid sit figura, prout
in hac arte sumitur vel habetur, et unde dicatur, et quot sunt genera
simplicium figurarum, et quomodo per eas longitudo vel brevitas
designetur.
Ad primum igitur dicimus, quod figura, prout hic sumitur, est
repraesentatio soni facta in debita quantitate secundum suum modum vel
secundum sui aequipollentiam. Aequipollentia et est dictio aequivoca,
sed hic sumitur pro caractere vel pro voce illitterata nihil per se
signans, eo quod ex sola voce non potest fieri concordantia ergo neque
cantus, cum omnis cantus per consonantias gradiatur, sed per duas vel per
plures; per quod patet quod vox composita in hac arte dignior est et
nobilior ipsa simplice, nam voces simplices sunt ad compositas
reducendae, sicut inferius declarabitur suo loco, et dicitur a fingendo.
Quomodo autem per eas longitudo vel brevitas designetur, declarabitur
supra textum.

----

8 et *pro* etiam *Sowa*   compositioni *pro* compositionis *Sowa*
10 medium *pro minimum Sowa*   crux *in marg.*   14 arte *add. in marg.*
24 simplici *pro* simplice *Sowa*

Chapter One

Part One

Look, now I shall give you the forms, etc. Now that the prologue is finished and the order of this book has been laid out above, the author undertakes and lays out in this place the more important part of his book, that is to say the tract, in which he will make mention of notational figures both collectively and individually. And it should be noted that it is not undeservedly that this chapter should be arranged before the others, since there are three very general species from which every genus of song results and occurs, that is to say notational figure, unit of time, and measure. Since therefore the notational figure is the cause and the beginning of every melody, and is measured under a fixed diminution of a unit of time or units of time, and is also said to be the fount and origin of the composition of this art -- as has been made clear above in that gloss: "Just as in each science one should first put the smallest unit," etc.* -- therefore at the outset we want to show the forms and proprieties of all the figures, and also how many units of time each of them for its part contains and keeps within itself. And so first it should be seen what a figure is, as it is used or occurs in this art, and why it is so named, and how many genera of single figures there are, and how length and shortness are designated by them.

First therefore we say that a notational sign, as it is used here, is the representation of a sound made for a requisite quantity according to its mode or according to its equipollence. Equipollence is an equivocal term, but it is used here to mean a character or an unwritten sounding note that signifies nothing by itself; because from one sounding note alone there can be neither concord nor melody, since every melody moves through consonances, two or more.* And from this it is clear that a composite sounding note in this art is more worthy and more noble than a single one, for single sounding notes must be reduced to composite ones, as will be stated below in the right place;* and it is said to occur by contriving. And how length or shortness are designated by them will be stated above the given text.

Et notandum est, quod huius figurae aliquando ponuntur sine littera,
aliquando cum littera; sine littera, ut in caudis seu neumis cantuum
variorum, cum littera, ut in motellis et consimilibus. Inter figuras
quae sunt sine littera et cum littera talis datur differentia, quoniam
illae quae sunt sine littera debent, prout amplius possunt, ad invicem
colligari, sed huius proprietas aliquando amittitur propter litteram
huius figuris associatam. Sed huius figurarum, tam litterae sociatarum
quam non, dantur divisiones seu differentiae ac etiam regulae
sussequentes. Figurarum igitur quaedam ligantur ad invicem quaedam non.
10 Figura ligata est, ubicumque fit multitudo punctorum simul iunctorum per

suos tractus, ut hic: ▪◣▎▐◣ . Figura non ligata fit penitus e
converso, ut hic: ◀▪♦ .
Hiis itaque expositis et finitis eo vero quod non est necesse modo
plura inquirere, ad divisionem litterae breviter accedamus. Haec igitur
praesens lectio in duas partes prout decet dividatur, in quarum prima
ostendit actor, de quo debet agere, in secunda exequitur. Prima pars
incipit **Ecce tibi formas** etc., secunda **Simplex longa** etc. Pars prior
remanet indivisa, sed secunda in duas dividitur, in quarum prima agit
20 actor de formatione simplicium figurarum, in secunda de protractionibus
ligatarum. Et quia ligatae vel compositae ducunt originem a simplicibus,
ideo patet ordo. Prima pars incipit **Simplex longa** etc., secunda **Ut bene
quaeque metas** etc. Item prima istarum in duas. In prima ostendit actor
quot sunt simplices figurae, in secunda procedit circa repraesentationem
temporum in eisdem. Et quia prius est aliquid in forma ostendere quam
cognoscere non provisum, ideo patet ordo. Prima pars incipit **Simplex
longa** etc., secunda **Quaelibet istarum** etc. Haec secunda in tres partes
propter breviloquium dividatur, in quarum prima docet actor
significationem earum fore in qualibet bipartitam. In secunda ostendit,
30 quot tempora quaelibet earum in se pro sua parte contineat et observet.
In tertia ostendit, qualiter per modorum species ordinatae ad
perfectionem cantuum operentur. Prima pars incipit **Quaelibet istarum**
etc., secunda **Tempora longa gerit** etc., tertia **Hiis proprias sedes** etc.
Istae partes remanent indivisae, sed illa in qua agit de simplicibus in
duas dividitur, in quarum prima ostendit, quot sunt simplices figurae; in
secunda exemplificat de eisdem. Prima incipit **Simplex longa** etc.,
secunda **Longa fit haec** etc. Et sic patet sententia et divisio leoninis.

Ecce, tibi[1] formas[2] dabo nunc cuiusque figurae.[3]
40   1 O lector vel cantor
        2 id est, protractiones proprietatesque
        3 id est, tam simplicis quam compositae

----
4 sine *add. super scriptum*   8 seu *et* etiam *add. super scriptum*
10 ligata *om. Sowa*   13 ◀▪[[▪]]♦   17 decet *pro* debet *Sowa*
18 **Sim(plex)** *sine sublinea in cod.*   21 ducuntur *pro* ducunt *Sowa*
25 quid *pro* aliquid *Sowa*   27 terties *pro* tres *Sowa*

And it should be noted that figures of this kind are sometimes placed without text and sometimes with text: without text for example in the end sections or melodic formulae of various melodies; with text for example in motets and similar things. The following difference exists between figures without text and those with text, that those which are without text must be joined together as much as possible; but this kind of propriety is sometimes lost on account of the text associated with figures of this kind. But for figures of this kind, both allied with a text and not, the following divisions or distinctions and also rules are given: Some of the figures are ligated to each other, and some are not. A ligated figure is whenever there occurs a number of written notes

joined together by their lines, as for example here:　　　. A figure that is not ligated occurs entirely in the reverse way, as for example here:　　　.

And so with these things having been expounded and finished -- for indeed it is not necessary now to investigate them further -- let us broach briefly the division of the text. So let this present reading be divided into two parts, as is proper, and in the first of them the author shows what he should deal with, and in the second it is accomplished. The first part begins **Look, now I shall give you the forms,** etc., the second **There are the single long,** etc. The first part remains undivided; but the second is divided into two parts, in the first of which the author deals with the formation of single figures, and in the second with the notations of ligated figures. And because ligated or composite figures take their origin from single figures, therefore the order is clear. The first part begins **There are the single long,** etc., the second **Pay attention to the boundaries,** etc. Also the first of these is divided into two parts. In the first the author shows how many single figures there are; in the second he goes on to deal with the representation of units of time in them. And because one should first show what the form of something is before becoming acquainted with what has not been explained before, the order is clear. The first part begins **There are the single long,** etc., the second **Each of those,** etc. This second part may be divided into three parts for the sake of brevity, and in the first of these the author teaches that the significance of each one is twofold. In the second he shows how many units of time each one of them for its part contains and keeps within itself. In the third part he shows how they are arranged through the species of the modes and how they work for the perfection of melodies. The first part begins **Each of those,** etc., the second **The larger long bears,** etc., the third **To these you should give,** etc. Those parts remain undivided, but the part in which he deals with single figures is divided into two parts, in the first of which he shows how many single figures there are, in the second he gives examples of them. The first begins **There are the single long,** etc., the second **The long occurs thus,** etc. And thus the meaning and division of the leonine verses is clear.

> **Look, now I shall give you[1] the forms[2] of each figure.[3]**
> 1 O reader or singer
> 2 that is, the notations and properties
> 3 that is, both of the single and of the composite

Quantaque de iure sit quaelibet, hinc[1] dabo normas.[2]
1 quasi post formarum notitiam
2 significationum sententiam reserabo
(fol. 137) Hic ostendit actor per diffinitionem, quid sit figura,
dicens: figura est repraesentatio soni facta in debita quantitate:
More figura soni debet quaecumque reponi.
Hic subiungit actor duas esse partes sive species figurarum:
Dat binas partes notularum, qui sapit[1] artes.[2]
1 id est, intelligit
2 liberales sive
Hic accedit ad species earundem, dicens omnes tales esse simplices
vel compositas:
Dicitur esse data vox simplex voxque ligata.
Modo accedit ad numerum simplicium, dicens esse tres figuras
simplices quo ad formam:
Simplex longa, brevis, vel semibrevis fore quaevis.
Fertur,[1] iunctura[2] vocum[3] fit mixta[4] figura.
1 id est, dicitur
2 id est, ligatura
3 suple plurium simplicium
4 id est, composita vel ligata
Regula est: omnis figura simplex portans tractum longiorem a dextra
parte quam a sinistra semper signat longitudinem:
Longaque quadrata manet a dextra sibi grata.
Cauda[1] fit illarum,[2] brevis est quadrata duarum.[3]
1 id est, tractus
2 id est, aliarum duarum
3 id est, illa quae est brevis quadrangularis efficitur
Regula semibrevium: omnis figura simplex oblique protracta
semibrevis apellatur:
Obliquo latere vult semibrevis residere.
Haec[1] careant caudis, nisi det plica[2] quando subaudis.[3]
1 sive tam brevis quam semibrevis
2 id est, nisi plica apponatur
3 id est, subaudiendo ponis
Modo exemplificat de eisdem et primo de longa, eo quod aliis
administrat originis fundamentum,
Longa fit haec ◀ talisque brevis ■ sit eique sodalis.
quippe ipsa est loco totius aliae partium seu membrorum.
Semibrevis forma sic ◆ , ut docet ordine norma.[1]
1 id est, praesens regula

Tres ita formari etc. Praeostensis formis et proprietatibus
simplicium figurarum hic vult actor ad notitiam plicae accedere in
eisdem, dicens, quod huius figuras plicari saepius invenimus. Unde in
primis videamus quid sit plica, deinde quomodo in huius figuris habeat

----

9 intellegit *pro* intelligit *Sowa*   29 simplex *om. Sowa*   32-35 *add.*
in marg.   39 loco totius aliae loco partium *cod*   vel *pro* seu *Sowa*

And here[1] I shall give the precepts as to how much each one is by law.[2]

    1 after the concept of their forms

    2 I shall unlock the meaning of their significances

(fol. 137) Here the author shows by means of a definition what a figure is, saying: A figure is the representation of a sound made for a requisite quantity:

Each figure must be put down by the usage of the sound.

Here the author adds that there are two parts or species of figures:

He who knows[1] the arts[2] gives two parts of the notes.

    1 that is, understands

    2 the liberal arts

Here he broaches their species, saying that all of them are either single or composite:

It is said that there are given both a single note and a ligated note.

Now he broaches the category of single figures, saying that there are three figures that are single as to their form:

There are the single long, the breve, and the semibreve.
It is held[1] that a mixed[4] figure occurs by a joining[2] of the notes.[3]

    1 that is, it is said

    2 that is, a ligature

    3 supply: of many single ones

    4 that is, composite or ligated

The rule is: Every single figure that carries a longer line on its right side than on its left always signifies length:

A squared long remains pleasing to itself on the right side.
A tail[1] occurs on those,[2] but of the two the breve is squared.[3]

    1 that is, a line

    2 that is, the other two

    3 that is, the one that is a breve is made rectangular

The rule of the semibreves: Every single figure that is notated obliquely is called a semibreve:

The semibreve wants to lie with an oblique side.
These[1] lack tails, unless the plica gives one[2] when you understand.[3]

    1 both the breve and the semibreve

    2 that is, unless a plica is added

    3 that is, when you understand and place one there

Now he gives examples of those, and first the long, because it provides the foundation of origin to the others,

The long occurs thus ▄ and thus the breve ▪ , and let it be a companion to it.

for indeed it is in the place of the whole of the other of the parts or portions.

The form of the semibreve is like this ♦, as the precept[1] teaches in order.

    1 that is, the present rule

Three notes should be formed, etc. Having already shown the shapes and proprieties of the single figures, the author wishes here to broach the concept of the plica in those figures, saying that we often find that figures of this kind are plicated. And so let us see first what a plica

ordinari et etiam quae sit eius repraesentatio sive forma.

Plica sic describitur: plica nihil aliud est quam signum dividens sonum in sono diverso. Repraesentatio plicae sive forma habet fieri nunc per unum tractum nunc per duos, et praecipue in simplicibus, et hoc dupliciter, aut ascendendo aut descendendo. Si autem plica fiat in simplicibus, duplex est eius differentia sive locus, quoniam aut cognoscitur in repraesentatione per dextram partem aut etiam per sinistram, unde textus **Longior a dextra** etc.

Hic igitur dicit actor, quod plica in longa simplice debet habere
10 longiorem tractum a dextra parte quam etiam a sinistra tam ascendendo

quam descendendo, sicut patet hic ▐ ▌▐ , in brevi vero simplice e converso, id est longiorem a sinistra parte quam a dextra, videlicet hic

▌ ▌▐ . Plicarum brevium et semibrevium idem est iudicium. Et nota, quod ratione longae simplicis in talibus nunc apponitur duplex tractus et praecipue descendendo, quia eaedem sunt caudae in plica longa et longa simplice a parte dextra descendendo, et ideo differentiae causa tractum duplicem in plica longa apponimus, <et> in brevibus siquidem, ut in
20 repraesentatione formae a longis <simplicibus> differant quemadmodum in effectu.

Quidam vero plicam brevem ascendendo protrahunt per duos tractus diversos, unum in dextra parte ascendendo signantem plicam et alium in sinistra descendendo, signantem, ut asserunt, brevitatem, protrahentes in

hunc modum ▌ , et hoc tam pro maiore brevi quam pro minore, quod protrahere ac etiam provulgare credimus puerile. Et hoc patet multiplici ratione. Una est quia aprobato usui sic repugnant evidente causa aliqua non obstante. Alia est quia in dispositione tractus, per quem dicunt
30 plicam in ea designari, plicae longae ascendenti nullatenus se opponit, quare male, cum opposite debeant se habere. Item quod neuter tractuum sic debeat ordinari, patet sic: ascensus et descensus in omnibus formaliter se opponunt. Descensus plicae in tali voce non directe ascensui se opponit; si ergo descensus in brevi <sic> protrahitur quoad plicam, talis ascensus in ea figurabitur indirecte. Sed descensus in ea directe et rationabiliter dicitur figurari secundum sententiam aprobatam et etiam quoad ipsos, quare ascensum talem credimus esse nullum, reputantes ipsos esse contrarios sibi ipsis. Item quando dicebant, quod per tractum in sinistra parte positum brevitas signabatur, falsum
40 similiter supponebant, quia tam breves quam semibreves per se positas protrahimus sine caudis, etenim si cauda talibus adderetur, potius longitudinem quam brevitatem designaret. Item magis videretur accedere ad naturam compositionis quam simplicitatis. Item talis cauda in compositis non semper signat brevitatem, sed longitudinem saepius introduxit.

----

2 plica [[sic]] nihil *cod.*   3 *crux in marg.*   9 simplici *pro* simplice *Sowa*   decet *pro* debet *Sowa*   12 simplici *pro* simplice *Sowa* 18 simplici *pro* simplice *Sowa*   20 a longis *add. in marg.* 24 descendendo *add. in marg.*, *om. Sowa*   26 tam *add. super scriptum* 27 hoc *add. super scriptum*   34 unde *pro* <sic> *cod.*   41 unde *pro* etenim *Sowa*   42 *inter* brevitatem *et* designaret *ras.* 44 brevitate *cod.*

is, and then how it is arranged in figures of this kind and also what is its representation or form.

A plica is described thus: A plica is nothing other than a sign dividing a sound into separate sounds. The representation or form of a plica occurs sometimes by means of one line, sometimes by means of two, and especially in single figures. And this occurs in two ways, either ascending or descending. If however a plica occurs in single figures, its distinction or place is of two kinds, since it is either recognized in representation by means of the right side or the left, whence the text **The plica is longer,** etc.

Therefore the author says here that the plica in a single long should have a longer line on the right side than on the left, both ascending and

descending, as can be seen here   ; but in the single breve the reverse, that is, longer on the left side than on the right, as here

. And the same is true of the plicas of breves and semibreves. And note that because of the single long a double line is added to those and especially descending, because the tails on the long plica and the single long are the same descending on the right side, and so in order to distinguish them we put a double line on the long plica, and indeed on the breves, so that they may differ from the single longs in the representation of their form as they do in their effect.

Some people* however notate the breve plica ascending with two separate lines, one on the right side ascending, signifying the plica, and another on the left side descending, signifying, they claim, its

shortness; and they notate it in this way   both for a larger breve and for a smaller. And we believe that doing this and also promulgating it are childish. And this is clear for many reasons. One is that they oppose approved usage in this way with no apparent reason. Another is that in the placement of the line by means of which they say the plica is designated, it is in no way the opposite of the plica of the ascending long, and so it is bad, since they should be the opposite of each other. Also it is clear that neither of the lines should be arranged in this way, because ascent and descent are the opposite of each other in all ways in their form. The descent of the plica in such a note is not directly the opposite of the ascent; if therefore the descent in the breve is notated this way as regards the plica, then this kind of ascent in it will be figured indirectly. But its descent is said to be drawn directly and rationally according to approved opinion and also according to those people themselves, and so we believe that an ascent of this kind is of no value, and consider those people to be contradicting themselves. Also when they said that shortness was signified by a line placed on the left side, they similarly brought in something false, because we notate both breves and semibreves placed by themselves without tails; for indeed if a tail were added to them, it would designate length rather than shortness. Also it would seem more to approach the nature of composite figures than that of single ones. Also such a tail in composite figures does not always signify shortness, but rather has more often introduced length.

Tres ita[1] formari debent poteruntque plicari.[2]

1 id est, sicut superius est expressum

2 quasi diceret: possibile est omnes tales plicari

Hiis[1] duplicem tractum, nunc unum[2] fert[3] plica factum.

1 sive tribus figuris quo ad artem sive usum

2 id est, unicum

3 id est, dat vel gerit

Longior a dextra plica[1] longae parte sinistra.[2]

1 tam ascendendo quam descendendo sive cum duplici tractu vel
uno, sicut patet hic

2 parte sive

Hanc[1] brevibus longas et semibreves[2] sibi iungas.

1 sive plicam tam ascendendo quam descendendo, sicut patet hic

2 sive maiores solum, ut hic

Semibrevem vere etc. Hic accedit actor ad expositionem plicae in semibrevibus practicam reserando, dicens, quod secundum usum a pluribus aprobatum nulla semibrevium per se posita plicata dicitur reperiri, nec in aliquo praedecessorum exemplo alicubi figurari. Quid autem sit nunc super hoc consulendum, ad hoc ut rei veritas apareat, videamus.

Plica, (fol. 137v) <ut> supra patuit, nihil aliud est quam signum dividens sonum in sono diverso. Per hoc igitur sequitur, quod ubicumque fit plicae additio, ibi est soni divisio, et ubi non fit vel potest fieri soni divisio vel decisio, ibi plica nullatenus potest addi. Semibrevium autem quaedem minor quaedam maior, prout inferius recitabitur, sunt repertae, quarum minor indivisibilis est in sono, eo quod non potest in sono amplius minorari, quare similiter nec plicari, quod concedimus. Maior autem per divisionem soni potest artificialiter diminui et decindi, quare similiter et plicari; et hoc sive sit per se posita sive cum socia colligata. Cum socia siquidem in figura binaria plicata saepius reperitur tam ascendendo quam descendendo, et licet per se posita plicari valeat et de iure, sicut provulgare proponimus alicubi per exempla, tamen antecessorum adhuc exemplorum copia ad nos pervenientium non admisit.

. . . **sed bisse** etc. Nota, quod hanc semibrevem maiorem bisse decrevimus appellari. Bisse namque sunt duae partes alicuius vel unius cuiusque rei in tria partitae tertia sublata. Maior semibrevis est huiusmodi, quia in se duas partes unius rectae brevis vel unius temporis repraesentat, quare bisse saepius apellamus.

Quasi diceret: nulla semibrevium per se posita vel inventa dicitur plicari quo ad usum; practica est:

----

15 videlicet *pro* ut *Sowa*   17 plicae *add. in marg.*   21 apareat *add.
super scriptum*   23-24 ubicumque fit fit *cod.,* ubiconque facit fit *Sowa*
29 soni *add. in marg.*   30 hec *pro* hoc *Sowa*   33 *inter* iure *et* sicut
ras.   alicubi *om. Sowa*   34 copiam *pro* copia *cod.*

Three notes should be formed this way[1] and can be plicated.[2]
1 that is, as has been stated above
2 he means that it is possible for all such notes to be plicated
The plica brings[3] to these[1] a double line, and sometimes one.[2]
1 to these three figures according to the art or usage
2 that is, only one
3 that is, gives or carries
The plica is longer on the right side of the long[1] than on the left.[2]
1 both ascending and descending, and whether with two lines or one, as can be seen here
2 side
You may join this[1] to breves, and also longs and semibreves.[2]
1 the plica both ascending and descending, as can be seen here
2 only larger ones, as here

Truly a plica, etc. Here the author broaches the exposition of the plica in semibreves, revealing the practice, and saying that, according to the usage that is approved by many, no semibreve placed by itself is said to be found plicated, nor is it figured that way anywhere in any example by our predecessors. Let us see, however, what should now be determined about this, so that the truth of the matter might appear.

The plica, (fol. 137v) as has been made clear above,* is nothing other than a sign dividing a sound into separate sounds. From this therefore it follows that whenever there occurs the addition of a plica, there is a division of the sound, and where a division or cutting apart of the sound does not occur or cannot occur, there a plica can in no way be added. However some semibreves are found that are smaller, some that are larger, as will be explained below; and of these the smaller is indivisible in sound, because it can not be made any smaller in sound, and so similarly it can not be plicated, which we concede. But the larger semibreve can be artificially diminished and cut apart by means of a division of the sound, and so similarly it can also be plicated, whether it is placed by itself or joined with a fellow. And indeed it is often found with a fellow in a plicated binary figure, both ascending and descending; and although when placed by itself it has the power to be plicated and rightly -- as we propose to promulgate elsewhere through examples -- nevertheless the bulk of examples of our forebears so far reaching us has not admitted it.

. . . **to the twin,** etc. Note that we have decided that this larger semibreve should be called twin. For twin means two parts of something or two parts of a certain thing divided into three with the third part removed. The larger semibreve is of this kind, since in itself it represents two parts of one breve that is correct or of one unit of time, and so we often call it twin.

He means to say that no semibreve placed or found by itself is said to be plicated as to its usage; the practice is:

Semibrevem vere per se plica nescit habere.
Usu,[1] sed bisse[2] placet[3] hanc[4] cum arte[5] dedisse.
1 sive communi
2 id est, maiori semibrevi
3 mihi sive
4 sive plicam
5 id est, per possibilitatem artis

Sensa tenens etc. Declarato superius, qualiter plica in figuris
10 simplicibus habeat ordinari, et quae sit eius repraesentatio sive forma,
ad hoc ut per eius formam praecognitam ad interiorem ipsius notitiam
facilius accedatur, ideoque in hoc loco vult actor eius naturam sub
breviloquio disserere pariter et effectum, ne per aliam materiae
continuationem a proposito resiliat contingenti, dicens, quod plica
secundum variam suorum tractuum dispositionem nunc in sono deprimitur aut
etiam elevatur; et sic mobilis in sonos varios subtiliter transmutata aut
per tonum vel semitonum aut ditonum vel semiditonum vel dyatessaron et si
licuerit dyapente, scematorum plurium quaerit amicabiliter armoniam.
Nota igitur, quod quemadmodum ista dictio *altum* aequivoce significata
20 varia repraesentat, similiter haec eadem signata in plica sensibiliter
reperimus. *Altum* namque in una significatione idem est quod sublime vel
elevatum, in alia idem est quod profundum vel depressum, in tertia idem
est quod mare vel mobile, in quarta idem est quod subtile vel ingeniosum;
unde versus:

   Altum sublime pontus subtile profundum.

Haec eadem significata in plica proprie poterunt reperiri. Plica
namque nunc elevatur, nunc deprimitur, nunc per soni divisionem mobilis
efficitur, tamquam aqua per impulsionem. Quae quidem mobilitas de sono
in sonum per varias concordantias, sicut superius iam dictum est,
30 subtiliter deportatur. Et hiis de causis plicam alti significationibus
voluimus comparare.

Sensa etc. Converte sic: **plica**, id est, tale signum vel talis soni
divisio; **tenens**, id est, in se naturaliter comprehendens; **sensa** id est,
significata; **alti**, id est, talis dictionis sumptae materialiter hic.
Plica, dico, **fit coma**, id est, crinis seu cauda, eo quod habet fieri cum
cauda vel tractu; **scematis**, id est, concordantiae alicuius. Scematis,
dico, **alti**, id est, subtilis vel subtiliter transformati; vel aliter
sic: plica **fit choma**, id est, membrum seu incisio vel decisio scematis
alti, eo quod habeat fieri propter consonantias decentius purpurandas vel
40 etiam variandas.

Da medium etc. Hic vult actor ostendere breviter, quantam plica in
figura qualibet soni accipiat portionem, dicens, quod nunc medium nunc
minus medii nunc aut plus dicitur importare. Medium soni siquidem nunc
importat et hoc est, ubicumque bina soni proportio aequaliter fit divisa,
utputa in minore longa et maiore brevi et maiore semibrevi, in quibus
sonus per plicam, quotienscumque ibi apponitur, proportionaliter
bipartitur. Nunc autem minus quam medium, utputa tertiam soni portionem

----

10-11 forma [[in hoc]] ad hoc *cod.*   11 percognitam *pro* praecognitam
Sowa   16 subtiliter *om. Sowa*   aut *om. Sowa*   17 semitonium *pro*
semitonum *Sowa*   36 scematio *pro* scematis *Sowa*   42 *crux in marg.*
43 siquidem *om. Sowa*   46 ibi *add. super scriptum*

Truly a plica does not know how to hold a semibreve by itself. But in usage[1] it is pleasing[3] to have given this[4] to the twin[2] with the art.[5]
1 common usage
2 that is, to the larger semibreve
3 to me
4 the plica
5 that is, through the possibility of the art

Holding the senses, etc. Since it has been stated above how the plica is arranged in single figures, and what is its representation or form -- in order that through a prior understanding of its form one might more easily approach a deeper knowledge of it -- therefore in this place the author wants to discuss briefly its nature and also its effect, lest by pursuing other material he retreat from the present subject. And he says that according to the different placement of its lines the plica sometimes is lowered in sound and sometimes raised, and being thus mobile it is shifted subtly to different sounds either by a tone or a semitone or by a ditone or a semiditone or a dyatessaron, or, if it is allowed, a dyapente; and it seeks in a friendly fashion the harmony of several patterns. Note therefore that in the same way that the term "altum" equivocally represents different meanings, similarly we find and perceive these same meanings in the plica. For "altum" in one meaning is the same as sublime or raised, in another is the same as deep or lowered, in a third is the same as the sea or something mobile, in a fourth is the same as subtle or clever. Whence comes the verse :
    "'Altum' is the sublime ocean, subtle and deep."*
These same meanings can properly be found in the plica. For the plica is sometimes raised, sometimes lowered, sometimes, being mobile, results from the division of sound, like water from some impulse. And this mobility is subtly moved about from sound to sound through different concords, as has already been said above. And for these reasons we wanted to compare the plica to the meanings of the word "altum."
    Holding the senses, etc. Interpret thus: **plica,** that is, this sign or this division of sound; **holding,** that is, naturally including in itself; **senses,** that is, meanings; **of "altum,"** that is, of such a term used materially here. The plica indeed **is the hair,** that is, a lock of hair or a tail, because it occurs with a tail or a line; **of the pattern,** that is, indeed, of any concord. Of the pattern indeed which is **"altum,"** that is, subtle or subtly transformed. Or in another way thus: the plica **is the hair,** that is, a portion or a cutting into or cutting apart of a subtle pattern, because it may occur on account of consonances that should be more properly embellished or varied.
    Give half, etc. Here the author wishes to show briefly what portion of sound the plica takes up in each figure, and he says that it is said to convey sometimes half, sometimes less than half, or sometimes more. Sometimes indeed it conveys half the sound and this is whenever a double proportion of sound is divided equally, for example in a smaller long and a larger breve and a larger semibreve, and in these the sound is bisected proportionally by the plica, whenever it is placed there. Sometimes, however, it conveys less than half. For example we have seen that a

in ea vidimus contineri, sicut patet in maiore longa, in qua plica
tempus unicum est adepta. Et hoc est vel quia plica solum tempus ad plus
dicitur continere vel quia in qualibet figura per plicam in sono duplici
bipartita vel divisa extremam soni sibi semper nasciscitur portionem.
Nunc autem plus quam soni medium optinebit, sicut patet in recta brevi,
quae si in duas partes per plicam quo ad sonum artificialiter dividatur,
tunc partes quoad sonos dicimus inaequales; nam sonorum prior minoris
semibrevis, alter maioris aequipollentiam repraesentat, sicut per
divisionem consimilem declarabitur inferius suo loco, quamvis quidam
10   asserant saepius e converso, quod una via contradicimus et de iure.
Talis ergo soni divisio in recta brevi, si per plicam habeat designari,
plica supremam vocis semper accipiet portionem, sive sit aequalis priori,
sive minor, sive maior. In recta brevi siquidem maior soni proportio
minorem sussequi reperitur, quare plicae fit specialiter attributa. Quod
autem minor maiorem in tali divisione nullatenus sussequatur, patet per
omnes figuras compositas et per oppositum figuratas, in quibus minores
semibreves aliis praeponuntur; patet etiam liquidius et per plicam, quae
in una qualibet figura certam et non variam semper soni accipit
portionem.
20

Sensa[1] **tenens alti,**[2] **plica fit coma**[3] **scematis alti.**[4]
1 id est, significata
2 id est, huius dictionis alti materialiter sumptae
3 id est, crinis vel membrum seu incisio
4 id est, subtilis
Da[1] **mediumque soni,**[2] **minus, aut plus, nunc sine**[3] **poni.**[4]
1 sive illi plicae
2 illius vocis cui adhaeret sive
3 id est, permitte
30   4 id est, addi

(fol. 138) **Quaelibet istarum** etc. Praeostensis superius formis seu
protractionibus simplicium figurarum, nec non qualiter plica in eis
habeat figurari, insuper quae sit eius efficacia sive virtus, et quantam
in qualibet figura semper accipiat portionem, ideoque actor in hoc loco
proponit innuere significationem cuiuslibet figurae fore in qualibet
bipartitam, quod per appropriationem denominationis ostendere nunc
intendit. Et nota quod quamvis sub bina significatione forma et eiusdem
repraesentatio sit consimilis et eadem, tamen quoad potestatem, artem,
40   regulam differunt, et naturam; per quod potest ostendi breviter sex esse
figuras simplices, quarum binae et binae eandem protractionis formam
retinent et important. Sed quia sub forma triplici variantur, ideo tres
simplices esse dicimus, quas etiam propter significationum differentias
aequivocas appellamus.
   Et nota, quod quidam errant, apponentes longiorem caudam maiori

----

1 plica *add. super scriptum*   6 dividitur *pro* dividatur *Sowa*
1-19 Nota quod plica in recta brevi continet minus frustrum licet
glosulae asserunt maius, cum totum [?] maius est, etc. *in marg. ab alia
manu*   16 per *add. super scriptum*   29 promitte *pro* permitte *Sowa*
38 intendum *pro* intendit *Sowa*   41 et binae *om. Sowa*   42 quia [[sub
quia]] sub *cod.*

third portion of the sound can be contained in it, as can be seen in the larger long, in which the plica has obtained a single unit of time. And this is either because the plica is said to contain only one unit of time at most, or because in each figure that is bisected or divided by the plica into two sounds the plica always receives the smallest portion of sound. Sometimes, however, it will obtain more than half of the sound, as can be seen in the correct breve, which, if it is artificially divided into two parts as to its sound by the plica, then we say that the parts are unequal as regards the sounds; for of these sounds the first represents the equipollence of the smaller semibreve, the second that of the larger, as will be stated below in the right place by means of a similar division; although some often claim the reverse, which we contradict properly and rightly. This kind of division of sound therefore in a correct breve, if it is designated by means of a plica, will always accept for the plica the last portion of the note, whether it is equal to the first portion, or smaller, or larger. Indeed in the correct breve the larger proportion of the sound is found to follow the smaller, and therefore it is specifically allocated to the plica. That in this kind of division the smaller may in no way follow the larger can be seen from all the composite figures and those figured in an opposite manner, in which the smaller semibreves are placed in front of the others. It can also be seen even more plainly from the plica, which in each figure always receives a fixed and invariable portion of the sound.

> **Holding the senses[1] of "altum,"[2] the plica is the hair[3] of the "altum"[4] pattern.**
> 1 that is, meanings
> 2 that is, of this expression "altum" used materially
> 3 that is, a lock of hair or a portion or a cutting into
> 4 that is, subtle
> **Give[1] half of the sound,[2] or sometimes allow[3] less to be placed,[4] or more.**
> 1 to that plica
> 2 of that note to which it is attached
> 3 that is, permit
> 4 that is, to be added

(fol. 138) **Each of those,** etc. Since the forms or notations of the single figures have been shown above, as well as how the plica is figured in them, and also what its efficacy or inherent quality is, and what size portion it always receives in each figure, therefore in this place the author proposes to suggest that the significance of each figure is twofold, which he now intends to show by appropriation of nomenclature. And note that although by a double significance a form and its representation are one and the same, yet they differ as to their power, art, rule, and nature. And through this it can be shown briefly that there are six single figures, which keep and convey the same form of notation by pairs. But because they are varied by three kinds of form, therefore we say that there are three single figures, which indeed on account of the differences of their significance we call equivocal.

And note that certain people* are in error who put a longer tail on

longae quam minori, praecipue quando tres semibreves eis prout decet
supponuntur, ad differentiam minoris et etiam e converso, in hunc modum

pro maiore longa protrahentes   ❙•• , pro minore autem sic   ❙•• , quod
non est ponere quoad artem, ne regula pro parte alicubi vitietur, ubi
dicitur **Forma quidem** etc., quoniam si differentia assignaretur inter eas
quo ad caudarum longitudinem seu etiam brevitatem, multofortius deberet
assignari quo ad corpus, cum corpus sit dignius in ipsis vocibus quam
sint caudae; sed non est sic assignare, ergo neque sic. Item si hoc
10 esset verum, ita necesse esset eandem differentiam vel consimili modo
factam assignari inter maiorem brevem et minorem, quando tres semibreves
ipsis similiter adiunguntur. Sed inter tales non differentiam assignant,
nec est etiam assignanda, quare nec in aliis ipsam volumus assignare, cum
de similibus simile iudicium sit agendum. Et nota, quod modorum
ordinatio variorum notitiam super hiis faciet manifestam, sicut facit
inter praedictas longas per se simpliciter ordinatas, sicut inferius in
tractatu semibrevium aparebit. Ad hoc autem plenius extirpandum possent
rationes multiplices introduci.
       . . . **minor aut maior** etc. Nos siquidem nonnullos vidimus
20 asserentes, quod inter tales voces minoritas et maioritas quoad nomen
nonquam debeant assignari, eo quod inter minoritatem et maioritatem, ut
dicunt, non est medium apponendum; sed inter tales contingit medium
reperire, utputa tractum vel intervallum vel consimile quid, quare una
maior et altera minor nullatenus debet dici. Ad quos respondimus, ne
earum obiectio frivola vel insolubilis videatur, dicentes, quod de tali
medio loqui possimus dupliciter. Est et enim quoddam medium, quod inest
utrique parti, ita quod utriusque naturam sapit pariter et importat; quod
quidem medium inter tales voces non evenit reperire, quia sic esset
triplex longae differentia et triplex brevis et triplex semibrevis, ita
30 quod una semper mediocris naturam saperet aliarum. Secus tamen est inter
tales voces, eo quod tali medio carere penitus sunt repertae. Et
secundum illud medium arguebant, et sic contra nos non arguunt vel
obiciunt etiam, sed pro nobis. Est et enim aliud medium, quod quandoque
interponitur, quandoque non. Et tale non impedit, quin voces eiusdem
formae ratione significationis per magis et minus differentes a magis vel
minus denominationem valeant importare, quippe cum signatum rei sit in
omnibus dignius sua voce, et a digniori debet res denominari, sicut
communiter recitatur; vel dicere possumus rationem talium esse
sophisticam et non veram, nam inter minoritatem et maioritatem nunc
40 medium reperitur, sicut patet in communi sermone, cum dicitur: *Hic est
minor, alter mediocris, iste maior*; et istud praecipue patet, cum additur
ordo vel materia. Nunc aut caret medio, sicut patet cum dicitur: *Minus
volumus prius, maius* etc. Et sic quandoque apponitur medium, quandoque
non, sed saepius evitatur.

----

12 differentiam *add. super scriptum*   24 decet *pro* debet *Sowa*
25 obiratio *pro* obiectio *Sowa*   37 decet *pro* debet *Sowa*   38 possimus
pro possumus *Sowa*   42 patet *add. super scriptum*

the larger long than on the smaller -- especially when three semibreves
are added to them properly -- in order to differentiate the smaller from

the larger, for they notate them this way for the larger long ♪•• but

in this way for the smaller ♪•• , which is not putting them according
to the art, lest the rule somewhere* where it says **Indeed the shape,** etc.
be violated. For if any distinction were to be made between them as to
the length or shortness of their tails, it should much rather be made as
to their bodies, since the body is more important in notes themselves
than are the tails; but no distinction is made this way, so it should not
be done that way either. Also if this were true, it would be necessary
to make the same distinction or distinguish in a similar way between the
larger breve and the smaller, when similarly three semibreves are joined
to them. But they do not make any distinction between those, nor indeed
should any be made, so we do not want to make any in the others either,
since about similar things a similar judgement should be made. And note
that the arrangement of the different modes will make the concept of
these things clear, as it does for the longs mentioned above, which are
arranged singly by themselves, as will appear below in the tract on
semibreves. But many reasons could be introduced to eradicate this more
fully.

. . . **the smaller or the larger,** etc. We indeed have seen some
people asserting* that between these notes their being smaller or larger
should never be distinguished as to name, because, they say, between
things that are smaller and things that are larger no middle ground
should be put; but, they say, it does happen that in these notes a middle
ground is found, for example a line, or a space, or something similar,
and so one should never be called larger and the other smaller. And we
answer them, lest their objection seem either trifling or insoluble, and
say that we may speak of such a middle ground in two ways. For there is
a certain middle, which is in each of the parts in such a way that it
partakes of and conveys the nature of each one equally. And indeed this
middle is not found in these notes, because then there would be three
distinctions of longs, and three of breves, and three of semibreves, in
such a way that one of the middle notes would always partake of the
nature of the others. But it is otherwise between these notes, because
they are found to lack completely such a middle ground. And they argued
according to that middle ground, and thus they are not arguing or
objecting against us, but for us. For there is also another middle,
which is sometimes placed in between and sometimes not. And this does
not prevent notes of the same form, that are different by means of their
significance as being larger or smaller, from having the power to convey
in their nomenclature their being larger and smaller, especially since
the meaning of a thing is in all things more important than its name, and
a thing should be named from what is more important, as is commonly
stated. Or we can say that the reason for such things is sophistical and
not true, for sometimes there is found a middle ground between smaller
and larger, as is clear from the common saying: "This is smaller, the
other is in the middle, and that is larger."* And this is especially
clear when order or material is added. Or sometimes it lacks a middle,
as is clear in the saying: "We want the smaller thing first, the larger
thing," etc. And thus sometimes the middle is put and sometimes not, but
more often it is avoided.

Quod autem tales voces sic differentiae causa possint et debeant apellari, patet sic: minoritas et maioritas assignantur inter res eiusdem generis secundum magis et minus differentes. Voces in musica, quae indifferenter se habent quoad formam, sunt huiusmodi, quare sic denominari nec inmerito meruerunt. Item quod sic debeant nominari, patet sic: *musica est scientia de numero relato ad sonum vel de numero est sonorum.* Cum ergo numeri in hoc differant, quod unus minor alter maior apellentur, similiter et vocum unam minorem et alteram maiorem poterimus apellare. Item patet sic et plenius: quicquid differt secundum magis et
10 minus sub identitate formae ac nominationis debet a magis et minus denominationem propriam importare. Voces in hac musica sunt huiusmodi, quare ipsas secundum magis et minus differentiae causa volumus apellare, ad hoc ut per talem nominationis apropriationem ab invicem cognoscantur.

> **Quaelibet istarum[1] minor aut maior manet[2] harum.[3]**
> 1 sive simplicium figurarum
> 2 ad hoc ut inter eas cognitio per differentiam oriatur
> 3 sive vocum

Quasi diceret: tam minor quam maior eandem formam inferunt et
20 important:

> **Forma quidem cari nonquam debet variari.**

Tempora longa etc. Quoniam actor in praecedentibus formas et protractiones simplicium figurarum descripsit, pariter et naturas, potestatem seu effectum cuiuslibet esse duplicem ostendendo, ideoque ad cognitionem earum quo ad repraesentationem temporis seu temporum in eis accedere nunc intendit, ostendendo quot tempora quaelibet earum in se pro sua parte contineat et observet. Gratia cuius in primis quid sit tempus prout in hac arte sumitur videamus.
30 Tempus igitur, prout hic sumitur, est morula, ubicumque recta brevis habet fieri. Et recta brevis est illa, quae unum solum tempus continet, et illud est indivisibile secundum illud praedictum, id est quo ad rectam brevem. Et nota, quod tempus potest tripliciter considerari et hoc proportionaliter, quoniam aut per vocem rectam aut cassam aut omissam. Vox recta est vox instrumentis naturalibus procreata. Vox cassa idem est quod sonus, non vox, artificialiter procreatus, sicut patet in musicis instrumentis, in quibus sonus nunc proportionaliter accipitur et habetur; vel vox quassa a *quassa* dicta est idem quod vox imperfecta aut etiam semiplena per sonos varios diminuta. Vox omissa fit per recreationem
40 spirituum et per pausationem aliquam praedictae voci aequi- (fol. 138v) pollentem. Illud siquidem tempus per vocem quassam, ut dictum est, divisibile est et imperfectum quoad semibreves, quae de semus, sema, semum, quod est imperfectus, imperfecta, imperfectum, dicuntur, quasi imperfectae breves.
Gratia cuius discutiendum de perfectione et imperfectione circa voces vel figuras, et praecipue circa longam maiorem et minorem, quoniam quidam

----

1 sic [[va]] differentiae *cod.*   10 decet *pro* debet *Sowa*
13 conoscantur *pro* cognoscantur *cod.*   24 descripserat pro descripsit
cod.   30-31 *crux in marg.*   42-43 semus .ma.mum. quod est imperfectus
.cta.ctum. *cod.*

But the fact that these notes may and should be called this way because of their difference is clear from the following: Being smaller and being larger are determined in things of the same genus according to whether they are more or less distinct. Notes in music, which occur indifferently as to their form, are of this kind, and so they not undeservedly deserve to be named in this way. Also the fact that they should be named in this way is clear from the following: "Music is the science of number as it relates to sound or about the number of sounds."* Since therefore numbers differ in the following way, that one is called smaller and the other larger, similarly we could also call one note smaller and the other larger. Also it is clear and more fully as follows: Whatever is different according to its being larger and smaller but with the same form and nomenclature should convey its being larger and smaller with the proper nomenclature. In this science of music notes are of this kind, and so we wish to call them according to their being larger or smaller because of their difference, so that they may be recognized from each other through this appropriation of nomenclature.

Each of those[1] remains the smaller or the larger[2] of these.[3]
1 the single figures
2 so that between them the recognition may arise by means of their distinction
3 notes

He means to say that both the smaller and the larger carry and convey the same shape:
Indeed the shape, dear ones, should never be varied.

The larger long, etc. Since the author has described in the foregoing the forms and notations of the single figures as well as their natures, showing that the power or effect of each one is twofold, he now intends to broach the understanding of them as regards the representation of a unit of time or units of time in them, showing how many units of time each one of them may contain and keep in itself. And for the sake of this let us see first what a unit of time is as it is used in this art.

A unit of time therefore as it is used here is a delay wherever a correct breve occurs. And a correct breve is that which contains only one unit of time, and that is indivisible according to what was said before regarding the correct breve. And note that a unit of time can be considered in three ways proportionally, that is either by means of a correct note or an empty note or one that is left out. A correct note is a note created on natural instruments. An empty note is the same as a sound -- not a sung note -- that is artificially created, as on musical instruments, in which the sound is sometimes proportionally perceived and occurs; or an empty note is so called from "quassa," which is the same as an imperfect note or a half-full one, diminished by means of different sounds. A note that is left out occurs through refreshing the breath and through some pause equi- (fol. 138v) pollent to the aforementioned note. Indeed that unit of time in an empty note, as has been said, is divisible and imperfect as to its semibreves, which are so called from the word "semi-," which means imperfect -- that is: imperfect breves.

And for the sake of this we should discuss perfection and imperfection in notes or figures and especially in the larger and smaller

in suis artibus maiorem longam perfectam solummodo vocaverunt, eo quod a perfectione trinae aequalitatis nomen habere sumpsit, et eo quod sub certa diminutione longitudinis unius per vocis accentum in mora trium temporum aequaliter proportionata manet, se ipsamque in novem partes diminuendo dupliciter partiens. Minorem autem longam imperfectam dicere praesumpserunt, eo quod non nisi duo tempora contineat, quamvis affinitatem in forma et proprietate habeat cum maiori longa. Et hoc asserunt tali siquidem ratione: nullus cantus perfectus potest fieri de imperfectis figuris, et hoc est quia nemo puras imperfectas pronuntiare

10 potest per se, quod concedimus, nam ex puris et veris imperfectis non posset cantus perfectus absque perfectarum consortio compilari. Sed quando concludebant minores longas esse penitus imperfectas ratione superius assignata, eo videlicet quod ex eis perfectus cantus non posset absque aliarum consortio compilari, dicimus respondentes, quod falsum supponebant, quia non sequitur propter hoc, quod illae voces sint omnes imperfectae, e quibus cantus per se non potest simpliciter ordinari. Quoniam si hoc esset verum, iam maiores breves essent similiter imperfectae, quod falsum est. Nam si recta brevis in uno tempore perficitur et ideo recta brevis dicitur et perfecta, multofortius et

20 maior brevis perfectior erit, quae duorum temporum aequalem proportionem continet et importat. Si ergo istae sunt perfectae, licet ex eis cantus per se non valeat ordinari, similiter et istas longas perfectas dicimus et de iure. Si autem quaerat aliquis, quare ex eis cantus per se non potuit ordinari, dicimus respondentes, quod hoc non potuit esse, quoniam si una earum immediate alii iungeretur, iam prior non esset minor longa sed maioris indueret potestatem iuxta regulam artis locis omnibus generalem, quae talis est: *longa ante longam valet tria tempora,* et in metro: **Longae cerne** etc. Et sic patet, quare una earum alteri immediate non potuit coadiungi.

30 Item quod nulla figura praeter semibreves dici debeat imperfecta potest satis rationabiliter declarari sic: perfectio et imperfectio differunt in forma protractionis quemadmodum in effectu, sicut patuit in brevibus et semibrevibus antedictis. Cum autem minor longa et maior in forma protractionis conveniant aliquo non obstante, licet in quantitate differant potestatis, nulla earum de iure dici poterit imperfecta, cum perfectionis formam retineant et important. Item nec in variatione nominis, quemadmodum semibrevis a brevi videlicet semilonga vocaretur, quare ipsam nonquam esse credimus imperfectam sed eam esse dicimus rectam longam et veram et insuper et perfectam. Maiorem autem longam in

40 potestate dicimus esse perfectiorem et temporum ampliatione, quare ipsam ultramensurabilem apellamus, sicut in capitulo declarabitur specierum.

Item quod minor longa recta longa et vera dici debeat et perfecta, patet sic: quemadmodum recta brevis est illa, cui si aliquid addatur vel sustrahatur iam non videbitur recta brevis, immo a sua rectitudine deviabit; similiter minor longa est illa, cui si aliquid addatur vel sustrahatur iam suae rectitudinis inde amittet. Cum autem minor brevis

----

6 non *add. super scriptum*   7 maiore *pro* maiori *Sowa*   20 aequalem *add. super scriptum*   21 licet ex eis per se *[add. super scriptum]* cantus *cod.*   23 quaerat [[quare]] aliquis *cod.*   30 imperfecta *add. super scriptum*   37 nominationis *pro* nominis *Sowa*   42 et vera *add. super scriptum*   45 quid *pro* aliquid *Sowa*   46 amittit *pro* amittet *Sowa*

long, since some people in their treatises* have called only the larger
long perfect, because, they say, it takes its name from the perfection of
triple equality, and because it remains under a fixed diminution of
length by means of the accentuation of one note in an equally
proportioned delay of three units of time, and distributes itself in two
ways by diminishing itself into nine parts. They have presumed to say,
however, that the smaller long is imperfect, because it only contains two
units of time, although it has an affinity in form and propriety with the
larger long.* And they assert this with the following rationale: No
perfect melody can be made out of imperfect figures, and this is because
no-one can utter pure imperfect figures by themselves;* which we concede,
for a perfect melody could not be put together from pure and true
imperfect figures without the accompaniment of perfect ones. But when
they concluded that smaller longs are completely imperfect because of the
reason given above, that is, because a perfect melody could not be put
together from them and without the accompaniment of the others, we say in
response that they were wrong, because it does not follow on this account
that all those notes are imperfect from which a melody by itself can not
be arranged. Since, if this were true, the larger breves would also be
imperfect, which is false. For if a correct breve is completed in one
unit of time and so is called a correct and perfect breve, so much the
more will a larger breve be more perfect, since it contains and conveys
an equal proportion of two units of time. If therefore those breves are
perfect, even though a melody by itself can not be arranged from them,
then similarly we also call the longs perfect, and rightly. If however
anyone asks why a melody by itself could not be arranged from them, we
say in response that this could not be, since if one of them were joined
immediately to another, now the first one would not be a smaller long but
would take on the power of the larger, according to the rule of the art
that is general in all places,* which is as follows: "A long before a
long is worth three units of time," and in verse: **Perceive those,** etc.*
And thus it is clear why one of them could not be joined immediately to
the other.

    Also the fact that none of the figures except the semibreves should
be called imperfect can be stated reasonably enough in this way:
Perfection and imperfection differ in the form of their notation in the
same way as they do in effect, as has been made clear in the breves and
semibreves mentioned above. Since however the smaller and the larger
long agree in the form of their notation if something does not stand in
the way, although they differ in the quantity of their power, none of
them could rightly be called imperfect, since they keep and convey the
form of perfection. Also they do not differ in their nomenclature, in
the same way that a semibreve is named from a breve that is semilong, and
so we believe that that note is never imperfect but we say that it is a
correct long and a true one and also even a perfect one. We say however
that the long that is larger in power is also more perfect in the
extending of its units of time, and so we call it beyond measuring, as
will be stated in the chapter on the species.

    Also the fact that the smaller long should be called the correct long
and true and perfect is clear from the following: Just as the correct
breve is that which, if something is added to it or taken away from it,
will no longer seem a correct breve but rather will deviate from its
correctness, in the same way the smaller long is that which, if something
is added to it or taken away from it, will thereby lose something of its

et minor longa in hoc conveniant, quod una aliam iuxta se semper exigat
aut suum aequipollens et etiam in additione et sustractione tamquam
correlative se habeant, ideo dicimus, quod si recta brevis in suo genere
sit perfecta, sic et minor longa perfecta merebitur apellari. Sed
perfecta in suo genere quo ad quantitatem unius temporis reperitur, quare
similiter et altera perfecta merebitur nuncupari.

    Item quod sit perfecta, patet per omnes figuras compositas et
perfectas, et praecipue in primo modo et secundo, quas perficit
terminando, quoniam si essent imperfectae, sicut in suis artibus
10 asserunt, non protraherentur perpendiculariter sed oblique, a qua
obliquitate imperfectionis nomen sumere meruerunt. Item quod sint
perfectae, patet etiam per dictum suum, cum dicunt, quod perfectus cantus
non potest fieri ex imperfectis figuris, quod concedimus ex hoc sic
arguentes contra ipsos: oppositorum oppositi sunt effectus; perfectio et
imperfectio ab invicem se opponunt et attenduntur circa finem. Ex hoc
sequitur, quod voces, quae in fine cantus perfecti ponuntur, cantum
perficiant et consumment. Longae minores sunt huiusmodi, quia primum
modum perficiunt et componunt, quare ipsas perfectas dicere nullatenus
dubitamus.

20   Item per talem comparationem quod sint perfectae patet. Musica
mensurabilis dicitur a mensura, sicut grammatica metrica a metros, quod
est mensura, quae inquam grammatica duas mensuras accentuum detinet et
importat, scilicet longum et brevem, quorum longus est duorum temporum,
brevis unius. Et sic sub illis duobus accentibus, inter quos nullum
medium fit repertum, rectam musicae mensuram reperiri dicimus et
perfectam. Sed hoc est longae minoris et brevis minoris proportio, quare
tales rectas esse dicimus et perfectas. Ad hunc autem errorem plenius
exstirpandum possent etiam rationes aliae introduci, sed earum copia nos
fatigat.

30

    (fol. 139) Hic ostendit actor, huius voces differunt in effectu:
       Tempora longa gerit maior tria, sed duo[1] quaerit.[2]
       1 sive tempora
       2 id est, acquirit
       Longa[1] minor, certa[2] lex haec sit ubique[3] reperta.
       1 id est, recta longa
       2 id est, secura et vera
       3 id est, in quolibet cantu vel modo
       Dat[1] brevis ecce minor tempus solum,[2] duo[3] maior.[4]
40   1 id est, in se continet vel importat
       2 id est, unicum
       3 tempora
       4 sive brevis
    Quasi diceret: tantum valet maior semibrevis per se, quantum duae
minores semibreves:
       Si minor est sema, maioris fert dupla scema.
- - - - - - - - - -

15 acceduntur *pro* attenduntur *Sowa*   17 consument *pro* consumment *Sowa*
quare *pro* quia *Sowa*   crux in marg.   21 metris *pro* metros *Sowa*
22 desinet *pro* detinet *Sowa*   24-26 Et sic sub illis duobus accentibus
inter quos non cadit medium recte mensurari dicitur et perfecte sic
rectam musicae mensuram reperiri dicimus et perfectam sub illis duobus
accentibus inter quos nullum medium fit repertum *cod.*   26 est *add.*
super scriptum

correctness. But since the smaller breve and the smaller long agree in this, that one always demands the other or something equipollent to it next to it, and also in addition and subtraction they are like correlatives, so we say that if the correct breve in its genus is perfect, so also the smaller long will deserve to be called perfect. But the breve is found as perfect in its genus as regards the quantity of one unit of time, and so similarly also the other one will deserve to be named perfect.

Also the fact that it is perfect is clear from all the composite and perfect figures and especially in the first mode and the second, for it completes these figures by ending them, since if they were imperfect as they assert in their treatises, they would not be notated perpendicularly but obliquely, and from this obliqueness they would deserve to take the name of imperfection. Also the fact that they are perfect is clear from their remark* when they say that a perfect melody can not be made from imperfect figures, which we concede; but from this we argue against them as follows: Opposites are the effects of opposites; perfection and imperfection are opposites of each other and are observed at the end. From this it follows that those notes which are placed at the end of a perfect melody complete the melody and consummate it. Smaller longs are of this kind, because they complete and make up the first mode, and so we do not hesitate at all to call them perfect.

Also it is clear that they are perfect from the following comparison. Measurable music is so called from measure, just as metrical grammar is so called from metre, which is also measure -- and so this grammar, as I say, retains and conveys two measures of accents, that is to say the long and the short, of which the long is of two units of time and the breve of one. And thus we say that it is in those two accents, between which no middle is found, that the correct and perfect measure of music is found. But this is the proportion of the smaller long and the smaller breve, which is why we say that they are correct and perfect. And other reasons could be introduced so that this error could be more fully eradicated, but the abundance of them tires us.

> (fol. 139) Here the author shows that notes of this kind differ in their effect:
>
> **The larger long bears three units of time, but what seeks[2] two[1]**
> 1 units of time
> 2 that is, acquires
> **Is the smaller long.[1] This fixed[2] law may be found everywhere.[3]**
> 1 that is, the correct long
> 2 that is, secure and true
> 3 that is, in any melody or mode
> **See, the smaller breve gives[1] only one[2] unit of time, the larger[4] gives two.[3]**
> 1 that is, contains in itself or conveys
> 2 that is, a single one
> 3 units of time
> 4 breve

He means to say that a larger semibreve by itself is worth as much as two smaller semibreves:

> **If the smaller is half, the pattern of the larger has two.**

Si minor est sema etc. converte sic: **Si minor sema,** id est, semibrevis minor; **est dupla,** id est, duplex vel duplata; **fert,** id est, repraesentat; **scema,** id est, ornatum quantitatis in proportione; **maioris,** sive semibrevis.

Quasi diceret: semibrevis maior in se repraesentat quantitatem duarum semibrevium minorum. Est et enim quaedam semibrevis in forma non per se sed cum aliis semibrevibus ordinata, quae quandoque quantitatem unius temporis, nunc duorum per accentus repraesentat, utputa quando tres semibreves loco unius longae duorum temporum sive trium accentaliter sunt
10 repertae. Sed de tali ibi non facimus mentionem quoniam metas suae significationis ac nominis transcendere non veretur. Et talem dicebant aliqui maiorem semibrevem proprie nuncupari atque ita decepti decidunt in errorem, eo quod transsumptive tunc et per accentus significationis alterius sive necessitatis causa sive ornatu musicae beneficium dicitur optinere vel occupare. Nos siquidem de illa seu de illis hic loquimur, quae nonquam suae significationis vel nominis metam transcendere sunt repertae.

Sic fit longa duplex etc. Hic recitat actor, quomodo per necessitatem contingit aliquando longam figuram sub eodem corpore bis se
20 ipsam repraesentare. Et hoc fit aut propter defectum planae musicae, ne per additionem aliquam corrumpatur seu etiam frangatur, vel quandoque propter ornatum musicae metricosum diutius adaptandum. Et nota, quod talis vox longa duplex dicitur in se sex tempora comprehendens, unde regula: longa duplex est illa cuius latitudo transit longitudinem, sicut littera manifestat.

Sic[1] fit longa duplex ▜ **ac[2] in se tempora fert[3] sex.**
1 id est, sicut praesens exemplum declarat
2 pro et
30 3 id est, repraesentat

Hiis proprias sedes etc. Hic vult actor ostendere, qualiter haec sex voces per sex modorum species ordinatae primo generaliter et de sui natura secundo accentaliter per convenientiam aliquam ad perfectionem omnium cantuum operentur, dicens **Longa capit ternam maior** etc. secundum tenorem textus et de propria natura et non per accentus; et sic de omnibus aliis secundum tenorem litterae dat exempla.

Sedem maiori etc. Hic ostendit qualiter et per accentus in aliis speciebus quam in propriis per convenientias aliquas sunt repertae, et
40 hoc aut propter colorem musicae competentius purpurandum aut propter superhabundantiam litterae.

Hiis[1] proprias sedes speciebus sex dare[2] debes.
1 sive vocibus supradictis
2 et hoc regulariter aut irregulariter, O cantor

----
1 **scema** *pro* **sema** *cod., corr. Sowa*   11 nominationis *pro* nominis *Sowa*
14 *inter* alterius *et* sive *ras.*   16 nominationis *pro* nominis *Sowa*
18 *crux in marg.*   29 etiam *pro* et *Sowa*   35 **maior** *om. Sowa*
38 etc. *add. super scriptum*

If the smaller is half, etc. Interpret thus: **the smaller half,** that is, a smaller semibreve; **two,** that is, double or doubled; **has,** that is, represents; **pattern,** that is, ornamented in the proportion of the quantity; **larger,** a larger semibreve.

He means to say that the larger semibreve represents in itself the quantity of two smaller semibreves. For there is also a certain semibreve that is not by itself in its form but is arranged with other semibreves, which sometimes represents the quantity of one unit of time through its accents and sometimes two, for example when three semibreves are found in place of one long of two units of time or three according to their accents. But we did not make mention of that one above since it is not afraid to transcend the boundaries of its significance and name. And some have said* that that one should properly be termed a larger semibreve, and being thus deceived they fall into error, because it is said to obtain or take possession of this benefit by transfer of terms and by means of the accents of another significance or because of necessity or to ornament the music. We indeed speak here about those which are never found to transcend the boundary of their significance or name.

Thus occurs the double long, etc. Here the author explains how it sometimes happens by necessity that a long figure represents itself twice in the same body. And this occurs either as a result of a defect in the plainsong, lest because of some addition it is corrupted or even broken, or sometimes as a result of adjusting for a long time to a metrical ornament of the music. And note that such a note that includes in itself six units of time is called a double long; whence the rule: A double long is that whose breadth is greater than its length, as the text shows.

> **Thus[1] occurs the double long** ▜ **and[2] it carries[3] in itself six units of time.**
> 1 that is, as the present example states
> 2 instead of: also
> 3 that is, represents

To these you should give, etc. Here the author wants to show how all these six notes are arranged by means of six species of modes, firstly in general and concerning their nature, and secondly according to their accents, and how they work by means of some accord to the perfection of all melodies; and he says **The larger long takes the third,** etc. according to the tenor of the text, and this is concerning their own nature and not by means of their accents; and thus he gives examples about all the others according to the tenor of the text.

I shall often give an abode, etc. Here he shows how they are also found by means of their accents in other species than in their own by means of some accords, and this is either because the rhetorical color of the music is more suitably embellished in this way or because of the over-abundance of the text.

> **To these[1] you should give[2] proper abodes in the six species.**
> 1 the above-mentioned notes
> 2 regularly or irregularly, O cantor

Longa[1] **capit ternam**[2] **maior**[3] **quintamque quaternam.**
1 et hoc proprie
2 id est, occupat speciem
3 id est, trium temporum sive
    Quasi diceret: longa minor in istis duabus est reperta:
Prima[1] **secunda choris sunt longae namque minoris.**
1 sive species et secunda
Sedem maiori specie dabo saepe priori.[1]
1 et hoc improprie et per accentus propter defectum litterae vel
propter affinitatem alicuius convenientiae
Hanc[1] **tamen asconde velud hic**[2] **sub lege secundae.**
1 subaudi longam maiorem
2 id est, in hoc exemplo:

Omnes

Nunc minor in terna[1] **reperitur vixque**[2] **quaterna.**[3]
1 specie sive
2 id est, nonquam, quamvis possibile sit
3 et hoc improprie et per accentus
Ecce dicit, quod brevis minor in qualibet specie locum proprium
retinebit:
Quaque brevis specie minor est data lege sophiae.
Sic[1] **quoque**[2] **semibrevis speciebus sit data**[3] **quaevis.**[4]
1 id est, similiter
2 id est, certe
3 et hoc potest esse proprie
4 id est, tam minor quam maior
Exceptio est et hoc, quia quinta species habet fieri ex omnibus
longis:
Hiis binis quintam vetat ars longis fore tinctam.
Maiorique brevi[1] **ternam**[2] **quartam quoque sevi.**[3]
1 sive a brevi duorum temporum
2 speciem sive
3 et hoc proprie
Maiorique brevi etc. converte sic: **quoque,** id est, certe; **sevi**
quartam speciem sive et ternam a maiore brevi.

(fol. 139v) **Ut bene quaeque metas** etc. Declaratis superius formis et
proprietatibus insuper et naturis simplicium figurarum, et quae et quot
et qualiter per sex modorum species ordinatae ad perfectionem cantuum
operentur, immediate proponit actor compositarum formas et proprietatum
differentias convenienter recitare, ad hoc ut ad cognitionem earum
propterea facilior sit accessus. Et notandum est primo, quod omnis

----
8 **speciei** *pro specie Sowa*   33 **fero** *pro* **fore** *cod., corr. Sowa*
35 a *add. ab alia manu*   44 *crux in marg.*   46 preterea *pro* propterea
Sowa

The larger[3] long[1] takes the third[2] and the fifth and fourth.
1 and this properly
2 that is, occupies the species
3 that is, of three units of time
He means to say that the smaller long is found in these two:
For indeed the first[1] and second in the group have the smaller long.
1 species, and the second
I shall often give an abode for the larger in the first species.[1]
1 and this is done improperly and by means of the accents, because of a defect of the text or because of the affinity of some accord
But hide this one[1] as here[2] under the law of the second species.
1 understand the larger long
2 that is, in this example:

Omnes

Sometimes the smaller is found in the third[1] and rarely[2] in the fourth.[3]
1 species
2 that is, never, although it is possible
3 and this is done improperly and by means of the accents
See, he says that the smaller breve will retain its proper place in any species:
In each species the smaller breve is given with the law of wisdom.
In this way[1] also[2] let each semibreve[4] be given[3] in the species.
1 that is, similarly
2 that is, certainly
3 and this can be properly
4 that is, both the smaller and the larger
And the exception is this, that the fifth species occurs with all longs:
The art forbids the fifth, with longs, to be colored by these two.
I have sown[3] the third[2] and also the fourth with the larger breve.[1]
1 with the breve of two units of time
2 species
3 and properly
I have sown, etc.: Interpret thus: **also**, that is, certainly; **the fourth** species and the third with the larger breve.

(fol. 139v) **Pay attention to the boundaries,** etc. Since the forms and proprieties and also the natures of the single figures have been stated above, and also which ones and how many and in what way they are arranged through six species of modes and work to the perfection of melodies, the author proposes immediately to explain appropriately the forms of the composite figures and the distinctions of their proprieties, so that there might therefore be easier access to the understanding of

figura composita vel ligata fit aut ascendendo aut etiam descendendo.
Per quod patet breviter quod figurae, quae sunt in eodem puncto positae,
non possunt facere figuram compositam vel ligatam. Et nota, quod illa
figura dicitur ascendere, cuius secundus punctus altior est primo,
descendere, cuius idem punctus inferior est primo, sicut inferius
declarabitur et per textum.

    In primis igitur binariae figurae differentias videamus, et scias,
quod sunt quinque, tres scilicet a parte principii et duae a parte finis.
A parte principii prima est cum proprietate tam ascendendo quam

10 descendendo, sive sit perfecta, ut hic [notation] , sive imperfecta, sic
[notation] . Secunda est sine proprietate tam ascendendo quam descendendo,

sive sit perfecta, ut hic [notation] , sive imperfecta, sic [notation] . Tertia est
per oppositum proprietatis, quae semper debet protrahi imperfecta tam
ascendendo quam descendendo, licet usus descendendo solum saepius
contradicat; quod autem protrahi debeant imperfectae tam ascendendo quam
descendendo, declarabitur inferius suo loco. Exemplum earum patet hic

[notation] . Usus autem sic protrahere consuevit solummodo descendendo

20 quamvis male [notation] .

    A parte principii dictum est, a parte finis omnes tales aut sunt
perfectae aut etiam imperfectae, sicut exempla postposita manifestant, et
haec exempla omnia subiacent illi versiculo: **Usa tenet iura** etc.

    Sequitur de ternaria figura, quae similiter quinque tenet
differentias usitatas, quarum prima est cum proprietate tam ascendendo

quam descendendo, sive sit perfecta, ut hic [notation] , sive

30 imperfecta, sic [notation] ; secunda est sine proprietate tam
ascendendo quam descendendo; et hoc totum cum perfectione, eo quod de
imperfectione ipsius nullatenus indigemus, quia ternaria imperfecta et
cum proprietate quoad quantitatem temporum idem facit, nec ad aliud se
extendit. Et alibi dicitur in arte, quod *nonquam debet poni aliqua*
figura sine proprietate, ubi potest poni cum proprietate, et alibi:
frustra habet fieri per duo, quod potest fieri per unum. Si aliquis
obiciat de binaria imperfecta eiusdem generis, eo quod similiter ratione
alterius binariae deberet aboleri, cum eandem quantitatem temporum
similiter repraesentent, dicimus, quod non est simile hinc et inde,

40 quoniam binaria figura cum proprietate et imperfecta nunc tria tempora
comprehendit, alia vero non nisi duo solummodo importabit. Et hac de
causa utraque istarum fuit necessaria. Quaelibet istarum siquidem tria
tempora continet neque magis neque minus, quare unam earum, scilicet
illam quae est sine proprietate, extirpamus, reliquam quae cum
proprietate protrahitur retinentes. Figuretur igitur haec secunda
differentia cum perfectione et sine proprietate tam ascendendo quam

descendendo sic [notation] ; tamen ars tales imperfectas bene

14 decet *pro* debet *Sowa*   23 preposita *pro* postposita *Sowa*   31-32 de
[[perf]] imperfectione *cod.*   32 *inter* indigemus *et* quia *ras.*
34 decet *pro debet Sowa*   35 *poni* [[sine prop]] *cum cod.*   48 *inter*
tales *et* imperfectas *ras.*

them. And it should be noted first that every composite or ligated
figure occurs either ascending or descending. From which it is clear in
short that figures which are placed on the same note can not make a
composite or ligated figure. And note that that figure whose second
written note is higher than the first is said to ascend, and that whose
second written note is lower than the first is said to descend, as will
be stated below and by means of the text.

Let us therefore first look at the distinctions of the binary figure;
and you should know that there are five, that is to say three with
respect to the beginning and two with respect to the end. With respect
to the beginning, the first distinction is with propriety both ascending
and descending, whether it is perfect as here   , or imperfect as
here   . The second is without propriety both ascending and

descending, whether it is perfect as here   , or imperfect as here
  . The third is with the opposite of propriety, and this must
always be notated as imperfect both ascending and descending, although
usage often indicates the contrary, as it only descends; and the fact
that these should be notated as imperfect both ascending and descending
will be stated below in the right place. An example of them is given

here   . In usage however it is usually notated in this way

descending only, although this is bad   .

With respect to the beginning has been spoken about; with respect to
the end all such figures are either perfect or imperfect, as the examples
given below display; and all these examples are under the line of verse:
The binary figure, etc.

There follows a discussion of the ternary figure, which similarly
holds five usual distinctions, of which the first is with propriety both
ascending and descending, whether it is perfect as here   ,

or imperfect as here   . The second is without propriety
both ascending and descending; and all of this is with perfection,
because we do not need anything about its imperfection, since the
imperfect ternary with propriety does the same as to its quantity of
units of time, and does not extend itself to anything else. And it is
said elsewhere in the treatise* that "no figure should ever be put
without propriety where it can be put with propriety," and elsewhere:*
"It is useless for anything to occur in two, which can occur in one." If
anyone makes an objection about the imperfect binary of the same genus,
that it should similarly be abolished for the same reason as the other
binary, since they both represent the same quantity of units of time, we
say that it is not the same thing for the one and for the other, since
the binary figure that is with propriety and imperfect sometimes includes
three units of time, but the other will convey only two. And for this
reason each of them was necessary. One of them indeed contains three
units of time, neither more nor less, and so we eradicate one of them,
that is to say that which is without propriety, and keep the one that
remains, which is notated with propriety. Therefore let this second
distinction with perfection and without propriety both ascending and

descending be figured in this way   ; nevertheless the art
could well permit such imperfect figures to be figured. The third

permitteret figurari. Tertia differentia est per oppositum figurata tam
ascendendo quam descendendo, sive sit perfecta, sic ▮ ▮ ▮ ▮ , sive
imperfecta, ut hic ▮ ▮ ▮ ▮ .
    Et sic sunt quinque, tres a parte principii et duae a parte finis.
Haec exempla subiacent illi versiculo: **Sic quoque quinque dabit** etc.
    Sequitur de quaternaria figura, quae quatuor habet differentias
usitatas et unam inusitatam et noviter exaltatam eo quod necessariam,
10   sicut inferius declarabitur suo loco. Prima igitur est cum proprietate
tam ascendendo quam descendendo, sive sit perfecta, ut hic ▮ ▮ ,
sive imperfecta, sic ▮ ▮ . Secunda de novo dicitur exaltata et
habet fieri sine proprietate tam ascendendo quam descendendo et hoc totum
cum perfectione sic ▮ ▮ . Tertia est per oppositum proprietatis tam
ascendendo quam descendendo, sive sit perfecta, ut hic ▮ ▮ , sive
imperfecta, sic ▮ ▮ . Et sic sunt quatuor differentiae usitatae
20   cum una inusitata, et haec exempla subiacent illi versiculo: **Quatuor
hinc cerne** etc.
    Sequitur de quinaria figura, quae tres habet differentias usitatas et
unam inusitatam. Unam a parte principii usitatam, quae protrahitur per
oppositum proprietatis, ut usui acquiescamus, quamvis competentius et
secundum artem seu artificium cum proprietate propria protrahi videretur,
protrahatur igitur per oppositum tam ascendendo quam descendendo ratione
organi specialis solum, sive sit perfecta, ut hic ▮ ▮ , sive
30   imperfecta, sic ▮ ▮ . Et sic sunt tres differentiae usitatae,
una a parte principii et duae a parte finis, alia inusitata, scilicet
quarta, sine proprietate propria figurata tam ascendendo quam
descendendo, et hoc totum cum perfectione, sicut hic ▮ ▮ .

    Sequitur de senaria, quae similiter tres habet differentias usitatas
et unam inusitatam. Prima est cum proprietate, sicut declarabitur
inferius suo loco, tam ascendendo quam descendendo, sive sit perfecta, ut
hic ▮ , (fol. 140) sive imperfecta, sic ▮ ▮ . Et sic sunt
40   tres differentiae usitatae, scilicet una a parte principii et duae a
parte finis; inusitata quidem sine proprietate propria figuratur tam
ascendendo quam descendendo, et hoc totum cum perfectione, sicut patet
hic ▮ ▮ .
    Sequitur de septenaria figura, quae tres habet tantummodo
differentias, nec amplius importabit, quarum prior est a parte principii
et cum proprietate semper tam ascendendo quam descendendo, sive sit
perfecta, ut hic ▮ , sive imperfecta, sic ▮ .

27-29 ratione organi specialis solum *add. in marg.*

distinction is figured by means of the opposite of propriety both
ascending and descending, whether it is perfect like this   ,
or imperfect like this   . And thus there are five
distinctions, three with respect to the beginning and two with respect to
the end. These examples are under the line of verse **Thus also the
ternary,** etc.

There follows a discussion of the fourfold figure, which has four
usual distinctions and one unusual one, which has recently been praised
as necessary, as will be stated below in the right place. The first
therefore is with propriety both ascending and descending, whether it is
perfect as here   , or imperfect as here   . The second is
said to be praised recently and occurs without propriety both ascending
and descending, and all of this is with perfection like this   .
The third is by means of the opposite of propriety both ascending and
descending, whether it is perfect as here   , or imperfect as here
  . And thus there are four usual distinctions with one unusual
one, and these examples go with the line of verse **Notice four here,** etc.

There follows a discussion of the fivefold figure, which has three
usual distinctions and one unusual one. Let us assent to the use of the
one that is usual with respect to the beginning, and this is notated by
means of the opposite of propriety -- although it would seem to be
notated more suitably and according to the art or theory with proper
propriety -- and so let it be notated by means of the opposite of
propriety both ascending and descending for the reason of special organum
alone, whether it is perfect as here   , or imperfect as here
  . And thus there are three usual distinctions, one with
respect to the beginning and two with respect to the end, and another,
that is to say a fourth, which is unusual and figured without proper
propriety both ascending and descending, and all of this is with
perfection, as here   .

There follows a discussion of the sixfold figure, which similarly has
three usual distinctions and one unusual one. The first is with
propriety, as will be stated below in the right place, both ascending and
descending, whether it is perfect as here   (fol. 140), or imperfect
as here   . And thus there are three usual distinctions, that
is to say one with respect to the beginning and two with respect to the
end. The unusual one indeed is figured without proper propriety both
ascending and descending, and all of this is with perfection, as is shown
here   .

There follows a discussion of the sevenfold figure, which has only
three distinctions, and will not convey any more, of which the first is
with respect to the beginning and always with propriety both ascending
and descending, whether it is perfect as here   , or imperfect as
here   .

Sequitur de octonaria, quae easdem differentias observat tam ascendendo quam descendendo, sive sit perfecta, ut hic ▰▰ , sive

imperfecta, sic ▰▰ .

De novenaria et denaria exempla nolumus provulgare, quoniam sunt ignotae, vel quia contra artis regulam constitutae, quae talis est, quod *omnis figurae cum proprietate positae penultima dicitur esse brevis;* sed si novenaria vel denaria proferrentur, penultima in eis semper semibrevis

10   esset data, et ideo earum exempla tacemus, ne impedimentum artis regulae inferamus. Possibile tamen est ipsas sic protrahi et etiam provulgari, eo quod longa maior usque in novem partes reperiri poterit diminuta.

Ut bene quaeque[1] metas[2] iunctarum respice metas.[3]
1 dicenda sive
2 id est, colligas
3 id est, differentias
Cernere[1] quas[2] poteris si glosae dogmata quaeris.
1 sive in glosulis

20   2 sive metas; et hoc est, quia ibi non est necesse has metrice compilare
Usa[1] tenet iura[2] binaria quinque[3] figura.
1 id est, usitata
2 id est, differentias
3 id est, de quinque existens
Sic[1] quoque[2] quinque dabit[3] ternaria[4] glosa normabit.[5]
1 id est, similiter
2 id est, certe
3 sicut binaria sive

30   4 sive figura
5 id est, declarabit
Quatuor[1] hinc cerne, sed quinque[2] do iura quaternae.[3]
1 sive differentias usitatas
2 sive quarum una est inusitata
3 sive figurae
Quinae[1] vel sextae iuncturae sunt ita[2] textae.[3]
1 id est, quinariae et senariae
2 id est, sicut glosula ostendit
3 id est, ordinatae

40   **Octo[1] septenae praesint[2] denisque novenae.[3]**
1 id est, octonaria
2 id est, praeponantur in ordine sive
3 si licuerit figurare sive

----

5 *ultimus punctus exempli ab alia manu super ras.*   6 nolimus exempla *pro* exempla nolumus *Sowa*   nolumus [[im]] provulgare *cod.*
8 *(bre)vis add. ab alia manu*   36 **Quinte** *pro* **Quinae** *Sowa*

There follows a discussion of the eightfold figure, which retains the same distinctions both ascending and descending, whether it is perfect as

here , or imperfect as here .

We do not wish to promulgate examples of the ninefold and tenfold figures, since they are unknown, or because they are constituted against the rule of the treatise,* which is as follows, that "of every figure placed with propriety the penultimate is said to be short;" but if the ninefold and tenfold figures are used, the penultimate in them would always be given as a semibreve, and so we keep quiet about examples of them, lest we bring forward a hindrance to the rule of the art. Nevertheless it is possible for these to be notated and even promulgated, because the larger long will be able to be found diminished into as many as nine parts.

Pay attention to the boundaries[3] of the figures that are joined, so that you can gather[2] each of them[1] well.
1 the things that should be said
2 that is, collect
3 that is, the distinctions
If you ask the rules of the gloss, it is to notice[1] those[2] which you can.
1 in the glosses
2 the boundaries; and this is because then it is not necessary to put them together in verse
The binary figure that is used[1] keeps five[3] laws.[2]
1 that is, the usual one
2 that is, distinctions
3 that is, existing in five forms
Thus[1] also[2] the ternary[4] will give five,[3] as the gloss will establish.[5]
1 that is, similarly
2 that is, certainly, like the binary
3 like the binary
4 figure
5 that is, will state
Notice four[1] here, but I give five[2] laws for the fourfold.[3]
1 usual distinctions
2 of which one is unusual
3 figure
Of the fifth[1] or sixth the joinings are woven[3] thus.[2]
1 that is, of the fivefold and sixfold figures
2 that is, as the gloss shows
3 that is, arranged
Let the seven, the eight,[1] and ninefold precede[2] the tenfold.[3]
1 that is, the eightfold figure
2 that is, let them be placed ahead in order
3 if one could notate these figures

\<Pars secunda\>

Disce ligatarum etc. Ostenso superius prosaice, quae et quot sunt differentiae figurarum ad invicem ligatarum, in hoc loco vult actor formas et proprietates et effectus omnium metrice declarare, breviter recitando quomodo et qualiter per eas longitudo et brevitas denotetur. Et nota, quod non inutile sive superfluum est primo universaliter ostendere formas seu protractiones huiusmodi figurarum sub metri breviloquio differentiarum numerum recitando vel assignando quam ad earum numerum accedatur, quippe cum prius sit ignorati formam ostendere vel praetendere quam ad incognitum accedere per effectum, eo quod levius est
10 manifestum rei per praesentiam detegere quam effectum formae incognitae seu non provisae simpliciter provulgare, sicut patet in oratione, quae prius debet legendo vel proferendo praetendi quam etiam convertendo. Simili modo est de figuris, quia prius debent in universo protrahi quam earum cognitio per effectum publice declaretur. Ideo pars praecedens sussequentibus necessaria istam praecedere iudicatur.

Haec igitur praesens lectio de qua in verbo agitur in duas partes breviter dividatur, in quarum prima ostendit actor de quo debet agere, in secunda exequitur. Prima pars incipit **Disce ligatarum** etc., secunda **Quando perfecta** etc. Pars praecedens remanet indivisa, sed secunda in
20 duas dividitur. In prima agit de figuris cum proprietate et perfectione, in secunda de imperfectis cum proprietate positis saepius et repertis. Ideo patet ordo: prima pars incipit **Quando perfecta** etc., secunda ibi **Imperfectarum** etc. Haec secunda in duas: in prima agit de imperfectis cum proprietate et sic in figura composita, in secunda de imperfectis simpliciter et per se. Et quia in prima agitur de imperfectis solummodo in figura et per accentus, in secunda de imperfectis naturaliter tam per formam quam etiam per effectum. Ideo patet ordo partis praeambulae ad sequentem.

Si quis autem obiciat, quod immo prius est agendum de imperfectis
30 naturaliter et per se quam de imperfectis secundum quid et per accentus, (fol. 140v) sicut primo agitur de proprietate in eis quam de improprietate, ad hoc dicimus respondentes, quod non sequitur in hoc loco, eo quod imperfectae naturaliter sunt in forma divisibiles, aliae vero non. Et quia hic agitur de perfectione in figura composita vel ligata, ideo post ipsam agendum est immediate de imperfectione ligatarum, cum inter perfectionem et imperfectionem circa idem non sit medium apponendum. Aliae siquidem imperfectae quo ad formam per se positae divisive in hoc ab aliis sunt remotae, quare ipsas post alias decrevimus ordinari.
40 Ideo patet ordo: prima pars incipit **Imperfectarum** etc., secunda **Nunc per se punxi** etc. Item prima istarum in duas: in prima agit de

----

12 decet *pro* debet *Sowa*   17 decet *pro* debet *Sowa*   26 figura [[solummodo]] et   32-33 in hoc hoco *cod.*   38 [[post alias]] post alias *cod.*   41 **punxi** *pro* **punxi** *Sowa*

Part Two

Learn about the ligatures, etc. Having shown above in prose which
and how many are the distinctions of the figures that are ligated to each
other, in this place the author wishes to state the forms and proprieties
and effects of all of them in verse, explaining briefly how and in what
way length and shortness may be denoted by them. And note that it is not
useless or superfluous first to show thoroughly the forms or notations of
figures of this kind briefly in verse, explaining or laying out their
distinctions, before broaching the number of them. And this is
especially so since one should first show or indicate the form of
something to someone who is unknowledgeable before broaching the effect
of the thing that is unknown, because it is easier to exhibit the
appearance of a thing immediately than just to promulgate the effect of
its form, when that form is unknown or unexpected. And this is clear,
for example, in a speech, which should first present something by reading
or performing it before interpreting it. It is the same with figures,
because they should first be notated completely before an understanding
of them by means of their effect may be publicly stated. And so it is
judged necessary that the preceding part should precede those things
which follow.

Therefore let this present reading which is being discussed be
divided briefly into two parts, in the first of which the author shows
what should be dealt with, and in the second it is accomplished. The
first part begins **Learn about the ligatures,** etc., the second **When a
perfect joining,** etc. The preceding part remains undivided, but the
second is divided into two parts. In the first he deals with figures
with propriety and perfection, in the second with imperfect figures that
are often placed and found with propriety. Hence the order: The first
part begins **When a perfect joining,** etc., the second at **The theory of
imperfect,** etc. This second part is divided into two. In the first he
deals with imperfect figures with propriety in composite figures, in the
second with imperfect figures singly and by themselves. And because in
the first part imperfect figures are dealt with only as to their figures
and by means of their accents, and in the second imperfect figures are
dealt with naturally both by means of their form and also by means of
their effect, therefore the order of the prefatory part to what follows
is clear.

If however anyone objects that imperfect figures naturally and
by themselves should be dealt with first rather than imperfect figures according to what they are and by means of their accents (fol.
140v) -- just as their propriety is dealt with first before their
impropriety -- we respond to this that it does not follow in this
situation, since imperfect figures are naturally divisible in form, but
the others are not. And because here perfection in the composite or
ligated figure is being dealt with, therefore after it the imperfection
of ligated figures should be dealt with immediately, since nothing should
be put in the middle between perfection and imperfection concerning this.
The other figures indeed that are imperfect as to their form and placed
by themselves are removed and separated in this from the others, and so
we have decided to arrange them after the others.

Thus the order is clear: The first part begins **The theory of
imperfect,** etc., the second **Now I have written,** etc. Also the first of

imperfectis cum proprietate, in secunda de imperfectis et sine
proprietate. Ideo patet ordo: prima pars incipit **Imperfectarum** etc.,
secunda **Quaevis utraque carens** etc. Istae partes remanent indivisae, sed
pars illa, in qua agit de perfectis et cum proprietate, in duas
dividitur. In prima agit de proprietate et perfectione in figuris
compositis, in secunda de plicis, quae in fine omnium figurarum locum
sibi retinent deputatum. Ideo patet ordo: prima pars incipit **Quando
perfecta** etc., secunda **Voceque composita** etc. Item prima istarum in
tres partes propter breviloquium dividatur, in quarum prima facit actor
mentionem de perfectis cum proprietate propria figuratis, in secunda de
eis quae sunt sine proprietate, in tertia et ultima de eis quae sunt per
oppositum figuratae. Prima igitur incipit **Quando perfecta**, secunda
Iuncturaeque datae, tertia **Opposito** etc. Et sic patet divisio leoninis.

> **Disce**[1] **ligaturum quae**[2] **proprietas**[3] **sit earum,**[4]
> 1 O cantor vel lector
> 2 id est, qualiter
> 3 sive propria vel non propria
> 4 sive ligatarum
> **Namque**[1] **per ascensum vel descensum dabo sensum.**
> 1 pro quia; et per hoc innuit actor, quod voces in eodem signo
> positae non possunt facere figuram compositam

Hic ostendit actor per regulam quid sit ascensus vel descensus,
dicens, quod illa figura dicitur ascendere cuius

> **Si primo punctum videas ascendere iunctum,**

secundus punctus altior est primo, sicut patet hic ▌▗▘▖▙ .
Alia regula de descensu: illa liga-

> **Esse ligatura scandens datur, atque figura.**

tura dicitur descendere, cuius secundus punctus inferior est primo,
sicut patet hic ▐▖ ▜▌ .

> **Tunc cum descendit, hic punctus ad infima tendit.**

Voces cerne etc. Hic accedit actor ad compositarum notitiam
figurarum, unde in primis notandum est, quod earum repraesentatio quo ad
signa, quibus ab invicem differunt, reperiri dicitur tripartita, quoniam
omnis figura aut protrahitur cum proprietate aut sine proprietate aut per
oppositum proprietatis. Sed siquidem tria signa omnium figurarum ad
invicem ligatarum nobis notitiam faciunt manifestam. Si quaeratur, quare
tot signa nobis sufficiant et non plura seu etiam pauciora, dicimus
respondentes, quod quemadmodum voces simplices, e quibus compositae
ducunt originis fundamentum, sunt in forma solummodo tripartitae, sic et
compositae triplicem variationis differentiam quo ad signa eas separantia
solummodo importabunt, ad hoc ut signa signatis respondeant recto modo.
Figurarum igitur quaedam ligantur cum proprietate, quaedam sine
proprietate, quaedam per oppositum proprietatis. Et nota, quod sine

----
7-8 **Quando perfecta** *sine sublinea in cod.*   8 **Voceque composita** *sine
sublinea in cod.*   etc. *add. Sowa*   12 **Quando perfecta** *sine sublinea
in cod.*   13 sic *add. in marg.*   15 **propproprietas** *cod.*   20 (Nam)que
add. ab alia manu   24 figure *pro* figura *Sowa*   28 (ligatu)r(a) *add.*
35 ad invicem *pro* ab invicem *Sowa*

these is divided into two: In the first part he deals with imperfect figures with propriety, in the second with imperfect figures without propriety. Thus the order is clear: The first part begins **The theory of imperfect**, etc., the second **The one that lacks both,** etc. Those parts remain undivided, but that part in which he deals with perfect figures with propriety is divided into two. In the first he deals with propriety and perfection in composite figures, in the second he deals with plicas, which keep an allotted place for themselves at the end of all figures. Thus the order is clear: The first part begins **When a perfect**, etc., the second **And the plica,** etc. Also let the first of these be divided into three parts for the sake of brevity, in the first of which the author makes mention of perfect figures with proper propriety, in the second those which are without propriety, in the third and last those which are with the opposite of propriety. Therefore the first begins **When a perfect**, etc., the second **And the joinings are given,** etc., the third **It will be given to the opposite,** etc. And thus the division of the leonine verses is clear.

> **Learn**[1] **about the ligatures what**[2] **the propriety**[3] **is of them,**[4]
> 1 O cantor or reader
> 2 that is, of what kind
> 3 proper or not proper
> 4 the ligatures
> **For**[1] **I shall give the meaning of them through their ascent or descent.**
> 1 instead of: because; and in this way the author suggests that
> notes placed at the same sign can not make a composite figure

Here the author shows by means of a rule what ascent or descent is, saying that that figure is said to ascend whose

> **If you see the written note that is joined to the first one ascend,**

second written note is higher than the first, as is shown here 🔳 .
Another rule about descent: That liga-

> **It is accepted as a climbing ligature and figure.**

ture is said to descend, whose second written note is lower than the first, as is shown here 🔳 🔳 .

> **Then when it descends, this note aims at the bottom.**

Perceive the notes, etc. Here the author broaches the concept of composite figures; and first it should be noted that the representation of them as to the signs whereby they are differentiated from each other is said to be found in three forms, since each figure is notated either with propriety or without propriety or by means of the opposite of propriety. And indeed three signs make the concept of all the figures ligated to each other clear to us. If it is asked why that many signs are sufficient for us and not more or even less, we say in response that in the same way that single notes from which the composite figures take the foundation of their origin are only made up of three forms, so also the composite figures will only convey three distinct differences as to the signs that separate them, so that the signs correspond to the things that are signified in the correct way. Some of the figures therefore are ligated with propriety, some without propriety, some by means of the opposite of propriety. And note that without propriety is to be deprived

proprietate est a proprietate propria privari penitus et repelli, per
oppositum est proprietate opposita se habere. Ex hoc igitur sic arguo
contra numerum antedictum: privari a proprietate et per oppositum
proprietatis se habere videntur esse idem, cum proprietati propriae sic
repugnent, quod eidem proprietati tam in significationibus quam in signis
contraria videantur. Si ergo sint eadem, unum ex hiis superfluere iam
videtur, eo quod verum oppositorum genus quo ad duo solummodo et non quo
ad tria se extendit. Cum ergo ibi sint tria et opposite se habeant, ut
probatur, unum ex hiis superfluit, sicut patet, et sic debet ab aliarum
10 consortio removeri. Solummodo dicimus, quod neutrumque istorum
superfluit, immo utriusque inventio necessaria iudicatur, sicut patuit
per praedicta et sicut inferius aparebit. Quando vero arguitur, quod
sunt idem, eo quod proprietati propriae se opponunt, dicimus, quod
repugnant non eodem modo sed diversis respectibus et naturis, quare non
sunt idem, immo similiter ab invicem se opponunt, sicut declarabitur
inferius et per textum. Quando vero obicitur, quod verum oppositorum
genus ad duo solummodo et non ad tria se extendit, dicimus, quod verum
est quo ad opposita simpliciter circa idem, et non quo ad opposita circa
diversa. Ista siquidem aliter et aliter ab invicem se opponunt, eo quod
20 in oppositione differunt tam circa significata quam circa signa, secundum
quod textus postea declarabit, quare neutrum superfluere iudicamus.

Hic dat actor regulam generalem de protractione omnium figurarum cum
proprietate ligatarum:
Voces cerne datas cum proprietate ligatas.
Regula est: omnis figura cum proprietate posita ascendendo debet

fieri sine tractu, sicut patet hic .
Ascensum iure sine tractu sume figurae.
30 Alia regula de descensu talis est: omnis figurae cum proprietate
propria figurata descendendo sua proprietas est, ut
Si sit descendens et proprietas ibi tendens,
(fol. 141) primus punctus ligaturae habeat tractum sub sinistro

latere descendentem, sicut patet hic .
Sub laevo latere caput optat caudam tenere.

Quando perfecta etc. Hic dat actor regulam generalem, ad omnes
figuras cum proprietate positas et perfectas singulariter se extendens,
40 quae talis est: omnis figurae cum proprietate positae et perfectae,
penultima dicitur esse brevis et ultima longa. Et nota, quod quia duplex
est brevis et duplex longa, de duplici aequipollentia est praesens regula
compilata, nam ad utramque aequipollentiam se extendit, sicut postea
variae species declarabunt. Littera per se patet.

Regula est generalis ad omnes figuras cum proprietate positas et
perfectas, quae talis est:

----
2 proprietati oppositae *cod.*   6 cantraria *pro* contraria *Sowa*
8 *primum* se *add. super scriptum*   extendat *pro* extendit *Sowa*
10 neutrum *pro* neutrumque *Sowa*   15 opponant *pro* opponunt *Sowa*
16 respondentibus *pro* respectibus *Sowa*   30 figura *pro* figurae *cod.*
42 longa quod de *cod.*

of proper propriety and also completely driven away from it, and by means
of the opposite of propriety is to occur with opposite propriety. From
this therefore I argue as follows against the number mentioned above: To
be deprived of propriety and to occur by means of the opposite of
propriety seem to be the same thing, since they reject proper propriety
in such a way that they seem contrary to that propriety both in
significances and in signs. If therefore they are the same, one of them
now seems superfluous, because a true genus of opposites extends itself
only to two things and not to three. Since therefore there are three
things there, and they occur as opposites, as proved, one of them is
superfluous, as is clear, and thus it should be removed from the company
of the others. We only say that neither of them is superfluous, rather
the invention of each one is judged to be necessary, as has been made
clear by the things that have been said before, and as will appear below.
And when it is argued that they are the same, because they are opposed to
proper propriety, we say that they reject it not in the same way but in
different respects and with different natures, and so they are not the
same, but rather they are also opposed to each other, as will be stated
below and by means of the text. But when it is objected that the true
genus of opposites extends only to two things and not to three, we say
that that is true as regards things that are opposite simply as to the
same thing, and not as regards things that are opposite as to different
things. Those things indeed are opposed to each other in quite different
ways, because they differ in their opposition both as to what they
signify and as to their signs, according to that which the text will
state later; and so we judge neither of them to be superfluous.

    Here the author gives a general rule about the notation of all
figures ligated with propriety:
        Perceive the notes given ligated with propriety.
The rule is: Every figure placed with propriety that ascends must

occur without a line as is shown here .
    Take the ascent of the figure by law without a line.
Another rule about descent is as follows: Of every figure that is
figured with proper propriety descending, its propriety is that
        If it is descending and its propriety is aiming there,
(fol. 141) the first written note of the ligature has a line

descending under the left side, as is shown here .
    The head wishes to hold its tail under the left side.

    When a perfect, etc. Here the author gives a general rule, which
applies particularly to all perfect figures placed with propriety, which
is as follows: Of every figure that is placed with propriety and is
perfect the penultimate note is said to be short and the last note long.
And note that because the breve is of two kinds and the long is of two
kinds the present rule is put together concerning both equipollences, for
it applies to both equipollences, as the different species will state
later. The text is clear by itself.

    There is a general rule which applies to all figures that are placed
with propriety and are perfect, which is this:

Quando perfecta iunctura fit atque refecta.
omnis figurae cum proprietate positae et perfectae penultima dicitur
esse brevis,
Proprietate brevis penultima vult fore quaevis.[1]
      1 nota sive minor sive maior
si sit longa minor sive maior.
Ultima longetur tibi regula vera fatetur.[1]
      1 quasi diceret: haec regula ubique dicitur esse vera

10   **Vox alii** etc. Hic accedit actor ad notitiam sive declarationem
regulae supradictae, per regulas speciales in primis de figura binaria
dans doctrinam, eo quod est praevia tamquam principium aliarum. Si quis
autem obiciat, quod in praecedenti regula de ipsa plenarie et praecipue
mentio fuit facta, quare nugatorium quid est iterum recitare, dicimus
respondentes, quod non est nugatorium recitare, immo utile et honestum,
quia regulam corroborat antedictam. Item, sicut praedictum est, debet
esse praevia tanquam principium aliarum, et alibi dicitur: *firmior enim
fit promissio duplici confirmatione.* Haec siquidem regula confirmatione
duplici roboratur, quare tanquam firmior competentius recitatur.

20
Haec est regula specialis verificans praecedentem, quae talis est:
omnis figura binaria cum proprietate posita et
Vox alii iuncta cum proprietateque puncta
perfecta dicitur habere penultimam brevem et ultimam longam. Nota
semper hic quaevis. Exemplum ▮▐▪ .
Et perfecta, brevis prior est longans ea quaevis.
Alia regula de figura ternaria eiusdem protractionis talis est:
omnis figura ternaria cum proprietate posita et perfecta
Si tribus addatur haec regula, prima vocatur.
30   dicitur habere primam longam minorem et mediam brevem minorem et

ultimam quamvis longam. Exemplum ▪▪▪ ◾◣ ┐ .
Longa minorque brevis haec, longa sit ultima quaevis.
Haec est autem exceptio regulae supradictae, eo quod in tertia specie
et in quarta aliter se habent in effectu:
Ternam quippe peto, quartam speciem prohibeto.
Haec est regula generalis ad omnes figuras cum proprietate positas et
perfectas excedentes numerum
Si qua ligans detur excedens tres redigetur.
40   trium in figura, quae talis est: omnis figura cum proprietate et
perfecta excedens tres ligatas est reducibilis ad numerum trium:
Illa trium numero primique modi fore spero.

Si qua ligans etc. Assignatis superius regulis tam generalibus quam
specialibus de figuris cum proprietate et perfectione positis et repertis

----
4 **penultia** cod.   10 **alii** [[iu]] etc. *cod.*   16 decet *pro* debet *Sowa*
25 ubi *pro* hic *Sowa*   30 brevem minore *cod.*   33 **miorque** *cod.*

When a perfect joining occurs and is made
Of every figure that is placed with propriety and is perfect the
penultimate note is said to be short,
With propriety, each penultimate[1] wants to be short.
1 note, whether smaller or larger
whether the long is smaller or larger.
The last note is lengthened, the true rule admits to you.[1]
1 he means to say that this rule is said to be true everywhere

A note joined to another, etc. Here the author comes to the concept
or statement of the above-mentioned rule, giving first the principle of
the binary figure through special rules, because it leads the way as the
basis for the others. But if anyone objects that in the preceding rule
mention was fully and particularly made about it, and that it is worthless to explain it again, we say in response that it is not worthless to
explain it, but rather it is useful and honorable, because it corrobo-
rates the above rule. Also, as has been said before, it should lead the
way as the basis for the others; and elsewhere it is said: "For a
promise is stronger with two confirmations."* Indeed this rule is
strengthened by two confirmations, and so it is quite suitable to explain
it, as it becomes stronger.

Here is a specific rule that verifies the preceding one, and it is as
follows: Every binary figure that is placed with propriety and
A note joined to another and written with propriety
is perfect is said to have the penultimate note short and the last
note long. Each of the notes is always like this. An example
.
And perfect, has a short before the one that is long.
Another rule about the ternary figure of the same notation is as
follows: Every ternary figure that is placed with propriety and is
perfect
If this rule is applied to three, the first is called
is said to have the first note as a smaller long and the middle note
as a smaller breve and the last note as any kind of long. An example
.
**A smaller long, then comes a breve, and the last long can be of
any kind.**
But there is an exception to the above-mentioned rule, because in the
third species and in the fourth they occur otherwise in their effect:
**Indeed I assail the third species, and I except the fourth
species.**
And there is a general rule which applies to all figures that are
placed with propriety and are perfect which exceed the number
If it happens that a ligature exceeds three, it is brought back.
of three notes in the figure, which is as follows: Every figure that
is with propriety and is perfect which exceeds three notes ligated is
reducible to the number of three.
**I hope that those will be in the number of three of the first
mode.**

If it happens, etc. Both the general and specific rules about
figures placed and found with propriety and perfection have been laid out

et praecipue quo ad figuram binariam et ternariam, eo quod priores sunt
et aliis digniores, et praecipue ternaria primi modi, quae inter ceteras
cum proprietate positas dicitur optinere dominii dignitatem, eo quod
omnis figura cum proprietate posita et perfecta excedens tres ligatas cum
proprietate et perfectione et etiam primi modi est ad tres praedictas
specialiter reducenda, seu ad aequipollentiam numeri earundem, quo ad
temporum quantitatem.

Quam poteris care etc. Hic accedit actor ad divisionem omnium
figurarum, quae sunt ad numerum trium praedictarum singulariter
reducendae, dicens: **Quatuor** etc. Hic dat doctrinam primae divisionis,
reducibilis ad tres, dicens: figura quaternaria cum proprietate posita
et perfecta, tam ascendendo, ut hic   , quam descendendo, sic

, est reducibilis ad numerum trium quo ad temporum
repraesentationem et etiam quantitatem. Nam de quatuor ligatis tres
priores sunt breves et aequales et ultima longa, iuxta regulam antedictam
Quando perfecta etc. Idem iudicium secundum multiplicationem vocum est
de reliquis faciendum, quoniam in omnibus penultima est brevis unius
temporis et ultima longa duorum et nunc trium. Si sint ibi plures
praecedentes vel praecedens totum ponimus pro longa. Quicquid excedere
fit repertum, si sint igitur ibi plures praecedentes, utputa duae vel
tres et etiam usque ad sex, omnes tales sunt in semibreves convertendae.

. . . **aut quinque** etc. Sequitur de reductione quinque ad numerum
trium praedictarum. Et quia de signo proprietatis suae contigit
dubitare, ideo vertamus nostrum propositum circa illud. Quidam istam
figuram quinariam (fol. 141v) per oppositum proprietatis protrahunt iuxta
usum. Ad quem usum siquidem confirmandum quaedam sussequens regula
poterit introduci, quae talis est: figurarum per oppositum protractarum
duae priores sunt semper semibreves inaequales. Figura quinaria est
huiusmodi, quia in ipsa sunt duae priores semibreves inaequales, ergo per
oppositum proprietatis merebitur figurari, ad hoc ut signa signatis
respondeant aequo iure. Isti tamen usui ars repugnat duplici vel
triplici regula seu etiam ratione, quarum prior est: omnis figura cum
proprietate posita et perfecta excedens tres ligatas cum proprietate et
perfectione est reducibilis ad tres ligatas vel ad numerum temporum
earundem. Quinaria figura excedit tres ligatas, et est reducibilis ad
numerum antedictum, ergo cum proprietate potius quam per oppositum est
etiam figuranda.

Item quod de proprietate propria debeat figurari, patet sic: nulla
figura in suo genere excedens tres est ad trium numerum eiusdem generis
reducenda, nisi cum proprietate propria figuretur, sicut praesens regula
manifestat. Ista siquidem est reducibilis ad numerum trium cum
proprietate quo ad temporum quantitatem, ergo cum proprietate et non per
oppositum protrahetur.

----

24 signo [[suae]] proprietatis *cod.*   43 (quantitatem) et nulla figura
nisi sit cum proprietate est reducibilis (ergo) *cod.*

above, and especially as regards the binary and ternary figures, because they are more important and more worthy than the others; and especially the ternary figure of the first mode, which is said to obtain the dignity of pre-eminence amongst the rest of the figures that are placed with propriety, because every figure that is placed with propriety and is perfect that exceeds three ligated notes with propriety and perfection of the first mode must be specifically reduced to the three notes mentioned, or to the equipollence of the number of them, as regards the quantity of the units of time.

And you could, dear one, etc. Here the author broaches the division of all figures which must be specifically reduced to the number of the three mentioned, and he says **Four,** etc. Here he gives the principle of the first division, reducible to three, saying that the fourfold figure that is placed with propriety and is perfect, both ascending as here

and descending as here   , is reducible to the number of three as regards the representation and also the quantity of units of time. For in four notes ligated the first three are breves and equal and the last is long in accordance with the abovementioned rule: **When a perfect,** etc. The same judgement according to the multiplication of the notes must be made about the rest, since in all of them the penultimate is a breve of one unit of time and the last is a long of two units of time and sometimes of three. We put the many notes that are preceding, if there are many there, or everything that is preceding, in the place of a long. Whatever is found exceeding that, if there are several notes preceding, for example two or three and even up to six -- all of these should be converted to semibreves.

. . . **or five,** etc. There follows a discussion of the reduction of five notes to the number three mentioned above. And because it happened that there was some doubt about the sign of its propriety, let us therefore change our proposition about that. Certain people* notate that fivefold figure (fol. 141v) by means of the opposite of propriety in accordance with usage. And a certain rule that follows will indeed be able to be introduced to confirm this usage, which is this: Of figures that are notated by means of the opposite of propriety the two first notes are always unequal semibreves.* The fivefold figure is of this kind, because the two first notes in it are unequal semibreves, and so it will deserve to be figured by means of the opposite of propriety, so that the signs correspond to the things that are signified with an equal law. Nevertheless the treatise rejects that usage with two or three rules or reasons, of which the first is: Every figure that is placed with propriety and is perfect that exceeds three ligated notes with propriety and perfection is reducible to three ligated notes or to the number of units of time that they have.* The fivefold figure exceeds three ligated notes, and is reducible to the aforementioned number, therefore it should be figured with propriety rather than by means of the opposite of propriety.

Also the fact that it should be figured with proper propriety is clear from the following: No figure of its genus that exceeds three notes should be reduced to the number of three of the same genus, unless it is figured with proper propriety,* as the present rule makes clear. This one indeed is reducible to the number of three with propriety as regards the quantity of units of time, therefore it will be notated with propriety and not by means of the opposite of propriety.

Quod autem nulla figura nisi sit cum proprietate propria ad numerum
trium sui generis sit possibiliter reducenda, patet per figuram
quaternariam sine proprietate et per quinariam et senariam eiusdem
generis, quamvis adhuc quam pluribus sint ignotae. Patet etiam per
figuram quaternariam opposite protractam et ab omnibus usitatam, quoniam
tales ad numerum trium sui generis nullatenus reducuntur nec etiam ad
numerum trium cum proprietate propria positarum. Ex quo ergo istae non
possunt ad aliquem praedictorum numerum introduci, sequitur quod quinaria
in quantum reducibilis est, sit cum proprietate propria figuranda, et sic
10 nonquam per oppositum secure credimus figurari.

Item nisi cum proprietate propria figuretur, nullam figuram cum
proprietate propria figuratam excedentem quatuor haberemus, et sic
praesens regula esset nulla, eo quod nisi ad figuram quaternariam cum
proprietate solummodo se haberet; sed se usque ad octonariam extendere
reperitur, quare liquet, quod omnes figurae ad trium numerum reducibiles
a quaternaria usque ad octonariam debent cum proprietate propria
artificialiter figurari, quod concedimus.

Et ad hoc etiam plenius confirmandum est expressa regula constituta,
quae alibi ordinatur, scilicet quod *nonquam debet poni aliqua figura sine*
20 *proprietate* vel per oppositum, *ubi potest poni cum proprietate*. Et hoc
est, quia proprietas in figuris ipsas seu librum purpurat et insignit,
improprietas autem deformitatem saepius introducit, ideoque nisi
necessitatis causa superesse cogatur, evitatur. Nota tantum, quod in ea
usui, qui per oppositum protrahit, cogimur consentire ratione duplici
sive causa. Una est, quia in ea opposite figurata videntur signa
signatis modo debito respondere, nam per tale signum nobis eius
significatio declaratur. Alia est, quia ad multiplicationem unius
oppositi sequitur multiplicatio alterius. Figurae cum proprietate et per
oppositum ab invicem se opponunt; sicut ergo figurae cum proprietate
30 multiplicantur, multiplicari poterunt sic et istae, quod concedere
cogimur quo ad istam quinariam et non ultra et hoc secundum organum
speciale.

Item tractus per oppositum in qualicumque figura duas priores
solummodo voces facit semibreves inaequales, nec in pluribus extendi suam
unquam novimus potestatem. Ideoque regulam de figuris per oppositum
usque ad ligaturam quinariam large et non secure satis extendimus usu
solito et rationibus praeostensis et hoc ratione organi specialis;
figuretur tamen haec cum proprietate tam ascendendo quam etiam

40
descendendo   . Et nota, quod in ea sunt duae
priores semibreves inaequales, ut supradictum est, et aliae duae rectae
breves et ultima longa.

Sequitur de senaria figura quam semper cum proprietate propria
figuramus rationibus superius assignatis. Usus tamen saepius per
oppositum more quinariae transfigurat. Sed usum in illa vel in ipsam
sequentibus nullatenus imitamur, eo quod nulla ratione certa vel regula

----

6 nullatenus *add. super scriptum*   7 trium *add. super scriptum*
19 decet *pro debet Sowa*   poni *add. super scriptum*   23 cogatur
scripsi, cognovit *Sowa*   31-32 et hoc secundum organum speciale *add. in
marg.*   37 et haec ratione *pro* et hoc ratione *Sowa*   38 etiam *om. Sowa*
41 *exempla in marg. partim*   47 nulla falsitus ratione *cod.*

But the fact that no figure can possibly be reduced to the number of three of its genus unless it is with proper propriety is clear from the fourfold figure without propriety and from the fivefold figure and the sixfold figure of the same genus, although thus far they are unknown to very many. It is also clear from the fourfold figure notated in an opposite fashion and in general use by everyone, since such figures are never reduced to the number of three of their kind nor even to the number of three placed with proper propriety. Therefore from the fact that these can not be brought to some number of the abovementioned, it follows that however much the fivefold figure is reducible, it should be figured with the proper propriety, and thus we safely believe that it should never be figured by means of the opposite of propriety.

Also unless it were figured with proper propriety, we would have no figure figured with proper propriety exceeding four and thus the present rule would be nothing, because it would only apply to the fourfold figure with propriety. But it is found to extend as far as the eightfold figure, and so it is evident that all figures that are reducible to the number of three from the fourfold figure up to the eightfold figure must be artificially figured with proper propriety, which we concede.

And a deliberate rule has been formulated to confirm this even more fully, which is laid out elsewhere;* that is to say that "a figure should never be put without propriety" or by means of the opposite of propriety "when it can be put with propriety." And this is because propriety in figures embellishes and adorns them or the book in which they occur, but impropriety often brings deformity, and so, unless it is forced to win over because of necessity, it is avoided. Only note that we are forced to consent to that usage of it which notates it with the opposite of propriety for two reasons or causes. One is that when it is figured in opposite fashion, the signs seem to correspond to the things that are signified in the appropriate manner, for with a sign like that its significance is stated to us. Another is that according to the multiplication of one opposite follows the multiplication of the other. Figures with propriety and figures by means of the opposite of propriety are the opposite of each other; therefore just as figures with propriety are multiplied, so these can also be multiplied, which we are forced to concede as regards that fivefold figure and not beyond, and this according to special organum.

Also the line of opposite propriety in any figure makes only the two first notes unequal semibreves, nor do we know that its power is ever extended further. And so we extend the rule about figures by means of the opposite of propriety broadly and not completely safely to the fivefold ligature, because of customary usage and the reasons shown above, and this is for the reason of special organum. Nevertheless let this be figured with propriety both ascending and also descending

. And note that the two first notes in it are unequal semibreves, as has been said above, and the other two are correct breves and the last is long.

There follows a discussion of the sixfold figure, which we always figure with proper propriety for the reasons laid out above. Usage however often transforms it into opposite propriety like the fivefold figure. But we do not at all imitate usage in that figure or in those that follow it, because although it can be seen in widespread use, it is

cernitur vagabundus et sic malus, et malus usus abholendus est et non per
imitationem augmentandus. Quod autem tractus per oppositum ei debeat
nullatenus coadiungi, patet per omnes figuras per oppositum figuratas,
utputa per binariam, ternariam, quaternariam, quinariam, in quibus eamdem
regulam retinet et effectum, nam duas priores semper facit semibreves
inaequales. In senaria siquidem vel in ipsam sequentibus hunc effectum
non potuit optinere, quare similiter nec hunc tractum, quod concedimus;
cum proprietate igitur tam ascendendo quam descendendo protrahimus in

10 hunc modum   . Et nota quod in hac senaria tres
priores sunt semibreves et aequales, et aliae duae rectae breves et
ultima longa, et sic ternariae numero aequipollent.

   Idem iudicium de septenaria et octonaria est habendum. Figuram
igitur septenariam, quoquo modo se habeat, protrahimus in hunc modum

              , octonariam vero sic   . In septenaria quinque priores
sunt semibreves, duo tempora continentes, quarum tres priores sunt
aequales et continent unum tempus et duae aliae inaequales, tempus aliud
continentes. Penultima vero cernitur recta brevis et ultima longa et sic
20 praedictarum trium numerum repraesentant. In octonaria quidem sex
priores sunt semibreves et aequales duo tempora per frustra aequalia
subtiliter decindentes et penultima brevis recta efficitur et ultima
vera longa, et sic ad trium numerum reducuntur.

   De novenaria quidem et denaria exempla nolumus provulgare, licet
possibile sit ipsas protrahere et proferre et ad praedictum numerum
reducere, eo quod longa maior, cui aequipollent longa et brevis, in novem
partes potest diminui vel decindi. Tamen aprobato usui repugnarent etiam
et regulae supradictae: **Quando perfecta** etc., ideoque de ipsis non
facimus mentionem. Littera patet.

30

        Quam[1] **poteris care**[2] **tot metis**[3] **multiplicare.**[4]
        1 sive ligaturam ternariam
        2 id est, dilecte
        3 id est, differentiis seu divisionibus
        4 id est, multiplicando dividere
        Quatuor[1] **aut quinque, sex, septem, non nego quinque.**[2]
        1 sive voces in figura, et sic de omnibus aliis, et hoc totum cum
proprietate et perfectione praeter quinariam, ut dictum est
        2 id est, illa figura
40   **Octo**[1] **tenet detur**[2] **ve novem,**[3] **quas**[4] **dena**[5] **sequetur.**
        1 id est, octonaria repraesentat
        2 id est, associetur
        3 id est, novenaria
        4 divisiones sive
        5 id est, denaria potest sequi

----

2 aumentandus *cod., corr. Sowa*   14 quoque *pro* quoquo *Sowa*   24 noveria
cod.

with no fixed reason or rule, and thus it is bad, and a bad usage should be abhorred and not increased by imitation. But the fact that a line of opposite propriety should in no way be added to it is clear from all the figures figured by means of the opposite of propriety, for example from the binary, ternary, fourfold, and fivefold figures, in which it keeps the same rule and effect, for it always makes the two first notes unequal semibreves. Indeed in the sixfold figure or in those that follow it it could not obtain this effect, and so similarly it could not have this line, which we concede. Therefore we draw it with propriety both

ascending and descending in this manner . And note that in this sixfold figure the three first notes are semibreves and equal, and the other two are correct breves and the last is a long, and thus they are equipollent to the number of a ternary figure.

The same judgement should be held about the sevenfold figure and the eightfold figure. Therefore we notate the sevenfold figure, whichever way it occurs, in this way , and the eightfold figure like this

. In the sevenfold figure the first five notes are semibreves, containing two units of time, and the first three semibreves are equal and contain one unit of time, and the two others are unequal, containing another unit of time. But the penultimate note is perceived as a correct breve and the last as a long, and thus they represent the number of three mentioned above. In the eightfold figure the first six notes are semibreves and equal, subtly cutting two units of time into equal pieces, and the penultimate note is made up of a correct breve and the last is a true long, and thus they are reduced to the number of three.

We do not wish to promulgate examples of the ninefold and tenfold figures, although it is possible to notate them and to perform them and to reduce them to the abovementioned number because the larger long, to which a long and a breve are equipollent, can be diminished or cut up into nine parts. Nevertheless they reject approved usage and also the abovementioned rule: **When a perfect,** etc., and so we do not make mention of them. Here is the text.

> **And you could, dear one,[2] multiply[4] it[1] by so many boundaries.[3]**
> 1 the ternary ligature
> 2 that is, beloved
> 3 that is, distinctions or divisions
> 4 that is, divide it by multiplying
> **Four[1] or five, six, seven, and, I repeat, five.[2]**
> 1 notes in the figure, and this applies to all the others, and all of this with propriety and perfection except the fivefold figure, as has been said
> 2 that is, that figure
> **The eight holds[1] or may be given[2] to the nine,[3] which[4] the ten will follow.[5]**
> 1 that is, the eightfold figure represents
> 2 that is, may be associated with
> 3 that is, the ninefold figure
> 4 the divisions
> 5 that is, the tenfold figure can follow

(fol. 142) **Binas[1] supremas si vis ex ordine demas.**
1 id est, novenariam et denariam, et hoc secundum usum artis
solitum et secundum tenorem cuiusdam regulae praecedentis in qua
continetur, quod in omni figura cum proprietate posita penultima
dicitur esse brevis, ad cuius instantiam novenaria figura et
denaria nullatenus habent esse
Hic subiungit actor rationem pro sua parte, quare debent ab aliarum
numero deponi:
Nam sunt ignotae plus octo mihi doceo te.
Haec[1] si perfectae sint proprietate refectae.[2]
1 supradictae divisiones sive
2 per hoc innuit satis plane, quod quinaria figura debet cum
proprietate figurari
Aequivalent[1] ternis primique modi[2] fore cernis.
1 id est, aequippollere debent
2 id est, figurae ternariae primi modi
More ligaturae manet ultima longa figurae.
Longam cumque brevi de praepositis tibi sevi.

Iuncturaeque datae etc. Exequto de figuris cum proprietate propria
figuratis etiam et perfectis, hic vult actor de figuris sine proprietate
propria positis facere mentionem, inde dans regulas generales, quarum
prior est de earum protractione, aliae sunt de earum repraesentationibus
et naturis.
    Et notandum, quod triplex est in figuris repraesentatio proprietatis,
per quam diversae differentiae figurarum ab invicem cognoscuntur, sicut
declaratum est superius manifeste. Unde istae figurae non dicuntur sine
proprietate eo quod omni proprietate careant, immo eo quod sua proprietas
proprietati figurarum praecedentium, quae cum proprietate propria
nominantur authonomatice, quia sunt aliis pulcriores, communiores et
etiam digniores in dispositione signorum, praecipue sit repugnans, sicut
declarabitur per exempla. Unde si quaeratur, quid sit proprietas, prout
huiusmodi figuris attribuitur, in communi dicendum est, quod proprietas,
prout in eis sumitur, est quaedam signorum differentia in figuris
variorum, quae nunc cum tractu efficitur et aliquando sine tractu,
effectus varios repraesentans.
    Sequitur de regulis huiusmodi figurarum sine proprietate, quarum
prior est de earum protractione, quae talis est, scilicet omnis figurae
sine proprietate positae ascendendo sua proprietas est, ut primus punctus
ligaturae habeat tractum sub sinistro latere descendentem, ut hic [image] ,
et sic de omnibus aliis ascendendo; descendendo autem, quod non habeat
sed debeat protrahi in hunc modum [image] , et sic de omnibus aliis
descendendo. Quidam tamen in suis artibus figuram binariam ascendendo
protrahebant sic [image] , antecessorum semitam relinquentes, de quo possunt

----

12 decet *pro* debet *Sowa*   17-18 *in marg. inferiore*   27 ducuntur *pro*
dicuntur *Sowa*   30 convenientiores *pro* communiores *Sowa*   31 signorum
[[et figurarum praecedentibus]] sit *cod.*   praecipue *add. super
scriptum*   33 attribuitur [[d]] in communi *cod.*   34 in figuris *add.
super scriptum, om. Sowa*   38 scilicet *om. Sowa*

(fol. 142) **If you want, you may remove the last two**[1] **from the order.**

1 that is, the ninefold and tenfold figures, and this is according to the customary usage of the art and according to the tenor of a certain preceding rule, in which is contained the statement that in every figure placed with propriety the penultimate note is said to be short; and to this demand the ninefold and tenfold figures in no way conform

Here the author adds a reason for his own part as to why they should be dropped from the category of the others:

For I teach you that more than eight are unknown to me.

These,[1] **if they are perfect, may be made with propriety.**[2]

1 the above-mentioned divisions

2 in this way he suggests quite clearly that the fivefold figure should be figured with propriety

They are equivalent[1] **to three, and of the first mode,**[2] **as you see.**

1 that is, they should be equipollent

2 that is, the ternary figure of the first mode

In the custom of the ligature the last long of the figure remains long.

I have sown for you a long with a breve from the things placed in front.*

And the joinings are given, etc. Having described the figures that are figured with proper propriety and are also perfect, here the author wishes to make mention of the figures that are placed without proper propriety, giving general rules about them, of which the first is about their notation, and the others are about their representations and natures.

And it should be noted that there are three ways of representing propriety in figures, through which the different distinctions of the figures are recognized in their turn, as has been stated clearly above. And these figures are not said to be without propriety because they lack all propriety; rather it is because their propriety especially rejects the propriety of the preceding figures, which are called with proper propriety by antonomasia, because they are more beautiful, more appropriate, and also more worthy in the disposition of their signs than the others, as will be stated through examples. And if it is asked what propriety is as it is allocated to figures of this kind, it should be commonly said that propriety as it is used in regard to them is a certain distinction in figures of different signs, representing different effects, which sometimes is accomplished with a line and sometimes without a line.

There follows a discussion of the rules about figures of this kind without propriety, of which the first is about their notation, which is as follows, namely that the propriety of every figure placed without propriety that is ascending is that the first written note of the ligature has a line descending under its left side as here ⬛, and likewise with all the others that are ascending. But if it is descending it does not have that line, but should be notated in this manner ⬛, and likewise with all the others that are descending. Nevertheless some people* in their treatises notated the binary figure ascending like this ⬛ , abandoning the path of their forebears, for which they can be

multipliciter blaphemari et per rationes manifestas. Quarum una est,
quia magistrorum deviant a praeceptis, inferentes artis regulae
nocumentum; alia est, quia nullam differentiam assignant in hoc inter
simplices et compositas. Nam talis figura magis accedit ad naturam
simplicium quam compositarum, nam ibi est simplex longa et simplex brevis
in protractionibus propriis ordinatae, quare male, cum compositae a
simplicibus differre debeant in protractionibus, in numero et natura, et
eo quod alibi dicit ars, quod *nonquam debet poni simplex vel non ligata*
ubi potest poni composita vel ligata. Si autem dicant, quod talis figura
10 sit composita, contra si esset composita aut protraheretur cum
proprietate vel sine proprietate vel per oppositum proprietatis. Cum
proprietate non protrahitur, quia ad earum protractionem vel naturam
propriam non accedit, immo etiam figura binaria cum proprietate isti
binariae totaliter se repugnat tam in forma propria quam effectu.

Item nec sine proprietate similiter figuratur, quia signum eis
artificialiter attributum neque formam eis debitam non importat. Si quis
dicat: immo figura binaria, quae sine proprietate protrahitur quo ad
artem, isto modo securius protrahi videretur, eo quod in ea secundum
ordinationem vocum quo ad sensum particularem tempora distinguntur, in
20 reliqua siquidem dignoscuntur signo proprio participante cum intellectu
potius quam cum sensu. Id autem quod cum sensu aprehenditur, sine labore
cernitur apprehendi, id autem quod cum intellectu non sine difficultate
et iudicio rationis, quare alia quae ad sensum pertinet, magis est
apetibilis et reliqua evitanda. Solummodo intellectus fundatur supra rem
et non sine ratione. Quae quidem ratio in sensu particulari et etiam in
omnibus dominatur, nam opus sine ratione vacuum est et inane. Illa autem
protractio ratione sophistica et non necessaria introducta artis
necessariam rationem impedit et doctrinam, quare debet penitus evitari.
Et hoc manifeste apparet per tractum in ea positum sub dextro latere
30 descendentem, quod in nulla figurarum compositarum evenit reperire.

Item nec per oppositum figurari iudicatur, quia in figuris per
oppositum figuratis est tractus supra caput prioris vocis figurae
cuiuslibet elevatus. Secus tamen est in ea, quare de earum numero nequit
esse.

Cum autem (fol. 142v) in protractione non participet cum aliqua de
praedictis, non erit composita iudicanda, eo quod si esset vere
composita, aliquas figuras alias sibi in specie protractionis consimiles
generaret, quod cum non faciat non est in compositarum numero reponenda.
Item nec est simplex quia ibi sunt duae voces ad invicem colligatae;
40 restat ergo quod a libro unientium deleatur.

A parte principii discussum est inter tales; ne autem aliquod vitium
lateat indiscussum circa finem talium figurarum aliqua prosequamur,
quoniam praedicti impositores antedictam figuram protrahebant
imperfectam, et non solum eam sed etiam figuram ternariam sine
proprietate propria positam solummodo ascendendo, figurantes eam in hunc

----
8 decet *pro debet Sowa*   18 eo *add. super scriptum*   28 decet *pro*
debet *Sowa*   29 apparetur *pro* apparet *Sowa*   36 vere *add. super*
scriptum   38 est in in compositarum *cod.*

reviled in many ways and for clear reasons. And one of them is that
they deviate from the precepts of the masters and bring harm to the rule
of the art; another is that in this way they mark out no distinction
between single and composite figures. For such a figure comes closer to
the nature of single figures than of composite ones, for that way there
are a single long and a single breve arranged in their proper notations,
and so it is bad, since composite figures should differ from single ones
in their notation, both in number and in nature, and because the treatise
says elsewhere* that "a single figure or a figure that is not ligated
should never be put where a composite or ligated one can be put." But if
they say that such a figure is composite -- on the contrary if it were
composite it would either be notated with propriety or without propriety
or by means of the opposite of propriety.

It is not notated with propriety, because it does not come close to
the notation or the proper nature of those with propriety, rather the
binary figure with propriety completely rejects that binary both in its
proper form and in its effect. Also neither is it figured similarly to
those without propriety, because the sign is artificially allocated to
them and does not convey the requisite form. Someone may rather say that
the binary figure, which is notated without propriety as regards the art,
would seem to be notated more safely in that way, because units of time
are distinguished in it according to the arrangement of the notes as
regards their particular sense, but in the other they are recognized with
the participation of the proper sign with the intellect rather than with
the senses. And that which is grasped with the senses is perceived to be
grasped without labor, but that which is grasped with the intellect is
grasped with difficulty and with the judgement of reason; and so the one
which pertains to the senses is more desirable, and the other should be
avoided. Only the intellect is based on the thing itself and is not
without reason. And this reason indeed dominates in the particular sense
and also in everything, for a work without reason is empty and hollow.
But that notation was introduced with a sophistical and unnecessary
reason and hinders the necessary reason and principle of the art, and so
it should be completely avoided. And this appears clearly from the line
placed in it descending under the right side, which is found to occur in
none of the composite figures.

Also it is not judged to be figured by means of the opposite of
propriety either, because in figures figured by means of the opposite of
propriety there is a line raised above the head of the first note of the
figure. But it is not so in this one, and so it can not be included as
one of their number.

And so, since (fol. 142v) it does not share in its notation with one
of the ones mentioned above, it should not be judged to be composite,
because if it were truly composite, it would generate some other figures
similar to it in the appearance of their notation, and since it does not
do this it should not be included in the category of composite figures.
Also it is not single either because there are two notes in it that are
connected to each other; it remains therefore that it may be deleted from
the book of figures that are alone.

With respect to the beginning was discussed among those figures; but
lest any offence remain not discussed concerning the end of such figures,
let us proceed with one of them, since the abovementioned imposters
notated the aforementioned figure as imperfect, and not only it but also
the ternary figure placed without proper propriety, but only ascending,

modum , et etiam quando figura ascendit in fine licet descendat a
parte principii, sicut patet hic ▚▘ . Et omnes alias, in quibus
ultimus punctus inferior est penultimo, iuxta artis nostrae
consuetudinem perfectas protrahunt et provulgant. Super quo etiam
videntur sibi ipsis esse contrarii et discordes, sicut bene poterit
declarari sic: ea quae eandem proprietatis speciem mediante qua ab
omnibus aliis differunt retinent, et quorum quantitas est eadem in
repraesentatione, numero et mensura, eandem protractionis differentiam
sub signis sibi debitis debent simpliciter importare. Figurae sine
10 proprietate positae sub signis sibi debitis sunt huiusmodi. Si ergo
quaelibet earum, in qua punctus ultimus inferior est penultimo, de sui
natura perfecta exigat figurari, quod ubique cernitur esse verum,
similiter figurae eiusdem differentiae vel speciei et eiusdem quantitatis
tam in numero quam in mensura, in quibus ultimus punctus altior est
penultimo, perfectae merebuntur figurari, quod concedimus, nam talis
dispositio est in omnibus concedenda. Ipsi autem quasdam perfectas
protrahebant et eiusdem differentiae alias imperfectas, prout supra
ostensum est, super quo debebant sibi ipsis contrarii iudicari et sic per
consequens nugatorii sunt dicendi.
20   Quod autem omnes figurae sine proprietate tam ascendendo quam
descendendo primitive sunt perfectae nec immerito figurandae, patet sic:
id perfectum in sua specie dicitur, cui nihil amplius sub tali
differentia potest addi, et a quo per diminutionem aliquid potest demi.
Figurae sine proprietate positae primitive sunt huiusmodi, ergo perfectae
figurari merebuntur. Nihil autem eis amplius potest addi, quia si quid
eis amplius adderetur quam id ad quod impositae sunt ad signandum, iam a
sua differentia propria deviarent, quare nihil possunt amplius continere.
Ipsae tamen possunt a tempore minorari per sustractionem artificialiter,
et tunc imperfectae debent totaliter ordinari, et sic quando continent id
30 quod possunt perfectae sunt, quando minus sunt similiter imperfectae.
Item notabile est, quod ubicumque est longitudo, ibi est perfectio in hac
arte, et ubi non est longitudo, ibi nec perfectio debet esse. Longitudo
namque causat perfectionem in figuris compositis in hac arte et ceterae
voces imperfectionem e contrario retinebunt. Differentia autem
perfectionis et imperfectionis per textum declarabitur inferius suo loco.
Hiis visis ad litteram accedamus.

        Hic subiungit actor regulam figurarum sine proprietate propria
        ligatarum, quarum regula in glosulis fit expressa:
40   **Iuncturaeque datae si sint sine proprietate:**
            In scandente[1] foris[2] tractus sub fronte[3] prioris
            1 id est, in illa, quae fit ascendendo
            2 id est, a sinistro latere
            3 id est, subtus frontem vel anteriorem partem, sicut patet hic

▜▘ ▜▘ ▛▘

----

6 declarare *pro* declarari *Sowa*   qua *add. super scriptum*   14 *secundum
in suppl. Sowa*   15 perfecta merebitur *cod.*   16 est *add. super
scriptum*   21 sint *pro* sunt *cod.*   25 fieri *pro* figurari *Sowa*   quis
pro quid *Sowa*   29 debent *add. super scriptum*   30 sint *pro* sunt *cod.*
32 decet *pro* debet *Sowa*   39 sit *pro* fit *Sowa*   42 sit *pro* fit *Sowa*

figuring it in this manner* , and also when the figure ascends at the end although it descends with respect to the beginning, as is shown here* . And all the others in which the last written note is lower than the penultimate they notate and promulgate as perfect in accordance with the customary practice of our art. And in this regard they seem to be contradictory to themselves and discordant, as could be stated well in this way: Those things which keep the same appearance of propriety with the help of which they differ from all others, and whose quantity is the same in representation, number, and measure, should simply convey the same distinction of notation with the signs that are requisite for them. Figures placed without propriety with signs that are requisite for them are of this kind. If therefore any one of them in which the last written note is lower than the penultimate demands to be figured as perfect according to its nature, which is perceived to be true everywhere, similarly figures of the same distinction or species and of the same quantity both in number and in measure, in which the last written note is higher than the penultimate, will deserve to be figured as perfect; which we concede, for such a disposition must be conceded in everything. But they notated certain figures as perfect and others of the same distinction as imperfect, as has been shown above, for which they should have been judged as contrary to themselves and thus as a consequence should be called worthless.

However the fact that all figures without propriety both ascending and descending are originally perfect and should deservedly be figured that way is clear from the following: That thing is said to be perfect in its appearance to which nothing further can be added under such a distinction and from which something can be taken away by diminution. Figures placed without propriety are originally of this kind, and will therefore deserve to be perfect. Nothing further can be added to them, because if anything were added to them beyond that to which they are bound for their significance, they would now deviate from their proper distinction, and so they can contain nothing more. They can however be diminished artificially in their time through subtraction and then they must be completely arranged as imperfect; and thus when they contain what they can they are perfect, and when they contain less they are similarly imperfect. Also it is notable that wherever there is length there is perfection in this art, and where there is not length there should not be perfection. For length causes perfection in composite figures in this art, and the other notes on the contrary will keep imperfection. The distinction of perfection and imperfection however will be stated below in the right place by means of the text. Now that these things have been seen, let us broach the text.

Here the author adds the rule of the figures ligated without proper propriety, and their rule is put forth in the glosses:
And the ligatures are given if they are without propriety:
In the climbing one[1] a line outside[2] under the front[3] of the first note
1 that is, in that one which occurs ascending
2 that is, from the left side
3 that is, below the front or the foremost part, as is clear here

Quasi diceret: quando illa figura fit descendendo nullum tractum
habebit, immo fit in hunc modum ▪▪ ▪▪ ◣ :
     Fit, nullum tractum descendens dat sibi factum.
    Hic explicat actor primam regulam de earum repraesentatione, dicens,
quod in omni figura sine proprietate posita
     Iunge duasque datae si sint sine proprietate.
prima est longa et ultima brevis tam ascendendo quam descendendo:
     Longa prior detur, brevis atque suprema tenetur.
    Alia regula: in figura ternaria sine proprietate et perfecta
penultima dicitur esse longa
     Tres ita si iungam mediam semper fore longam
et duae exteriores sunt breves. Exemplum earum patet hic, ascendendo

sic   ♪ ♪   , descendendo sic ◥ ◣ .
     Dico, breves aliae sunt semper lege sophiae.

    Quatuor etc. Hic vult actor quandam inserere regulam a paucis non
tamen generaliter usitatam, eo quod de ea provecti in musica saepius
altercarunt. Haec autem regula est de figura sine proprietate
quaternaria, quae sic dignoscitur figurari tam ascendendo quam

descendendo ♪▪ ◣ .
    Quidam enim dicunt istam figuram ad suum ternarium esse (fol. 143)
reducibilem, et sic fatentur eam quatuor tempora solummodo continere
iuxta sui ternarii quantitatem. Dicunt namque omnem figuram quoquo modo
figuratam et excedentem tres in numero esse suo ternario reducendam, quod
de figuris cum proprietate positis et perfectis solummodo credimus esse
verum, et hoc supra declaravimus manifeste. Ad hanc igitur altercationem
et opinionem talium disserendam breviter est sciendum, quod nulla figura
excedens tres nisi sit cum proprietate et perfectione est ad suum
ternarium reducenda, quod declarare possumus multis rationibus et
exemplis.
    Et primo per figuras cum proprietate imperfectas, quae nec arte nec
usu sunt reducibiles ad suum ternarium imperfectum, quoniam omnis figura
cum proprietate et imperfecta excedens tres quatuor tempora continet, et
suum ternarium non continet nisi tria. Istud autem probatione alia non
indiget, quia notorium est apud omnes musicos providos et discretos.
Item patet similiter per figuras per oppositum proprietatis ligatas,
quarum nulla ad suum ternarium usualiter fit reducta, immo quaelibet
excedens tres, si cum signo unico fuerit figurata, more imperfectarum cum
proprietate suum ternarium unico tempore superabit. Et sic ad eum
nullatenus reducetur, quoniam omnis reductio est per aequipollentiam
facienda. Si quis autem dicat: immo est reducenda; contra si
reduceretur, more et ordinatione figurarum cum proprietate et perfectarum
reduceretur. Sed in reductione earum non moventur seu mutantur nec
penultima nec ultima, immo in suo statu et loco integre remanent sicut
ante, quod in istis posset fieri nullo modo. Item in reducibilibus ad
tres fit resecatio et vocum multiplicatio ratione primae vocis sui

----

1 sit *pro* fit *Sowa*   descendens *pro* descendendo *Sowa*   25 quoque *pro*
quoquo *Sowa*

He means to say that when that figure occurs descending it will have
no line, rather it occurs in this manner ▪ ◣ ◪ :
    Occurs, but the one that descends gives itself no line.
Here the author explains the first rule about the representation of
them, saying that in every figure placed without propriety
    And join two if they are given without propriety.
the first is a long and the last one is a breve, both ascending and
descending:
    A long is given as the first, and a breve is held as the last.
Another rule: In a ternary figure that is without propriety and
perfect the penultimate is said to be long
    If I join three in this way, the middle one will always be long
and the two outside ones are breves. Here is an example of them,

ascending like this   ▐ ▗   , and descending like this ◣ ◪ .
    I say, and the others are always breves, with the law of wisdom.

This precept, etc. Here the author wants to introduce a certain rule
which is nevertheless not in general use by a few people, because being
advanced in music they have often quarreled about it. And this rule is
about the fourfold figure without propriety, which is recognized as being

figured as follows both ascending and descending ▟▖ ◪ .
    For some people say* that that figure is reducible to its ternary
form, (fol.143) and thus they admit that it only contains four units of
time in accordance with the quantity of its ternary form. For they say
that every figure figured in any way that exceeds three in number should
be reduced to its ternary form, which we believe to be true only of
figures that are placed with propriety and are perfect, and we have
stated this clearly above.* As regards this quarrel therefore and the
arguable view of these people, it should be known briefly that no figure
that exceeds three should be reduced to its ternary form unless it is
with propriety and perfection, which we can state with many reasons and
examples.
    And first is the example of imperfect figures with propriety, which
neither in theory nor in usage are reducible to their imperfect ternary
form, since every figure that is with propriety and imperfect that
exceeds three contains four units of time, and its ternary form only
contains three. And that needs no other proof, because it is well known
amongst all prudent and discerning musicians. Also it is clear similarly
from the example of figures ligated by means of the opposite of
propriety, none of which are usually reduced to their ternary form;
rather each one that exceeds three, if it is figured with a single sign,
will surpass its ternary form by a single unit of time in the manner of
imperfect figures with propriety. And thus it is in no way reduced to
the ternary, since every reduction should be made by means of
equipollence. Someone however might say rather that it should be
reduced; on the contrary, if it were reduced, it would be reduced in the
manner and arrangement of figures that are with propriety and perfect.
But in the reduction of them neither the penultimate nor the last note is
moved or changed; rather they remain exactly the same as before in their
state and place, which in these figures could not occur in any way. Also
in those that are reducible to three there is a cutting-up and
multiplication of the notes because of the first note of their ternary

ternarii. Hoc autem non potest fieri in figuris per oppositum figuratis ratione primae vocis sui ternarii, quoniam est minor semibrevis et indivisibilis, restat ergo quod nullatenus reducantur. Item si essent omnes tales reducibiles, ut dicebant, figurarum sufficientiam nullatenus haberemus, immo etiam in aequivocationis dubium et ignorantiae fallaciam saepius caderemus, quare reductiones varias evitamus, uni solummodo adhaerentes. Item si vere reducerentur, reductio deberet tenere in perfectis et non in imperfectis. Sed teneret utrobique, quare male, quia de imperfectis ad imperfectas non est reductio facienda, neque etiam de
10 imperfectis ad perfectas nec e converso, eo quod se habent in opositione et oppositorum opposita sunt effectus.

Ad opinionem illorum, qui dicebant istam figuram sine proprietate continere quatuor tempora divisive, respondemus dicentes, quod non potest esse, quoniam si verum esset, necesse esset eam protrahere imperfectam, quia nulla perfectio in figuris compositis sine longitudine aliqua debet esse vel potest. Et si eam protrahant imperfectam, non erit reducibilis ratione antedicta. Nos vero in praedicta figura oppositionem figurae quaternariae cum proprietate et perfectione quo ad dispositionem duarum vocum ultimae scilicet et penultimae considerantes, ipsius penultimam
20 dicimus esse longam et omnes alias rectas breves, et sic more binariae et ternariae figuris cum proprietate positis repugnabit. Et etiam primam vocem illius quaternariae per semibreves in figura quinaria et senaria resecamus, sicut textus series declarabit. Littera per se patet.

Hic subiungit actor aliam regulam quamvis inusitatam de figura quaternaria:

Quatuor haec norma coniungit nunc ita forma .

Quas[1] si vis[2] brevia quorundam teste sophia.[3]
30 1 quatuor supple
2 id est, si talium opinioni acquiescas
3 id est, doctrina
Vult[1] tamen hoc tegma,[2] quod longa[3] sit antesuprema.[4]
1 id est, docet
2 id est, haec doctrina
3 et aliae breves sive
4 id est, ultima
Primam nunc tendo[1] per semibreves minuendo.[2]
1 id est, per divisionem multiplico
40 2 id est, resecando
Cum[1] iunctura[2] datur quinaria[3] sena[4] sequatur.[5]
1 pro quando
2 sive ligatura
3 sine proprietate
4 id est, senaria
5 id est, addatur

----

8 in *add. super scriptum*   15 decet *pro* debet *Sowa*   18 duarum *add. super scriptum*   23 resecamur *pro* resecamus *Sowa*   37 ulterima *pro* ultima *Sowa*

form. And this can not occur in figures figured by means of the opposite of propriety because of the first note of their ternary form, which is a smaller semibreve and indivisible; it remains therefore that they may in no way be reduced. Also if all such figures were reducible as they said, we would in no way have enough figures, rather we would often fall into the doubt of equivocation and the mistake of ignorance, and so we avoid these different reductions, keeping to one only. Also if they are reduced truly, the reduction would have to obtain in perfect figures and not in imperfect ones. But it obtains for both of them and so it is bad, because reduction should not be made from imperfect to imperfect figures nor from imperfect to perfect nor the reverse, because they occur in opposition, and opposites are the effects of opposites.

To the opinion of those who said that this figure without propriety contains four units of time separately,* we say in response that it can not be, since if it were true it would be necessary to notate it as imperfect, because there should not be, nor can there be, any perfection in composite figures without some length. And if they notate it as imperfect, it will not be reducible for the reason given above. But we, considering the opposition in the abovementioned figure of the fourfold figure with propriety and perfection as regards the disposition of the two notes, that is to say the last and the penultimate, we say that its penultimate is long and that all the others are correct breves, and thus in the manner of the binary and ternary it will reject figures placed with propriety. And we also cut the first note of that fourfold figure up into semibreves in the fivefold and sixfold figures, as the sequence of the text will state. The text is clear by itself.

Here the author adds another rule, although it is an unusual one, about the fourfold figure:

This precept now joins together four in the following form

.

Which,[1] if you want,[2] are short things, for which the wisdom[3] is a witness.
1 supply: four
2 that is, if you agree with the view of those people
3 that is, this principle
But this device[2] wishes[1] that the one before the end[4] be a long.[3]
1 that is, teaches
2 that is, this principle
3 and the others breves
4 that is, the last
Sometimes I stretch out[1] the first note, diminishing it[2] through semibreves.
1 that is, I multiply it by dividing it
2 that is, cutting it up
Since[1] the joining[2] is given, let the fivefold[3] follow[5] and the six.[4]
1 instead of when
2 the ligature
3 without propriety
4 that is, the sixfold figure
5 that is, let it be added

Cum iunctura datur etc. Exemplum quinariae patet hic ,

senariae autem sic . Istae autem duae ultimae sunt inusitatae et
ideo quam pluribus sunt ignotae, et licet parum proficiant, de ipsis
tamen facimus mentionem, quia possibile et leve est ipsas protrahere.
Sed quid levissimum est proferre, notandum et est etiam, quod nullus
debet uti figuris sine proprietate positis imperfectis nec eas figurare
excepta binaria. Et licet sit possibile ipsas protrahere quo ad artem,
ipsis tamen nullatenus indigemus, quia figuris cum proprietate positis
10 imperfectis pari numero aequipollent. Et ars docet, quod *nonquam debet
poni aliqua figura sine proprietate, ubi potest poni cum proprietate,*
ideoque ipsas penitus extirpamus.

(fol. 143v) **Nescio**[1] **plus cari**[2] **sine proprietate ligari.**[3]
1 id est, ignoro
2 id est, O cantores
3 id est, figurari

Opposito dabitur etc. Declaratis supra protractionibus et naturis
20 figurarum cum proprietate et sine proprietate propria positarum, et
assignata inter eas differentia competenti, hic vult actor accedere ad
notitiam figurarum per oppositum protractarum, de earum forma seu
proprietate primo dans regulam generalem, quae talis est: in omni figura
per oppositum figurata sua proprietas est, ut primus punctus ligaturae,
sive sit perfecta sive imperfecta, habeat tractum supra caput positum in
sinistro latere ascendendo, sive figura ascendat, ut hic , sive

descendat, sic . Quidam tamen quorundam veterum vestigia
sussequentes ternariam figuram per oppositum figurandam sine proprietate
30 et imperfectam et etiam quandoque perfectam in solo ascensu continuo

protraxerunt in hunc modum , et hoc praecipue reperitur in
Alleluya de *Hic Martius*. Et sic expertes iudicio rationis ac
ignorantiae nubilo excaecati figurarum signa propria et protractiones
ratione inopinabili corrumpebant. Ideoque talium vestigia a provectis
etiam sunt maxime praecavenda, ne more insipientium tanquam caeci
procedere videantur. Sed quia plures sunt pictores quam scriptores et
delirantes quam cantores et etiam stolidi quam provecti, ideo cum talibus
non est rationibus insistendum, sed ulterius procedendum ordinationem seu
40 aequipollentiam modi prae manibus habiti firmiter observando. Nullus
enim cantus directe compositus a modo incepto potest ita privari, quin
sit ad eum per aequippollentias vel convenientias ibi positas
proportionaliter reducendus. Et talis ordinatio usque ad pausationem,
quae finis punctorum dicitur, est in omnibus cantuum dispositionibus
observanda; post quam pausam modus alius et nova aequipollentiarum
variatio pro voluntate imponentium poterit ordinari. Et talis iterum

----
7 decet *pro* debet *Sowa*   10 decet *pro debet Sowa*   12 extirpandas *pro*
extirpamus *Sowa*   19 **Opposito dabitur** *sine sublinea in cod.*
23-25 *crux in marg.*   30 imperfecta *pro* imperfectam *Sowa*   perfecta
pro perfectam *Sowa*   32 reperi *cod.*, reperiri *Sowa*   35 a *add. super
scriptum*   40 *in marg.:* nota   41 quia *pro* quin *Sowa*   46 variatio
iterum *in marg.*

Since the joining is given, etc. Here is an example of the fivefold

figure ⬛ , and here is an example of the sixfold figure ⬛ .
These last two, however, are unusual and so they are unknown to quite a
large number of people, and although they are of little advantage,
nevertheless we make mention of them, because it is possible and easy to
notate them. But what is very easy to mention is that it should also be
noted that nobody should use figures that are placed without propriety
and are imperfect, nor figure them, except for the binary. And although
it is possible to notate them as regards the art, yet we never need them,
because they are equipollent in an equal number to figures that are
placed with propriety and are imperfect. And the treatise teaches* that
"no figure without propriety should ever be put where one can be put with
propriety," and so we completely eradicate those.

> (fol. 143v) **I do not know,**[1] **dear ones,**[2] **that any more should be**
> **ligated**[3] **without propriety.**
> 1 that is, I have no knowledge
> 2 that is, O cantors
> 3 that is, figured

It will be given to the opposite, etc. Having stated above the
notations and natures of the figures placed with propriety and without
proper propriety, and having laid out a suitable distinction between
them, here the author wants to broach the concept of figures notated by
means of the opposite of propriety, first giving a general rule about
their form or propriety, which is as follows: In every figure figured by
means of the opposite of propriety its propriety is that the first
written note of the ligature, whether it is perfect or imperfect, has a
line placed above its head on the left side ascending, whether the figure

ascends as here ⬛ , or descends as here ⬛ . But some
people,* following in the footsteps of certain of the ancients, have
continually notated the ternary figure that should be figured by means of
the opposite of propriety as without propriety and imperfect and even

sometimes as perfect only in the ascent, in this manner ⬛ , and
this is especially found in the "Alleluya" of "Hic Martinus." And being
thus devoid of the judgement of reason and blinded by a cloud of
ignorance they corrupted the proper signs of the figures and their
notations for an inconceivable reason. And so the footsteps of these
people should be very carefully avoided by the advanced, lest in the
manner of senseless people they seem to proceed as though blind. But
because there are more embroiderers than writers and madmen than singers
and also more stupid people than advanced ones, so with them one should
not insist with reasons, but one should proceed further, firmly observing
the arrangement or equipollence of the mode that is held in front of
one's hands. For no melody that is straightforwardly composed can be so
removed from the mode that it can not be proportionally reduced to it
through equipollences or accords placed there. And such an arrangement
must be observed in all dispositions of melodies up to the pause which is
called the end of the written notes; and after this pause another mode
and a new variation of equipollences will be able to be arranged
according to the wishes of those who are putting them down. And again

aequipollentia ad novi modi maneriem reducetur.

An alii punctus etc. Hic vult actor de figura binaria per oppositum figurata facere mentionem, de qua non inutile est in hoc loco tripliciter dubitare, primo utrum perfecta figurari debeat an etiam imperfecta, cum in ea usus contrarius habeatur, secundo utrum ipsa imperfecta inter perfectarum numerum debeat ordinari, tertio utrum in ea tempus unicum continente voces in proportione temporis sint aequales aut etiam inaequales; et si inaequales, utrum minus frustrum debeat praecedere et maius sussequi necessario aut pro voluntate mutua e converso, sicut quam plures asserere sunt reperti. Deinde utrum pro maiore brevi in aequipollentiis possint supponere, sicut quidam in suis artibus asserere non formidant, dicentes de ea: *prima autem minor semibrevis dicitur, secunda vero maior, vel e converso, ita quod ambae nisi solo tempore mensurantur, nisi quod aliquando pro altera brevi ponantur, tunc enim in ea duo tempora compleantur.*

Circa primum igitur dubitabile quaeritur, utrum perfecta debeat figurari. Et primo arguitur sic: perfectum est id a quo perfectio alia ducit originis fundamentum. Figurae per oppositum figuratae excedentes binariam perfectae possunt absque dubio reperiri. Ergo ipsa binaria erit perfecta nec immerito figuranda, cum sine ipsa aliae nullatenus possint esse, ipsa namque aliis fundamentum originis administrat. Item ad idem deficiente causa deficit et effectus, ipsa enim est causa aliarum, ut praeostensum est, ergo si non esset perfecta, aliae ab ea descendentes perfectae nullatenus possent esse. Sed perfectae saepius positae sunt et de iure, ergo et ipsa binaria perfecta tenebitur figurari.

Si istud concedatur, contra imperfectum est id quod imperfectionem de sui natura signat et quod pro imperfectione semper supponere fit repertum. Figura binaria est huiusmodi, ergo imperfecta merebitur figurari. Quomodo autem significet imperfectionem patet sic: voces ex quibus efficitur sunt ambae semibreves inaequales et sic imperfectae. Sed ex puris imperfectis de se naturaliter non potest perfectio resultare nec etiam generari, restat ergo quod figurari debeat imperfecta. Item, sicut dictum est supra, longitudo in figuris compositis causat perfectionem, sed ibi non est longitudinem reperire ergo neque perfectionem nec in forma nec etiam in effectu, quod concedimus, ad argumenta in oppositum respondentes.

Et primo ad primum quando dicitur sic: perfectum est id a quo perfectio etc., figura binaria est huiusmodi, ergo etc., dicimus, quod verum est id esse perfectum, a quo perfectio causatur etiam in figura composita et ubique. Sed quando dicitur: figura binaria per oppositum est huiusmodi, dicimus, quod falsum est semper. Nulla enim perfectio in figuris causari potest a vocibus imperfectis; quando postea dicebatur, quod sunt principia originalia aliarum et sic nisi essent perfectae, perfectas nullatenus generarent, dicendum est, quod perfectio non causatur a principiis rerum sed potius a fine. Unde quamvis ipsa binaria

----

2 **An alii punctus** *sine sublinea in cod.*   16 quare *pro* quaeritur *Sowa* 17 arguitur quod sic *cod.*   19 Igitur *pro* Ergo *Sowa*   29 signari *pro* figurari *Sowa*   Quatenus *pro* Quomodo *Sowa*   30 efficitur *add. super scriptum*   39 perfectum *add. super scriptum*   43 sunt *add. super scriptum*

such an equipollence will be reduced to the style of the new mode.

Look at the joinings there, etc. Here the author wishes to make mention of the binary figure that is figured by means of the opposite of propriety, and it is not useless in this place to have some doubts about it in three ways: firstly whether it should be figured as perfect or imperfect, since both, contrary, usages occur for it; secondly whether, being imperfect, it should be put in the category of perfect figures; and thirdly whether, since it contains a single unit of time, the notes in the proportion of the unit of time are equal or unequal; and if they are unequal, whether necessarily the smaller piece should precede and the larger follow, or whether it could be the reverse by mutual agreement, as very many are found to assert. Then there is the question as to whether they can substitute for a larger breve in equipollences, as some are not afraid to assert* in their treatises, and they say about it: "The first note is said to be a smaller semibreve, and the second a larger one, or the reverse, in such a way that both are only measured by one unit of time, unless sometimes they are put in the place of an alternate breve, in which case two units of time are filled up by it."

Concerning the first doubt, therefore, the question is whether it should be figured as perfect. And first it is argued as follows: A perfect thing is that from which some perfection draws the foundation of its origin. Figures figured by means of the opposite of propriety that exceed a binary can be found as perfect without doubt. Therefore the binary will be perfect and should deservedly be figured that way, since without it the others could in no way exist, for it provides the foundation of the origin for the others. Also in the same way if the cause is missing the effect is also missing, for this figure is the cause of the others, as has been shown above, and so if it were not perfect, the others descending from it could in no way be perfect. But they are often placed as perfect and rightly, so this binary also is held to be figured as perfect.

If that is conceded, on the other hand an imperfect thing is that which signifies imperfection from its own nature and which is always found to substitute for imperfection. The binary figure is of this kind, therefore it will deserve to be figured as imperfect. But how it may signify imperfection is clear from the following: The notes from which it is made up are both unequal semibreves and thus imperfect. But perfection can not naturally by itself result or be generated from pure imperfect things, and it therefore remains that it must be figured as imperfect. Also, as has been said above,* length in composite figures causes perfection; but one does not find length in it and therefore one does not find perfection in it, either in its form or in its effect, which we concede in our answer to the opposing arguments.

And firstly in response to the first argument which says: Perfect is that from which perfection etc., and: A binary figure is of this kind, therefore etc.; we say that it is true that that thing is perfect from which perfection is caused both in the composite figure and everywhere. But when it says that the binary figure by means of the opposite of propriety is of this kind, we say that that is always false. For no perfection in figures can be caused by imperfect notes; and when later it said that they are the original beginnings of the others and that thus unless they were perfect they would in no way generate perfect figures, it should be said that perfection is not caused by the beginnings of things but rather by their end. And so although this binary figure is

sit prior et originalis causa ordine numerorum, non tamen est causa
finalis in eis, a qua causa existente perfecta tales figurae perfectionem
sumere meruerunt.

Ad aliud, ubi dicitur deficiente causa etc., dicimus, quod verum est,
sed quando concluditur sic: si non esset perfecta etc., dicimus, quod
non est verum. Ad perfectionem enim aliarum non sequitur propter hoc
perfectio (fol. 144) in eadem, immo talis possibilitas sequeretur potius
e converso. Ipsa namque perfecta nullatenus potest esse, quia ex
partibus constituitur imperfectis, sicut patet supra. Unde cum non
10 perfecta modo aliquo possit esse, sequitur, quod perfectio in figuris
eiusdem differentiae causetur per adiunctum veniens aliunde, a quo
siquidem coadiuncto causatur, si sit perfectio in eisdem. Et hac de
causa non sequitur, quod si figurae eiusdem speciei seu differentiae
illam binariam excedentes sint perfectae, propter hoc illa binaria sit
perfecta. Super quo quidam etiam modernorum possunt et publice
reprehendi et sibi ipsis contrarii nuncupari, eo quod ipsam binariam
ascendendo protrahunt imperfectam, et perfectam communiter descendendo,
quare male, cum earum proportio et natura sit consimilis et aequalis in
signis, numero et mensura; ex quo sequitur, quod forma talium in figura,
20 si imperfecta usu et arte poni debeat ascendendo, similiter descendendo
poni vel protrahi tenebitur imperfecta, licet usus non sane intelligentium perfectam protrahat descendendo.

Ad quaestionem quae posset hic fieri, quare de ipsa, cum protrahi
debeat imperfecta, facit actor mentionem in numero perfectarum, dicimus,
quod hoc fuit duplici ratione. Una est, eo quod est causa originalis
aliarum signo eiusdem differentiae signatarum. Secunda est, ne videretur
in ordinatione numeri praecavisse numerum ternarium vel quaternarium
binario praeponendo.

Ad aliud etiam quod posset quaeri, utrum voces in ea sint in
30 quantitate consimiles et mensura, quod a provectis in arte causatoribus
audivimus confiteri, contra quos talem praetendimus rationem: ista
figura valet solummodo rectam brevem; quam quidem brevem si contingat in
frustra dividi vel discerni, aut dividetur in duo vel in tria et non in
plus secundum vocem humanam. Unde si contingat eam in tria frustra
dividere, erunt in quantitate ita minima quod non erunt amplius
dividenda. Ex quo frustra esse aequalia proportionaliter arbitrantur,
quia nulla eorum potest amplius in instrumentis naturalibus minorari. Si
ergo in tria minima aequalia dividatur, in duo aequalia proportionaliter
non poterit minorari vel etiam resecari, quia si sic oporteret quod
40 frustrum illius ternarii medium in duo aequalia secaretur et sic minutum
proportionaliter frustris aliis incorporaretur, quod nullatenus potest
esse. Restat ergo quod si recta brevis vel suum aequippollens in duo
frustra dividatur, necesse est illa esse inaequalia in mensura. Sed
figura binaria per oppositum figurata rectae brevi proportionaliter
aequippollet, ergo frustra in ea inaequalia sunt habenda, quod verum est.

De quorum dispositione contingit similiter dubitare, eo quod quidam

----

2 exeunte *pro* existente *Sowa*   5 quando *add. super scriptum*
11 causetur perfectio per *cod.*   14 perfectae quod propter *cod.*
15 publice *add. super scriptum*   16 sic *pro* sibi *Sowa*   21 talis *pro*
vel *Sowa*   21-22 intellective *pro* intelligentium *Sowa*   35 in
quantitate *add. super scriptum*   41-42 quod nullatenus potest esse *add.
in marg.*   43 dividantur *pro* dividatur *cod.*

the prior and original cause in the order of numbers, yet it is not the final cause in them, and it is from the existence of this perfect cause that such figures deserve to take their perfection.

To the other statement that says: If the cause is missing etc., we say that it is true, but when it ends thus: If it were not perfect etc., we say that it is not true. For because of the perfection of the others it does not follow that there is perfection (fol. 144) in this; rather such a possibility would follow from the reverse. For indeed this can in no way be perfect, because it is made up of imperfect parts, as is clear above. And so since it can not be perfect in any way, it follows that perfection may be caused in figures of the same distinction by means of something joined to them that comes from elsewhere, and indeed it is from this that is joined to them that it is caused, if there is perfection in them. And for this reason it does not follow, that if figures of the same appearance or distinction exceeding that binary figure are perfect, for this reason that binary figure is perfect. And on this subject indeed certain of the moderns can also be publicly censured and thus termed contrary to themselves, because they notate this binary figure ascending as imperfect, and descending generally as perfect, which is bad, since their proportion and nature are similar and equal in their signs, number, and measure; from which it follows that the form of such figures, if it should be put as imperfect according to usage and art ascending, will be held to be put or notated as similarly imperfect descending, although the usage of not very intelligent people notates it descending as perfect.

To the question which could be raised here as to why the author makes mention of this figure in the category of perfect figures when it should be notated as imperfect, we say that this is for two reasons. One is that it is the original cause of the others with the sign of the same distinction as those figures that are signified. The second is lest in the numerical arrangement it seem that the ternary or fourfold number had been left out by putting the binary first.

Also regarding the other question which could be raised, as to whether the notes in that figure are similar in quantity and measure, which we have heard being claimed by those who are advanced and active in the art, we put forward the following reason against them: This figure is worth only a correct breve, and if indeed it happens that this breve is divided or separated into pieces, it will be divided either into two or three, and not more, according to the capacities of the human voice. And so if it happens that it is divided into three pieces, they will be so minimal in quantity that they will not be able to be divided further. And from this the pieces are judged to be proportionally equal, because none of them can be made any smaller on natural instruments. If therefore it is divided into three equal minimal parts, it will not be able to be made smaller or cut up proportionally into two equal parts, because if it were thus necessary that the middle piece of that ternary figure were cut into two equal parts, being thus diminished it would be incorporated proportionally by the other pieces, which can in no way happen. It remains therefore that if a correct breve or its equipollent is divided into two pieces, it is necessary that they are unequal in measure. But the binary figure figured by means of the opposite of propriety is proportionally equipollent to a correct breve, and therefore its pieces must be considered as unequal, which is true.

About the disposition of them it happens similarly that there are

dicunt in ista figura minorem semibrevem praecedere et maiorem sussequi
vel penitus e converso pro mutua cantantium voluntate. Et isti opinioni
videtur maxima pars canentium adhaerere. Unde magister Lambertus de tali
figura dicit: *prima autem semibrevis minor dicitur, secunda vero maior,*
vel e converso, ita quod ambae nisi solo tempore mensurentur, quod
contradici potest multiplici ratione. Una est, quia sic videretur unum
corpus indifferenter pro alio reperiri et e converso, quod non potest
fieri. Unum namque corpus non potest in alium transmutari neque idem
esse, quod aliud erat prius. Item si talis transmutatio esset vera,
10 esset habenda inter corpora aequalia in quantitate et non inter
inaequalia. Ista sunt inaequalia in quantitate temporis et mensura,
quare dicimus unum non posse transmutari in aliud nec pro eo reperiri nec
etiam loco sui, eo quod saepius inter cantores varios maxima vocum
discrepantia posset super hoc generari, quia dum unus maiorem semibrevem
proferret, forte alius minorem in aequipollentia provulgaret, vel etiam
in eodem cantu et eodem sono idem posset accidere inter eos et sic
cacephationem id est vocum discrepantiam generans, quod est vitium
evitandum. Item si verum esset, ista transmutatio posset similiter
reperiri in omnibus figuris aliis per oppositum figuratis, quemadmodum in
20 binaria. Quod non potest esse, nec est etiam opinandum, quare similiter
nec illa. Item si verum esset, manifeste posset declarari per semibreves
hoquetatas, inter quas nonquam maior praecedere fit reperta, quod
reperiretur saepius si talis transmutatio esset vera, ideoque
impossibilem arbitramur. Item hoc esset contra naturam omnium aliarum
figurarum, in quibus vox quaelibet locum sibi proprium atque sonum absque
transpositione aliqua possidet et importat. Item alibi dicit ars:
brevium et semibrevium idem est in ordinatione iudicium. Sed ubicumque
minor brevis et maior conveniunt in figura vel una post alteram
ordinatur, semper minor praecedit et maior sussequitur, et nullatenus e
30 converso, quare similiter conversionem semibrevium pro eodem tempore
supponentium credimus esse nullam.

Ad quaestionem quae posset fieri, utrum possint supponere pro maiore
brevi in aequippollentia, sicut quidam asserunt <in> suis libris,
dicimus, quod non est sane talibus adhaerendum, quia si sic supponerent,
a sua natura propria et officio deviarent, et sic inaequales in
aequippollentia naturaliter pro aequalibus supponerent. Et pars pro
toto, id est imperfectum pro perfecto, poni videretur ratione seu
necessitate aliqua non cogente, quare sic facere non credimus esse verum.
Ideoque loco talis aequipollentiae figuram sine proprietate binariam et
40 imperfectam ponimus, sicut infra declarabitur suo loco.

Opposito[1] **dabitur tractum sursumque**[2] **potitur,**
1 id est, figurae datae per oppositum
2 id est, supra caput positum
Fronte[1] **per ascensum vel descensum**[2] **noto tensum.**[3]

----

1 illa *pro* ista *Sowa*   17 generarens *pro* generans *cod.*, generantes *Sowa*
est *add. super scriptum, om. Sowa*   23 veri *pro* vera *Sowa*
28 communiunt *pro* conveniunt *Sowa*

doubts, because some people say* that in that figure the smaller
semibreve precedes and the larger one follows or the reverse according to
the mutual wishes of those who are singing. And it seems that the
largest number of singers agrees with that view. And Master Lambertus
says* about that figure: "The first semibreve is said to be smaller, and
the second larger, or the reverse, in such a way that both may be
measured by a single unit of time;" which can be contradicted for many
reasons. One is that in this way one body would seem to be found in
place of another indifferently, and the reverse, which can not happen.
For indeed one body can not be changed into another, nor can something be
the same, when before it was different. Also if such a change were true
it would have to occur between bodies that are equal in quantity and not
between bodies that are unequal. These are unequal in quantity of time
and in measure, and so we say that one can not be changed into another
nor can it be found instead of it or indeed in its place, because the
greatest discord of voices could often be generated on this account
between different singers, because while one might be performing a larger
semibreve, perhaps the other might bring forth a smaller semibreve in
equipollence; or even in the same melody and on the same sound the same
could happen between them, thus generating a cacophony, that is a discord
of the voices, which is a vice that should be avoided. Also if it were
true, that change could similarly be found in all other figures figured
by means of the opposite of propriety, in the same way as in the binary.
But that can not be, nor is it even conceivable, and so similarly nor can
that. Again if it were true, it could clearly be stated by means of the
semibreves in hocket, amongst which the larger semibreve is never found
to precede, which would be found often if such a change were true, and so
we judge it to be impossible. Also this would be against the nature of
all the other figures, in which each note possesses a place that is its
own and conveys a sound without being transferred. Also the treatise
says elsewhere that one should judge the same way about the arrangement
of both breves and semibreves. But whenever the smaller breve and the
larger breve come together in a figure, or one is arranged after the
other, the smaller one always precedes and the larger one follows and
never the reverse, and so similarly we believe that the inversion of
semibreves that are substituted for the same unit of time is void.

To the question which could be raised, whether they can substitute
for a larger breve in equipollence, as some people assert* in their
books, we say that it is not proper to comply with such things, because
if they would substitute in this way, they would deviate from their own
nature and function, and thus notes that are naturally unequal in their
equipollence would substitute for equal notes. And a part would seem to
be put for the whole, that is imperfect for perfect, without the
compulsion of any reason or necessity, and so we do not believe it to be
a true thing to do this. Therefore in the place of such equipollence we
put a binary figure that is without propriety and imperfect as will be
stated below in the right place.

It will be given to the opposite[1] **and receives a line above,**[2]
1 that is, to the figure given by means of the opposite of
propriety
2 that is, placed above the head
With the front[1] **being known through the stretching out**[3] **of the
ascent or descent.**[2]

1 id est, anteriori parte

2 id est, tam ascendendo quam descendendo

3 id est, appositum

(fol. 144v) **An[1] alii punctus sit, ibi sic respice iunctus.**

1 pro utrum; regula est, quod omnis figura binaria et per oppositum figurata duas semibreves continet inaequales

Semibreves[1] esse tales reor esse necesse.

1 subaudi inaequales; prima namque minor semibrevis dicitur et altera maior. Exemplum earum patet hic ▮▮ .

10   **Si tribus haec detur lex,[1] ultima longa[2] vocetur**

1 id est, regula

2 duorum temporum

Exemplum istius figurae ternariae patet hic ▮▮▮▮ .

Cum perfecta datur, si non,[1] brevis illa[2] locatur.

1 perfecta

2 ultima sive

Si prius explores sunt semibrevesque priores.

Quatuor etc. Hic vult actor aliam inserere regulam pro doctrina, usu
20 et actoritate cantantium communiter approbatam seu etiam roboratam,
scilicet figuram quaternariam et perfectam per oppositum figuratam
figurari ac specialiter reperiri sub natura et dispositione organi
specialis. Hoc est dictu: ipsa figura quaternaria figurata per
oppositum et perfecta semper in dispositione organi specialis nasciscitur
sibi esse; id est, quotienscumque in cantu aliquo ordinatur, supra
burdonem tenoris aedificari cernitur a natura et sub dispositione organi
specialis, hac de causa dicitur se habere, quia quo ad ultimam et
penultimam rectae proportionis metas excedere non veretur, quod est
proprium organi specialis. Cognoscitur namque organum speciale per
30 penultimam et ultimam et per concordantiam et maxime per figuram, et eo
quod procedit secundum modum non tamen rectum vel sub affecta proportione
mensurae traditum; nam per eum longitudo vel brevitas sub recta
proportionis habitudine non traditur observanda, nisi secundum quod
cantans in aedificatione armonica suae voci melius viderit expedire.
Sub qua siquidem aedificatione ista maxime inter figuras alias saepius
habet locum. In ipsa namque licet penultima sit brevis a natura, quia
non est reducibilis ad suum ternarium, sicut aliqui crediderunt,
similiter et ultima longa, tamen in eis non est recta proportio
brevitatis vel longitudinis attributa, ideoque ipsa ante finem punctorum
40 et maxime supra burdonem in cantibus organicis saepius ordinatur, et
etiam in multis locis aliis pro voluntate mutua imponentium habet esse.
Huius autem repraesentatio pateat hiis exemplis ▮▮ ▮▮ ▮▮ ▮ .

----

8 inaequale *pro* inaequales *cod., corr.* Sowa   11 id est, regula *om.*
Sowa   15 perfecta *om. Sowa*   16 ultima sive *super* **brevis** *in cod.*
21 quaternariam perfectam et per *Sowa*   et *add. super scriptum*
perfectam *add. in marg.*   27 hac de tam *pro* hac de causa *Sowa*

1 that is, the front part
2 that is, both ascending and descending
3 that is, the situation
(fol. 144v) **Look at the joinings there, to see if**[1] **there is a written note for the other one.**
1 instead of: whether; the rule is that every figure that is binary and figured by means of the opposite of propriety contains two unequal semibreves
I think it is necessary that the semibreves[1] **be of that kind.**
1 understand: unequal; for indeed the first is said to be a smaller semibreve and the second a larger. An example of them is given here ▮▮ .
If this law[1] **is given for three, let the last one be called a long,**[2]
1 that is, the rule
2 of two units of time
An example of this ternary figure is given here ▮▮▮▮ .
When it is given as perfect; if not,[1] **that**[2] **one is placed as a breve.**
1 perfect
2 last
If you investigate first, the first notes are semibreves.

Four, etc. Here the author wishes to introduce another rule which is generally approved or even confirmed for the principle, use, and authority of singers, which is that there is a fourfold figure that is perfect and figured by means of the opposite of propriety that is figured and found specifically under the nature and disposition of special organum. That is to say: The fourfold figure that is figured by means of the opposite of propriety and is perfect always arises and occurs in the disposition of special organum; that is, whenever it is arranged in some melody, it is perceived to be built above the drone of the tenor from the nature and under the disposition of special organum, and it is said to occur in this way because as regards the last and penultimate notes it is not afraid to exceed the boundaries of correct proportion, which is a property of special organum. For indeed special organum is recognized by its penultimate and last notes and by concord and especially by figure, and because it proceeds according to a mode that is not a correct one or is delivered under a changed proportion of measure. For through this mode length or brevity are not delivered with the correct condition of proportion being observed, except according to that which the singer in the harmonic building of his voice has seen to be useful and better. And indeed in that building process this figure particularly from amongst the other figures more often holds a place. For indeed in this figure the penultimate note may be a breve naturally, because it is not reducible to its ternary form, as some have believed, and similarly also the last note is long. Nevertheless the correct proportion of brevity or length is not allocated in them, and so this figure is often arranged before the end of the written notes and especially over the drone in organal melodies, and also occurs in many other places according to the mutual wishes of those who are putting them down. But let the representation of this be clear from these examples

▮▮ ▮▮ ▮▮ ▮ .

Alia regula data per modum doctrinae:

> **Quatuor hoc tractu perfectas[1] ut fit in actu**

1 id est, per oppositum; exemplum earum patet hic

> **Punxi,[1] praesente sed asilo[2] dupla[3] tenente.[4]**

1 id est, figuravi
2 id est, burdone
3 id est, organum duplex vel speciale
4 doctrina est

> **Huius[1] qui quinque plus fert ita,[2] dogma relinque.[3]**

1 sive actoris
2 id est, qui dicit quinque sic protrahi vel saltem plus quinque
3 id est, evita

Modo subiungit rationem, quare figurae per oppositum non debent excedere quinque in figura:

> **Iunctas nolo dari sine proprietate, locari**

Quasi diceret: nonquam debet poni aliqua figura sine proprietate, ubi potest poni cum proprietate:

> **Si possint a te melius cum proprietate.**

Punctus praecedens etc. Exequto de figuris et proprietatibus omnium figurarum ligatarum et de earum quantitatibus et naturis, et hoc secundum varias differentias a parte principii, hic vult actor assignare earum differentias quo ad finem, dicens, quod duae sunt solummodo differentiae earundem. Omnes namque aut sunt perfectae aut etiam imperfectae, super quo talis regula est habenda: illa figura perfecta dicitur figura, cuius ultimus punctus stat perpendiculariter supra penultimum in ascendente circa finem, sicut patet hic   , vel cuius ultimus punctus adiungitur directe penultimo in figura descendente circa finem, sicut patet hic   , et in consimilibus exemplis per libri seriem declaratis.

Et notandum, quod figurae quandoque bene possunt habere duplicem ascensum et duplicem descensum, vel unum ascensum et unum descensum, vel penitus e converso, vel possunt haberi per continuum ascensum vel continuum descensum. Exemplum ascensus continui patet hic   , et in consimilibus, exemplum descensus continui patet hic   , et sic de similibus. In aliis autem figuris potest esse unus ascensus et unus descensus, vel e converso. Exemplum prioris patet hic   , exemplum alterius sic   . Exemplum aliarum figurarum in quibus potest haberi duplex ascensus vel duplex descensus datur hic, et primo de duplici ascensu sic   , de duplici descensu sic   . Unde notandum est, quod quemadmodum secundus punctus ligaturae facit ascensum vel descensum a parte principii, ita et ultimus punctus respectu penultimi a parte

----

3 *exemplum datum est supra*   17 decet *pro* debet *Sowa*   33-34 duplicem ascensum et duplicem ascensum *cod., corr. Sowa*   35 continum ascensum *cod., corr. Sowa*

Another rule given in the manner of a principle:

> **Four perfect notes[1] with this line, as occurs in actuality,**

1 that is, with opposite propriety;
here is an example of them

> **Have I written,[1] but with the present refuge[2] holding[4] two things.[3]**

1 that is, I have figured
2 that is, the drone
3 that is, double or special organum
4 it is the principle

> **Leave[3] the doctrine of him[1] who brings in more than five in this way.[2]**

1 the author
2 that is, who says that five can be notated in this way, or at least more than five
3 that is, avoid

Now he adds a reason why figures by means of the opposite of propriety must not exceed five notes in the figure:

> **I do not wish notes that are joined to be given without propriety,**

He means to say that no figure should ever be put without propriety, when it can be put with propriety:

> **If they can be placed better by you with propriety.**

If the preceding note, etc. Having described the figures and proprieties of all ligated figures and their quantities and natures, and this according to their different distinctions with respect to their beginning, here the author wishes to lay out their distinctions as regards their end, saying that they have only two distinctions. For indeed all of them are either perfect or imperfect, and on this subject the following rule obtains: That figure is said to be a perfect figure whose last written note stands perpendicularly above the penultimate written note in the ascent at the end, as is shown here , or whose last written note is joined directly to the penultimate written note in the figure as it descends at the end, as is shown here and in similar examples stated through the sequence of the book.

And it should be noted that figures can sometimes properly have a double ascent and a double descent, or a single ascent and a single descent, or completely the reverse, or can occur by means of continuous ascent or continuous descent. An example of continuous ascent is shown here and in similar examples, an example of continuous descent is shown here and in this way for similar examples. In other figures however there can be a single ascent and a single descent, or the reverse. An example of the former is shown here , an example of the latter here . An example of the other figures in which there can occur a double ascent or double descent is given here, firstly the double ascent , and then the double descent . And from this it should be noted that just as the second written note of the ligature makes its ascent or descent with respect to the beginning, so also does the last written note regarding the penultimate with respect to the end.

finis. De descensu vel ascensu mediocri non est mentio facienda.

(fol. 145) Regula est, quasi vellet 'dicere: in quacumque figura
composita vel ligata ultimus punctus
Punctus precedens si supremo si bene cedens
directe stat vel adiungitur penultimo, ista figura dicitur esse

perfecta. Exemplum perfectarum patet hic: ▌▐▪◣▪ .
Sit, tunc punctorum perfecta figura fit horum.

10   Regula de imperfectis talis est: in quacumque figura ultimus punctus
oblique protrahitur vel
Obliquoque modo cum supremum tibi nodo,
ultimus cum penultimo, talis dicitur esse imperfecta. Exemplum

imperfectarum patet hic: ▪◣◢▪ ▐ .
Si bene censetur tunc imperfecta vocetur.

Voceque composita etc. Assignata superius differentia inter figuras
perfectas et imperfectas quae finem faciunt figurarum, ideo actor in hoc
20   loco vult de plica in figuris compositis facere mentionem. Quae quidem
plica in omni figura, sive sit simplex sive composita, sive perfecta sive
etiam imperfecta, extremum latus possidet, id est dextrum, tam in signo
etiam quam effectu. Possibile namque est ipsam ponere aut reperire in
omni genere figurarum, in quibus semper supremam soni sibi accipit
portionem. In quibus siquidem potest dupliciter ordinari, aut secundum
ascensum aut secundum descensum, sicut patuit in tractatu simplicium, ubi
declaratum fuit, quid sit plica et quae sit eius repraesentatio sive
forma, maxime in simplicibus, ideoque non licet hic talia repetere sed
supplere.
30   In hoc loco potest quaeri, quare hic facit actor de plica inter
compositas mentionem tam perfectas quam etiam imperfectas, postea qua de
causa in figuris perfectis, in quibus ultimus punctus altior est
penultimo, ratione plicae ibi positae vel adiunctae, talis figura semper
figuretur imperfecta, cum perfecta remaneat illa, in qua ultimus punctus
inferior est penultimo, licet ei plica similiter adiungatur, quamvis
praedictae figurae sint eiusdem proprietatis et naturae.
Circa primum procedamus: quaeritur quare actor de plica in figuris
compositis hic faciat mentionem, cum in fine se habeat figurarum, videtur
enim quod ibi locum non habeat competentem, cum competenter non sit adhuc
40   satisfactum de omni genere figurarum, quia actor adhuc imperfectarum
notitiam nullatenus declaravit. Et sic videtur, quod de plica in eis
adhuc mentionem facere minime teneatur, cum prius sit agendum de
essentiali quam de suo accidente.
Respondemus dicentes, quod quaestio rationabiliter procedit, tamen
actor consideravit quod de figuris ligatis ad invicem et perfectis
satisfecerat competenter, quare de plica in eis habita immediate se
voluit expedire, cum ex eis causetur, in quibus principaliter habet esse
tanquam accidens in subiecto, quare de ea actor hic debuit facere

----
3 quacumcumque *cod.*   5 **(supremo) si (bene)** *add. super scriptum;* **sed**
Sowa   10 quociensconque *pro* quacumque *Sowa*   13-15 imperfecta exempla
patent hic exemplum *cod.*   21 *super* [[simplex]] ligata *cod.*   37 quare
pro quaeritur *Sowa*   39 vel *pro* ibi *Sowa*

No mention need be made about the descent or ascent of the middle note.

(fol. 145) The rule is, as he means to say: In whichever composite or ligated figure the last note
If the preceding note yields properly to the last one,
stands or is joined directly to the penultimate, that figure is said to be perfect. An example of perfect figures is given here:

Then a perfect figure is made out of these notes.
The rule about imperfect figures is as follows: Whenever in a figure the last note is notated obliquely, or
And when I tie the last one for you in an oblique manner,
the last note is notated with the penultimate, such a figure is said to be imperfect. An example of imperfect figures is given here:

If it is considered well done, then let it be called imperfect.

And the plica, etc. Having laid out above the difference between the perfect and the imperfect figures which make the end of the figures, therefore in this place the author wishes to make mention of the plica in composite figures. And indeed this plica possesses the last side, that is the right side, of the figure both in its sign and also in its effect in every figure, whether it is single or composite or perfect or imperfect. For indeed it is possible to place it or find it in all genera of figures, in which it always takes for itself the last portion of the sound. And in these indeed it can be arranged in two ways, either according to ascent or according to descent, as has been made clear in the tract on single figures, where it was stated what a plica is and what its representation or form is, especially in single figures, and so it is not permitted to repeat these things here but to add to them.

In this place it can be asked why the author makes mention of the plica here among composite figures both perfect and imperfect, and also why, in perfect figures in which the last note is higher than the penultimate, because of the plica that is placed or added there, such a figure is always figured as imperfect, when that one remains perfect in which the last note is lower than the penultimate, although a plica is similarly joined to it, and although the aforementioned figures are of the same propriety and nature.

Let us proceed with the first question: It is asked why the author makes mention of the plica here amongst the composite figures, when it occurs at the end of the figures. For it seems that it does not have a suitable place here, since sufficient and suitable explanation has not yet been made about all genera of figures, because the author has still in no way stated the concept of imperfect figures. And thus it seems that it is not at all relevant to make mention of the plica amongst these, since first one should deal with the essential before the extraneous.

We say in response that the question proceeds rationally, and yet the author has decided that he has sufficiently and suitably made explanation about figures that are ligated to each other and are perfect, and so he wanted to discuss immediately the plica that occurs in them, since it is a result of them, and it occurs principally in them like an

mentionem. Et quia plica tam in perfectis quam in imperfectis eandem
proprietatem in signo retinet et natura, ideo causa brevitatis, et quia
sic facere debuit, de plica tam perfectarum quam imperfectarum se expedit
una vice. Item formam perfectarum et imperfectarum immediate superius
declaravit, quare immediate plicae in eis habitae notitiam disserere
tenebatur.

Si quaeratur postea quare omnes puncti ascendentes, quos plica
tangit, protrahi debeant imperfecti, licet perfectos de iure protrahere
deberemus, cum perfectis descendentibus aequippolleant in officio et
10   natura, solummodo perfecti esse nullatenus potuerunt impedimento duplici
hoc obstante. Unum est, quoniam si tales puncti essent perfecti, plica
si eis adderetur, aut poneretur in dextro latere aut etiam sinistro. Si
dicatur in dextro, quod est proprium plicae, contra licet ibi plica
posset protrahi ascendendo, non tamen ibi esse poterat descendendo, quia
non est ibi locum proprium vel vacuum reperire. Et non est ponere plicam
in aliqua figura, quin in ea possit dupliciter ordinari ascendendo
videlicet aut etiam descendendo, ideoque dextrum latus non potuit in
talibus optinere. Item nec debuit, quia locum interiorem non potest
aprehendere; sed in talibus figuris dextrum latus est interius et nonquam
20   exterius, quare ibi plica nullatenus potest esse. Item nec in sinistro,
quia hoc esset contra naturam suam, in figuris compositis vel ligatis
dextrum namque latus retinet a natura. Item nec ibi esse debuit, quia
nonquam habet sedem in parte anteriori sed in posteriori, sicut supra
declaratum est. Sed sinistra pars in talibus est anterior et prior, ideo
ipsam non potuit retinere, quia a sua natura posteriorem locum occupat
tam in signo proprio quam in sono, ex quo ergo sic esse vel sic non
potuit. Necessarium fuit tales punctos protrahi imperfectos, ad hoc ut
plica in eis locum debitum optineret et sic (fol. 145v) patet causa seu
ratio, quare sic oportuit ordinare.

30   Notandum est ergo, quod plica in talibus eandem naturam retinet et
effectum, quem retinent perfectae in forma perfectionis propria et
natura. Sed quia ingens dubitatio posset esse, quae esset differentia
assignanda inter tales imperfectas in forma, licet perfectae maneant in
effectu, et inter imperfectas in forma, officio et natura, cum eandem
formam et signum inferant hinc et inde, respondemus, quod licet in forma
non differant, differunt tamen in dispositione locorum; ubi autem habet
esse perfecta talis in effectu et non in forma, ibi imperfecta in forma
et effectu nullatenus est habenda, nec etiam e converso, quia nonquam
inter perfectas figuras debet plicari aliqua imperfecta in effectu, nec
40   etiam inter imperfectas naturaliter debet imperfecta ratione plicae
solummodo ordinari, licet formam necessario induat earundem. Et sic
inter tales modus et ordinatio figurarum provectis et sibi praecaventibus
notitiam facient manifestam, sine quibus plica nonquam alicubi poterit
inveniri. Et sic et non aliter est tale dubium removendum.

- - - - - - - - - -

4 et imperfectarum *add. in marg.*   12 addereretur *cod.*   etiam *add.*
super scriptum   20 ibi *add. super scriptum, om. Sowa*   39 decet *pro*
debet *Sowa*   40 decet *pro* debet *Sowa*   41 earundem *super* [[aliarum]]
cod., earum *pro* earundem *Sowa*   42 figurarum [[inter tales]] provectis
cod.

accidental property in a subject, and so the author ought to make mention of it here. And because the plica keeps the same propriety in its sign and nature, both in perfect figures and in imperfect ones, so for reasons of brevity, and because he ought to do this, he discusses the plica of both perfect and imperfect figures in immediate succession. Also he has stated the form of perfect and imperfect figures immediately above, and so it was decided to expound the concept of the plica that occurs in them immediately.

If then it is asked why all ascending written notes which the plica touches should be notated as imperfect, although rightly we should notate them as perfect, since they are equipollent to perfect descending notes in function and nature, we say only that they could in no way be perfect because of these two hindrances standing in the way: One is that if such notes were perfect, if a plica were added to them, it would either be placed on the right side or on the left. If it is said to be on the right side, which is proper for a plica, the obstacle is that although a plica could be notated there ascending, it could not be notated there descending, because that is not the proper place and there is no room to be found there. And one should not put a plica in any figure unless it can be arranged in two ways, that is ascending and descending, and so the right side could not be used in such notes. Also it should not, because it can not take a place on the inside of the figure; but in such figures the right side is on the inside and never on the outside, and so there can in no way be a plica there. Also it can not be on the left side either because this would be against its nature, for indeed in composite or ligated figures it keeps the right side by its nature. Also it should not be there either, because it never has its position at the front part but at the back part, as has been stated above. But the left part in such notes is at the front and first, and so it could not keep that part, because by its nature it occupies the back place both in its own sign and in the sound, and as a result therefore it could not be either in this way or that. It was necessary therefore to notate such notes as imperfect, so that the plica in them would obtain its requisite place, and that is (fol. 145v) the cause or reason why it had to be arranged this way.

It should be noted therefore that the plica in such notes keeps the same nature and effect which perfect figures keep in the proper form of their perfection and in their nature. But because a huge doubt could arise as to what distinction should be laid out between such figures that are imperfect in their form, although they remain perfect in their effect, and those that are imperfect in their form, function, and nature, since both the former and the latter present the same form and sign, we answer that although they do not differ in their form, they nonetheless differ in the disposition of their places; for in the place where such a figure occurs that is perfect in effect but not in form, in that place one that is imperfect in both form and effect should never occur, nor the reverse, because never should any figure that is imperfect in effect be plicated among perfect figures, nor should a figure that is imperfect only by reason of its plica be arranged among figures that are naturally imperfect, although it may take on their form by necessity. And thus between such figures their mode and arrangement will make their concept clear to those who are advanced and take precautions for themselves, and without these things the plica could never be found anywhere. And in this way and in no other should such doubt be removed.

Quia vero in omni genere figurarum potest plica dupliciter ordinari, ascendendo videlicet et etiam descendendo, ideo de ipsius dispositione naturaliter in perfectis, licet aliquae earum, ut supradictum est, in forma appareant imperfectae, sicut discussum est, exemplificandum est et primo de imperfectis in forma et non in effectu, ad hoc ut perfectarum naturam et effectum sapere videantur. Exemplum plicae ascendentis et

descendentis in talibus patet hic ⟨musical figures⟩ . Exemplum eiusdem plicae in figuris perfectis, in quibus ultimus punctus inferior

10 est penultimo, patet hic ⟨musical figures⟩ , et sic de similibus perfectis, licet sint sine proprietate vel per oppositum figuratae, sive figurae sint ternariae vel quaternariae vel ultra.

Praeostensis exemplis in perfectis officio et natura, licet forma in aliquibus sit repugnans, exemplum plicae in figuris imperfectis naturaliter et officio et natura pateat hic tam ascendendo quam descendendo. In figuris ascendentibus, in quibus plica potest dupliciter

ordinari sic ⟨musical figures⟩ . Exemplum earundem in figuris, in
20 quibus ultimus punctus inferior est penultimo, patere potest hic

⟨musical figures⟩ . Et sic de omnibus figuris imperfectis, quoquo modo se habeant, exemplificandum est. Hiis visis ad litteram breviter sit accessus.

(fol. 146) Quasi diceret: plica cuilibet figurae compositae licentialiter et secundum artem poterit coadiungi:
    Voceque composita plica sit quacumque petita.
    Iuncturasque[1] premis[2] cauda[3] nunc sponte[4] supremis.[5]
30   1 id est, figuras compositas
    2 O cantor sive
    3 illius plicae
    4 id est, spontanea voluntate
    5 sive vocibus
    Quas[1] secat[2] inque sono vario plica, tunc ubi pono.
    1 supremas sive
    2 id est, dividit; regula est: plica nihil aliud est quam signum dividens sonum in sono diverso
Hic assignat actor differentiam plicarum inter simplices voces et
40 compositas:
    Cuique plicae iunctae reliquis tractum dabo, punctae
    Per se[1] nunc duplex[2] tractus sit, nunc ibi simplex.[3]
    1 id est, per unicam vocem
    2 et praecipue descendendo
    3 et praecipue ascendendo
Hic dat actor doctrinam de plica in figuris compositis ascendendo,

----

2 ipsavis *pro* ipsius *Sowa*   3 earum *add. super scriptum*   8 in talibus *add. in marg.*   9 plicae [[in natura]] in figuris *cod.*   14 Pretensis *pro* Preostensis *Sowa*   19 *ultima figura deest Sowa*   23 quoque *pro* quoquo *Sowa*   24 breviter [[licet glosulae]] sit *cod.*   27 arte *pro* artem *cod.*

But because in all genera of figures the plica can be arranged in two
ways,* that is to say both ascending and descending, therefore its
natural disposition in perfect figures should be exemplified, although
some of them, as has been said above, appear imperfect in form, as has
been discussed. And firstly we should exemplify the figures that are
imperfect in form and not in effect so that they seem to partake of the
nature and effect of perfect figures. An example of the plica both
ascending and descending in these figures is given here

. An example of the same plica in perfect figures
in which the last note is lower than the penultimate is given here

, and in this way for similar perfect figures
although they are without propriety or figured by means of the opposite
of propriety, whether the figures are ternary or fourfold or more.

Having already shown examples in figures that are perfect in function
and nature, although in some of them the form may be contrary, let us
give an example of both an ascending and a descending plica in figures
that are naturally imperfect both in function and nature. In ascending
figures, in which the plica can be arranged in two ways, like this

. An example of the same ones in figures in
which the last note is lower than the penultimate can be seen here

. And in this way all imperfect figures,
whichever way they occur, should be exemplified. Now that these things
have been seen, let us go on briefly to the text.

(fol. 146) He means to say that the plica will be able to be added to
any composite figure freely and according to the art:
And the plica may be sought by any composite note.
And you mark[2] the joinings[1] with the tail,[3] and sometimes
freely[4] at the last ones.[5]
1 that is, the composite figures
2 O cantor
3 of the plica
4 that is, with free will
5 notes
Sometimes when I put it, the plica cuts[2] them[1] into different
sounds.
1 the last notes
2 that is, divides; the rule is: The plica is nothing other
than a sign that divides a sound into different sounds
Here the author lays out the difference between plicas on single and
composite notes:
To any plica joined to others I shall give a line, but for one
written
By itself[1] there is sometimes a double line,[2] sometimes a single
one.[3]
1 that is, by means of a single note
2 and especially descending
3 and especially ascending
Here the author gives the principle of the ascending plica in

dicens: regula est: omnes puncti ascendentes
   Scandentes punctos oblique vult dare cunctos,
quos plica tangit, debent oblique regulariter et artificialiter
figurari:
   Lex plica quos tangit, quam nulla parenthesis angit.[1]
   1 id est, differentia interponitur
   Omnibus aequalis[1] extremis[2] esto[3] sodalis,
   1 id est, non diversa
   2 sive tam perfectis quam imperfectis quo ad formam suam solum et
10   non quo ad effectum
   3 sive plica
Ecce dicit, quod plicae virtus seu differentia inter tales per modum
et figurarum aequipollentiam cognoscetur:
   Lexque figurarum dabit illic nosse plicarum.

   Binas perfectas etc. Expedita serie figurarum in suo genere
perfectarum et plicarum similiter, eo quod finem possident figurarum, in
hoc loco vult actor quoddam incidens de bene esse inserere, recitando
modum scribentium et cantorum contra artem saepius usitatum in motellis
20 solummodo aut in conductis supra litteram, scilicet figuram binariam cum
proprietate positam et perfectam pro eadem binaria imperfecta usualiter
reperiri; quod est ponere contra artem, eo quod binaria figura cum
proprietate posita et perfecta de sui natura brevem et longam
artificialiter comprehendit. Binaria siquidem imperfecta unius longae
solummodo aequipollentiam continet et importat. Per hoc igitur liquidum
est et apertum, quod nonquam deberet una earum loco alterius collocari,
quod concedere non repugno. Tamen illorum qui sic ponere consueverunt
propositum penitus non condemno, immo in uno approbo duplici ratione.
   Quarum prior est solus usus et licentia peritorum usui attributa;
30 alia est, quare in motellis et in conductis seu organis supra litteram
ita fit, quia imperfecta figura impedita est et deformis maxime
descendendo et praecipue quando continet dyatessaron aut etiam dyapente
vel consimile quid, propter quod saepius evitatur. Figura siquidem
perfecta formosa est et librum purpurat et insignit. Hinc est, quare
ipsa saepius utitur reliqua evitando quo ad descensum solum, vix aut
nonquam quo ad ascensum.
   Quid sit autem nunc super hiis disponendum ad hoc ut partim arti et
partim usui deferamus, nota, quod ascendendo semper protrahimus
imperfectam, eo quod non est nimis deformis nec etiam impedita;
40 descendendo similiter imperfectam figuramus, quando facit tonum aut
semitonum sive ditonum aut semiditonum et hoc large. Si autem faciat
dyatessaron aut dyapente, primam cum proprietate et ultimam in formam
semibrevis protrahimus in hunc modum ⌶╫ et sic nec impedita nec
deformis nec perfecta nec imperfecta penitus reperitur. Tamen semibrevis
in forma, quae ibi apponitur, repraesentat quod figurari debeat
imperfecta. Et sic ubique supra litteram figuramus. In hoquetis autem
et in caudis cantuum aliorum nonquam debet poni figura perfecta pro
imperfecta, nec etiam e converso, quoniam tota virtus figurarum

----

6 interponis *cod.*   9 solummodo *pro* solum *Sowa*   34 quare *add. in
marg.*   37 aut *pro* autem *Sowa*   41 semitonium *Sowa*

composite figures, saying that the rule is: All ascending written notes

The law wants to give all climbing written notes obliquely,

that the plica touches must be figured according to the rules and artificially in an oblique fashion:

Which the plica touches, and no parenthesis troubles it.[1]

1 that is, distinction is interposed

To all last notes[2] let it[3] be an equal[1] partner,

1 that is, not disparate

2 both perfect and imperfect as to their form only and not as to their effect

3 the plica

Here he says that the quality or distinction of the plica will be recognized among these things by the mode and equipollence of the figures:

And the law of the figures will provide in that regard the understanding of the plicas.

Sometimes you see, etc. Having discussed the sequence of the figures that are perfect in their genus and similarly the plicas, because they possess the end of the figures, in this place the author wishes to introduce something incidental about their proper existence, explaining the method that is against the art but often in use by writers and cantors but only in motets or in conductus above a text, which is that a binary figure that is placed with propriety and is perfect is usually found instead of the same binary figure that is imperfect; and that is to place it against the theory, because the binary figure that is placed with propriety and is perfect artificially includes a breve and a long from its nature, but the binary that is imperfect only contains and conveys the equipollence of one long. Because of this therefore it is patent and obvious that one of them should never be put in the place of the other, which I do not shrink from conceding. And yet I do not completely condemn the purpose of those who are accustomed to placing it in that way; rather I approve it in one way for two reasons.

And the first of these is usage alone and the freedom marked out for the usage of the skilled. The second is that in motets and in conductus or organa above a text it happens that the imperfect figure is obstructed and deformed, especially descending and particularly when it contains a dyatessaron or a dyapente or something similar, and for that reason it is often avoided. But the perfect figure is beautiful, and embellishes and adorns the book. And that is why it is often used, avoiding the other as to descent only, but scarcely or never as to ascent.

As to what should now be determined about these things so that we may defer partly to the theory and partly to usage, note that we always notate it as imperfect ascending, because it is not too deformed or obstructed; and we figure it similarly as imperfect descending, when it makes a tone or a semitone or a ditone or a semiditone and we do this liberally. But if it makes a dyatessaron or a dyapente, we notate the first note with propriety and the last note in the form of a semibreve in this manner   , and thus it is found neither completely obstructed nor deformed nor perfect nor imperfect. And yet the semibreve in the form that is put there represents that it should be figured as imperfect. And we figure it that way everywhere over a text. But in hockets and in the end sections of other melodies no perfect figure should ever be put

quarumlibet ibi consistit et traditur praecipue et illic specifice
reperitur. Littera per se patet.

   Binas[1] perfectas supra textum[2] quandoque spectas
   1 sive voces in compositione perfectas et cum proprietate
   2 id est, litteram tam motellorum quam aliorum cantuum
   Usu[1] non arte[2] quis[3] nunc[4] volo cedere[5] parte.
   1 sive communi
   2 id est, non artificialiter
   3 id est, quibus
   4 id est, quandoque
   5 id est, partim acquiescere vel locum dare

  (fol. 146v) **Imperfectarum** etc. Quoniam actor in praecedentibus
figurarum omnium perfectarum virtutem declaravit et naturam, ideoque ad
imperfectarum cognitionem accedere nunc intendit, de qualibet per ordinem
faciens mentionem, et primo de binaria et ternaria eiusdem generis, eo
quod saepius eandem vim retinent et important. Dicit ergo in primis,
quod figura binaria cum proprietate posita et imperfecta, similiter et
ternaria eiusdem generis, uni longae trium temporum artificialiter
aequippollent. In hoc tamen differunt quod si sola brevis vel suum
aequippollens figuram binariam subsequitur, tunc illa binaria nisi duo
tempora continebit.
  Exemplum illius binariae figurae, quae trium temporum aequi-
ppollentiam repraesentat, sine littera patet hic tam ascendendo quam
descendendo  .
  Cum littera tam ascendendo quam descendendo patet hic:

       Vox in rama

  Exemplum illius binariae, quam sola brevis sequitur, sine littera
tam ascendendo quam descendendo patet hic ▪ ▪ ▶ ▪ , cum littera tam
ascendendo quam descendendo patet hic:

       Cum gaudio

  Exemplum ternariae eiusdem generis sine littera patet hic
▪▪ ▶ ▶ ▪ , cum littera patet sic:

       Plorans clama

Et non refert utrum longa vel brevis ipsam ternariam sussequatur.
  Quidam novi impositores quasdam figurarum formas varias protrahunt et
----

15 declaraverat *pro* declaravit *cod.* 18 eam *pro* eandem *cod.*
24 figurae *add. super scriptum* 29-31 *exemplum sic in marg.*
41 exemplum [[illius]] ternariae *cod.* 48 Et non refert . . .
sussequatur *om. Sowa*

in place of an imperfect nor the reverse, since the whole quality of any
figure consists in that and is especially handed down and specifically
found in that. The text is clear by itself.

> **Sometimes you see two perfect notes[1] over the text[2]**
> 1 notes in the composite figure that are perfect and with
> propriety
> 2 that is, the text both of motets and of other melodies
> **To which[3] I now[4] want to yield[5] partly in usage[1] and not in
> art.[2]**
> 1 common usage
> 2 that is, not artificially
> 3 that is, to those
> 4 that is, sometimes
> 5 that is, to acquiesce partly or give a place to

(fol. 146v) **The theory of imperfect,** etc. Since the author has
stated the quality and nature of all perfect figures in the preceding, he
therefore intends now to broach the understanding of imperfect figures,
making mention of each one in order; and first the binary and ternary
figures of the same genus, because they often keep and convey the same
force. Therefore he says first that the binary figure that is placed
with propriety and is imperfect, as well as the ternary figure of the
same genus, are equipollent artificially to one long of three units of
time. Yet they differ in this, that if a single breve or its equipollent
follows the binary figure, then that binary will only contain two units
of time.

An example of that binary figure which represents the equipollence of
three units of time is given here without text both ascending and
descending 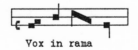 .
Here is an example both ascending and descending with text:

Vox in rama

Here is an example of that binary figure followed by a single breve,
without text both ascending and descending  , and with text
both ascending and descending:

Cum gaudio

Here is an example of the ternary figure of the same genus without
text  , and with text:

Plorans clama

And it does not matter whether a long or a breve follows that ternary
figure.

Certain new writers* notate and promulgate certain different forms of

provulgant, quae quamvis proferri valeant et etiam figurari, tamen artis
rationibus inferunt nocumentum. Unde quamvis has paciar, non tamen de
hiis in metro faciam mentionem, quia licet aliquorum usus accipiat,
tamen artificium non admittit. Haec sunt autem protractiones talium

figurarum: prima ternaria sic fit ▟ ▙ ▟ , alia quaternaria sic

protrahitur quo ad ipsos ▟ ▙ .

    Quod autem nec istae nec illae secundum artem sic valeant figurari,
10 patet lucida ratione. Omne illud, quod ab altero procreatur, debet
repraesentare in forma seu in suo genere naturam suae originis ac etiam
fundamentum. Ex hoc sic arguo, omnis figura a parte principii habet
signum suae proprietatis, per quod in suo genere ab aliis cognoscatur, et
a parte finis similiter per quod perfecta vel imperfecta videatur. Istae
siquidem non habent signa a parte principii, per quod in suo genere ab
aliis cognoscantur. Ergo istas proprie figuratas non credimus, sed
potius abusivas. Item omnis figura composita trahit originem suae
protractionis a figura binaria eiusdem generis seu protractionis. Sed
non est ponere aliquam figuram binariam sic protractam nec etiam sic
20 prolatam, ergo nec ternaria vel quaternaria figurari sic poterit quo
ad artem, quod concedimus.

    Item nulla figura perfecta primo per figuras ita dispositas potest
artificialiter protrahi nec componi, ergo per locum a simili nec etiam
imperfecta, cum omnis differentia inter ipsas a fine solum et non a
principio vel medio oriatur, quod concedimus, dicentes, quod non sunt
verae compositiones figurarum sed etiam abusivae. Item quod non possint
stare patet sic: duo opposita non possunt esse simul et semel in eodem;
ibi est proprietas et per oppositum in uno corpore, quod videtur esse
impossibile, eo quod ab invicem se opponunt, ergo male etc. Nota tamen
30 ne fallaris, quod si tales figurae tibi occurrerint: si sit ternaria,
prima sine tractu brevis est, ut asserunt; si habeat tractum a dextra
parte sicut longa, longa erit et duae aliae semibreves. In quaternaria
prima et ultima sunt breves et mediae semibreves. Littera patet.

        Imperfectarum[1] datur[2] hic ars[3] compositarum.[4]
        1 figurarum sive
        2 id est, ostenditur
        3 id est, introductio
        4 ad differentiam simplicium
40   **Imperfecta[1] quidem[2] si proprietas sit ibidem,[3]**
        1 sive figura
        2 id est, certe, ut hic tam ascendendo quam descendendo

        ▟ ▜ | ▟ ▜

        3 id est, in ipsa figura

----

10 decet *pro* debet *Sowa*   13 ab aliis *add. super scriptum*   26-29 Item
quod non . . . ergo male etc. *add. in marg.*   27 seu *pro* semel *Sowa*
32 et duae aliae semibreves *add. in marg.*

the figures, which, although they can be performed and also figured, yet bring harm to the reasonings of the art. And so although I shall agree to these, I shall not make mention of them in the verse, because although the usage of some people may accept them, yet theory does not admit them. These however are the notations of such figures: first the ternary

occurs like this ⬛▮ ▮⬛ ▮▮ , and then as regards them the fourfold

figure is notated like this ⬛▮▮ ▮▮⬛ .

That neither the former nor the latter however should be figured in this way is clear for an obvious reason. Everything that is created from something else must represent in its form or in its genus the nature and also the foundation of its origin. And from this I argue as follows, that every figure with respect to its beginning has a sign of its propriety, from which it may be distinguished from others of its genus, and also a sign at its end, by which it may be seen as perfect or imperfect. But those figures indeed do not have signs at their beginning by which they may be distinguished from others in their genus. Therefore we do not believe that they are properly figured, but rather are inappropriate. Also every composite figure draws the origin of its notation from the binary figure of the same genus or notation. But one should not put any binary figure notated in this way or performed in this way, therefore neither the ternary or fourfold figure will be able to be figured this way as regards the art, which we concede.

Also no perfect figure can be artificially notated or put together firstly with figures disposed in this way, therefore on similar grounds neither can an imperfect figure, since every distinction between them arises only from the end and not from the beginning or the middle, which we concede, saying that those are not true ways of putting figures together, but are improper. Also that they can not stand in this way is clear from the following: Two opposites can not exist at one and the same time in the same thing, and in those there is both propriety and the opposite of propriety in one body, which seems to be impossible, because they are the opposite of each other, therefore it is badly done, etc. But lest you make a mistake, note that if you come across such figures: if it is a ternary, the first note without a line is a breve, as they assert; if it has a line on its right side like a long, it will be a long and the two others will be semibreves. In the fourfold figure the first and last notes are breves, and the middle ones are semibreves. Here is the text.

The theory[3] of imperfect[1] composite[4] ones is given[2] here:
1 figures
2 that is, is shown
3 that is, introduction
4 as distinct from single ones
An imperfect[1] indeed,[2] if there is propriety in the same place,[3]
1 figure
2 that is, certainly; as here, both ascending and descending

⬛▮ ▮⬛ | ⬛▮ ▮⬛

3 that is, in the figure

Longam¹ portendit,² subdi³ longam⁴ sibi prendit.
1 aut minorem aut maiorem sive
2 id est, ostendit
3 id est, immediate postponi
4 hoc est in se trium temporum sive

Modo specificat:

Iuncturae binae¹ manet haec data lex² quoque ternae.³
1 id est, binariae
2 id est, ista regula
3 id est, ternariae solum

Tempora bina¹ geret binaria cui brevis² haeret.³
1 id est, longam minorem vel aequipollentiam
2 sive figura
3 ut hic

Quaevis utraque carens, etc. Facta superius mentione de figuris compositis imperfectis et cum proprietate repertis, hic vult actor de imperfectis proprietate propria carentibus notitiam declarare, dicens, quod figura ternaria imperfecta et per oppositum figurata minori longae singulariter aequippollet tam ascendendo quam descendendo, ut hic

. Quaternaria siquidem eiusdem formae maiori longae vel suo aequippollenti respondet tam ascendendo quam descendendo, sicut patet hic . Si autem haec quaternaria figura per licentiam nec per artem bis per oppositum figuretur, sicut patet in hoc exemplo de *In omni fratre*

tuo et alibi , duo tempora continebit quamvis securius et
ve

decentius sic figuraretur .

Pro maiore brevi, etc. Hic vult actor quandam doctrinam inserere de aequipollentia maioris brevis, de qua nondum mentio superius fuit facta, dicens, quod utile est et expediens figuram binariam sine proprietate positam et imperfectam pro ipsa aequipollentialiter reperire vel figurare, eo quod duo tempora solum continet, neque amplius neque minus poterit importare, similiter nec illa, quare sic facere credimus quid securum. Quidam tamen in suis artibus dicunt, quod quemadmodum figura binaria per oppositum figurata supponitur pro minore brevi, ita et pro maiore, dicentes de illa, quod solo tempore mensuratur, nisi quod si aliquando pro altera brevi ponatur, tunc (fol. 147) ea duo tempora compleantur. Quod frivolum credimus figurare et etiam provulgare, quod patet sic: quemadmodum pausa unius temporis pro maiore brevi non potest supponi, sic voces unius temporis poni non poterunt pro eadem. Sed semibreves in figura sunt huiusmodi, quia unum tempus solummodo repraesentant, sicut supra patuit per exempla, ergo poni non poterunt pro eadem. Si autem pro ea poni non valeant et secure, restat quod pro ea

----

3 id est *add. super scriptum*   16 [[**Proprietate**]] *pro* **Quaevis utraque** *cod.*   22 formae *add. super scriptum*   29 figurarentur *pro* figuraretur *cod., corr. Sowa*   31 superius mentio *pro* mentio superius *Sowa* 37 supponit *pro* supponitur *cod., corr. Sowa*   39 ei *pro* ea *Sowa*

Indicates[2] a long,[1] and takes for itself a long[4] to be appended.[3]

1 either smaller or larger
2 that is, it shows
3 that is, put immediately after it
4 this is one of three units of time

Now he specifies:

This law[2] remains given to the twin[1] ligature and also to the triple.[3]

1 that is, the binary
2 that is, this rule
3 that is, and the ternary only

The binary carries two units of time[1] to which the breve[2] is attached.[3]

1 that is, the smaller long or its equipollent
2 figure
3 as here

The one that lacks both, etc. Having made mention above of imperfect composite figures found with propriety, here the author wishes to state the concept of imperfect figures that lack proper propriety, saying that the imperfect ternary figure figured by means of the opposite of propriety is specifically equipollent to a smaller long both ascending and descending, as here . Indeed the fourfold figure of the same form corresponds to the larger long or its equipollent both ascending and descending, as can be seen here . But if this fourfold figure, through license and not according to the art, is figured by means of the opposite of propriety twice, as can be seen in this example of "In omni fratre tuo," and elsewhere or , it will contain two units of time, although it would be figured more safely and more properly in this way .

Nevertheless, etc. Here the author wishes to introduce a certain principle about the equipollence of the larger breve which has not yet been mentioned above, and he says that it is useful and advantageous to find or figure the binary figure that is placed without propriety and is imperfect equipollently in place of it, because it only contains two units of time, and will not be able to convey more or less, and similarly nor can that, and so we believe that it is a safe thing to do it this way. Nevertheless some people* in their treatises say that just as the binary figure figured by means of the opposite of propriety is substituted for the smaller breve, so it should be for the larger, and they say about it that it is measured by a single unit of time, except that if sometimes it is put instead of an alternate breve, then (fol. 147) two units of time are filled up by it. But we believe that it is silly to figure it this way and to promulgate it, which can be seen as follows: Just as a rest of one unit of time can not be substituted for a larger breve, so the notes of one unit of time can not be put in the place of it. And the semibreves in the figure are of this kind, because they only represent one unit of time, as has been shown above through examples, and therefore they could not be put in the place of it. But if

ponamus quicquid ei sub recta proportione sciverimus verasciter et absque dubio conferendum. Sed haec est figura binaria sine proprietate et imperfecta, quare ipsam pro maiore brevi in aequipollentia collocamus.

Quaevis utraque[1] carens pro longa[2] vult[3] fore parens,[4]
1 id est, tam proprietate quam perfectione
2 sive pro minore sive pro maiore
3 sive figura
4 et hoc specifice, ut hic

10 **Sed pro maiori[1] quadruplex vox[2] proque[3] minori[4]**
1 sive longa, quae tria tempora continet
2 id est, figura quaternaria
3 vel pro suo aequipollente
4 longa sive
Si sit meta[1] trium, breve supposita sibi solum.

1 id est, ligatura, ut hic
Huic[1] duo tempora das si tractum bis ita tradas.
1 subaudi figurae quaternariae imperfectae bis per oppositum

20 figuratae, ut hic
Ecce dat actor doctrinam de aequipollentia maioris brevis, de qua dubium resultabat:
Pro maiore brevi tamen hanc ▌▌ ▄ dare consulo sevi.

Vox imperfecta etc. Hic assignat actor quandam doctrinam ad omnes imperfectas figuras, de quibus non fecit mentionem superius, se habentem, quae talis est: omnis figura imperfecta cum proprietate sibi proprie distributa excedens tres cum proprietate et imperfectione aequipollere
30 dicitur ternariae figurae sine proprietate positae, quae in secundo modo proprie reperitur. Cuius ratio est: sicut omnes figurae cum proprietate positae et perfectae excedentes tres perfectas cum proprietate propria figuratas sunt ad numerum trium eiusdem generis quoad quantitatem temporum reducendae, sic possibile est et permissibile omnes imperfectas cum proprietate propria praeter quinariam figuratas ad numerum trium sine proprietate protractarum quo ad numerum temporum et etiam quantitatem aequippollentialiter comparari. Haec siquidem reductio hic traditur ad hoc ut imperfectarum omnium figurarum notitia specifice pateat universis.
Et per hoc est notandum, quod imperfectae minus quam perfectae
40 solummodo continent unum tempus. Et per hoc potest etiam concludere, quod tertia species, quarta et quinta, quoad longas suas in figuris compositis sunt ultramensurabiles, eo quod non possunt eas sic positas convertere in imperfectas quo ad formam, quoniam dubium esset, utrum

----
2 hoc *pro* haec *Sowa*   5 [[**Proprietate**]] *pro* **Quaevis utraque** *cod.*
10 **maiore** *pro* **maiori** *Sowa*   **minore** *pro* **minori** *Sowa*   15 *super*
supposita *et* **solum** *glos. ras.*   33 sunt omnes ad *cod.*   35 proprie
pro propria *Sowa*   41 longas *add. super scriptum*

they can not be put in the place of it safely, it remains that we may put
in its place whatever we know truly and without doubt to be comparable to
it under the correct proportion. And this is the binary figure that is
without propriety and imperfect, and so we establish that in the place of
the larger breve in equipollence.

**The one[3] that lacks both[1] wants to be the kindred[4] in the place
of the long,[2]**
1 that is, lacking both propriety and perfection
2 either the smaller or the larger
3 the figure
4 and specifically, as here
**But in the place of a larger one;[1] and the quadruple note[2] is in
the place of[3] a smaller one.[4]**
1 a long which contains three units of time
2 that is, the fourfold figure
3 or in the place of its equipollent
4 long
**If there is a boundary[1] of three, only a breve will be
substituted for it.**
1 that is, a ligature as here
**You give two units of time to this one[1] if you bestow on it a
line twice.**
1 understand: the fourfold imperfect figure figured by means of

the opposite of propriety twice, as here
Here the author gives the principle of the equipollence of the larger
breve about which there arose some doubt:
**Nevertheless I advise you to sow this figure   in the
place of the larger breve.**

Let the imperfect note, etc. Here the author lays out a certain
principle which applies to all imperfect figures which he has not
mentioned above, which is as follows: Every imperfect figure that is
distributed properly with propriety that exceeds three notes with
propriety and imperfection is said to be equipollent to the ternary
figure placed without propriety which is properly found in the second
mode. And the reason is this: Just as all figures that are placed with
propriety and are perfect that exceed three perfect notes figured with
proper propriety should be reduced to the number of three of the same
genus as regards their quantity of units of time, so it is possible and
permissible to compare equipollently all imperfect notes that are figured
with proper propriety beyond the fivefold figure to the number of three
that are notated without propriety as to the number of units of time and
also the quantity. Indeed this reduction is given here so that the
concept of all imperfect figures may be specifically made clear to
everyone.

And by this means it should be noted that imperfect figures less than
perfect figures only contain one unit of time. And through this it can
also be concluded that the third, fourth, and fifth species are beyond
measuring as regards their longs in composite figures, because they can
not change them when they are placed in that way into ones that are
imperfect as to their form, since there would be doubt whether such a
figure would be put for the quantity of three units of time, or whether

talis figura pro quantitate trium temporum poneretur, an figuram
ternariam tertiae speciei sive quartae faceret imperfectam.   Unde si
istae tres species sub recta mensura sicut tres aliae ponerentur, simili
modo suas figuras compositas facerent imperfectas, quod cum in forma non
faciant licet in diminutione temporum facere bene possent.   Ideo ipsas
rectam mensuram excedere nuncupamus, eo quod si eis superfluum mensurae,
id est unum tempus, sustrahatur, ad huc sub perfectione formae propria
protrahentur.

> Hic igitur de quaternaria figura cum proprietate posita et imperfecta
10 in primis exemplificandum est tam ascendendo quam descendendo, qualiter

protrahatur et etiam cognoscatur: .   Exemplum quinariae per
oppositum figuratae, ne usui partim et arti contrarii videamur, patet hic

.   Exemplum senariae patet hic   .   Exemplum

septenariae patet sic   , octonariae sic   .

> Ne mireris omnes figuras posse poni imperfectas, quippe cum omnis
20 figura duplicem habeat differentiam circa finem, sicut patuit in
praedictis.   Littera per se patet.

> **Vox imperfecta[1] superans tres esto reducta**
> 1 id est, figura cum proprietate et imperfecta, ut quaternaria,
> quinaria, senaria, et sic de aliis
> **Ad tres[1] coniunctas sine proprietateque punctas.**
> 1 figuras sive, sicut in secundo modo contingit reperire, ut
> hic

30 **Nunc per se punxi** etc.   Exequto superius de figuris ad invicem
colligatis, quae de sui natura propria figuram ligatam faciunt et
componunt, ideoque de semibrevibus positis divisive vult actor facere
mentionem, quae quamvis descendendo ab invicem separentur, tamen in se
ligaturae naturam sapiunt et important, sicut in figuris patuit
antedictis.

> Notandum est igitur, quod in sussidium omnium figurarum et praecipue
propter colores musicae decentius purpurandos ac etiam variandos tres
semibreves divisive descendendo sociae sunt repertae, aliquando per se et
aliquando cum aliis sive simplicibus sive compositis adiunguntur.   Cum
40 autem per se positae sunt inventae, nunc cum caudis nunc sine caudis
positas invenimus; unde sciendum est, quod quotienscumque caudas eis
apponimus, longitudinem repraesentant, si autem invenias sine caudis,
procul dubio brevitatem, secundum quod textus litterae specifice
recitabit.

----

3 [[tertiae]] *cod.*, tres *add. super scriptum*   36 est *om. Sowa*

it would make the ternary figure of the third or fourth species imperfect. And so if these three species were put in the correct measure like the three others, in a similar way they would make their composite figures imperfect, which, although they do not do it in their form, they could properly do in the diminution of their units of time. And so we name them as exceeding the correct measure, because if the extra amount of measure, that is one unit of time, is removed, they will then be notated under the proper perfection of form.

Here therefore we must first exemplify the fourfold figure that is placed with propriety and is imperfect both ascending and descending; how it is notated and also how it is recognized: . An example of the fivefold figure figured by means of the opposite of propriety, lest we seem contrary partly to usage and to the art, is given here

. An example of the sixfold figure is given here . An example of the sevenfold figure is given here , and of the eightfold here .

Do not wonder at the fact that all figures can be placed as imperfect, especially since all figures have two distinctions at their end, as has been made clear in the aforementioned. The text is clear by itself.

> **Let the imperfect note[1] that surpasses three be reduced**
> 1 that is, a figure that is with propriety and is imperfect, such as the fourfold, the fivefold, the sixfold, and likewise with the others
> **To three[1] that are joined together and written without propriety.**
> 1 figures, just as it happens to occur in the second mode, as here

Now I have written, etc. Since the author has discussed above the figures that are connected to each other, which make and form from their own nature a ligated figure, he therefore wishes to make mention of semibreves placed individually, which, although they are separated from each other descending, yet partake of and convey the meaning of the nature of a ligature as it has been made clear in the figures mentioned above.

It should be noted therefore that for the assistance of all figures, and especially for the purpose of embellishing and varying the rhetorical colors of music more properly, three semibreves descending individually are found together, sometimes by themselves and sometimes joined to other figures, either single or composite. And when they are found placed by themselves we sometimes find them placed with tails and sometimes without tails. And it should be known that whenever we put tails on them they represent length, but if you find them without tails they definitely represent brevity, just as the content of the text will specifically explain.

Nunc[1] per se punxi[2] tres semibreves[3] quoque[4] iunxi
1 id est, quandoque
2 id est, figuravi
3 aut aequales aut inaequales
4 id est, similiter
(fol. 147v) **Nunc aliis.[1] Tractum nunc prima respice factum:**
1 sive figuris tam simplicibus quam compositis, perfectis vel
imperfectis, sicut exempla declarabunt postea
Nunc[1] datur extremae,[2] nunc illis[3] undique deme.
1 id est, quandoque
2 sive voci
3 id est, tam primae quam ultimae
Hinc[1] tibi dogma dabo sensumque meum reserabo.[2]
1 id est, quando debebunt habere tractum vel non
2 id est, opinionem meam declarabo

Quando tenent longae etc. Hic vult actor harum trium semibrevium
proprietatem specificare pariter et naturam, inde dans regulas speciales,
quarum prior est: quotienscumque tres semibreves descendendo suo ordine
dispositae pro longa simplice sunt repertae, proprietas earum est quod
prima illarum habeat tractum sive caudam obliquo modo factam sub sinistro
latere descendendo, sicut patet hic ⬦. Et nota, quod duae priores
voces valent unum tempus, et ultima valet tantum quantum duae
praecedentes, nunc autem e converso, et hoc est, quando pro longa duorum
temporum vel pro aliquo sibi aequipollente tantummodo sunt repertae. Si
autem pro longa trium temporum vel pro aliquo sibi aequipollente
specialiter reponantur, et sub eadem forma seu protractione, tunc ultima
earum duo tempora continebit, et duae praecedentes unicum retinebunt,
nunc autem penitus e converso, et tunc prior earum a pluribus protrahitur
recta longa, prout inferius recitabitur supra textum.

Vidi fore saepius imma etc. Hic recitat actor opinionem quorundam
apponentium caudam ultimae earundem, et hoc praecipue quando pro longa
maiore repertae sunt, sicut patet hic ⬦. Quod autem talis tractus
sive cauda nonquam ibi debeat coadiungi, patet duplici ratione, quarum
una est: nulla differentia est in forma inter maiorem longam et minorem,
licet in effectu quantitatis differant et natura. Ergo per locum a
simili nec inter tres semibreves pro ipsis positas quo ad formam erit
differentiam assignare. Immo posset aliquis dicere: differentia
assignanda est. Differentia assignatur inter aliquas figuras pro ipsis
longis positas et repertas, sicut supra patuit hiis exemplis
◤ ◣ ◥ ◢   et consimilibus, quare similiter assignari debuit inter
se antedictas.
Ad quod obiectum respondimus dicentes, quod non est simile hinc et

----

13 [[Hinc tibi dogma dabit modus harum et reserabit]] *cod.*
20 simiplici *pro* simplice *Sowa*   32-33 et hoc . . . repertae sunt *add.*
in marg.   quando praecipue *cod.*   34 debeat [[quoadiu]] coadiungi
cod.   40 longis *add. in marg.*

Now[1] I have written[2] three semibreves[3] by themselves, and I have also[4] joined them
1 that is, sometimes
2 that is, I have figured
3 either equal or unequal
4 that is, similarly
(fol. 147v) Sometimes to other ones.[1] Now look at the line made on the first one.
1 figures both single and composite, perfect or imperfect, as the examples will state afterwards
Now[1] it is given to the last.[2] Now take it away everywhere from them.[3]
1 that is, sometimes
2 note
3 that is, both from the first and the last
I shall give you the doctrine on this matter[1] and I shall reveal my meaning.[2]
1 that is, when they should have a line or not
2 that is, I shall state my view

When they hold, etc. Here the author wishes to specify the propriety of these three semibreves and at the same time also their nature, giving specific rules in that regard, of which the first is: Whenever three semibreves descending arranged in order are found in the place of a single long, their propriety is that the first of them has a line or tail, made in an oblique fashion descending under the left side, as is shown here . And note that the two first notes are worth one unit of time, and the last is worth as much as the two preceding. And sometimes it is the reverse, but this is only when they are found in the place of a long of two units of time or in the place of something equipollent to it. But if they are put specifically in the place of a long of three units of time or in the place of something equipollent to that and in the same form or notation, then the last of them will contain two units of time and the two preceding will keep only one. But sometimes it is completely the reverse, and then the first of them is notated by many people as a correct long, as will be explained below over the text.

     . . . but I have seen it often on the last, etc. Here the author explains the view of certain people* who put a tail on the last one of them, and this is especially when they are found in the place of a larger long, as is shown here . But the fact that such a line or tail should never be added there is clear for two reasons. The first of these is that there is no difference in form between the larger long and the smaller, although they do differ in the effect of their quantity and in their nature. Therefore on similar grounds neither will it be right to assign a difference as to their form between three semibreves put in their place. On the other hand someone could say: A difference should be assigned. A difference is assigned between some figures put and found in the place of those longs, as has been shown above in these examples   and in similar ones, and so it should be assigned similarly between those mentioned above.

     We respond to this objection by saying that the one case is not the same as the other, since a difference should be assigned between the

inde, quoniam inter illas debuit assignari differentia, nullatenus inter
istas. Necesse enim fuit inter figuras compositas differentiam
assignare, per quam una ab altera quo ad repraesentationem temporum
cognoscatur, sed hoc est per signa a parte principii et non finis. Nam
per finem perfectio vel imperfectio designatur, et hoc sine tractu aliquo
sive cauda, per principium autem repraesentatio figurarum cum cauda
pluries aliquando sine cauda. Ex quo sequitur, quod si necesse sit inter
tales differentiam assignare, hoc erit a parte principii et non finis.
Quod autem a parte principii non sit necesse differentiam assignare inter
10   eas quo ad formam, patet sic: duae priores earum eandem prolationem
vocis inferunt et eandem temporis quantitatem pro utraque aequipollentia,
quare debent suae protractionis formam similem importare. Secus autem
est de aliis figuris, quoniam non eandem prolationem vocis a parte
principii nec eundem effectum inferunt. Et ideo variationem formmae
habere per signa dissimilia meruerunt. Alia est autem ratio quare non
debent habere tractum sive caudam sic positam circa finem, scilicet
propter plicam, quae in fine omnium figurarum suum possidet dominatum, et
in illis praecipue descendendo, aliter non potuit figurari. Ad cuius
differentiam, talem caudam in fine semibrevium decrevimus aboleri.

20
         Quando tenent¹ longae² sedem, caudam modo³ punge
         1 sive huius semibreves, regula est
         2 sive sive maioris sive minoris
         3 id est, quandoque
         Obliquae¹ prima; vidi fore saepius imma.²
         1 sicut patet hic
         2 hic recitat actor opinionem eorum, qui apponebant in fine
         sic
    Modo subiungit rationem, dicens, quod sic saepius plicari potest,
30   ut hic :
         Quod male¹ credo dari² quia sic vult saepe plicari.
         1 id est, non sane vel secure
         2 id est, dici
         Dum tamen haec longae¹ sedem teneant, ita² punge.
         1 sive maioris sive minoris sive
         2 id est, sicut hic
    Et sic deviant a figura:
         Primam nunc tendunt¹ ita   cum tria tempora prendunt.²
         1 id est, prolongant
40   2 id est, comprehendunt
         Cui¹ duo tempora des,² aliis³ unum quoque trades.⁴
         1 priori sive
         2 id est, faveas
         3 sive duabus
         4 id est, relinques vel mancipabis

----
2 fuit *add. in marg.*   8 tales se differentiam *cod.*   differentiam
[[in eas]] assignare *cod.*   10-11 prolationis [[volo]] vocem *cod.*
14 formmae *cod.*   23 *primum* sive *om. Sowa*   34 **hee** *pro* **haec** *cod.*
35 *ultimum* sive *om. Sowa*   38 **nunc ita tendunt** *Sowa*   41 **Qui** *pro* **Cui**
Sowa   44 sive duabus [[aliis]] *cod.*

latter, but not between the former. For it is necessary to assign a
difference between composite figures, by which one may be recognized from
the other as regards the representation of units of time, but this is by
means of signs with respect to the beginning and not the end. For it is
by the end that perfection and imperfection are designated and this is
without any line or tail; but the representation of figures by the
beginning is often with a tail and sometimes without a tail. From which
it follows that if it is necessary to assign a difference between such
notes, this will be with respect to the beginning and not the end. But
the fact that it is not necessary to lay out a difference between them as
to their form with respect to the beginning, is clear from the following:
The two first notes bear the same performance of the voice and the same
quantity of time for each equipollence, and so they must convey a
similar form for their notation. But it is otherwise with the other
figures since they do not bear the same performance of the voice with
respect to the beginning nor the same effect. And so they deserve to
have a difference of form by means of dissimilar signs. But there is
another reason why these semibreves should not have a line or tail placed
in this way at the end, and that is on account of the plica, which
posesses its domain at the end of all figures, and especially in those
descending, for it could not be figured otherwise. And for the purpose
of this distinction, we have decided that such a tail at the end of the
semibreves should be abolished.

> **When they[1] hold the position of a long,[2] now[3] write a tail**
> 1 semibreves of this kind, the rule is
> 2 either larger or smaller
> 3 that is, sometimes
> **On the first note of the oblique figure;[1] but I have seen it
> often on the last note.[2]**
> 1 as is shown here
> 2 here the author explains the view of those who put it at the
> end like this

Now he adds a reason, saying that it can often be plicated in this
way, as here :

> **And I believe that this is badly[1] done[2] because it is in this
> way that it often wants to be plicated.**
> 1 that is, not sensibly or safely
> 2 that is, said
> **Yet while they hold the position of the long,[1] write them thus.[2]**
> 1 either the larger or smaller
> 2 that is, like this

And they deviate in this way from the figure:

> **They stretch[1] the first note now in this way when they take[2]
> three units of time.**
> 1 that is, they prolong
> 2 that is, comprise
> **And to that[1] you may give[2] two units of time, and you will also
> bestow[4] one on the others.[3]**
> 1 the first note
> 2 that is, you may favor it with
> 3 the other two
> 4 that is, you will leave or deliver

Regula est: tres semibreves suo ordine positae sine caudis unum
tempus tantummodo repraesentant, ut hic ♦♦ :
  Pro quae brevi dantur sine caudis quando locantur.
  (fol. 148) **Sic[1] per se pones, hinc[2] cum reliquis[3] ita[4] dones.**
  1 id est, sicut superius est expressum
  2 id est, postea
  3 id est, quando cum aliis adiunges
  4 id est, sicut sequitur
  Parte manent[1] prima, media[2] nunc, nunc et imma.[3]
  1 sicut patebit immediate post
  2 sive parte
  3 id est, posteriori vel inferiori
  Nunc ita praecedunt[1] aliis,[2] velut hic[3] quoque cedunt
  1 id est, praecedere possunt
  2 sive in figura composita
  3 id est, in hoc exemplo ♦♦■   ♦♦♩
  Saepe brevi iunctae sibi[1] vel longae[2] dabo sponte.
  1 sicut supra exemplificatum est vel sic ♦♦■
  2 sive figurae vel voci, ut hic ♦♦♩
  Cumque valent longam[1] tractum sibi tunc ita iungam.
  1 id est, quandocumque pro longa aliqua supponere sunt repertae
  sic ♦♦■

  Has aliis cinctas etc. Hic vult actor expedire se breviter de huius
semibrevibus circumdatis ab aliis hinc et inde, dicens, quod omnes tales
sine caudis positae sunt inventae.
  Hinc tibi dogma etc. Ecce dicit, quod modus, in quo sic positae sunt
repertae, notitiam super hiis faciet manifestam, utrum hic pro brevi sint
positae, vel pro longa. Nam in primo modo inter duas longas positae
continent unum tempus, ut hic ♩♦♦♩. In secundo modo inter duas breves
positae duo tempora repraesentant, sicut hic ⌐♦♦■. In tertio modo et
quarto et in quinto, si evenerit reperire, tria tempora continebunt; in
tertio sicut hic ♩♦♦♩, et hoc quando inter duas longas singulariter
reponuntur. In quarto modo vel quinto vix aut nonquam a duabus longis
circumdatas has poteris reperire. Et nota, quod si in tertio modo seu
quarto pro minore brevi supponantur, unum tempus continebunt, si pro
maiore, duo tempora reservabunt. In sexto autem modo ubique nisi solo

tempore mensurantur, sicut patet hic ⌐♦♦■ ⌐♦♦■ ⌐♦♦■. Littera plana est.
  Regula est: quotienscumque huius semibreves ab aliis circumdantur
sine caudis sunt repertae:
  Has aliis cinctas sine caudis respice tinctas.

----

12 posteriore *pro* posteriori *Sowa*   inferiore *pro* inferiori *Sowa*
13 **ita** *add. super scriptum*   21 quandoque *pro* quandocumque *Sowa*
28 supra *pro* super *Sowa*   faciet *add. in marg.*   36 supponant *pro*
supponantur *cod.*   37 ubicumque *pro* ubique *cod.*

The rule is: Three semibreves placed in order without tails only represent one unit of time, as here ♦♦ :

And when they are positioned in the place of a breve they are given without tails.

(fol. 148) **You will put them thus[1] by themselves, then[2] you may give them in this way[4] with the rest.[3]**

1 that is, as has been expressed above

2 that is, afterwards

3 that is, when you join them with others

4 that is, as follows

They remain[1] with the first part, now with the middle,[2] and now with the last.[3]

1 as will be shown immediately after

2 part

3 that is, the posterior or lower

Now in this way they precede[1] the others,[2] as they also yield here[3]

1 that is, they can precede

2 in a composite figure

3 that is, in this example ♦♦■   ♦♦┐

Often to a breve joined to them,[1] or, I shall willingly add, a long.[2]

1 as has been exemplified above, or like this ♦♦■

2 figure or note, as here ♦♦┐

When they are worth a long[1] then I shall join a line to them like this.

1 that is, whenever they are found substituting for any long, like this ♦♦■

Look at these, etc. Here the author wishes to discuss briefly semibreves of this kind surrounded by others on both sides, saying that all of them are found placed without tails.

Then the mode, etc. Here he says that the mode in which they are found placed in this way will make the concept of them clear, whether they are put here in the place of a breve, or in the place of a long. For in the first mode, when they are placed between two longs, they contain one unit of time, as here ¶♦♦┐ . In the second mode, when they are placed between two breves, they represent two units of time, as here ┌♦♦■ . In the third mode, and the fourth and the fifth, if it happens that they are found there, they will contain three units of time; in the third like this ¶♦♦┐ , and this is when they are placed singly between two longs. In the fourth mode or the fifth you will scarcely or never be able to find them surrounded by two longs. And note that if in the third mode or the fourth they are substituting for a smaller breve, they will contain one unit of time; if for a larger, they will keep two units of time. But in the sixth mode they are always only measured by one unit of

time, as is shown here ┌♦♦■ ┌♦♦■ ┌♦♦■ . Here is the text.

The rule is: Whenever semibreves of this kind are surrounded by other notes they are found without tails:

Look at these, surrounded by other notes and furnished without tails.

Hinc[1] **tibi**[2] **dogma**[3] **dabit modus**[4] **harum et reserabit,**[5]
1 vel et
2 O cantor
3 id est, doctrinam
4 species in qua reperientur
5 id est, reserando manifestabit
An[1] **prolongari**[2] **teneantur**[3] **vel breviari.**[4]
1 pro utrum
2 id est, pro longa poni
10   3 id est, teneri debeantur
4 id est, pro aliqua brevi poni; et nota, quod pro utraque
possunt poni

Cum seris has longe etc. Ostenso superius quomodo et qualiter huius
semibreves aliis praeponuntur, et quomodo nunc ab aliis circumdantur,
ideo in hoc loco vult actor ostendere, qualiter aliis adiunguntur,
dicens, quod simplex longa eis quandoque praecedere reperitur, sicut hic
⬛, quandoque tamen figura composita praecedere cernitur, sicut patet
20 hic ⬛ ; quandoque sola brevis et hoc est dupliciter, quoniam aut illa
figura ascendens est aut descendens. Si ascendens, tunc illa brevis
nullum debet habere tractum sive caudam sed debet fieri in hunc modum
⬛ . Si sit descendens, tunc brevis praecedens debet habere tractum
sive caudam a sinistro latere descendentem tanquam figura binaria cum
proprietate posita, pro qua praesens suponere iam videtur, et sic eius
naturam debet sapere ac virtutem. Descendendo igitur sic protrahatur
⬛ , et sic omnium figurarum quibus possent adiungi. Necesse est
circumstantias inspicere et considerare, quoniam figuras quibus
associantur nonquam variant neque mutant, unde textus: **Nonquam**
30 **mutentur** etc.
Exemplum qualiter diversis protractionibus figurarum poterunt
coadiungi patet hic, primo de figuris cum proprietate propria figuratis,
ut hic ⬛ ⬛ ⬛ ⬛ ; si cum figuris sine proprietate, sic debent
protrahi ⬛ ⬛ . Nota tamen, quod cum figuris sine proprietate
positis non sunt securius adiungendae, eo quod figurae cum proprietate
positae sive perfectae sive imperfectae et sub certo numero distributae
cum semibrevibus loco aliarum competentius supponere sunt repertae. Et
hoc iuxta id quod alibi dicitur in arte, quod *nonquam debet poni aliqua*
40 *figura sine proprietate, ubi potest poni cum proprietate,* unde metrum
supra **Iunctas nolo dari** etc.
Exemplum qualiter cum figuris per oppositum figuratis varie
protrahuntur, patet hic ⬛ ⬛ ⬛ et sic de aliis.

----

5 reperirentur *pro* reperientur *Sowa*   15 *inter* nunc *et* ab *ras.*
16 actor *om. Sowa*   18 tamen in figura *cod.*   22 sed decet fieri *pro*
sed debet fieri *Sowa*   23 decet *pro* debet *Sowa*   25 supponere *pro*
suponere *Sowa*   26 decet *pro* debet *Sowa*   28 inspirere *pro* inspicere
cod., corr. Sowa   32 cum *add. super scriptum*   34 ex. *add. in marg.*
37 sub [[certo]] certo *cod.*   39 decet *pro debet Sowa*

Then[1] the mode[4] will give and disclose[5] to you[2] the doctrine[3] for these,
1 or: and
2 O singer
3 that is, the principle
4 the species in which they will be found
5 that is, will make clear by disclosing
If[1] they may be considered[3] to be prolonged[2] or shortened.[4]
1 instead of: whether
2 that is, put in the place of a long
3 that is, ought to be considered
4 that is, put in the place of some breve; and note that they can be put in the place of either

Since you entwine these with a long, etc. Having shown above how and in what way semibreves of this kind are put in front of others, and how sometimes they are surrounded by others, therefore in this place the author wishes to show in what way they are joined to others, saying that a single long is sometimes found preceding them, as here ▜•⸪ , but sometimes is perceived to precede them in a composite figure, as is shown here ▛•⸪ . Sometimes a single breve is found, and that can be in two ways, since that figure is either ascending or descending. If it is ascending, then that breve must have no line or tail but should occur in this way ▪•⸪ . If it is descending, then the breve that is in front should have a line or tail descending from the left side like the binary figure placed with propriety, for which the present figure is seen now to be a substitute and thus should partake of its nature and quality. Therefore it may be notated like this descending ▐•⸪ , and similarly for all the figures to which they may be joined. It is necessary to look at the circumstances and examine them, since they never vary or change the figures with which they are associated; whence the text: **Never may the notes be changed,** etc.

An example of how they could be joined to different notations of figures is given here, firstly figures figured with proper propriety as here ▟•⸪ ▛•⸪ ▛•⸪ ▙•⸪ . But if they are joined to figures without propriety, they should be notated like this ▐•⸪ ◥•⸪ . But note that they can not be joined safely to figures placed without propriety, because figures placed with propriety -- whether perfect or imperfect -- and distributed under a fixed number are found to substitute for them more suitably when they are with semibreves in place of the others. And this is in accordance with what is said elsewhere in the treatise,* that "no figure should ever be put without propriety where one can be put with propriety," whence the verse above: **I do not wish notes that are joined,** etc.

An example of the different way in which they are notated with figures figured by means of the opposite of propriety is given here ▙•⸪ ◥•⸪ ◣•⸪ , and similarly for the others.

Cum[1] seris[2] has[3] longae,[4] iuncturam tunc ita ♪⋰ punge.
1 pro quando
2 id est, iungis
3 sive semibreves
4 quantacumque sit, sive minor sive maior
Si brevis[1] ante datur hic tractus ei[2] sociatur,
1 sive vox sola in figura, sicut patet hic ⌐⋰
2 sive brevi
Cum[1] iunctura cadit,[2] sed scandens[3] hunc[4] sibi radit.
10   1 pro quando
2 id est, ligatura descendit
3 sive ligatura
4 tractum sive, ut hic ■⋰
(fol. 148v) **Has[1] quoque secure cuivis coniunge figurae.[2]**
1 sive tres semibreves
2 id est, cuilibet figurae sive perfectae sive imperfectae
Nota tamen, quod imperfectae ad perfectionis numerum introducuntur:
Sed plus cum semis quas complent iure ligatis.
Per hoc datur intelligi, quod nonquam voces quibus adiunguntur plus
20   vel minus importabunt:
Nonquam mutentur voces quibus arte tenentur.
Quasi diceret: nec propter aliam vocem mutabuntur:
Altera nec mutet vox has ne regula[1] mutet.
1 id est, ordinatio regularis

Saepe plicam etc. Notandum est, quod quotienscumque tres semibreves
pro longa aliqua sunt repertae, tunc earum ultima poterit plicari, sive
sit ascendens sive etiam descendens, sive sint per se positae, ut hic
⋰ ⋰ , sive cum aliis coadiunctae, sicut hic ♪⋰ ■⋰ ◣⋰ ◣⋰ , et
30 sic de aliis.
Scandere etc. converte sic: **sperne,** id est, non consenti; **tres
semibreves minores,** id est, aequales; **scandere,** id est, sursum erigi
divisive, nisi sint cum littera; **fores,** id est, metas spatiorum et
linearum, et hoc sine littera. Nota tamen, quod duae in figura per
oppositum figurata et cum plica ascendente istud idem secundum
aequipollentiam repraesentant. Littera per se patet.

Saepe plicam sternis[1] cum pro longa fore cernis.[2]
1 id est, multotiens paras vel ponis
40   2 ex hoc sequitur quod pro brevi nonquam plicentur
Scandere[1] sperne fores[2] tres semibrevesque minores.
1 id est, ascendere divisive notae
2 id est, metas spatiorum et linearum et sine littera

----
9 **scandes** *pro* **scandens** *cod*.   14 **cuius** *pro* **cuivis** *Sowa*   17 introducunt
pro introducuntur *cod*.   18 **ligetis** *pro* **ligatis** *cod*.   19 intellegi *pro*
intelligi *Sowa*   28 ascendendo *pro* ascendens *Sowa*   descendendo *pro*
descendens *Sowa*   33 sit *pro* sint *Sowa*   36 representat *pro*
repraesentant *cod*.   42 nota *pro* notae *cod*.

Since[1] you entwine[2] these[3] with a long,[4] write the joining then in this way ⁊⸙ .
1 instead of when
2 that is, you join
3 semibreves
4 whatever size it is, whether smaller or larger
If a breve[1] is given before, this line is joined to it,[2]
1 a note alone in the figure, as is shown here ⌐⸙
2 the breve
Since[1] the ligature falls,[2] but a climbing one[3] erases this[4] from itself.
1 instead of: when
2 that is, the ligature descends
3 ligature
4 the line, as here ▪⸙
(fol. 148v) Join these[1] also safely to any figure.[2]
1 three semibreves
2 that is, to any figure whether perfect or imperfect
But note that imperfect figures are brought in to the category of perfection:
But they fill those according to the law when there are more ligated with semibreves.
In this way the understanding is given that never will the notes to which they are joined convey more or less:
Never may the notes by changed to which they are held in the art.
He means to say that neither will they be changed on account of another note:
Nor may another note change them, lest the rule[1] change them.
1 that is, the regular arrangement

You often stretch out a plica, etc. It should be noted that whenever three semibreves are found in the place of some long, the last of them will be able to be plicated, whether it is ascending or descending, and whether they are placed by themselves as here ⋀⸙ ⋀⸙ , or joined with others, as here ⁊⸙ ▪⸙ ⌐⸙ ⌐⸙ , and similarly with the others.
And prevent, etc. interpret thus: **prevent,** that is, do not allow; **three smaller semibreves,** that is, equal ones; **from climbing,** that is, from being set above separately, unless they are with text; **the threshold,** that is, the boundaries of the spaces and lines, and this is without text. But note that two notes in a figure figured by means of the opposite of propriety and ascending with a plica represent that same thing according to its equipollence. The text is clear by itself.

You often stretch out a plica[1] when you see them standing in the place of a long.[2]
1 that is, many times you prepare or place it
2 it follows from this that they may never be plicated when they stand in the place of a breve
And prevent three smaller semibreves from climbing[1] over the threshold.[2]
1 that is, from ascending as separate notes
2 that is, the boundaries of the spaces and lines, and that is without text

Quasi diceret: plica maiori semibrevi duarum in figura poterit id
suplere, sicut supra patuit suo loco ▐◗ :
    Sed plica maiorique duum data tam valet ori.
Ecce ostendit, qualiter supra litteram divisive scandere ab aliquibus
sunt repertae, ut hic:

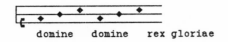

domine   domine   rex gloriae

10

    Scandere divise supra textum sunt ita visae.

   Nonquam ponatur etc. Hic assignat actor quandam regulam, quae talis
est, scilicet quod nonquam debet poni aliqua figura simplex vel non
ligata, ubi potest poni composita vel ligata, quoniam formosior est
compositio, brevior et aptior, dignior atque generalior in hac arte quam
vox simplex per se posita, dum tamen possit cum aliis regulariter
ordinari. Et hoc est quia voces simplices sunt partes, quarum compositio
est totum. Unde cum totum sit dignius suis partibus, quas ponendo

20 terminat et coniungit seu disponit, ideoque figuras compositas nobiliores
dicimus quo ad artem, et sic digniores, quare simplices ad ipsas
principaliter sunt reducendae. Exemplum qualiter simplices ad compositas

reducuntur patet hic ◖▪◗◖ | ◗◖◗ .
   Iure reducetur etc. Hic declarat actor aliam regulam, per quam
praecedens lucide confirmatur, quae talis est: omnis figura simplex, et
hoc propter litteram vel aliquam aliam superhabundantiam, quemadmodum in
motellis et conductis cum littera et similibus, debet reduci ad figuram
compositam in toto vel in parte secundum perfectiones modorum vel

30 imperfectiones. Et hoc est quia modus sive maneries per figuram
compositam et nonquam per simplicem cognoscitur et etiam compilatur,
secundum quod patebit inferius in capitulo specierum. Littera patet.

   Regula est, quod nonquam debet poni aliqua figura simplex vel <non>
ligata, ubi potest poni composita vel ligata:
    Nonquam ponatur simplex ubi iura sequatur
Hic subiungit rationem, dicens, quod figura composita formosior est
simplice:
    Artis composita,[1] quia sic vult esse polita.
40   1 sive figura
Alia regula est corroborans antedictam, quae talis est: omnes voces
simplices
    Iure reducetur vox simplex, si qua locetur,
sunt ad compositas vel ad earum numerum reducendae.
    Compositae cartae vel toto vel quasi parte.[1]
    1 id est, vel in toto vel in parte

----

1 id *om. Sowa*   2 *ex. in marg*   3 **duarum** *pro* **duum** *Sowa*   **tam** *om. Sowa*
4 scandere *om. Sowa*   7-9 *ex. in marg.*   15 decet *pro* debet *Sowa*
19 simplices sunt [[ad composi]] sunt partes *cod.*   25 [[fine]] *sub ex.*
cod.   29 decet *pro* debet *Sowa*   35 decet *pro* debet *Sowa*   <non>
suppl. Sowa   39 simplici *pro* simplice *Sowa*

He means to say that the plica will be able to supply it for the
larger semibreve in a figure of two, as has been shown above in
the right place ⌐⌐ :
     But a plica can be given and arise for the larger of two.
See, he shows how they are found by some to climb separately over a
text, as here:

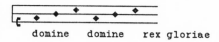

                domine   domine   rex gloriae

          In this way they are seen to climb separately over a text.

     A single one may never be put, etc. Here the author lays out a
certain rule, which is as follows, namely that no single or non-ligated
figure should be put where a composite or ligated figure can be put,
since the composite occurrence of figures is more beautiful, shorter, and
more appropriate, more worthy, and more general in this art than a single
note placed by itself, as long as it can be arranged regularly with other
notes. And this is because single notes are parts, of which the
composite occurrence is the whole. And since the whole is more worthy
than its parts, which in placing it ends and joins together or
distributes, therefore we say that composite figures are more noble as
regards the art, and thus more worthy; and so single figures must be
reduced to them principally. An example of how single figures are

reduced to composite ones is given here ⌐ ⌐ ⌐ ⌐ | ⌐ ⌐ .
     A single note will be reduced, etc. Here the author states another
rule, by which the preceding is plainly confirmed, which is as follows:
Every single figure, and this is on account of the text or some other
over-abundance -- as in motets and conductus with text and similar things
-- should be reduced to a composite figure in whole or in part according
to the perfections or imperfections of the modes. And this is because
mode or manner is recognized by a composite figure and never by a single
one, and it is even put together that way, according to what will be made
clear below in the chapter on the species. Here is the text:

     The rule is that no single or non-ligated figure should ever be put
     where a composite or ligated one can be put:
          A single one may never be put where may follow the laws
     Here he adds a reason saying that the composite figure is more
     beautiful than the single one:
          **Of the art the composite one,[1] because it wants to be elegant in
          this way.**
          1 figure
     There is another rule that corroborates the previous one, which is as
     follows: All single notes
          **The single note will be reduced by law, if there is one
          positioned there,**
     must be reduced to composite ones or to the number of them
          To composite writing either wholly or partly.[1]
          1 that is, either in whole or in part

\<Capitulum secundum\>

Est mensura modus etc. Quoniam actor in praecedenti capitulo
figurarum tam simplicium quam compositarum proprietates proportionesque
nec non et differentias declaravit pariter et naturas, ideoque in hoc
loco secundum capitulum aggreditur sui libri, in quo modorum sive
specierum series nec \<non\> et regulae multiplices insuper et hoquetorum
genera continentur. Et est notandum, quod praecedens capitulum ante
istud ratione multiplici debuit ordinari, quod patet sic: superius dictum
est de omni genere figurarum et de earum quantitatibus et naturis, (fol.
149) ex quibus modus sive maneries efficitur et consistit, quare non sine
10 causa praecedens capitulum ordinari debuit ante istud, nam praeambulae
partes sussequentibus fundamentum originis administrant. Item partes
praeambulae orthographiam delucidant huius artis, sussequentes
ordinationem earum plenarie repraesentant. Sicut ergo in omni scientia
est ponere primum et minimum, utpote in gramatica orthographiam et sic de
aliis, similiter et in musica figuras seu voces, quae orthographiam
illius repraesentant, per certas regulas inde datas, quare non immerito
praecedens capitulum ordinari decrevimus ante istud. Item patet sic:
omne vinculum posterius est eis, quae debent vinciri hoc vinculo. Modus
sive maneries est vinculum figurarum, quare dicimus, quod modorum
20 capitulum figurarum capitulo est et rationabiliter apponendum. Et quia
in praesenti capitulo agitur de modis, per quos omnium cantuum genera
artificiose ac regulariter componuntur, quae sub mensurabili musica sunt
reperta, ideoque in primis quid sit modus sive species videamus, et unde
dicatur modus, et quot sunt modorum species adinventae, et quare tot et
non plures, et quare taliter ordinantur.

Ad primum igitur dicimus, quod modus sive species est quicquid currit
per debitam mensuram longarum vel brevium notularum, et dicitur a
moderando, eo quod omnia cantuum genera moderando dividat et decindat,
vel componat. Et sciendum est, quod sex sunt modi sive species huius
30 artis nec plures nec pauciores, sicut enim sunt sex proportiones vocum
sive simplicium figurarum, ex quibus tota musica compilatur, ad quarum

----

5 \<non\> *suppl. Sowa*   8-9 naturis [[ex quibus]] ex quibus *cod.*
20 et est *pro* est et *Sowa*   22 et *pro* ac *Sowa*   25 e *super* plur[[a]]s

Chapter Two

Mode is the true measuring, etc. Since the author in the preceding chapter has stated the proprieties and proportions of both single and composite figures and also their distinctions and their natures as well, in this place therefore he undertakes the second chapter of his book, in which the sequence of the modes or species as well as the many rules and also the genera of hockets are contained. And it should be noted that the preceding chapter had to be arranged before this one for many reasons, as follows: Above have been discussed all kinds of figures and their quantities and natures (fol. 149) from which mode or manner is made up and consists, and so it is not without reason that the preceding chapter had to be arranged before this one, for introductory parts provide the foundation of origin to subsequent ones. Also the introductory parts clarify the orthography of this art, and the subsequent ones represent the arrangement of them in full. Therefore just as in every science one should first put the smallest thing, for example orthography in grammar and similarly with the others, so in music one should first put the figures or notes given through fixed rules, for these represent its orthography;* and so it was not undeservedly that we decided that the preceding chapter should be arranged before this one.

Also it is clear in this way: Every bond comes after those things which should be bound by this bond. Mode or manner is the bond of the figures, and so we say that the chapter on the modes should rationally also be put after the chapter on the figures. And because the present chapter deals with the modes, by means of which the genera of all melodies which are found in measurable music are put together artfully and according to the rules, therefore let us see first what is a mode or a species, and why a mode is so named, and how many species of modes have been devised, and why there are just so many and not more, and why they are arranged in such a fashion.

Firstly therefore we say that mode or species is whatever runs through the requisite measure of long or short notes, and it is so named from the word regulating [*moderando*], because it divides and cuts apart, or puts together, all genera of melodies by regulating them. And it should be known that there are six modes or species of this art, and not more or less, just as there are six proportions of notes or single

185

similitudinem tantum sex dicimus esse modos. Item sex sunt consonantiae
generales in hac musica, sicut patebit inferius suo loco, per quas tota
musica modulatur, quae per modorum series distribuitur et artatur, ad
quarum similitudinem sex esse dicimus species huius artis. Item musica
procedit per numerum senarium, sicut patuit per vocum numerum antedictum,
et per proportiones varias earundem, similiter et per convenientias seu
consonantias huius artis, similiter et per sex species sive modos. Item
sex sufficiunt, ergo non amplioribus indigemus, eo quod frustra habet
fieri per duo quod potest fieri per unum. Item antecessores nostri,
10 musicae mensurabilis inventores, sex modorum species statuerunt, quorum
vestigia nos insecuti tanquam ab actoritate sex dicimus esse modos,
scilicet primum, secundum, tertium, quartum, quintum, sextum, unicuique
denominationem propriam imponentes.

   Primus igitur dicitur primus, quia levior est et communior omnibus
aliis, item prior quia dignior et generalior omnibus aliis est. Et hoc
est quia in se generaliores et nobiliores figuras continet, ad quas
ceterae figurae cum proprietate positae et perfectae sunt specialiter ac
artificialiter reducendae, sicut in tractatu patuit figurarum. Item quod
primus dici debeat sic aparet: *musica est de numero sonorum, vel de*
20 *numero relato ad sonum.* Sicut ergo in numeris binarius est primum
principium, quia unitas non est numerus, similiter in musica, modus, qui
binarius est in pari proportione numeri, primum principium optinebit.
Sed modus, quem primum dicimus, est huiusmodi, eo quod longa in ipso, a
qua incipit et in qua similiter terminatur, est in proportione temporum
binaria, ergo primus et rationabiliter meruit appellari.

   Et nota, quod tres eorum possunt autentici nuncupari, eo quod in
perfectiores figuras perfectionem suam terminant et distingunt, nam a
longa ducunt originem et finem recipiunt in eandem. Et isti sunt primus,
tertius et quintus. Alii vero plagales poterunt apellari, id est
30 collaterales et minus digniores, eo quod ab imperfectis figuris vel sine
proprietate propria figuratis perfectionem suam terminant et concludunt.
Et isti sunt secundus, quartus et sextus, nam a brevi incipiunt et in
brevem finem recipiunt et adoptant. Nota tamen, quod sunt imperfectae
solummodo quo ad formam.

   Secundus quidem dicitur secundus, quia opponit primo quoad
ordinationem temporum et etiam figurarum, et hoc est ut opposita iuxta se
posita plenius elucescant. Tertius autem tertius appellatur et
ultramensurabilis, quia excedit rectam mensuram. Recta mensura procedit
ab aequalitate, ultra mensuram poni dicitur a superhabundantia et
40 inaequalitate. Numerus par procedit ab aequalitate proportionis, impar
ab inaequalitate. Et sic tertius modus propter sui inaequalitatem, id
est quia ultra mensuram se habet, tertius apellatur, vel tertius dicitur
a trina aequalitate temporum, quam in se continet propria longa tertii
modi, vel tertius dicitur propter ternarium numerum et continuum in
figura. Quartus dicitur quartus, quia in dispositione figurarum tertio
se opponit. Quintus dicitur quintus, quia de se non potest facere
figuram compositam vel ligatam. Figura namque composita in hac arte

----

14 dicitur *add. super scriptum*   15 primus *pro* prior *Sowa*
28-29 primus [[secundus]] tertius *cod.*   30 *post* figuris *ras.*
33 sunt *add. super scriptum*   36 in hoc *pro* hoc est *Sowa*

figures from which the whole of music is made up, and so in conformity
with this we say that there are only six modes. Also there are six
general consonances in music, as will be made clear below in the right
place, through which the whole of music, which is distributed and
restricted by means of the sequence of the modes, is produced, and in
conformity with this we say that there are six species of this art. Also
music proceeds by means of the number six, as has been shown by the
number of notes which has just been mentioned, and by the different
proportions of them, and also by means of the accords or consonances of
this art, and by means of the six species or modes. Also six are enough
and so we do not need more, because it is in vain that something occurs
by means of two that can occur by means of one.* Also our forebears, the
inventors of measurable music, established six species of modes, and we
follow in their tracks as authorities and say that there are six modes,
that is to say the first, second, third, fourth, fifth, and sixth,
placing the proper nomenclature on each one.

So the first is called the first, because it is easier and more
common than all the others, and also because it is more worthy and more
general than all the others. And this is because it contains in itself
more general and more noble figures, to which the rest of the figures
that are placed with propriety and are perfect are reduced specifically
and artificially, as has been shown in the tract on the figures. Also
the fact that it should be called the first appears as follows: "Music
is about the number of sounds or about number as it relates to sound."*
Therefore just as in numbers the binary is the first beginning, because
unity is not a number, so in music the mode which is binary in an equal
proportion of number will obtain the first beginning. And the mode which
we call the first is of this kind, because the long from which it begins
and at which similarly it ends is in the binary proportion of units of
time, therefore it deserves rationally to be called the first.

And note that three of them can be termed authentic,* because they
end and distinguish their perfection in more perfect figures, for they
draw their origin from a long and bring their ending to the same. And
these are the first, third, and fifth. The others indeed can be called
plagal, that is collateral and less worthy, because they end and finish
their perfection with figures that are imperfect or figured without
proper propriety. And these are the second, fourth, and sixth, for they
begin from a breve and bring and take their end at a breve. But note
that they are only imperfect as to their form.

Indeed the second is called the second because it is the opposite of
the first as regards the arrangement of its units of time and also its
figures, and this is so that being opposites placed next to each other
they may shine forth more clearly. The third is called the third and
beyond measuring because it exceeds correct measure. Correct measure
proceeds from equality; beyond measure is said to be placed from over-
abundance and inequality. Equal number proceeds from equality of
proportion; unequal from inequality. And thus the third mode is named
the third on account of its inequality, that is because it occurs beyond
measure; or it is called the third from the threefold equality of the
units of time which the proper long of the third mode contains in itself;
or it is called the third on account of the continuous ternary number in
its figures. The fourth is called the fourth because it is the opposite
of the third in the disposition of its figures. The fifth is called the
fifth because a composite or ligated figure can not be made from it. For

generalior est et nobilior quam simplex, eo quod figurae simplices sunt
ad compositas reducendae, sicut textus antea declaravit. Et ideo
supradictae species quintam praecedere meruerunt. Vel quinta dicitur
quia est vinculum et columpna, a quo aliae tanquam a tenore saepius
fulsiuntur et supra quod resonant dulciter modulatae, et ideo tanquam
vinculum aliis dicitur haec praeponi. Vel quintus dicitur quia sic
placuit institutori, quod quinta species vocaretur. Sexta et ultima
sexta dicitur vel sexto loco ponitur quia quintae opponitur. Quinta
namque est ex omnibus longis, sexta ex omnibus brevibus, et sic
10 sussequetur eo quod cernitur minus digna. Vel sexta et ultima dicitur,
quia ex imperfectis figuris compositis suo modo proprio figuratur. Omnes
siquidem aliae species per perfectas artificialiter protrahuntur, unde
sicut perfectum ante imperfectum sic praeambulae species sive modi istam
praecedere debuerunt. Et sic patet in universo quot sunt species huius
artis et quare taliter ordinantur.

   Haec igitur praesens lectio in duas partes breviter dividatur, in
quarum prima describit actor modum sive maneriem specierum, de quibus est
(fol. 149v) in sequentibus tractaturus. In secunda ostendit sex esse
modi sive species huius artis. Prima pars incipit **Est mensura modus**
20 etc., secunda **Sex species horum** etc. Haec secunda in duas: in prima
agit de numero specierum, in secunda de prima specie dat doctrinam.
Prima incipit **Sex species horum** etc., secunda **Si sit perfecta** etc. Item
prima istarum in duas: in prima sex esse modorum species manifestat, in
secunda per prosae testimonium hoc confirmat quoddam incidens aponendo.
Prima pars incipit ubi dicit **Sex species horum** etc., secunda **Sic recitat
prosa** etc. Et sic patet divisio leoninis.

   Est mensura[1] **modus,**[2] **verax brevium**[3] **notularum**[4]
   1 id est, recta proportio
30 2 id est, maneries
   3 et etiam semibrevium
   4 id est, vocum
   Vel productarum[1] **cuius**[2] **dat dogmata**[3] **nodus.**[4]
   1 sive notularum
   2 sive modi
   3 id est, introductiones
   4 id est, regula

   Sex species horum etc. Hic vult actor specierum numerum recitare,
40 dicens, quod sex sunt species adinventae, sicut glosarum sententia
superius declaravit.
   Quarum mensura etc. Hic dicit actor, quod praedictarum sex specierum
tres in recta mensura se habentes et tres ultramensurabiles nuncupantur.
Recta mensura, ut hic accipitur, est quicquid sub certa et aequali
proportione temporis unius ad minus, vel duorum ad plus, accipitur et
metitur. Ultra mensuram siquidem vocamus quicquid sub impari numero in

----

6 hic proponi *pro* haec praeponi *Sowa*   39 [[est]] **Sex species** *cod.*

indeed the composite figure in this art is more general and more noble
than the single one, because single figures must be reduced to composite
ones, as the text has stated before. And therefore the abovementioned
species deserve to precede the fifth. Or it is called the fifth because
it is the bond and column by which the others are often supported as by
the tenor, and above which they sound, sweetly sung, and therefore this
one is said to be put first like a chain for the others. Or it is called
the fifth because it pleased the person who set it up that it should be
named the fifth species. The sixth and last is called the sixth or is put
in the sixth place because it is the opposite of the fifth. For indeed
the fifth is made up of all longs and the sixth of all breves, and thus
it follows because it is perceived as less worthy. Or it is called the
sixth and last, because it is figured from imperfect composite figures in
its own manner. Indeed all the other species are notated artificially
with perfect figures, and so, as perfect precedes imperfect, thus the
introductory species or modes should precede this one. And thus it is
clear throughout how many species there are of this art and why they are
arranged in this way.

Therefore let this present reading be divided briefly into two parts,
in the first of which the author describes the mode or manner of the
species, with which he is (fol. 149v) about to deal in the following.
The first part begins **Mode is the true measuring**, etc., the second **The
reader states that there are six**, etc. This second part is divided into
two: In the first he deals with the number of the species, in the second
he gives the principle of the first species. The first part begins **The
reader states that there are six**, etc., the second **If it is the first**,
etc. Also the first of these is divided into two: In the first he shows
that there are six species of the modes, in the second he confirms this
through the testimony of the prose, adding something incidental. The
first part begins where he says **The reader states that there are six**,
etc., the second **Thus recites the prose**, etc. And thus the division of
the leonine verses is clear.

> **Mode[2] is the true measuring[1] of the breves[3] of the notemarks,[4]**
> 1 that is, the correct proportion
> 2 that is, manner
> 3 and also the semibreves
> 4 that is, the notes
> **Or of those[1] that are produced, whose[2] principles[3] are given by
> the bond.[4]**
> 1 notes
> 2 the mode's
> 3 that is, introductions
> 4 that is, the rule

The reader states that there are six, etc. Here the author wishes to
recite the number of the species, saying that six species have been
devised, as the meaning of the glosses above has stated.

Of which they say, etc. Here the author says that of the aforementioned six species three are said to occur in correct measure and three
are called beyond measuring. Correct measure as it is used here is
whatever is accepted and measured under a fixed and equal proportion of
one unit of time at least, and two at most. And indeed we call beyond
measure whatever includes the proportion of more units of time in an

longitudine, vel sub pari numero in brevitate, plurium proportionem
temporum comprehendit. Item quod recta mensura sub aequalitate duorum
temporum ad plus et unius ad minus solummodo habeatur, patet per
gramaticam metricam, quae sub tali proportione accentuum ac temporum
reperitur. Item patet sic: illud recte mensuratum dicitur, cui si
aliquid addatur vel sustrahatur, iam a sua rectitudine deviabit, sicut
patet in recta longa et recta brevi. Illud siquidem ultramensurabile
dicitur, quod rectam mensuram sub aliqua proportione excedere reperitur,
sicut patet in maiore longa et maiore brevi. Nam si unicuique temporis
10 proportio sustrahatur, absque substractione formae ac nominis, rectam
mensuram induere sunt repertae. Et sic patet differentia inter tales.

    Sex species[1] **horum lector dat esse modorum,**[2]
    1 id est, divisiones
    2 sive manerierum, sub quibus omne genus cantuum continetur
    Quarum[1] **mensura**[2] **tres dicunt**[3] **currere pura.**[4]
    1 sive specierum
    2 id est, proportione
    3 id est, magistri asserunt
20   4 id est, vera et recta
  Et haec sunt scilicet prima, secunda et sexta:
    Prima, secunda quidem, quis[1] **sexta**[2] **locatur**[3] **ibidem.**
    1 id est, quibus
    2 sive species
    3 id est, adiungitur
    Esse brios[1] **vera**[2] **datur**[3] **istis;**[4] **hoc bene spera.**[5]
    1 id est, mensura
    2 id est, recta
    3 id est, dicitur
30   4 sive tribus supradictis speciebus
    5 id est, considera
    Ultra mensuram[1] **sunt tres aliae, dare curam**
    1 sive rectam, quia sub certa proportione mensurae sunt repertae
    Hiis[1] **melius cura, si vis bene scire futura.**[2]
    1 sive tribus, quae secuntur
    2 id est, ea quae dicenda sunt
    Tertia[1] **quarta datur,**[2] **et eisdem**[3] **quinta**[4] **locatur.**[5]
    1 sive species
    2 id est, adiungitur
40   3 sive duabus
    4 sive species
    5 id est, apponitur
    Sic recitat prosa[1] **studio multiplice**[2] **rosa,**[3]
    1 id est, ars prosaice compilata
    2 id est, valde commendabili
    3 id est, elimata

----

6 quid *pro* aliquid *Sowa* 43 **multiplici** *pro* **multiplice** *Sowa*

uneven number in length or an even number in brevity. Also the fact that
correct measure may only exist under the equality of two units of time at
most and one at least is clear from grammatical meter, which is found
under this same proportion of accents and units of time. Also it is
clear as follows: That thing is said to be correctly measured, which, if
something is added to it or taken away from it, will now deviate from its
correctness, as is clear in the correct long and the correct breve.
Indeed that thing is called beyond measuring which is found to exceed
correct measure under some proportion, as is clear in the larger long and
the larger breve. For if a proportion of time is taken away from any one
of them without taking away their form and name, they are found to take
on correct measure. And thus the difference between them is clear.

The reader states that there are six species[1] of these modes,[2]
1 that is, divisions
2 manners, within which all genera of melodies are contained
Of which[1] they say[3] that three run with pure[4] measure.[2]
1 species
2 that is, proportion
3 that is, the masters assert
4 that is, true and correct
And these are the first, second, and sixth:
**The first and second indeed, with which[1] the sixth[2] is also
positioned.[3]**
1 that is, to which
2 species
3 that is, is added
True[2] meter[1] is stated[3] to be in these;[4] hope for[5] this well.
1 that is, measure*
2 that is, correct
3 that is, is said
4 the three species mentioned above
5 that is, consider
There are three others beyond measure,[1] be careful
1 correct measure; because they are found under a fixed
proportion of measure
**To be more careful about these,[1] if you want to know future
things[2] well.**
1 the three which follow
2 that is, those things which must be said
**The third[1] is given[2] to the fourth, and with those[3] the fifth[4] is
positioned.[5]**
1 species
2 that is, is joined
3 two
4 species
5 that is, is added
Thus recites the prose,[1] worn[3] by much[2] hard work,
1 that is, the treatise put together in prose
2 that is, very commendable
3 that is, polished

Quae[1] **male**[2] **lactavit hunc**[3] **illam qui laceravit.**[4]
1 sive prosa
2 id est, ad damnum suum
3 sive clericum vel magistrum
4 id est, reprehendere praesumpsit

Silva vetus etc. Methaphora sumpta est ab arboribus: sicut ille
oberrans dicitur, qui fructificantes arbores seu terram fructiferam
destruit et desertat, quae sibi et aliis bona de quibus debet vivere
habundandus administrat, sic illum errantem reputat actor iste, qui
doctrinam seu documenta negligit de quibus sumpsit copiosius alimentum.
Cum autem sunt nonnulli artem prosae commendabilis destructores, suamque
in hoc fatuitatem perfectam proprie provulgantes, quos actor percipiens
elationis animo gloriari, ipsos non praesumptionis vitio nec livoris
stimulo simpliciter et methaphorice redarguit admonendo, ne per tales
sophisticas rationes alios velint de ceteris perlicere fraudulenter.

Methaphora:
Silva[1] **vetus stabat nulla violata securi.**
1 id est, prosa, in qua documenta plurima praebebantur
Hii[1] **modo**[2] **securi**[3] **sunt carpere**[4] **quos faciebat.**[5]
1 sive clerici
2 id est, nuper
3 id est, audaces
4 id est, reprehendere
5 id est, documentis informabat
(fol. 150) **Proch dolor,**[1] **O quaedam**[2] **licet edere, non tamen edam.**[3]
1 id est, quantus dolor est quod ipsam vilipendunt; exclamatio est
2 id est, differentia
3 id est, dicam
Modo subiungit rationem, dicens: vox unius vox nullius:
Nullius unius sermo est si sit quoque dius.[1]
1 id est, verus
Degenerare[1] **nego prosam**[2] **sequar, hosque**[3] **relego.**
1 id est, oberrando deviare
2 de qua sumpsi pluries documenta
3 sive clericos vel magistros
Musa[1] **sile propera**[2] **precor assint carmina**[3] **vera.**
1 id est, doctrina
2 id est, noli moram facere alios blaphemando vel etiam acusando
3 sive sua
Et mea[1] **quaeque dabo compendia**[2] **iam properabo.**[3]
1 sive carmina
2 id est, abbreviationes, quas dare intendo
3 id est, breviter agrediar

----

7 Metaphora *pro* Methaphora *Sowa*   9 decet *pro* debet *Sowa*   13 propria
pro proprie *cod.*   15 metaphysice *pro* methaphorice *Sowa*   16 cetero *pro*
ceteris *Sowa*   21 **faciabat** *pro* **faciebat** *Sowa*   29 extera *pro* exclamatio
Sowa

Which[1] **has unfortunately**[2] **suckled him**[3] **who has mutilated**[4] **it.**
1 the prose
2 that is, to its own ruin
3 the cleric or master
4 that is, has dared to censure

The old forest, etc. The metaphor is taken from trees: Just as he
who destroys and ruins fruitful trees or fertile ground -- which provide
him and others with good things from which he could live abundantly -- is
said to be in serious error, so this author considers him to be in error
who neglects the principle or the lessons from which he has copiously
taken his nourishment. But since there are some destroyers of the art of
the praiseworthy prose, who are appropriately exhibiting their own
perfect foolishness in this way, whom the author perceives to be exulting
in their own pride, he refutes them, guided not by the vice of presumption nor by the stimulus of envy but simply and metaphorically, and gives
them warning, lest by means of these sophistical reasonings they want
others to take similar license falsely about the things that remain.

A metaphor:
The old forest[1] **was standing safely with no injury.**
1 that is, the prose, in which very many lessons were supplied
These men[1] **now**[2] **are safe**[3] **to complain**[4] **whom it made.**[5]
1 clerics
2 that is, recently
3 that is, daring
4 that is, find fault
5 that is, informed with its lessons
(fol.150) **Alas, what sorrow!**[1] **O what**[2] **it would be if I could
utter it, and yet I shall not utter it.**[3]
1 that is, what a sorrow it is that they despise it; this is an
exclamation
2 that is, a difference
3 that is, say it
Now he adds a reason, saying that the voice of one person is like
nobody's voice:
The speech of one is that of none, even if it is divine.[1]
1 that is, true
I refuse to dishonor[1] **it, and I shall follow the prose,**[2] **and
banish these people.**[3]
1 that is, deviate from it in error
2 from which I have taken lessons many times
3 the clerics or masters
Silent Muse,[1] **hurry,**[2] **I pray, and let true poems**[3] **be present,**
1 that is, principle
2 that is, make no delay in reviling those others or accusing
them
3 the Muse's
Both mine[1] **and certain summaries**[2] **I shall now hurry**[3] **to give.**
1 the poems
2 that is, the abbreviations which I intend to give
3 that is, I shall undertake briefly

Si sit perfecta etc. Declarata superius serie specierum et quare sunt sex species solummodo et non plures et quare taliter ordinantur, ideoque actor in hoc loco ad cognitionem earum accedere nunc intendit divisionem breviter inserendo. Haec igitur praesens lectio in duas partes dividatur, in quarum prima agit actor de speciebus perfectis, tam in suo genere, quam in genere figurarum, in secunda de speciebus imperfectis in genere figurarum, licet in suo genere sint perfectae. Ideo patet ordo partis praeambulae ad sequentem: prima pars incipit ubi dicit **Si sit perfecta** etc., secunda ibi **Dic speciem sextam** etc. Haec

10 secunda remanet indivisa, sed pars prior in duas dividitur. In prima agit de speciebus de sui natura figuram compositam facientibus, in secunda de speciebus figuram non compositam facientibus. Et quia figura composita in hac arte dignior est et generalior quam sit simplex, nam simplices, ut supra patuit, sunt ad compositas reducendae tanquam pars ad totum, ideo patet ordo. Prima pars incipit ubi dicit **Si sit perfecta** etc., secunda ibi **A longis quinta** etc. Item prima in duas. In prima agit de speciebus in recta mensura se habentibus, in secunda de speciebus ultra mensuram se habentibus, et quia recta mensura in se nihil superfluum in se nihil continet diminutum, ultramensurabilis siquidem a

20 superhabundantia nominatur. Et sic recta mensura a regularitate procedit, ultramensurabilis ab irregularitate. Sicut ergo regulare ante irregulare, ita pars prima ante secundam. Prima pars incipit **Si sit perfecta** etc., secunda ibi **Tertia quae sequitur** etc. Haec secunda in duas: in prima agit de tertia specie, in secunda de quarta. Et sic patet ordo: prima incipit **Tertia quae sequitur** etc., secunda **Opponit quarta** etc. Istae partes remanent indivisae, sed pars principior in duas: in prima agit de prima specie, in secunda de secunda specie dat doctrinam; prima incipit **Si sit perfecta** etc., secunda ibi **Ut didici quondam** etc. Item prima in duas: in prima ostendit actor modum et

30 seriem primae speciei, in secunda tres regulas in ea subicit, per quas eius effectus cognoscitur et habetur. Prima pars incipit **Si sit perfecta** etc., secunda **Norma triplex dabitur** etc. Haec secunda in tres partes propter breviloquium dividatur secundum trium differentias regularum: in prima agit de generaliori regula, in secunda et tertia de specialibus regulis. Prima quidem generalior est, quia se extendit ad omnia genera specierum, et haec incipit **Longe cerne** etc., secunda ibi **Pausaque sit tanta** etc., tertia **Ordo servandus** etc. Et sic patet sententia et divisio leoninis.

Si sit perfecta etc. Notandum est breviter, quod omnis modorum

40 species aut est perfecta aut etiam imperfecta. Perfecta dicitur illa maneries seu species, quando finit per talem quantitatem temporum sicut per illam in qua incipit. Quarta tamen a brevi unius temporis incipit et in brevem duorum terminatur. Et nota, quod quemadmodum duae semibreves ad perfectionem unius temporis seu rectae brevis operantur, sic et duae breves inaequales ad perfectionem unius longae ultramensurabilis

----

16 **E** *pro* **A** *cod.*   21 a *pro* ab *cod.*   25 prima pars *Sowa*
26 principalior *pro* principior *Sowa*   34 generaliore *pro* generaliori
Sowa   37 **servandus** [[etc]] etc. *cod.*   39 **Si sit perfecta** *sine sublinea in cod.*   41 temporum [[et etiam figurarum]] sicut *cod.*

If it is the first, etc. Having stated above the sequence of the species and why there are only six species and not more, and why they are arranged in this way, therefore in this place the author now intends to broach the understanding of them, briefly adding the way the text is divided. Therefore let this present reading be divided into two parts, in the first of which the author deals with perfect species, both in their own category and in the category of figures, and in the second with imperfect species in the category of figures, although as regards their own category they are perfect. Therefore the order of the introductory part to what follows is clear: The first part begins where it says **If it is the first**, etc., the second **Say that the sixth**, etc. This second part remains undivided, but the first part is divided into two. In the first part he deals with species that make a composite figure from their own nature, and in the second with species that make a figure that is not composite. And because in this art the composite figure is more worthy and more general than the single figure -- for single figures, as has been shown above, should be reduced to composites as a part to a whole -- therefore the order is clear. The first part begins where it says **If it is the first**, etc., the second **The fifth species**, etc. Also the first part is divided into two. In the first he deals with species that occur in correct measure, in the second with species that occur beyond measure; and because correct measure contains in itself nothing superfluous, nor does it contain in itself anything diminished, beyond measuring indeed is so named from over-abundance. And thus correct measure proceeds from regularity, and beyond measuring from irregularity. Therefore just as regular comes before irregular, so the first part comes before the second. The first part begins **If it is the first**, etc., the second **The third which follows**, etc. This second part is divided into two: In the first he deals with the third species, in the second with the fourth. And thus the order is clear: The first part begins **The third which follows**, etc., the second **The fourth species is the opposite**, etc. These parts remain undivided, but the first part is divided into two: In the first he deals with the first species, in the second he gives the principle of the second species; the first part begins **If it is the first**, etc., the second **As I learned once**, etc. Also the first part is divided into two: In the first the author shows the mode and the sequence of the first species, in the second he supplies three rules for it, by means of which its effect is recognized and understood. The first part begins **If it is the first**, etc., the second **Three precepts are given**, etc. Let this second part be divided into three parts for the purposes of brevity according to the differences of the three rules: In the first he deals with a more general rule, in the second and third with specific rules. Indeed the first is more general because it extends itself to all genera of species, and this begins **Perceive those that are given**, etc.; the second begins at **The pause is just as big**, etc., the third **The order should be kept**, etc. And thus the meaning and division of the leonine verses is clear.

If it is the first, etc. It should be noted briefly that every species of mode is either perfect or imperfect. A manner or species is said to be perfect when it finishes with the same quantity of units of time as that with which it begins. The fourth however begins with a breve of one unit of time and ends with a breve of two units of time. And note that just as two semibreves have the effect of a perfection of one unit of time or a correct breve, so also two unequal breves have the

operantur.   Imperfecta quidem fit species sive modus, quando finit per
aliam vocem et etiam quantitatem.   Et nota, quod si in principio alicuius
modi inveniantur plures breves vel semibreves, vel aliquid aliud aequippollens pro longa vel loco ipsius vel pro brevi, tales enim diminutiones
debent computari pro longa vel pro brevi, nec offendunt quin species sint
perfectae.

   Vox prior etc.   Hic intendit actor primae speciei notitiam breviter
declarare, dicens, quod prima species est illa quae a recta longa incipit
et recta brevi et longa, et sic usque in infinitum potentialiter, sive
10 per simplices figuras sive per compositas, tam sine littera quam cum
littera.

   Cum littera sicut patet hic et in aliis exemplis:

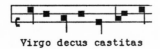

Virgo decus castitas

   Sine littera, ut in tenoribus vel neumis cantuum.

   Et nota, quod aequipollenta in omnibus modis intelligenda sunt.
20 Aequipollenta, dico, ut si non sequatur longa vel brevis, suo loco
accipiatur illud quod loco earum reperitur.

   Exemplum primae speciei sine littera patet hic:

Alleluya

   Norma triplex etc.   Hic dat actor regulam generalem per omnes species
30 sive cantus, quae talis est: longa ante longam valet tria tempora, vel
longam et brevem.

   Pausaque sit etc.   Alia regula est in omni perfecta specie generalis:
tanta est pausa quanta est penultima.   In tertia quidem specie et quarta
duae breves loco penultimae reponuntur.   In ista siquidem prima specie
tam cum littera quam sine littera semper (fol. 150v) brevis est
penultima, ergo similiter et pausa, quod concedimus.   Si quaeratur,
quare plus assimulatur potius penultimae quam ultimae, dicimus, quod
duplex est ad hoc ratio introducta.   Una est, quia omnis pausa perfecta
contrariatur semper suo modo praecedenti, unde si assimularetur ultimae
40 non contrariaretur ei, quare etc.   Item ultima nunc perfecta nunc
imperfecta ante pausam reperitur et sic incerta; pausatio quidem in
quolibet modo perfecto est certa et perfecta et sic ultimae nullatenus
est aequalis.   Penultima siquidem certa est et discretionem facit
certissimam inter modos, quare pausa ei in similitudine conformatur.

   Ordo etc.   Notandum est, quod quilibet modus habet suum ordinem, unde
alibi dicitur: *in omnibus debet ordo servari.*

   Tres ibi etc.   Hic introducit actor practice qualiter primus modus in

----

2 quantite *pro* quantitatem *cod.*   18 Sine littera . . . neumis cantuum
add. in marg.   19 modis [[aequipollenta]] intelligenda *cod.*
20 sequitur *pro* sequatur *Sowa*   37 pociens *pro* potius *Sowa*   39 si *add.*
super scriptum   40 quare etc. *add. super scriptum*   46 decet *pro debet*
Sowa

effect of a perfection of one long that is beyond measuring. An
imperfect species or mode occurs when it finishes with a different note
and quantity. And note that if several breves or semibreves are found at
the beginning of some mode -- or something else equipollent to a long, or
in its place or in the place of a breve -- then such diminutions should
be counted in place of a long or in place of a breve, and they do not
violate the perfection of the species.

The first note, etc. Here the author intends to state briefly the
concept of the first species, saying that the first species is that which
begins from a correct long and a correct breve and a long, and so on
potentially to infinity, whether with single figures or composite
figures, and both without a text and with a text.

With a text, as is shown here and in other examples:

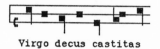

Virgo decus castitas

Without a text, for example in tenors or the melodic formulas of
melodies.

And note that things that are equipollent should be understood in all
modes. By things that are equipollent I mean that if a long or a breve
does not follow, then in their place that which is found in their place
may be accepted.

An example of the first species without text is shown here:

Alleluya

Three precepts are given, etc. Here the author gives a rule that is
generally applicable to all the species or melodies, which is as follows:
A long before a long is worth three units of time, or a long and a breve.

The pause is just as big, etc. Another rule is generally applicable
in every perfect species: The pause is the same length as the
penultimate note. Indeed in the third and fourth species two breves are
put in the place of the penultimate. And indeed in this first species,
both with a text and without a text, (fol. 150v) the penultimate is
always a breve, and therefore similarly so is the pause, which we
concede. If it is asked why it is similar to the penultimate rather than
to the last note, we say that there are two reasons that can be
introduced on this account. One is that every perfect pause always
contradicts its preceding mode; and if it were similar to the last note
it would not contradict it, and so, etc. Also the last note is sometimes
found to be perfect, sometimes imperfect, before a pause, and is thus
unfixed; but indeed the pause in any perfect mode is fixed and perfect
and thus is in no way equal to the last note. The penultimate note
indeed is fixed and makes a very fixed separation between the modes, and
that is why the pause resembles and conforms to it.

The order, etc. It should be noted that any mode has its order, and
so it is said elsewhere:* "In all things must order be kept."

Now I tie three, etc. Here the author introduces in a practical way

figura composita debeat ordinari, dicens, quod figura ternaria cum
proprietate et perfecta debet praecedere vel praeponi, et binaria eiusdem
generis immediate sussequi, nisi pausa propria supponatur, nunc autem
impropria quoad ipsum, sive longa aliqua reperitur. Et non refert utrum
binaria bis vel ter vel pluries ternariam sussequatur. Si quaeratur,
quare ternaria figura semper praecedit binariae, eo quod secundum
ordinationem numeri fieri debeat e converso, et quod binaria ternariae
proprietatis differentiam administrat, solummodo dicimus, quod ista
ternaria huiusmodi speciei notitiam perfectionemque in se continet et
10   penitus repraesentat, quod non facit binaria, quare tanquam dignior
primum locum debuit optinere. Item ternaria trianguli portionem in se
continet et perfecte, et est totum, cuius membrum binaria liquet esse,
quare non sine ratione praecedere recensetur; vel quia a longa incipit et
in eadem replicatur, quod est ipsius modi proprium, alia vero non, quare
etc.

    Si sit perfecta[1] species prior arteque recta,[2]
    1 hoc dicitur ad differentiam imperfectae
    2 id est, artificialiter ordinata, nisi sine proprietate
20   figuretur, quod quandoque accidit
    Vox[1] prior est longa, brevis[2] haec, terna quoque longa.[3]
    1 sive sive sit in figura composita sive per se
    2 unius temporis sive
    3 sive sit minor sive maior
    Lex[1] sic praecedat dum[2] cantus fine[3] recedat.
    1 id est, ordinatio regularis
    2 pro donec
    3 id est, finem perfectum attingat
  Quasi diceret: tres ibi dantur regulae generales:
30   **Norma triplex dabitur quarum prior haec[1] reperitur:**
    1 id est, ista, quae sussequitur
    Longae cerne[1] data,[2] si longa sit immediata,[3]
    1 id est, perpende
    2 id est, concessa vel adiuncta
    3 ita quod non sit medium inter eas
    Tunc[1] primam vere tria tempora dico[2] tenere.[3]
    1 id est, quando nullum medium inter eas est repertum
    2 id est, assero
    3 id est, possidere
40   Quasi diceret: ubicumque longa ante longam reperitur, prior tria
tempora continebit:
    Regula fit talis quocumque modo generalis.
  Alia regula est et in omni specie similiter generalis: tanta est
pausa quanta est penultima:
    Pausaque sit tanta fertur penultima quanta.

----

2 decet *pro* debet *Sowa*   11 ternaria[[m]] *cod.*   12 perfectionem *pro*
perfecte *Sowa*   18 dicit *pro* dicitur *Sowa*   21 **ternam** *pro* **terna** *cod.*
22 *primum* sive *om. Sowa*   39 possiderere *cod.*   42 **quoque** *pro* **quocumque**
Sowa

how the first mode should be arranged in a composite figure, saying that
a ternary figure that is with propriety and is perfect must precede or be
put first, and a binary figure of the same genus follow immediately,
unless a proper pause, or sometimes one that is improper as regards the
mode, is added, or some long is found. And it does not matter whether
two, three, or more binary figures follow the ternary figure. If it is
asked why the ternary figure always precedes the binary -- because
according to the ordering of numbers it should be the reverse, and
because the binary provides the difference in propriety of the ternary --
we only say that this ternary contains the concept and perfection of this
kind of species in itself, and completely represents it, which the binary
figure does not do, and so since it is more worthy it should hold the
first place. Also the ternary figure contains in itself a share of the
triangle and does so perfectly, and is a whole, of which the binary can
be a portion, and so it is not without reason that it is considered right
that it should precede. Or because it begins with a long and is repeated
with a long, and that is proper to this mode; but the other figure is
not, and so, etc.

> **If it is the first species, and it is perfect[1] and correct by
> art,[2]**
> 1 this is said to distinguish it from the imperfect
> 2 that is, artificially arranged, unless it is figured without
> propriety, which sometimes happens
> **The first note[1] is a long, the next one a breve,[2] and the third
> also long.[3]**
> 1 whether it is in a composite figure or by itself
> 2 of one unit of time
> 3 whether it is smaller or larger
> **Let the law[1] excel in this way, while[2] the melody withdraws at
> the end.[3]**
> 1 that is, the regular arrangement
> 2 instead of: until
> 3 that is, reaches a perfect ending

He means to say that three general rules are given for it:

> **Three precepts are given, of which this[1] is the first that is
> found:**
> 1 that is, this one that follows
> **Perceive[1] those that are given to[2] the long; if the long is
> immediate,[3]**
> 1 that is, consider
> 2 that is, put with or added to
> 3 in such a way that there is nothing in between them
> **Then[1] I say[2] indeed that the first will hold[3] three units of
> time.**
> 1 that is, when there is nothing found in between them
> 2 that is, I assert
> 3 that is, possess

He means to say that whenever a long is found before a long, the
first will contain three units of time:

> **Such a rule is general to any mode.**

There is another rule which is also general to every species: the
pause is the same size as the penultimate note:

> **The pause is just as big as the penultimate.**

Sed brevis¹ est iure quod denotat ordo figurae.²

1 in ista specie penultima est, ergo similiter et pausa

2 id est, ordinatio figurarum

Corripe¹ sic pausam,² noli plus quaerere causam.³

1 O cantor vel lector

2 huius speciei

3 quasi diceret: non est super hoc inquirendum

Ordo¹ servandus sit in omnibus atque notandus,

1 id est, numerus punctorum ante pausam, et hoc praecipue quo ad

10   temporum ordinationem et numerum

Modo subiungit rationem, dicens: et sive pari numero vel impari; eo
quod illud quod est in pari, debet concordari omni quod fit in
impari:

Namque suum numerum retinet quaevis specierum.

Tres¹ ibi nunc cordo² post binas³ ut docet ordo.⁴

1 sive cum proprietate et perfectione

2 id est, iungo

3 sive sequentes

4 id est, ordinatio regularis

20

Ut didici etc. Hic accedit ad notitiam secundae speciei, ostendendo
in primis qualiter primae speciei secundum vocum transpositionem se
opponit, dicens, quod quemadmodum prima species est illa, quae procedit a
longa et brevi et longa et sic usque in infinitum, similiter et secunda
est illa, quae procedit ex brevi et longa et brevi et sic usque in
infinitum potentialiter. Et nota, quod in prima specie vel secunda omnes
longae sunt duorum temporum et brevis unius, secundum quod textus
litterae manifestat.

Saepe duas ternis etc. Hic dat actor doctrinam qualiter secunda
30 species se habeat in figuris, dicens, quod binaria figura debet
praecedere ternariae, ad hoc ut in dispositione figurarum prima et
secunda ab invicem se opponant. Et non refert utrum binaria cum
proprietate posita bis vel ter vel pluries praecedat ternariae sine
proprietate. Et illa ternaria debet in fine reponi semper ante pausam
vel sola potest esse pausatione undique perlustrata.

Exemplum qualiter disponitur figura binaria ante ternariam patet hic:

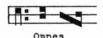

Omnes

40

Exemplum illius speciei cum littera patet hic:

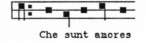

Che sunt amores

----

8 [[**Ordo notat verum servatus sex specierum**]]   12 decet *pro* debet *Sowa*
14 **unum** *pro* **suum** *Sowa*   30 decet *pro* debet *Sowa*   31 in *add. super
scriptum*   34 decet *pro* debet *Sowa*   35 pausatio *pro* pausatione *Sowa*

But it is a breve[1] by law, as the order of the figure[2] indicates.
1 the penultimate in that species, and therefore so is the pause
2 that is, the arrangement of the figures
Take hold[1] of the pause[2] in this way, and do not seek any more for the reason.[3]
1 O cantor or reader
2 of this species
3 he means to say that one should not ask questions on this topic
The order[1] should be kept and noted in all of them,
1 that is, the number of written notes before a pause, and especially as regards the arrangement and number of the units of time
Now he adds a reason, saying that it is either with an even number or with an uneven one, because that which is in the even position must concord with everything that occurs in the uneven position:
For each of the species keeps its number.
Now I tie[2] three[1] there after the twos,[3] as the order[4] teaches.
1 with propriety and perfection
2 that is, I join
3 the ones that follow
4 that is, the regular arrangement

As I learned, etc. Here he broaches the concept of the second species, showing first how it is the opposite of the first species according to the transposition of the notes, saying that just as the first species is that which proceeds from a long and a breve and a long, and so on to infinity, so similarly the second is that which proceeds from a breve and a long and a breve, and so on potentially to infinity. And note that in the first species and the second all the longs are of two units of time and the breve is of one, according to what the text shows.

Often you see twos, etc. Here the author gives the principle as to how the second species occurs in the figures, saying that the binary figure must precede the ternary so that in the disposition of their figures the first and the second species are the opposite of each other. And it does not matter whether the binary that is placed with propriety precedes the ternary without propriety twice or three times or many times. And that ternary figure must always be placed at the end before the pause, or it can be alone, with the pause distributed on both sides.

An example of how the binary figure is placed before the ternary is given here:

Omnes

An example of that species with text is given here:

Che sunt amores

Exemplum qualiter ternaria per se posita reperitur patet hic:

Omnes

Ut didici[1] **quondam speciem dic**[2] **esse secundam.**
1 sive a magistris et ab arte
2 O lector vel cantor
Oppositam[1] **certe**[2] **primae quis**[3] **noscere**[4] **per te,**
1 id est, opposite ordinatam
2 id est, in rei veritate
3 id est, potes
4 id est, cognoscere
Nam[1] **brevis**[2] **est longae**[3] **praetexta,**[4] **brevem quoque iunge.**[5]
1 pro quia
2 sive vox
3 duorum temporum sive
4 id est, praeposita
5 sive illi longae
(fol. 151) **Lex sic procedat,**[1] **dum cantus fine recedat.**
1 id est, regula supradicta in hac specie propria est et etiam generalis
Pausaque[1] **longetur**[2] **cum longans penultima detur.**
1 et hoc duorum temporum solum
2 hoc, dico, specie existente perfecta
Unum datque[1] **brevis tempus solum,**[2] **duo**[3] **quaevis**
1 sicut exempla praeposita manifestant
2 id est, unicum
3 secundum suum modum sive
Longa,[1] **sed hac specie**[2] **prima quoque lege sophiae,**[3]
1 propria sive
2 id est, ista secunda et prima
3 id est, artis
Nota practicam: regula est: figura binaria cum proprietate debet ternariae sine proprietate praeponi:

Saepe duas ternis velut hic  **praecedere cernis.**
Vox[1] **brevis hunc morem**[2] **finit, sic**[3] **longa priorem.**[4]
1 id est, figura vel punctus
2 id est, istum secundum modum
3 pro sicut
4 sive speciem

Tertia quae sequitur etc. Hic exequitur actor de speciebus sive modis ultra mensuram se habentibus; quod autem ultra mensuram se habere videantur, satis patuit per praedicta. Nam sicut supradictum est, recta

----

1 per se [[posi]] posita *cod.*   sic *pro* hic *Sowa*   11 **Oppositam**
[[**primae**]] **certe** *cod.*   14 potest *pro* potes *Sowa*   36 decet *pro* debet
Sowa

An example of how the ternary figure is found placed by itself is given here:

Omnes

As I learned[1] once, say[2] that there is a second species.
1 from masters and from the treatise
2 O reader or cantor
You can[3] know[4] by yourself that it is certainly[2] the opposite[1] of the first,
1 that is, arranged in the opposite fashion
2 that is, in the truth of the matter
3 that is, you are able to
4 that is, understand
For[1] the breve[2] is put before[4] the long,[3] and also add a breve.[5]
1 instead of: because
2 note
3 of two units of time
4 that is, placed in front of
5 to that long
(fol. 151) Let the law proceed in this way,[1] until the composition withdraws at the end.
1 that is, the abovementioned rule is proper and general in this species
And let the pause[1] be lengthened[2] when the penultimate is given as lengthened.
1 and this only of two units of time
2 I say that this applies to the perfect species
And the breve gives[1] only one[2] unit of time, and two[3] for each
1 as the examples given above show
2 that is, a single
3 according to its mode
Long,[1] but in this species[2] and also the first, by the law of wisdom,[3]
1 proper long
2 that is, this second one and the first
3 that is, the art
Note the practice: The rule is: The binary figure with propriety must be put before the ternary without propriety:

Often you see twos as here ![notation] **precede the threes.**
The breve note[1] finishes this method,[2] as[3] the long finishes the first one.[4]
1 that is, figure or written note
2 that is, this second mode
3 instead of: just as
4 species

The third which follows, etc. Here the author describes the species or modes that are beyond measure; and the fact that they seem to be beyond measure has been made clear enough by the things mentioned above.

mensura sub duplici proportione accentuum solummodo reperitur, sicut
patet in gramatica metrica et in gramatica de accentu, in qua tempus
regulariter consideratur secundum longum et brevem. Longitudo autem
illic duorum temporum continet quantitatem, brevitas vero unius temporis
morulam repraesentat, et sic sub illis duobus accentibus in hac arte
rectam mensuram longitudinis et etiam brevitatis solummodo reputamus,
quicquid autem talem longitudinis mensuram ac etiam brevitatis excedere
reperitur ultramensurabile nuncupantes, utputa longam trium temporum et
brevem duorum, quae in ista tertia specie et in quarta specifice

10 reponuntur. Item quod ultramensurabiles sint repertae patet sic:
mensurabile dicitur illud esse, quod, recte mensuratum secundum suum
nomen, nihil in se superflui nihil in se continet diminuti. Longa duorum
temporum et brevis unius sunt huiusmodi, eo quod in diminutione a sua
rectitudine deviarent, quare sub recta mensura positas nec immerito
nuncupamus. Reliquas vero superfluum continentes ultramensurabiles
decrevimus apellari, sicut sunt longa maior et brevis maior. Quod autem
ex superhabundantia ultramensurabiles videantur, patet per diminutionem
earundem. Nam si quaelibet diminutionem unius temporis patiatur, tunc
absque variatione nominationis rectam denominationem et propriam

20 retinebit, ideoque ipsas ultramensurabiles apellamus. Et sic ibi
dupliciter loquimur de mensura, scilicet prout in se nihil continet
superfluum aut etiam diminutum vel prout in ea necessitatis causa sive
approbata consuetudine quid superfluere reperitur. Quare autem
praeambulae species hanc praecedere debuerunt, patuit per praedicta.
Haec autem species est, quae procedit ex una longa et duabus brevibus et
altera longa, tam sine littera quam cum littera.

    Sine littera ut hic:

30

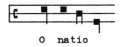

    Cum littera sic:

o natio

40   **Tertia**[1] **quae sequitur**[2] **superare brios**[3] **reperitur.**
    1 sive species
    2 istam secundam
    3 id est, rectam mensuram, quamvis sic mensuretur
    Terna[1] **namque**[2] **sinis brevibus praecedere binis**
    1 sive specie
    2 pro quia
  Modo subiungit, quare mensuram excedunt:
      Longam,[1] **post**[2] **vere petit altera longa**[3] **sedere.**
      1 sive trium temporum
50   2 sive illas duas breves
      3 sive maior

----

22 ac *pro* aut *Sowa*   43 mensuratur *pro* mensuretur *Sowa*   44 **finis** *pro*
sinis *Sowa*

For, as has been said above, correct measure is only found in two proportions of accents, as is clear in the grammar of metrics and in the grammar of accent, in which time is regularly considered according to long and short. And there length contains the quantity of two units of time, and brevity represents a delay of one unit of time, and in this art the only way we calculate the correct measure of length and brevity is with those two accents. But whatever is found to exceed such a measuring of length and brevity we call beyond measuring, for example a long of three units of time and a breve of two, which are specifically used in this third and fourth species. Also the fact that they are found as beyond measuring is clear from the following: A measurable thing is said to be that which is correctly measured, as its name implies, and contains nothing in itself that is superfluous or diminished. A long of two units of time and a breve of one are of this kind, because, if they were diminished, they would deviate from their correctness, and so we term them as deservedly put in the category of correct measure. We have decided that the rest that contain something superfluous should be called beyond measuring, and such are the larger long and the larger breve. But the fact that they seem to be beyond measuring from over-abundance is clear from diminishing them. For if one of them undergoes a diminution of one unit of time, then without variation of name it will keep the correct and proper nomenclature; and so we call them beyond measuring. And thus in that case we speak in two ways about measure, that is to say in as much as it contains nothing superfluous or diminished in itself, and in as much as something is found to be superfluous in it as a result of necessity or approved custom. And the reason why the introductory species ought to precede this one, has been made clear above. And this species proceeds from one long and two breves and another long, both without text and with text.

Without text as here:

With text as here:

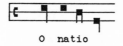

O natio

The third[1] which follows[2] is found to excel the meter.[3]
1 species
2 that second one
3 that is, correct measure, although it is measured this way
For[2] indeed in the third[1] you allow two breves to be preceded by
1 species
2 instead of: because
Now he adds the reason why they exceed the measure:
A long,[1] and after[2] indeed another long[3] wants to sit.
1 of three units of time
2 those two breves
3 a larger one

Opponit etc. Exemplum illius patet hic et sine littera:  .

    Opponit[1] **quarta species huic,**[2] **respice cartam.**[3]

    1 in ordinatione vocum sive

    2 id est, tertiae

    3 id est, sicut liber recitat per exempla

Ecce ostendit qualiter in dispositione vocum tertiae se opponit:

    Duplice namque brevi longam ratus undique sevi.

Hic dat actor regulam de longis et brevibus, dicens quod longa vera vel

10   **Ternae vel quartae speciei longa fit arte,**

propria in hiis speciebus est trium temporum.

    Tempora terna gerens, quae quinta tenet sibi quaerens.[1]

    1 id est, acquirens

    De brevibus[1] **vere prior**[2] **unum tempus habere**[3]

    1 sive supradictis

    2 sive brevis

    3 id est, importare

    Dicitur, illa[1] **gerit duo tempora lex ita quaerit.**

    1 id est, altera brevis, et sic rectam mensuram excedere

20   reperitur

Sola brevis etc. In tertia specie vel in quarta talis regula reperitur: quotienscumque sola brevis unius temporis alicui longae praeponitur, illa longa nisi duo tempora continebit, eo quod brevis praecedens ab ipsa surripitur aut propter superhabundantiam litterae aut propter colorem musicae variandae.

Propter superhabundantiam litterae, sicut patet hic:

30

Ave regina etc.

Aut propter colorem musicae purpurandae vel variandae sic:

40   **Si longae plures** etc. Alia regula est in tertia specie nunc inventa, quae talis est: quotienscumque quatuor breves et minores inter duas longas sunt repertae, longa sussequens nisi duo tempora continebit, eo quod brevis ultima sibi immediate praeposita sustrahitur ab eadem. Longa vero praecedens tria tempora continebit, et debet signari per tractulum,

----

2 **carta** *pro* **cartam** *cod.*   7 **Duplici** *pro* **Duplice** *Sowa*   23 reperitur [[vel]] quotienscumque *cod.*   25 ipsa [[subri]] surripitur *cod.*
34 purpuradae *pro* purpurandae *cod.*   44 decet *pro* debet *Sowa*

The fourth species, etc. An example of that one is given here and without text:  .

> **The fourth species is the opposite[1] of this,[2] have regard for these pages.[3]**
>
> 1 in the arrangement of the notes
> 2 that is, the third
> 3 that is, just as the book recites by means of examples

See, he shows how it is the opposite of the third species in the disposition of its notes:

> **For indeed I thought that the long should be preceded everywhere by two breves.**

Here the author gives a rule about longs and breves, saying that the true long or

> **In the third or fourth species the long occurs by art,**

proper long in these species is of three units of time.

> **Bearing three units of time, which the fifth also seeks[1] and has for itself.**
>
> 1 that is, acquires

> **Of the[1] breves indeed the first[2] is said to have[3] one unit of time,**
>
> 1 abovementioned
> 2 breve
> 3 that is, convey

> **But that one[1] bears two units of time, as the law requires.**
>
> 1 that is, the other breve; and thus it is found to exceed correct measure

When a single breve, etc. In the third species or in the fourth the following rule is found: Whenever a single breve of one unit of time is put in front of any long, that long will only contain two units of time, because the preceding breve is taken away from it, either on account of the over-abundance of text, or on account of a rhetorical device to vary the music.

On account of the over-abundance of text is shown here:

Ave regina etc.

And on account of a rhetorical device to embellish or vary the music is shown here:

If you put several, etc. Another rule is now discovered in the third species, which is as follows: Whenever four smaller breves are found between two longs, the following long will only contain two units of time, because the last breve put immediately before it is taken from it. But the preceding long will contain three units of time and must be

qui vocatur divisio modorum, sicut patet hic:

dex ele ma tot motur emble

Regula est: quotienscumque sola brevis uni longae praeponitur in
hiis speciebus, <illa longa nisi duo tempora continebit>:
Sola brevis longae praetexta breves quoque iunge
10   (fol. 151v) **Huic,[1] duo tempora fert,[2] prior unum nam brevis
aufert.[3]**
1 sive longae
2 subintellige longa illa
3 hic ostendit, quare solum uno tempore mensuratur
Doctrina est, quasi diceret: si plures breves, utputa quatuor et
aequales, in tertia specie vel in quarta
Si longae plures praeponas hoc bene cures:
alicui longae praeponantur, accidit nunc, quod ultima sustrahit illi
longae solum tempus, et sic nisi duo tempora continebit:
20   **Proxima fine quidem nunc tempus tollit eidem.**

A longis quinta etc. Actor dicit, quod quinta species, quae
ultramensurabilis est, ex omnibus longis undique perlustratur, ut patet
hic:

manere

30   Et nota, quod duplex longa ob defectum planae musicae, aut propter
colorem eiusdem ibi saepius reperitur, aut in duplo cantu sic:

In bethlehem

aut in tenore
et hoc assidue,
sicut patet hic:

40
A longis[1] quinta species est undique tincta.
1 sive figuris et simplicibus, nisi abusive causa brevitatis in
figura ternaria sint positae
Hic dat actor doctrinam de pausis istarum trium specierum, dicens,
In specie terna quintam coniunge quaterna
quod si sit perfecta et prout decet ordinata tria tempora continebit:

3-5 *sine tractulo in cod.*   22 **A** *om. Sowa*   33-38 *ex. in marg.*
46 quod si[[t]] sit *cod.*

marked by a small line, which is called the division of the modes, as is shown here:

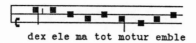

dex ele ma tot motur emble

The rule is: Whenever a single breve is put before one long in these species, that long will only contain two units of time:

When a single breve is put before a long, also add breves
(fol. 151v) To it,[1] then it[2] carries two units of time, for the
first breve takes away one.[3]
1 the long
2 understand: that long
3 here he shows why it is only measured by one unit of time

He means to say that the principle is: If several breves, for example four equal ones, in the third species or in the fourth

If you put several before a long take good care of this:
are put before some long, it happens now that the last one takes away from that long a single unit of time and thus it will only contain two units of time:

The one next to the end indeed now takes away a unit of time
from it.

The fifth species, etc. The author says that the fifth species, which is beyond measuring, is filled up throughout with all longs, as is shown here:

manere

And note that because of a defect in the plainsong or on account of a rhetorical device in it, a double long is often found there, either in the duplum melody, like this:

or in the tenor
and this is constantly,
as is shown here:

In bethlehem

The fifth species is colored throughout by longs.[1]
1 in single figures, unless they are inappropriately put in a ternary figure for reasons of brevity

Here the author gives the principle of the pauses of these three species, saying

In the third species and the fourth, and add the fifth,
that if it is perfect and arranged as it should be, it will contain three units of time:

Nec plus praebebit, tria tempora pausa tenebit.
Hac specie[1] longam duplicem[2] sic[3] quandoque[4] pungam,
1 id est, in hac quinta
2 id est, sex tempora continentem
3 sicut hic: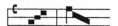

4 id est, propter defectum planae musicae vel litterae
Hic ostendit actor ubi saepius reperitur:
Namque suo more sedem petit usque[1] tenore.
10   1 id est, assidue
Nunc[1] duplo[2] constat[3] *In Bethleem*[4] tibi[5] monstrat.
1 id est, quandoque
2 id est, secundo cantu
3 id est, reponitur
4 id est, ille motellus
5 O cantor

Dic speciem sextam etc. Hic accedit actor ad notitiam sextae
speciei, quae ex omnibus rectis brevibus seminatur, tam sine littera,
20 ut hic:

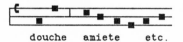

quam cum littera, sicut patet hic:

douche   amiete   etc.

30

Hac quatuor etc. Hic subiungit actor breviter notitiam ipsius quo ad
figurarum ordinem in eadem, dicens, quod sexta species in figuris debet
ordinari per figuram quaternariam imperfectam ternariae imperfectae
praecedentem. Et non refert utrum ternaria bis vel ter vel pluries
sussequatur, sicut praesens exemplum plenarie manifestat sic:

40   Quomodo autem per ternariam imperfectam per se positam gradiatur,
superius est ostensum. Quare autem ultima nominatur, patuit per
praedicta.

Dic[1] speciem sextam[2] rectis brevibus[3] fore textam.
1 O cantor
2 et ultimam sive
3 per hoc excludit maiores breves

27-29 *ex. in marg.*   32 decet *pro* debet *Sowa*   41 nominetur *pro*
nominatur *cod.*   47 maiore *pro* maiores *cod.*

The pause will hold three units of time, and will not supply more.

In this species[1] **I shall sometimes**[4] **draw a double long,**[2] **in this way,**[3]

1 that is, in this fifth species

2 that is, containing six units of time

3 as here:

4 that is, on account of a defect in the plainsong or in the text

Here the author shows where it is often found:

For indeed in its manner it seeks a location everywhere[1] **in the tenor.**

1 that is, constantly

Now[1] **it stands**[3] **in the duplum,**[2] **as "In Bethlehem"**[4] **shows you.**[5]

1 that is, sometimes

2 that is, the second melody

3 that is, it is placed

4 that is, that motet

5 O cantor

Say that the sixth species, etc. Here the author broaches the concept of the sixth species, which is produced entirely from correct breves, both without text, as here:

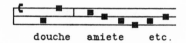

and with text, as is shown here:

In this you see four, etc. Here the author adds briefly the concept of it as to its order of figures, saying that the sixth species should be arranged in its figures with an imperfect fourfold figure preceding an imperfect ternary figure. And it does not matter whether the ternary follows twice or three times or several times, as the present example shows fully:

How it moves through an imperfect ternary figure placed by itself, however, has been shown above. And why it is named the last has been shown above.

Say[1] **that the sixth**[2] **species is woven from correct breves.**[3]

1 O cantor

2 and last

3 in saying this he excludes larger breves

> Hac[1] quatuor[2] ternis brevibus[3] praecedere[4] cernis
> 1 sive specie
> 2 cum proprietate et imperfectas
> 3 similiter cum proprietate et imperfectis
> 4 in figura composita sive
> Ac[1] imperfectas[2] has omnes dic fore lectas.
> 1 pro et
> 2 sive tam quaternariae quam ternariae debent protrahi
> imperfectae

10

Non sibi pausa etc., eo quod aequale. Modi principium et finis non recipiunt contrarietatem quare neque pausam, cum pausa contrarietur semper suo modo praecedenti.

> **Non sibi pausa datur prior hinc ve secunda legatur.**
> **Pausa dabit nosse specierum sex tibi posse.**
> Nota, quod si modus est perfectus, et pausa similiter, ac etiam e
> converso:
> **Cernere perfectae si sint vel non bene[1] rectae.**

20   1 id est, artificialiter

Ordo notat verum etc. In prohemio sive prologo huius libri superius audivistis, quomodo quidam in suis artibus noviter exaltatis prosam huius musicae mensurabilis per singula capitula destruebant, quorum reprehentio me compellit hoc opus suscipere describendum. Dicebant et enim in suo modorum capitulo novem esse modos sive species huius artis ad similitudinem novem instrumentorum naturalium, haec verbula subiungentes: *ad quorum modorum cognitionem discernendam, et multorum etiam errorem destruendum, tres liberaliores excipiuntur, scilicet primus, quartus et*

30 *septimus.* Cetera propter breviloquium praetermitto. Sed sciendum, quod ex ordinatione figurarum suas species componebant. Primum ita siquidem describebant: primus modus dicitur, qui tantum componitur ex perfectis figuris, qui quintus est quo ad nos. Secundum enim dicebant quem primum nominamus et sic de aliis, secundum quod in suis artibus continetur. Octavum siquidem dicebant fieri ex omnibus semibrevibus inaequalibus positis in figura vel sine secundum tamen numerum binarium ordinatis; nonum enim ex tribus semibrevibus et aequalibus. Quod autem sic disponere sit inutile et etiam contra ipsos, patet multiplici ratione.
Una est quia si hoc esset verum, non essent solummodo novem modi immo

40 etiam infinitus esset numerus eorundem, cum infinitae figurae et vario modo dispositae nunc simplices nunc compositae inter duas pausas habeant reperiri seu etiam ordinari. Item patet per dictum suum, quod octavus et nonus esse non possint, etiam quo ad ipsos sic: perfectus cantus non potest fieri nisi per perfectum modum, et perfectus modus nisi <per> perfectas figuras seu voces. Semibreves tam minores quam maiores sunt penitus imperfectae, ergo perfectum modum possunt nullatenus generare. Cum autem in omni re perfectae et imperfectae a parte finis sint solummodo perpendendae, dicimus, quod sicut vox perfecta perfectum modum

----

1 *in marg.:* quatuor hic   3 imperfecta *pro* imperfectas *cod.*
4 imperfecte *pro* imperfectis *Sowa*   7 etiam *pro* et *Sowa*   11-13 *in
marg.*   15 *inter versus*   24-25 *inter* reprehentio *et* me *ras.*   26 modo
pro modorum *Sowa*   35 fieri *om. Sowa*   44 <per> *suppl. Sowa*

In this[1] you see four[2] precede[4] three breves,[3]
1 species
2 with propriety and imperfect
3 also with propriety and imperfect
4 in a composite figure
And[1] say that all these should be read as imperfect.[2]
1 instead of: also
2 both the fourfold and ternary figures should be notated as imperfect

A pause is not given, etc., because it is equal. The beginning and end of the mode are not in contrast, and so neither is the pause, since the pause is always the contrary of the mode that precedes it.

A pause is not given to it as the first or second is appointed.
The pause will give you the ability to know the six species,
Note that if the mode is perfect then so is the pause, and also the reverse:
And to see if they are perfect or not properly[1] correct.
1 that is, artificially

Keeping the order, etc. In the introduction or prologue of this book above you have heard how some people in their treatises which have been recently praised were destroying the prose work on this measurable music in every single chapter, and the need to censure them forces me to take up the task of writing this work. For they were saying in their chapter on the modes* that there are nine modes or species of this art in conformity with the nine natural instruments, adding these words: "In order to gain clear knowledge of these modes, and destroy the error of many people, three of the more liberal are selected, that is to say the first, fourth, and seventh."* The rest I leave out for the sake of brevity. But it should be known that they were putting together their species from the arrangement of the figures. Indeed they described the first as follows: The first mode is said to be the one which is only made up of perfect figures. And this is the fifth according to us. For they said that the second is the one which we name the first and so on for the others, according to what is contained in their treatises. Indeed they said that the eighth is made up entirely of unequal semibreves placed in a figure or without a figure but arranged according to the binary number.* The ninth is made up of three equal semibreves.* But the fact that it is useless and contrary to the modes to put them this way, is clear for many reasons.
One is that if this were true, there would not only be nine modes but rather an infinite number of them, since an infinite number of figures, put in different ways, sometimes single, sometimes composite, could be found to occur or be arranged between two pauses. Also it is clear from their own saying that the eighth and ninth mode could not exist, even according to their own words: A perfect melody can not occur except by means of a perfect mode,* and a perfect mode can not occur except by means of perfect figures or notes.* Both smaller and larger semibreves are completely imperfect, therefore they can in no way generate a perfect mode. Since therefore in every regard figures are only to be reckoned as perfect and imperfect with respect to their end, we say that just as a

perficit et componit, similiter imperfecta illum modum faciet
imperfectum. Semibreves sunt huiusmodi, ergo planum est, quod octavus et
nonus modus sunt semper et penitus imperfecti. Si dicant, quod semper
sunt perfecti, contra si unum correlativorum non inest nec alterum iam
manebit. Perfectum et imperfectum tanquam correlative (fol. 152) se
habent eo quod unum ducit originem ab altero, nam a diminutione
perfectionis sumpsit imperfectio sibi nomen. Ergo si octavus et nonus in
suo genere perfecti nullatenus possunt esse, nec etiam imperfecti, ergo
per consequens neque modi. Sed planum est ipsos nonquam perfectionis
10   induere potestatem, eo quod ex imperfectis vocibus componuntur, quare
similiter neque cantus perfectus ex eis absque aliarum consortio poterit
compilari. Si igitur tales voces perfectum cantum non perficiant, ergo
similiter neque modum, quod concedimus.

     Item in ista musica non est modus secundum nos, qui non potest per
suas figuras proprias seu voces prout exigit ordinatas a principio usque
in finem cantum aliquem componere et perficere, absque figuris seu
adiutorio aliorum. Quintus, sextus, octavus, nonus secundum
dispositionem eorum, qui ita disponere praesumpserunt, nonquam cantum
aliquem secundum se a principio usque ad finem deducere sunt reperti,
20   ergo neque modos dicimus reperiri, cum modi ab effectu suum nomen debeant
importare. Nos siquidem tales cantuum dispositiones ex ˈquibus modos suos
perficiunt et componunt, modorum contrarias apellamus. Et de talibus
immediate proponimus facere mentionem, ad hoc ut lucidius pateant
antedicta et altercatio rationum ex opositis introducta. Littera per se
patet.

     Hic subiungit actor, quod recta ordinatio preservata modorum notitiam
manifestat:
          Ordo notat verum servatus sex specierum.
30   **Quique[1] novem dicunt[2] artis[3] species maledicunt.[4]**
          1 id est, illi novi impositores
          2 id est, asserunt
          3 sive huius
          4 id est, maledicere praesumunt
          Ne credas dictis illorum[1] tam male fictis.[2]
          1 id est, noli dictis eorum acquiescere, eo quod contra artem et
          sententiam meliorum
          2 id est, compositis
     Hic ostendit actor per regulam, quod nonquam debet fieri per duo quod
40   potest fieri per unum:
          Per duo nec frustra quod in unum quis dare frustra.

     Mixtim conveniunt etc. Hic vult actor breviter specierum
convenientias declarare dicens sex esse modos sive species, ex quibus
omne genus cantuum conficitur et habetur. Et nota, quod quemadmodum ex
quatuor elementis seu humoribus efficitur unum corpus per mundanam
musicam aut humanam, sic per convenientias huiusmodi specierum potest

----

2 est *add. super scriptum*   3 et *om. Sowa*   4 imperfecti *pro* perfecti
cod.   7 nomen [[tunc]] ergo *cod.*   8 generi *pro* genere *Sowa*
22 conficiunt *pro* perficiunt *cod., corr. Sowa*   31 compositores *pro*
impositores *Sowa*   39 decet *pro* debet *Sowa*

perfect note completes and puts together a perfect mode, so an imperfect note will make that mode imperfect. Semibreves are of this kind, therefore it is obvious that the eighth and ninth mode are always completely imperfect. If they say that they are always perfect -- on the contrary, if one of the correlatives is not in it then the other will no longer remain. Perfect and imperfect occur as correlatives, (fol. 152) because one draws its origin from the other, for imperfection takes its name from the diminution of perfection. Therefore if the eighth and ninth mode in their genus can in no way be perfect, and also not imperfect, therefore as a result they can not be modes. But it is obvious that they never take on the power of perfection, because they are made up of imperfect notes, and so similarly neither can a perfect melody be made up from them without the company of other notes. If therefore such notes may not complete a perfect melody, so similarly they may not complete a mode, which we concede.

Also in music, according to us, that is not a mode which can not put together and complete some melody from the beginning to the end by means of its own figures or notes arranged as it requires, and without the figures or help of other modes. The fifth, sixth, eighth and ninth mode, according to the placement of those who have presumed to place them in this way, are never found to go through any composition in their own way from the beginning to the end, and therefore we say that they do not exist as modes, since modes must convey their name from their effect. Indeed we call such placements of melodies, from which they complete and make up their modes, the contrary of modes. And we propose to make mention of such things immediately, so that the things mentioned before, as well as the contest of reasons introduced from opposites, may be clear and more plain. The text is clear by itself.

> Here the author adds that keeping the correct arrangement of the modes makes the concept clear:
>> **Keeping the order indicates the truth of the six species.**
>> **And those[1] who say[2] that there are nine species of the art[3] speak slander.[4]**
>> 1 that is, those new imposters
>> 2 that is, assert
>> 3 of this art
>> 4 that is, presume to speak slander
>> **Do not believe the words of those people,[1] which are so badly contrived.[2]**
>> 1 that is, do not agree to their words, because they are against the art and the opinion of better people
>> 2 put together
> Here the author shows, by means of a rule, that something should never occur by means of two when it can occur by means of one:*
>> **You give in vain by means of two pieces what you can give in one.**

In a mixed fashion, etc. Here the author wishes to state briefly the accords of the species, saying that there are six modes or species from which every genus of composition is put together and occurs. And note that just as one body is made up of the four elements or humors, by means of music of the universe or music of man,* so, by means of the accords of species of this kind, one melody or more that are aiming towards the same

unus cantus seu etiam plures ad eundem finem tendentes tanquam sub uno
corpore melodiam cantuum generare. Et sic de duplici convenientia loqui
proponimus in praesenti, aut secundum convenientiam eiusdem modi aut
plurium circa plures cantus ad eundem finem tendentes consideratam, aut
secundum convenientiam plurium modorum ad perfectionem unius cantus
communiter attributam.

   Aut igitur talis convenientia habet fieri circa unum cantum aut circa
plures. Si circa unum, nota, quod istae sex species per convenientiam
aliquam possunt cantum unicum statuere pro dispositione mutua
10 componentis. Et non refert utrum secunda species seu tertia et sic de
aliis in tali cantu priori vel alii praeponantur, aut etiam e converso,
vel utrum tales species sint ibi perfectae vel imperfectae vel sub
propriis figuris aut etiam alienis, dum tamen voces cohaereant seu
conveniant tenori modi alicuius supposito competenter. Et nota, quod
talis cantus sive tales, si sint ibi plures, debent iudicari de eodem
modo de quo est tenor, si sit ibi reperire. Et de tali cantuum
dispositione aliqui stupefacti modos suos statuere voluerunt. Nos
siquidem tales cantus de eodem modo de quo tenor est iudicamus, eo quod
sit dignior pars, nam ab ipso ducunt omnes alii originem, quibus esse
20 decernitur fundamentum. Ex quo sequitur, quod sit dignior pars et a
digniori debet res denominari, quare non sine causa cantus supra ipsum
compositus et confectus a tenore suum nomen merebitur importare.

   Si autem talis convenientia per cantus varios sit reperta, hoc erit
dupliciter, quoniam aut rectus modus ad rectum modum aut ad modum per
ultra mensuram, aut e converso. Si rectus ad rectum, hoc erit
dupliciter, quoniam aut ad se ipsum aut ad reliquum. Si ad se ipsum, sic
erit primus contra primum aut secundus contra secundum aut sextus contra
sextum. Si ad reliquum, sic erit dupliciter, quoniam aut primus contra
sextum, aut secundus, aut penitus e converso. Si modus rectus ad modum
30 per ultra mensuram, hoc erit dupliciter, quoniam aut primus contra
quintum aut secundus contra tertium sive quartum seu etiam quintum, aut
penitus e converso, aut sextus contra quemlibet ordinabitur, aut e
converso. Si autem modus per ultra mensuram ad modum per ultra mensuram,
conveniat et decenter, hoc erit dupliciter, quoniam aut ad se ipsum aut
ad reliquum. Si ad se ipsum, sic erit tertius contra tertium aut quartus
contra quartum aut quintus ad se ipsum. Si ad reliquum, sic erit tertius
contra quartum sive quintum aut quartus contra utrumque, aut penitus e
converso. Et nota, quod licet isti sex modi ad perfectionem unius cantus
sive plurium conveniant aut simpliciter sive mixtim, nonquam tamen primus
40 modus contra tertium sive quartum in variis cantibus poterit convenire,
nec etiam e converso, figurarum repugnantia sive vocum in eis contraria
hoc obstante.

   Plurimus ordo etc. Hic recitat modorum seriem inter pausationes quo
ad punctorum numerum nullatenus comprehendi, eo quod quandoque perfecti
quandoque imperfecti quandoque sub pari numero et aliquotiens sub impari,

----

1 etiam *add. super scriptum, om.* Sowa   3-4 aut plurium *add. super
scriptum*   9 [[possunt]] *cod.*   12-14 *crux in marg.*   14 communiant
pro conveniant Sowa   18 modo *om.* Sowa   21 digniore *pro* digniori Sowa
decet *pro* debet Sowa   22 suo *pro* suum *cod.*   32 quem licet *pro*
quemlibet Sowa   38 isti [[cantus]] sex *cod.*   cantus *add. in marg.*
39-40 primus [[cantus]] modus *cod.*

ending can generate a musical sound of melodies as though in a single body. And so we propose to speak of two accords at present, either regarding the accord of the same mode or of several modes, this accord being considered in the case of several melodies aiming towards the same ending, or regarding the accord of several modes, this accord being commonly attributed to the perfection of one melody.

This kind of accord therefore occurs either in the case of one melody or in the case of several. If it is in the case of one melody, note that these six species by means of some accord can establish a single melody by the mutual arrangement of the person who is putting it together. And it does not matter whether the second species or the third, and so on for the others, are put before the first or any other in such a melody, or the reverse, or whether such species are perfect or imperfect in it, or with their own figures or strange ones, as long as the notes suitably agree or accord with the tenor that is put beneath the mode. And note that such a melody, or melodies if there are more, must be judged by the same mode from which the tenor is made, if there is one found there. And some senseless people have wished to establish their modes from this kind of ordering of the melodies.* But we indeed judge such melodies from the same mode from which the tenor is made, because it is the more worthy part, for from it all the others draw their origin, and it is perceived to be the foundation to them. From which it follows that it is the more worthy part, and a thing should be named from what is more worthy, and so it is not without cause that the melody put together and made up above it will deserve to convey its name from its tenor.

But if such an accord is found through various melodies it will be in two ways, that is either with correct mode against correct mode or with correct mode against a mode that is beyond measure, or the reverse. If it is with correct against correct, it will be in two ways, that is either against itself or against one of the others. If against itself, then it will be first against first, or second against second, or sixth against sixth. If against one of the others, then it will be in two ways, that is either first or second against sixth or completely the reverse. If correct mode against mode beyond measure, this will be in two ways, that is either first against fifth, or second against third or fourth or fifth, or completely the reverse, or sixth against any one that can be arranged, or the reverse. But if it is mode beyond measure against mode beyond measure, and it accords properly, this will be in two ways, that is either against itself or against one of the others. If against itself, then it will be the third against the third, or the fourth against the fourth, or the fifth against itself. If against one of the others, then it will be the third against the fourth or fifth, or the fourth against either of the others, or completely the reverse. And note that although these six modes accord either singly or in a mixed fashion for the perfection of one melody or of several, yet never will the first mode be able to accord with the third or the fourth in various melodies, nor the reverse, since the incompatibility of the figures or notes in these modes stands in the way of this.

Very many orders, etc. Here he explains that the sequence of the modes between pauses as to the number of their written notes can in no way be recounted, because they are found everywhere sometimes as perfect, sometimes imperfect, sometimes with an even number and at other times with an odd number, either greater or smaller, according to the mutual

secundum magis et minus, quoad componentium mutuam voluntatem undique
sunt reperti. Et sic ordinationis numerus tot capitorum sententiis
mutuatus quo ad punctorum numerum est incertus, quamvis quidam dicant:
primus ordo primi modi perfectus; secundus, tertius, quartus vel etiam
imperfectus, et sic in aliis modis, quod dicere nihil est. Unde
venerabilis magister noster Henricus de Daubuef ait versu:

> *Tot sunt cantores et cantus fabulatores,*
> *Quod cantus mores deserit atque fores.*

10

    Maneries praesto etc. Hic dicit actor, quod quotienscumque plures
cantus et varii supra aliquem tenorem secundum diversas species et
numeros componuntur, talis confectio specierum a tenore nasciscitur sibi
nomen. Converte igitur sic: **tenor,** id est, infimus cantus sive
suppositus; **praesto,** id est, praesens; **esto,** id est, sit; **maneries,** id
est, modus; **hiis,** suple cantibus supra ordinatis.

    Mixtim[1] conveniunt[2] species sex indeque fiunt[3]
    1 id est, convenienter
20   2 id est, concordant, et hoc dupliciter aut in eodem cantu aut
    etiam in diversis
    3 id est, componuntur
    Cantus,[1] ad numerum[2] recitatque reductio verum,
    1 sive varii
    2 id est, metrum vel mensuram punctorum et actuum a principio
    usque ad finem
    (fol. 152v) **An[1] bene formentur[2] vel non quocumque locentur.[3]**
    1 pro utrum
    2 illi cantus sive
30   3 id est, sive sint sub pari numero vel impari
Quasi diceret: prima species contra tertiam speciem sive quartam
nonquam poterit convenire:
    Non valet in ternam prior addi sive quaternam.
Quasi diceret: omnis cantus debet iudicari de eodem modo de quo est
tenor:
    Maneries praesto tenor hiis, quia dignior, esto.[1]
    1 id est, sit
    Plurimus[1] ordo datur specierum nam variatur
    1 id est, multiplex, quia quandoque est perfectus, quandoque
40   imperfectus, quandoque sub pari numero, aliquando sub impari
    Ut placet actori[1] nec erit numerabilis ori.[2]
    1 id est, sicut impositor ordinat pro mutua voluntate
    2 et hoc propter confusionem variationis

    Quolibet esse modo etc. Expeditis convenientiis nec non et ordinibus
specierum, de quibus alibi declarabitur per exempla, ideoque in hoc loco

----

1 componentium [[num]] mutuam *cod.*   1-2 undique sunt reperti *add. in
marg.*   5 nichil est dicere *pro* dicere nihil est *Sowa*   8-9 *in marg.:*
Versus   12 cantus et varii *add. in marg.*   34 decet *pro* debet *Sowa*
45 nec non *om. Sowa*

wishes of those who are putting them together. And thus the number of
the arrangement obtained with the opinions of so many heads is uncertain
as to the number of written notes, although some may say: The first
order of the first mode is perfect, the second, third, and fourth are
imperfect, and so on with the other modes;* which is to say nothing. And
so our revered master Henricus de Daubuef* says in verse:

> "There are so many cantors and makers of melody,
> That melody abandons its customs and hearth."*

Let the tenor, etc. Here the author says that whenever several
different melodies are put together above some tenor according to diverse
species and numbers, such a compilation of species takes its name from
the tenor. Therefore interpret as follows: **the tenor,** that is, the
lowest melody or the melody put underneath; **now,** that is, at present; **be,**
that is, let it be; **the manner,** that is, the mode; **to these,** supply:
melodies arranged above.

> **In a mixed fashion[1] the six species are in accord,[2] and from
> there arise[3]**
> 1 that is, appropriately
> 2 that is, they are in concord; and this is in two ways, either
> in the same melody or in different ones
> 3 that is, are put together
> **Melodies,[1] and the reduction recites the truth as to the
> number,[2]**
> 1 various ones
> 2 that is, the meter or measure of the written and actual notes
> from the beginning to the end
> (fol. 152v) **If[1] they are well formed[2] or not, wherever they may
> be placed.[3]**
> 1 instead of: whether
> 2 those melodies
> 3 that is, whether they are with an even number or an odd number

He means to say that the first species against the third species or
the fourth will never be able to be in accord:

> **The first can not be added to the third or the fourth.**

He means to say that every melody must be judged from the same mode
from which the tenor is made:

> **Let the tenor now be[1] the manner to these, because it is more
> worthy.**
> 1 that is, may it be
> **Very many[1] orders for the species are given, for they are varied**
> 1 that is, many different kinds; because sometimes they are
> perfect, sometimes imperfect, sometimes with an even number, and
> other times with an odd number
> **As the author pleases,[1] and they will not be able to be counted
> by the voice.[2]**
> 1 that is, as the one who is putting them down arranges them
> according to mutual wishes
> 2 and this is on account of the confusion of the variety

To any mode is given, etc. Having discussed the accords as well as
the orders of the modes, which will be stated elsewhere through examples,

vult actor specierum sive modorum aequipollentias per diversa cantuum
genera declarare, et praecipue per hoquetos, in quibus omne genus
aequipollentiae reperitur. Nam ut dicit prosa, aequipollenta in omnibus
modis intelligenda sunt. Aequipollenta, dico, ut si non inveniatur longa
vel brevis, suo loco accipiatur illud, quod loco brevis vel longae
repertum est. Et quia tres sunt voces simplices vel figurae, quarum
quaelibet in se duplicem efficaciam retinet et naturam, sicut superius
est expressum, ideoque de duplici aequipollentiae specie erit
exemplificandum inferius suo loco, quare talia praetermittimus in
10   praesenti, ne exemplorum copia tam prolixa fastidium generet aut inducat.
     Haec siquidem lectio in duas partes breviter dividatur ad hoc ut per
divisionis sententiam ludicius pateant recitanda. Nam in prima parte
agit actor de aequippollentia specierum, in secunda de pausis, quae
multum conferunt ad cognitionem earundem. Prima igitur incipit **Quolibet
esse modo** etc., secunda **Tempora tot pausa** etc. Item prima istarum in
duas: in prima agit de aequipollentia omnium figurarum generaliter sive
mixtim, in secunda specialiter, sicut per hoquetorum genera disponuntur.
Prima **Quolibet esse modo**, secunda **Semibreves detis** etc. Haec secunda in
duas: in prima agit de semibrevibus hoquetatis, gratia quarum hic agitur
20   de hoquetis; in secunda de dispositione horum in longo modo. Et quia
semibreves hoquetatae sunt motivum primum, quare de hoquetis hic facimus
mentionem, ideo patet ordo. Prima pars incipit **Semibreves**, secunda **Si
modus est certe** etc. Haec secunda in duas: in prima agit de hoquetis
sine littera, in secunda de transmutatione motellorum, ostendendo
qualiter de modo in alium artificialiter transmutantur. Et quia pars
praecedens aequipollentiarum notitiam manifestat, pars sussequens
doctrinam reserat motellorum, ostendendo qualiter secundum modos habeant
transmutari. Et sic pars prima est propinqua sententiae praecedentis,
secunda vero remota. Ideo patet ordo: prima pars incipit **Si modus est
30   certe** etc., secunda **Sic brevis efficitur** etc. Item prima istarum in
duas: in prima agit de hoquetis iuxta vocum aequipollentiam resecatis,
in secunda de hoquetis per voces absque resecatione positas ordinatis.
Et quia vocum resecatio per aequipollentiam reseratur, vocum non
resecatio per convenientias, solum dispositionem sequitur aliarum. Ideo
patet ordo: prima pars incipit **Si modus est certe longus** etc., <secunda>
Si modus hic terne etc., et <sic> patet divisio et sententia leoninis.

     Quolibet[1] **esse modo datur aequiparantia**[2] **nodo.**[3]
     1 sive perfecto sive imperfecto
40   2 id est, sunt aequipollentiae accedendae
     3 id est, regula

6-7 *crux in marg.*   7 efficiatam *pro* efficaciam *Sowa*   15 etc. *post* **modo**
add. Sowa   21 motuum *pro* motivum *Sowa*   34 sequitur aliarum aliarum
ideo *cod.*

therefore in this place the author wishes to state the equipollences of the species or modes by means of different genera of melodies, and especially by means of hockets in which every genus of equipollence is found. For as the prose treatise says,* equipollent things must be understood in all modes. By equipollent things I mean that if a long or a breve is not used, then in its place is accepted that which is found in the place of a breve or a long. And because there are three single notes or figures, each of which keeps in itself two kinds of efficacy and nature, as has been expressed above, therefore two species of equipollence will be exemplified below in the right place, and so we leave out such things at the present lest such a copious abundance of examples generate or induce contempt.

Indeed let this reading be divided briefly into two parts so that through the meaning of the division those things which must be explained may become clear and more plain. For in the first part the author deals with the equipollence of the species, and in the second with pauses, which contribute much to the understanding of the species. Therefore the first part begins **To any mode is given**, etc., and the second **Let the pause hold**, etc. Also the first of these is divided into two parts: In the first he deals with the equipollence of all figures generally or in a mixed fashion, and in the second he deals specifically with them as they are placed by means of the genera of hockets. The first begins **To any mode is given**, etc., the second **You may give semibreves**, etc. This second part is divided into two parts: In the first he deals with hocketed semibreves, and because of this he deals here with hockets; in the second he deals with their placement in a long mode. And because hocketed semibreves are the prime motive as to why we make mention of hockets here, that is why the order is that way. The first part begins **You may give semibreves**, the second **If the mode**, etc. This second part is divided into two parts: in the first he deals with hockets without text, in the second with the transformation of motets, showing how they are artificially transformed from one mode into another. And because the preceding part displays the concept of equipollences, the following part discloses the principle of motets, showing how they may be transformed according to the modes. And thus the first part is near to the preceding meaning, but the second part is far. Therefore the order is clear: The first part begins **If the mode**, etc., the second **Thus the breve is made up**, etc. Also the first of these is divided into two parts: in the first he deals with hockets that are cut up in accordance with the equipollence of their notes, in the second with hockets that are arranged with notes that are placed without cutting up. And because the cutting up of the notes is disclosed through equipollence, and the system of not cutting up the notes through the accords, it only follows the placement of the others. Thus the order is clear: The first part begins **If the mode**, etc., the second **Look and see**, etc., and thus the division and meaning of the leonine verses is clear.

> **To any mode**[1] is given equivalence[2] by knot.[3]
> 1 whether perfect or imperfect
> 2 that is, there are equipollences to be accomplished
> 3 that is, by rule

Dante[1] breves dabimus, vel semibreves[2] reperimus
1 id est, ordinando favente tam minores quam maiores
2 sive sive minores sive maiores
Undique[1] vel pausam pro longa[2] respice causam.[3]
1 id est, in quolibet modo vel cantu
2 sive maiori sive minori
3 id est, considera rationem

    Pro brevibus etc. Hic exequitur actor de aequipollentia brevium et
10 semibrevium figurarum, gratia quarum de omni aequipollentiarum genere
breviter distingamus et primo de aequipollentia longae, eo quod
fundamentum originis aliis administrat. Et nota, quod quia duplex est
eius efficacia sive virtus, ideo de duplici aequipollentiarum genere
videamus. Si sit ergo longa, aut est maior aut minor; si maior, tria
tempora repraesentat; et nota, quod loco ipsius quandoque propter
superhabundantiam litterae aut propter colorem musicae tres breves
reperiri poterunt et aequales, nunc aut duae inaequales, quarum ultima
duo tempora continebit, nunc aut longa duorum temporum <et recta brevis>
aut e converso, nunc aut recta brevis et pausa duorum temporum vel e
20 converso, vel duae rectae breves et pausa unius temporis aut e converso,
nunc aut pausa trium temporum, vel duae semibreves inaequales vel tres et
aequales et duae rectae breves, aut e converso, nunc aut sola brevis et
tres semibreves duorum temporum aut unius propter aliam brevem sequentem
vel pausulam, aut penitus e converso, aut sex semibreves vel minus, plus
etiam usque ad novem semibreves, et sic in omni genere aequipollentiarum
poterit provocari.
    Idem iudicium de aliis simplicibus pro quantitate temporum et actuum
in eis est habendum. Exempla quidem per hoquetos varios atque cantus tam
sine littera quam cum littera sunt quaerenda, quia si exemplorum copia
30 hic modo publice traderetur, confusionem induceret et gravamen. Tamen si
quis altius hoc perpendat, in exemplis hoquetorum fere singula poterit
reperire, nam in eis tota virtus musicae mensurabilis et natura districte
traditur et efficaci studio compilatur. Littera per se patet.

    (fol. 153) **Pro brevibus[1] pausas[2] vel semibreves[3] fore clausas[4]**
1 tam pro maioribus quam minoribus
2 sive breves
3 sive maiores sive minores
4 id est, positas vel inclusas
40 **Invenire potest cantor[1] cui discere prodest.[2]**
1 id est, si curam apposuerit; et hoc tam cum littera quam sine
littera
2 id est, proficit

----

30 tradere[[n]]tur *cod.*   33 efficacia *pro* efficaci *Sowa*

In giving[1] it we will give breves or find semibreves[2]
1 that is, by arranging it and in favoring both smaller and
larger ones
2 either smaller or larger ones
Or a pause everywhere[1] in place of a long;[2] have regard for the
cause.[3]
1 that is, in any mode or melody
2 whether larger or smaller
3 that is, consider the reason

Instead of breves, etc. Here the author describes the equipollence
of breve and semibreve figures, by means of which we may distinguish
briefly every genus of equipollence; and firstly the equipollence of the
long, because it provides the foundation of origin to the others. And
note that because its efficacy or quality is of two kinds, therefore we
may consider two genera of equipollence. If it is long it is either
larger or smaller; if larger it represents three units of time. And note
that in its place sometimes, on account of the over-abundance of text or
a rhetorical device of the music, three equal breves can be found;
sometimes two unequal breves, of which the last will contain two units of
time; sometimes a long of two units of time and a correct breve, or the
reverse; sometimes a correct breve and a pause of two units of time, or
the reverse; or two correct breves and a pause of one unit of time, or
the reverse; sometimes a pause of three units of time; or two unequal
semibreves or three equal ones and two correct breves, or the reverse;
sometimes a single breve and three semibreves of two units of time or of
one unit of time on account of another breve following it or a small
pause, or completely the reverse; or six semibreves or less, or even more
up to nine semibreves; and it will be able to be produced in this way in
every genus of equipollence.
    The same judgement should be held about the other single figures as
regards the quantity of units of time and actual notes in them. Indeed
examples should be sought by means of various hockets and melodies both
without text and with text, because if an abundance of examples were
given publicly here now, it would induce confusion and inconvenience.
But if anyone reckons this more deeply, he will be able to find almost
every single thing in examples of hockets, for in them the whole quality
and nature of measurable music is concisely handed down and brought
together by effective labor. The text is clear by itself.

(fol.153) **Instead of breves[1] he can find pauses[2] or semibreves[3]
encompassed[4] there** --
1 instead of both larger ones and smaller ones
2 breve pauses
3 larger or smaller
4 that is, placed or included
The singer[1] who benefits from[2] learning.
1 that is, if he takes trouble, and this is both with a text and
without a text
2 that is, takes advantage of

Semibreves¹ detis² per pausas³ nunc⁴ in hoquetis.⁵
1 sive tam minores quam maiores
2 O cantores
3 sive semibreves
4 id est, quandoque
5 id est, in omni cantu hoquetato

    Quis debes care etc. Quoniam actor in praecedentibus de hiis, quae faciunt ad esse huiusmodi specierum, fecit mentionem, utputa de
10 convenientiis et aequipollentiis earundem, ideoque in hoc loco de eis, quae faciunt ad bene esse earum, utpote ad convenientias et aequipollentias nec non et ordinem distinguendum, intendit actor propositum declarare, videlicet de hoquetis, per quos omnis aequipollentia sive convenientia figurarum omneque genus et efficacia cognitioque virtus et natura earum perfecte dignoscitur et habetur. Quae quidem hoquetatio a nobis et aliis anthonomasice nuncupari poterit armonia.
    Et nota, quod *armonia*, ut dicit Ysidorus, *est modulatio vocis et concordia plurimorum sonorum vel coaptatio*, quae audientium mentes
20 excitat et delectat, scientes et cantantes imbuit et informat ad omne genus cantuum perfectius cognoscendum et proferendum et leviter componendum. Attendas igitur, mi dilecte, tu qui tantae dulcedinis ac modulationis cupis aquas potabiles exaurire, ut ea quae secuntur aure vigili uringinis suscipias, cordis armariolo pacifice reponendo, ne quod a paucis cognitum et honorifice reservatum est provulgatum communiter iam vilescat.
    Scias igitur quod illa hoquetatio fit aut per resecationem vocum aut sine resecatione. Si sit sine resecatione, hoc erit dupliciter, quoniam aut cum littera vel sine. Si cum littera, sic erit secundum primum modum
30 vel secundum vel tertium etc., aut secundum convenientiam unius modi cum altero vel pluribus, et hoc per mutuationem vocum et pausationum subtiliter hinc et inde; et quandoque potest ibi resecatio reperiri, tamen hoc est raro. Si sit sine littera, eadem est vocum altrinsecatio sed saepius mutuanda ac etiam resecanda.
    Si sit autem per resecationem vocum, hoc erit dupliciter, quoniam aut supra tenorem alicuius modi vel plurium, aut sine tenore aliquo seu etiam fundamento. Si supra tenorem sit talis resecatio ordinata, hoc erit sine littera, nisi aliquando eveniat in motellis, sicut patet in *Poure socors* vel consimilibus. Et nota quod talis altrinsecatio fit bis vel ter vel
40 pluries continue pro voluntate mutua imponentis, aut per discantus apositionem saepius intermissa <est>. Et hoc dupliciter, aut per voces utrinque simplices vel compositas, aut ex una parte sunt simplices et ex altera compositae. Et nota, quod talis vocum resecatio fit per longas rectas vel breves, quandoque regulariter ordinatas, quandoque irregulariter, sicut textus postea declarabit; aut fit etiam per semibreves inaequales recto ordine dispositas et regulariter ordinatas, aut etiam irregulariter quo ad dispositionem variatam, sicut textus

----

9 fecerat *pro* fecit *cod.*   16 authonomatice *pro* anthonomasice *Sowa*
19 plurimum *pro* plurimorum *Sowa*   21 perfectius *add. in marg., om. Sowa*
24 reponendo [[honorifice]] ne *cod.*   25 paucis [[honori]] cognitum *cod.*
37 haec *pro* hoc *Sowa*   38 conveniat *pro* eveniat *Sowa*   en *pro* in *cod.*
secors *pro* socors *Sowa*   42 compositae *pro* compositas *cod.*

You may give[2] **semibreves**[1] **by means of pauses**[3] **now**[4] **in hockets.**[5]
1 both smaller and larger
2 O cantors
3 semibreve pauses
4 that is, sometimes
5 that is, in every melody that is hocketed

For those, dear one, etc. Since the author in the preceding discussions made mention of these things which make for the existence of species of this kind, for example the accords and equipollences of them, therefore in this place the author intends to state his argument about those things which make for the proper existence of them, so that the accords and equipollences as well as the order can be distinguished; that is to say about hockets, by means of which every equipollence or accord of the figures and every genus and efficacy and understanding and quality and nature of them is perfectly recognized and occurs. And indeed this hocketing can by antonomasia be called harmony by us and by others.

And note that "harmony," as Isidore says,* "is the production of sound by the voice and the concord or fitting together of very many sounds," which stirs and pleases the minds of those who hear it, and inspires and instructs knowledgeable people and singers to understand more perfectly, and to perform and easily put together every genus of melody. You should pay attention therefore, my beloved, you who desire to drain the thirst-quenching waters of so much sweetness and sound, so that you may take up those things which follow with the alert ear of desire, and put them peacefully in the book-case of your heart, lest something that is understood by few and honorably reserved should be widely promulgated and now become worthless.

You should know therefore that hocketing occurs either by means of the cutting up of the notes or without cutting them up. If it is without cutting them up, it will be in two ways, either with text or without. If with text, then it will be according to the first mode or the second or third etc., either according to the accord of one mode with another or with several, and by means of the exchange of notes and pauses subtly from one to the other; and sometimes cutting up can be found there, but only rarely. If it is without text, it has the same cutting up of the notes in both parts, but it should be exchanged and cut up more often.

If it is by means of the cutting up of the notes, it will be in two ways, either above the tenor of some mode or several modes, or without any tenor or foundation. If this kind of cutting up is arranged above a tenor, this will be without text, unless sometimes it happens in motets, as is clear in "Poure secours" or similar ones. And note that such a cutting up in both parts occurs twice or three times or several times continuously, according to the mutual wish of the person who is putting it down, or is often interrupted by means of the placement of the discant. And this occurs in two ways, either by means of notes that are single or composite in both parts, or that are single in one and composite in the other. And note that this kind of cutting up of the notes occurs by means of correct longs or breves, sometimes regularly arranged, sometimes irregularly, as the text will state afterwards; also it either occurs by means of unequal semibreves placed in a correct order and regularly arranged, or indeed irregularly with a varied placement, as the text will explain next. But if it is without the proper tenor of some

proxime recitabit. Si sit autem sine tenore proprio alicuius modi, tunc
tam longas quam breves quam etiam semibreves irregulariter et inordinate
positas reperimus, similiter et confuse, ita quod vix aut nonquam ad
certum aequipollentiae numerum quo ad modum aliquem vel maneriem
reducuntur. De singulis tamen dispositionibus eorundem supra litteram
sive textum copiam tradimus exemplorum, de regularibus praecipue certas
regulas assignantes, et primo de semibrevibus hoquetatis quam de longis
seu brevibus facientes mentionem, eo quod sunt causa quare de hoquetis
hic facimus mentionem, quia nonquam in diversis cantibus per varias
10 aequippollentias disponuntur nisi fuerit in hoquetis.

Nota igitur, quod semibreves inaequales per pausulas in diversis
cantibus positas hoquetando debent sic artificialiter ordinari, scilicet
quod minor semibrevis et sua pausula sint in triplo, maior autem et sua
pausula sint in duplo, id est secundo cantu, tenore tamen in talibus
existente. In quadruplo siquidem haec omnia confuse posita reperimus, et
hoc est, quia quadruplum cuilibet cantuum nititur adulari.

Sit minor etc. Exemplum qualiter huius semibreves in brevi modo
debent artificialiter hoquetari patet hic:

20

In seculum

30

Confuse etc. Exemplum earundem irregulariter positarum sine tenore
saepius et confuse patet in hoc exemplo de *Ave Maria:*

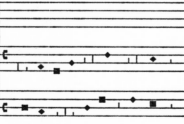

Amen

40

Primo quando modo etc. Exemplum qualiter huius semibreves supra

----

2 longae *pro* longas *cod.*   9 quare *pro* quia *Sowa*   13 autem *add. super
scriptum*   45 **modo** *sine sublinea in cod.*   semibreve *pro* semibreves
cod.

mode, then we find both longs and breves and also semibreves placed
irregularly and out of order, and also in a confused fashion, in such a
way that they are scarcely or never reduced to a fixed number of
equipollence as regards some mode or manner. But we provide a large
number of examples of individual placements of these over a text,
assigning fixed rules, especially of the regular ones, and firstly of
semibreves in hocket, before making mention of longs or breves, because
they are the reason why we make mention of hockets here, since they are
never placed in diverse melodies by means of different equipollences
unless it be in hockets.

   Note therefore that unequal semibreves that are hocketing by means of
little pauses placed in diverse melodies must be arranged artificially in
this way, that is that the smaller semibreve and its little pause are in
the triplum, but the larger semibreve and its little pause are in the
duplum, that is the second melody, when there is a tenor in such compositions. In the quadruplum indeed we find all these things placed in a
confused fashion, and that is because the quadruplum strives to emulate
any one of the melodies.

   Let the smaller, etc. An example of how semibreves of this kind in a
short mode must be hocketed artificially is given here:

In seculum

   You hocket them, etc. An example of the same semibreves placed
irregularly often without tenor and in a confused fashion is given in
this example of "Ave Maria":

Amen

   When they are in the first mode, etc. An example of how semibreves
of this kind above a tenor of the first mode are hocketed regularly is

tenorem primi modi regulariter hoquetantur patet hic:

Manere

Hic proponit dare doctrinam de omni genere hoquetorum:
  Quis[1] debes care sic semibreves variare,
  1 id est, quibus hoquetis
Hic subiungit actor, quomodo huius semibreves in pausulas saepius
convertuntur:
  Dum tamen in pausas per cantus ordine pausas.
  Sit minor[1] in triplo,[2] maior[3] velud est data duplo.[4]
  1 sive semibrevis
  2 id est, tertio cantu
  3 sive semibrevis
  4 id est, secundo cantu tenore tamen supposito

(fol. 153v) **Confuse spretas** etc. Hic vult actor ostendere qualiter
huius semibreves per cantus varios et praecipue per hoquetos positae sunt
confuse, sicut patet in triplo de *Manere* brevis modi, et in aliquibus
conductis sine tenore proprio hoquetatis, ut in *Ave Maria* hoquetato. Et
nota, quod talis hoquetatio fit pro mutua instituentium voluntate aut
continue aut etiam intermisse aut per simplices voces aut per compositas.
  Si talis igitur hoquetatio sit reperta, est perfecta quo est de se,
aut etiam imperfecta. Si sit perfecta, tunc talis hoquetatio fit per
altrinsecationem resecationum ab uno cantu in alterum continue mutuatam,
sicut exempla praeposita manifestant. Si sit imperfecta, tunc ex sola
parte resecatio fit reperta, sicut patet in hoc exemplo:

Manere

Et scias quod talem vocum resecationem discantus saepius interrumpit.

----

1 hoquetatur *pro* hoquetantur *cod*.   19 **tamen** *add. super scriptum*

given here:

Manere

Here he proposes to give the principle about all genera of hockets:
**For those,[1] dear one, you ought to vary the semibreves in this
way,**
1 that is, for those hockets

Here the author adds how semibreves of this kind are often converted
into little pauses:
**As long as you pause with the pauses in the order of the melody.
Let the smaller[1] be in the triplum,[2] and the larger[3] as is it
given in the duplum.[4]**
1 semibreve
2 that is, the third melody
3 semibreve
4 that is, the second melody with the tenor put underneath

(fol. 153v) **You hocket them,** etc. Here the author wishes to show how
semibreves of this kind are put in confused fashion in various melodies
and especially in hockets, as is shown in the triplum of "Manere" of the
short mode, and in some conductus hocketed without a proper tenor, as in
the hocketed "Ave Maria." And note that this kind of hocketing occurs,
according to the mutual wishes of those who are putting it down, either
continuously or interruptedly, or with single notes or composite ones.
    If this kind of hocketing is found, it is perfect as regards itself,
or imperfect. If it is perfect, then this kind of hocketing occurs by
means of a system of cutting up in both parts that is exchanged continuously from one melody to the other, as the examples put beforehand
show. If it is imperfect, then the cutting up is found in one part only,
as is shown in this example:

Manere

And you should know that the discant often interrupts this kind of

Sunt tamen nonnulli artis huius peritiam ignorantes, qui absque secura
legis serie cantus et hoquetos conficiunt pro mutua voluntate regu-
laritatis semita derelicta, quorum sequi vestigia non curamus, immo
postponimus, specialiter inhaerentes approbatis rationibus et sententiis
magistrorum. Littera per se patet.

Confuse[1] spretas non ordine[2] legis[3] hoquetas.[4]
1 id est, confuso modo datas
2 regulari sive
10   3 id est, regulae supradictae
4 id est, hoquetare convenit
Per hoc dat actor intelligere, quod brevis modus a longo saepius
extorquetur:
Cum[1] brevis e longo modus ortus adest ita pungo.
1 pro quando
Regula est: quemadmodum semibreves ordinantur in brevi modo, sic et
in primo, et per hoc patet, quod non ordinantur semper aliunde:
Primo quando modo sunt ut prius ordine nodo.
Quasi diceret: possibile est et leve unus modus in alium
20   transmutari:
De quinto primum facio nunc sive secundum.
Hic dicit, quod non est vis facienda quis eorum ab altero derivetur:
Ordine retrogrado mihi cum licet ordine trado.

Si modus est certe etc. Facta superius mentione de semibrevibus
hoquetatis quomodo et qualiter habeant ordinari, et hoc in brevi modo,
utputa in primo modo et secundo, hic vult actor longi modi seriem
declarare, dicens, quod eadem series vel ordinatio, quae data est de
semibrevibus hoquetatis, est etiam facienda de minore brevi et minore
30   longa in longo modo ad invicem hoquetatis, id est, quod minor brevis sit
in triplo et minor longa sit in duplo. Et sicut praedictae semibreves
aliquando mutuantur, mutuatae sunt pari numero sic et istae, nam et istae
saepius praeordinatae, eo quod brevis modus a longo regulariter et naturaliter oriatur, alternationis sive variationis viam aliis introducens.
Exemplum quomodo et qualiter huius longae et breves in longo modo
debent regulariter ordinari vel hoquetari patet hic:

40

In seculum

----
4 proponimus *pro* postponimus *Sowa*   21 **De primum quinto** *Sowa*   28 et
pro vel *Sowa*   36 debeant *pro* debent *Sowa*

cutting up of the notes. Yet there are some who have no knowledge of any skill in this art, who put together melodies and hockets according to their mutual wishes without any secure sequence in the law, and abandon the path of regularity, and we do not care to follow in their footsteps, rather we reject them, keeping specifically to the approved reasons and opinions of the masters. The text is clear by itself.

> **You hocket[4] them separated and in a confused fashion[1] without the order[2] of the law.[3]**
> 1 that is, given in a confused way
> 2 the regular order
> 3 that is, the above-mentioned rule
> 4 that is, you agree to hocket them

In this the author gives one to understand that the short mode is often extracted from the long mode:

> **Since[1] the short mode that arises from the long is present, I draw it this way.**
> 1 instead of: when

The rule is: Just as semibreves are arranged in the short mode so they are in the first mode, and in this way it is clear that they are not always arranged from elsewhere:

> **When they are in the first mode, I tie them in the order as before.**

He means to say that it is possible and easy for one mode to be transformed into another:

> **From the fifth mode now I make the first or the second.**

Here he says that no argument should be made as to which of them may be derived from the other:

> **When I give it in this order, I can give it in a backwards order.**

If the mode, etc. Having made mention above of hocketed semibreves and how and in what way they occur and are arranged in the short mode, for example in the first mode and the second, here the author wishes to state the sequence of the long mode, saying that the same sequence or arrangement which is given for hocketed semibreves should also be made for the smaller breve and smaller long which are hocketed in turn in the long mode; that is that the smaller breve is in the triplum and the smaller long is in the duplum. And just as the aforementioned semibreves are sometimes exchanged, these too are exchanged in this way in an even number, for these too are often arranged beforehand, because the short mode may regularly and naturally arise from the long, introducing the way of alternation or variation to the others.

An example of how and in what way the longs and breves of this kind in the long mode should be regularly arranged or hocketed is given here:

In seculum

Nunc alternantur etc. Hic dat actor doctrinam, quod non semper supradictae voces tam longae quam breves et semibreves regulariter ordinantur.

Exemplum qualiter a regula deviant antedicta patet hic:

Portare

Si modus[1] est certe longus,[2] per eos[3] sit aperte[4]
1 nota quo ad tenorem
2 id est, quintae speciei
3 sive hoquetos
4 et hoc regulariter
Longa minor duplo, brevis ut minor est data triplo.[1]
1 et hoc est, quia brevis pausa praeveniens ei sustrahit unum tempus
Quamlibet[1] istarum quadruplo reperis notularum.
1 id est, tam minor quam maior in quadruplo sunt repertae
Hic datur doctrina, quod regulae supradictae non tenent in aliquibus hoquetis:
Nunc alternantur per cantus quando vagantur,
Ecce ostendit, quare regula generalis nequit super hiis confirmari:
Hinc nequit esse data generalis lex neque grata.

Si modus hic terne etc. Quoniam in praedictis recitavit actor resecationum vocum notitiam in hoquetis, ad hoc ut per eam modorum aequipollentiae plenius habeantur, quia ibi praecipue et specialiter exprimuntur, ideoque ad notitiam hoquetorum per resecationem vocum nullatenus traditorum immo secundum voces proprias sui modi vult actor facere mentionem.

Et nota, quod partes praeambulae sunt quasi de esse huius capituli, eo quod per eas modorum aequipollentiae et resecationes ac alternationes simplicium figurarum generaliter declarantur. Haec siquidem partes hic quasi de bene esse immo doctrinae gratia reponuntur, et etiam ne quis opinari praesumeret, quod omnes voces hoquetatae per resecationem mutue ponerentur, quare vocum perfectarum et per suos modos proprie positarum

----

1-2 semper in supradictae *cod.*   2 quam [[bre]] breves *cod.*   34 hoc [[per]] ut *cod.*

Sometimes they are interchanged, etc. Here the author gives the
principle that the abovementioned notes, both longs and breves and
semibreves, are not always regularly arranged.

An example of how they might deviate from the rule mentioned before
is given here:

Portare

**If the mode[1] is certainly long,[2] through them[3] there may be
openly[4]**
1 note that this is as regards the tenor
2 that is, of the fifth species
3 hockets
4 and regularly
**A smaller long in the duplum, when a smaller breve is given in
the triplum.[1]**
1 and this is because the breve pause coming before it takes
away one unit of time
You find any[1] of these notes in the quadruplum.
1 that is, both the smaller and the larger are found in the
quadruplum
Here the principle is given that the abovementioned rules do not
apply in some hockets:

**Sometimes they are interchanged through the compositions when
they wander,**
Here he shows why a general rule can not be confirmed about these
matters:

Hence a general law can not be given or be acceptable.

Look and see, etc. Since in the things that have been said above
the author has explained the concept of the cutting up of notes in
hockets, so that by means of this concept the equipollences of the modes
may be more fully understood -- because it is in that that they are
especially and specifically expressed -- therefore the author wishes to
make mention of the concept of the hockets that do not have in any way a
cutting up of their notes, but rather are given according to the proper
notes of their mode.

And note that the introductory parts are, as it were, about the
essence of this chapter, because it is through them that the
equipollences of the modes and the cuttings up and alternations of the
single figures are generally stated. And these parts indeed are put
here, as it were, about the proper existence or rather for the benefit of
the principle, and also lest anyone presume to think that all hocketed
notes should be placed mutually by means of cutting up, which is why he
displays the concept of notes that are perfect and placed properly by

absque resecatione aliqua notitiam manifestat. Et hoc praecipue et
expresse per tertiam speciem hoquetatam, dicens, quod in ea et in aliis
speciebus perfectis sit longarum et brevium hoquetatio pro voluntate
mutua ordinata, sicut patet hic et in similibus:

Pro patribus

Alia doctrina vel regula in tertia specie ordinata sive in quarta:
    Si modus hic ternae speciei sit, fore cerne.
    (fol. 154) **Longam[1] maiorem per cantus[2] tolle[3] minorem.**
    1 absque diminutione temporum sive
    2 omnes subaudi
    3 quia in illa specie tunc nullatenus hoquetatur
    Sic[1] variata brevis[2] vult cantibus[3] hiis fore quaevis.
    1 id est, taliter
    2 sive tam minor quam maior
    3 id est, in hoquetis absque resecatione vocum ordinatis
    Diversis metis[1] has[2] ut placet alterutretis.
    1 id est, pausis
    2 sive tam longas quam breves de uno cantu in alium, sicut
    placet
Quasi diceret: quaelibet specierum secundum suum rectum modum per
suas voces mutue sic poterit hoquetari:
    More suo verum petit hoc quaevis specierum.

Cetera compone etc. Hic vult actor ostendere qualiter alternationem
vocum mutue distributam discantus appositio saepius interrumpit, dicens,
quod non solum talis hoquetatio per se posita simpliciter reperitur, immo
discantus ordinatio secundum maneriem aliquam sive modum per aequipollentiarum convenientiam ibi pluries fit reperta, ad hoc ut armoniae
modulatio gratiosior et dulcior videatur.

    Cetera[1] compone velud exigit ars[2] ratione
    1 subaudi quae non hoquetantur tam in resecatis quam non
    2 id est, regularis ordinatio discantus secundum aliquem modum

----

4 mutue *pro* mutua *Sowa*   32 poteris *pro* poterit *Sowa*

means of their modes but without any cutting up. And this is especially
and expressly by means of the third hocketed mode, for he says that in it
and in the other perfect species there may be a hocketing of longs and
breves arranged according to mutual wishes, as is clear here and in
similar examples:

Pro patribus

Another principle or rule arranged in the third species or in the
fourth:
    Look and see if this is the mode of the third species.
    (fol.154) **Take away[3] the larger long[1] and the smaller through the
melodies.[2]**
    1 without a diminution of units of time
    2 understand: all melodies
    3 because in that species then it is in no way hocketed
    Thus[1] any breve[2] wishes to be varied in these melodies.[3]
    1 that is, in this way
    2 both smaller and larger
    3 that is, in hockets arranged without any cutting up of the
notes
    **You may alternate these[2] as you please with different
boundaries.[1]**
    1 that is, pauses
    2 both longs and breves from one composition to another as you
please
He means to say that any of the species will be able to be hocketed
mutually in this way according to its correct mode by means of its
notes:
    In its own way each of the species seeks this truth.

    Put together the others, etc. Here the author wishes to show how the
addition of the discant often interrupts the alternation of voices
distributed mutually, saying that not only is such hocketing found singly
placed by itself, but rather the arrangement of the discant is several
times found there according to some manner or mode by means of the accord
of the equipollences, so that the sound of the harmony may seem more
pleasant and sweeter.

    Put together the others[1] as the art[2] demands, as if by reason
    1 understand: those which are not hocketed, both in ones that
are cut up and those that are not
    2 that is, the regular arrangement of the discant according to
some mode

Tanquam discantus,[1] hos qui regit ordine[2] cantus.
1 sive per se regulariter componeretur
2 quo ad reductionem aequipollentiarum ad aliquem modum

Sic brevis etc. Executo superius de hoquetis in brevi modo positis
similiter et in longo, eo quod per eos omne genus aequipollentiae
declaratur, et quia duplex est ordinatio eorundem, et hoc totum sine
littera, sicut praecedens eruditio demonstravit, ideoque ad cognitionem
motellorum, in quibus similiter duplex maneries est reperta, actor
10 accedere nunc intendit, ad hoc ut de omni cantuum genere notitia
perfectior habeatur, dicens in primis, quod longus modus in motellis pro
mutua voluntate instituentium ordinatur secundum convenientiam et
ordinem specierum, et ideo de tali, cum ad beneplacitum componentium
ordinetur, non est hic mentio facienda. Brevis vero, qui a longo ducit
originem et importat, difficilior est quo ad artem, nam cantantes ipsum
componere nescientes nonnonquam impedit et perturbat. Ad hoc autem ut
ipsius notitia sive cognitio leviter habeatur, nota utrum tenor in longo
modo sit tertiae speciei sive quartae, saepissime tamen quintae. Nam si
sit tertiae sive quartae et hoc regulariter iuxta artem, in sextam
20 speciem simpliciter convertetur nihil aliud addito nihilque aliud
transmutato. Idem iudicium in motellis et ubique, sive sint sine littera
sive cum littera, est in talibus observandum, et sic efficitur brevis
modus.
     Sciendum tamen est, quod omnes voces in talibus per aequipollentiam
distributae sive per convenientiam aliquam a regularitate modi propria
deviantes, sunt in semibreves convertendae, utputa si brevis et longa
duorum temporum aut e converso pro longa trium temporum sint repertae,
necesse est enim ipsas converti in duas semibreves inaequales; si autem
tres breves, in tres semibreves et aequales. Et sic de reliquis idem
30 iudicium est habendum.
     Si tenor hiis quintae etc. Hic subiungit actor, qualiter brevis
modus a quinta specie dicitur extorqueri, dicens, quod quinta species in
secundam convertitur utrobique, sicut patet in fine huius glosulae lucide
per exempla.
     Semibrevesque satas etc. Ecce dicit, quod omnes voces per
aequipollentiam datae propter superhabundantiam litterae aut propter
ornatum musicae sunt in semibreves convertendae, sicut patebit inferius
in illo exemplo *sub Herodis* et in similibus.   Si quis autem memoriae
commendaverit hanc doctrinam, omnes motellos ex tertia specie sive quarta
40 similiter et ex quinta compositos et confectos de longo modo in brevem
aut etiam e converso absque labore convertere poterit pro mutua
voluntate, nisi semibrevium superfluitas propter superhabundantiam
litterae alicubi hoc excludat, sicut patet in illo motello *Par une
matinee* et in similibus.
     Sic brevis etc. Exemplum qualiter brevis modus in sextam speciem
conversus a tertia specie vel a quarta per conversionem simplicem
extorquetur patet hiis exemplis:

----
10 ut *add. super scriptum*   18 saepiissime *pro* saepissime *cod.*
19 *inter* in *et* sextam *ras.*   21 sit *pro* sint *cod.*   40 brevi *pro* brevem
cod.   45 **Sic brevis** *sine sublinea in cod.*

Of the discant,¹ which rules these melodies by order.²
1 as if it were put together regularly by itself
2 as regards the reduction of the equipollences to some mode

Thus the short, etc. Having described above hockets placed in the
short mode as well as in the long, because it is through them that every
genus of equipollence is stated, and because their arrangement is of two
kinds -- and this is all without text as the preceding explanation has
demonstrated -- therefore the author now intends to broach the
understanding of motets, in which similarly two kinds of manner are
found, so that a more perfect concept of all genera of melodies may be
gained. And he says at first that in motets the long mode is arranged
according to the mutual wishes of those who are organizing it and
according to the accord and order of the species, and therefore no
mention needs to be made about it here, since it is arranged at the
pleasure of those who are putting it together. But the short mode, which
draws and conveys its origin from the long, is more difficult as regards
the art, for sometimes it hinders and disturbs singers who do not know
how to put it together. But in order that the concept or understanding
of it may be easily gained, note whether the tenor in the long mode is of
the third species or the fourth, or very often the fifth. For if is of
the third or fourth and it is regular in accordance with the art, it is
simply converted into the sixth species with nothing else added and
nothing else transformed. The same judgement should be observed about
such things in motets and everywhere, whether they are without text or
with text; and that is how the short mode is accomplished.

Nevertheless it should be known that in such things all notes
distributed by means of equipollence, or deviating from the proper
regularity of the mode by means of some accord, are to be converted into
semibreves -- for example if a breve and a long of two units of time or
the reverse are found in place of a long of three units of time, for it
is necessary for those to be converted into two unequal semibreves; but
if there are three breves, they would be converted into three equal
semibreves. And the same judgement is to be held in this way for the
rest.

If the tenor in these, etc. Here the author adds how the short mode
is said to be extracted from the fifth species, saying that the fifth
species is converted into the second in both parts, as is shown clearly
by means of examples at the end of this gloss.

And say that the notes, etc. Here he says that all notes given
through equipollence on account of the over-abundance of the text or the
ornamentation of the music are to be converted into semibreves, as will
be shown below in the example "Sub Herodis" and in similar examples.
But if someone committed this principle to memory, he could convert all
motets put together and made up from the third species or the fourth and
similarly from the fifth from the long mode to the short, and also the
reverse, according to mutual wishes and without labor, unless an excess
of semibreves on account of an over-abundance of text elsewhere excludes
this, as is shown in the motet "Par une matinee" and in similar ones.

Thus the short, etc. An example of how the short mode is converted
into the sixth species and extracted from the third species or the fourth
by a simple conversion is given in these examples:

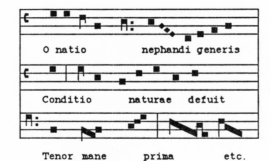

10

Exemplum qualiter per convenientiam tertiae speciei sive quartae atque quintae eadem conversio regulariter reperitur, utputa tertiae vel quartae in sextam et quintae in secundam, et etiam qualiter aequipollentiae ibi repertae sunt in semibreves convertendae, patet hic et sic de omnibus aliis:

20

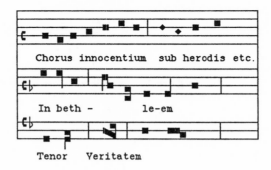

Sic brevis[1] efficitur[2] e longo,[3] qui reperitur[4]
30   1 sive modus
        2 id est, componitur vel formatur
        3 sive modo
        4 sive brevis modus
Motellis,[1] sextae speciei[2] sint ibi[3] textae
        1 id est, ubique cum littera
        2 quo ad brevem modum sive
        3 id est, in illo brevi modo
Voces[1] quae ternae fuerant longae, ve quaternae.[2]
        1 tam simplices quam compositae sive
40   2 id est, quando inveniebantur in tertia specie sive quarta
Si tenor[1] hiis quintae fuerat nunc esto secundae,[2]
        1 id est, primus cantus, qui aliis esse dicitur fundamentum
        2 per talem conversionem sive
        (fol. 154v) **Nam[1] petit[2] ex quinta fieri tunc lege[3] secunda.[4]**
        1 pro quia
        2 ratio est, quoniam quinta species in secundam est ubique
        convertenda
        3 id est, regulariter
        4 sive species

----

40 inveniebant *pro* inveniebantur *cod.*   44 **tunc** [[**sponte vel**]] **lege** *cod.*
46 **ubiconque** *pro* **ubique** *Sowa*

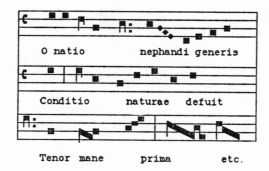

An example is given here of how the same conversion is found regularly by means of the accord of the third species or the fourth and the fifth, for example a conversion of the third or fourth into the sixth, and the fifth into the second, and also how the equipollences found there should be converted into semibreves; and the same applies to all the others:

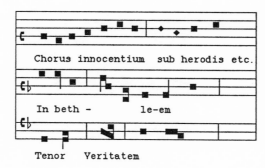

Thus the short[1] is made up[2] from the long,[3] which is found[4]
1 mode
2 that is, is put together or formed
3 mode
4 the short mode
In motets,[1] if there are woven there,[3] of the sixth species,[2]
1 that is, everywhere with text
2 as regards the short mode
3 that is, in that short mode
Notes[1] which were of the third long species, or the fourth.[2]
1 both single and composite
2 that is, when they were found in the third species or the fourth
If the tenor[1] in these was of the fifth species, now let it be of the second,[2]
1 that is, the first melody, which is said to be the foundation for the others
2 through such a conversion
(fol. 154v) For[1] it seeks[2] from the fifth then to become the second[4] by the law.[3]
1 instead of: because
2 the reason is that the fifth species should always be converted into the second
3 that is, regularly
4 species

Quasi diceret: omnes voces a recto ordine deviantes sunt in semibreves convertendae:

Semibrevesque satas dic voces aequiperatas.

Quasi diceret: eadem conversio est de longa duplice facienda respectu diminutionis, eo quod convertitur in brevem et longam secundum secundam speciem:

Hoc duplicem longam minuendo dogmate pungam.

----

4 duplici *pro* duplice Sowa   5-6 eo quod . . . secundam speciem *add. in marg.*77

He means to say that all notes that deviate from the correct order should be converted into semibreves:

And say that the notes that are ploughed in equally are sown as semibreves.

He means to say that the same conversion should be made with the double long with respect to its diminution, because it is converted into a breve and a long according to the second species:

I shall draw the double long, diminishing it by the doctrine.

\<Capitulum tertium\>

Tempora tot pausa etc. Quoniam actor in praecedentibus hoquetorum
modum et seriem nec non et altrinsecationem eorum lucide declaravit,
ostendendo etiam qualiter omne genus cantuum possit et artificialiter de
uno modo in alium transmutari, utputa de longo in brevem et etiam e
converso, ideoque de pausis in talibus positis et repertis et modo simili
mutuatis vult efficaciam reserere breviter et naturam, eo quod per eas
fit nobis certa cognitio praedictorum, dicens breviter, quod pausa in
talibus voci pro qua dabitur proportionaliter aequipollet.

10 **Tempora[1] tot pausa teneat[2] quot dat sibi clausa[3]**
      1 id est, tantam quantitatem temporum seu temporis
      2 id est, contineat vel repraesentet
      3 id est, in se inclusa
      Vox[1] pro qua dabimus, nec ei plus addere scimus.[2]
      1 sive sive sit longa sive brevis sive semibrevis
      2 quasi diceret: nihil amplius importabit

   Hic dabo pausarum etc. Declarato superius capitulo specierum nec non
et hoquetorum serie declarata tam brevium quam longorum, ostendendo etiam
20 qualiter brevis modus a longo vel e converso per diversa cantuum genera
oriatur, in hoc loco vult actor exponere tertium capitulum sui libri,
quod de pausarum generibus conficitur et naturis. Et est notandum, quod
non sine ratione immediate adiungitur praecedenti, quod sic patet: in
praecedenti capitulo declaratur specierum notitia et etiam hoquetorum,
quae quidem notitia parum aut nihil proficeret sine pausis, eo quod per
eas modorum differentia distinguitur et etiam omnium figurarum. Item

----

4 transmutari *add. in marg.*   6 naturam [[dicens]] eo quod *cod.*

242

Chapter Three

Let the pause hold, etc. Since in the preceding discussion the author has clearly stated the method and sequence of hockets as well as their cutting up in both parts, showing also how every genus of melody can be transformed artificially from one mode into another, for example from a long into a short mode and also the reverse, therefore he wishes to disclose briefly the efficacy and nature of pauses placed and found in these and exchanged in a similar way, because it is through them that a fixed understanding of the aforementioned matters comes to us; and he says briefly that a pause in these is equipollent to a note in the place of which it will be given proportionally.

> **Let the pause hold[2] as many units of time[1] as, enclosed in it,[3]**
> 1 that is, as much quantity of several units or a single unit of time
> 2 that is, let it contain or represent
> 3 that is, included in it
> **The note[1] gives, which we shall give in its place, and we know that we should not add more to it.[2]**
> 1 whether it is a long or a breve or a semibreve
> 2 he means to say that it will convey nothing more

Here I shall give the species of the pauses, etc. Since the chapter on the species has been given above, and the sequence of hockets both short and long has been stated, showing also how the short mode arises from the long, or the reverse, by means of different genera of melodies, in this place the author wishes to set forth the third chapter of his book which is made up of the genera and natures of pauses. And it should be noted that it is not without reason that it is joined immediately to the preceding one, and the reason is this: In the preceding chapter the concept of the species and hockets is stated, and indeed this concept would be of little or no use without pauses, because it is through them that the distinction of the modes and of all the figures is differen-

voces cantantium absque recreatione spirituum praegravatae nonquam
perfectum finem attingerent sine ipsis, ideoque ipsas, sicut patet
necessarias, post modorum capitulum decrevimus ordinari, eo quod per
eas specierum distinctio nec non et convenientia plenius habeatur.

Item sicut nomen exigit verbum ad hoc ut oratio sit perfecta, sic
etiam modorum species per pausarum differentias ad perfectionem cantuum
ordinantur; ad quod praecipue denotandum pausarum capitulum subiungitur
praecedenti. Item nota, quod modus et pausa correlative se habent, sicut
patuit per praedicta, ubi dictum fuit: *si modus est perfectus, et*
10 *pausatio est perfecta; si imperfectus, imperfecta.* Et sic patet quare
hic debuit ordinari.

Et quia hic agitur de pausis, ideoque in primis videamus quid sit
pausa, et quae sit causa inventionis ipsius; quot sint eius differentiae
patebit inferius suo loco. Ad primum igitur dicimus: pausa est divisio
soni facta in debita quantitate, vel pausa est recreatio spiritus
fatigati sicut punctuatio. Pausa inventa fuit ut modorum differentias
circa perfectas et imperfectas declararet, aut propter recreationem
spiritus fatigati, aut propter duram vocum collisionem seu discordantiam
evitandam, aut ut per eam variae modorum species convenirent.

20 Hiis breviter expeditis, ad divisionem litterae accedamus. Haec
igitur praesens lectio in duas partes principaliter dividatur, in quarum
prima ostendit actor de quo debet agere, in secunda exequitur. Prima
incipit **Hic dabo pausarum** etc., secunda **In bina specie** etc. Haec secunda
in duas: in prima agit de hiis quae faciunt ad esse huius capituli, in
secunda de eis quae faciunt ad bene esse. Ideo patet ordo: prima pars
incipit **In bina specie** etc., secunda **Hic suspirorum**. Item prima istarum
in duas, in quarum prima dividit pausam in simplicem et compositam, in
secunda procedit circa perfectionem et imperfectionem eiusdem. Prima
igitur incipit **In bina specie** etc., secunda **Ante modum talem** etc. Haec
30 secunda in duas: in prima agit de perfectione et imperfectione circa
pausas, in secunda ostendit quantum spatii vel spatiorum continere debeat
unaquaeque. Prima pars incipit **Ante modum** etc., secunda **Semibrevis
pausa** etc. Item illa, in qua dividit pausas in simplices et compositas,
in duas dividitur, nam in prima agit de divisione pausarum, in secunda
exemplificat de eisdem. Prima incipit **In bina specie** etc., secunda
Simplicium forma etc. Et sic patet sententia et divisio leoninis.
Littera per se patet.

Hic[1] dabo pausarum species,[2] et quanta[3] sit harum.
40 1 id est, in hoc capitulo
2 id est, differentias
3 quoad quantitatem temporum sive

----

22 ostendat *pro* ostendit *cod*.   decet *pro* debet *Sowa*
28 imperfectionem [[earum]] vel eiusdem *cod*.   31 pausam *pro*
pausas *Sowa*   33 ista *pro* illa *Sowa*   40 id est *om. Sowa*

tiated. Also the voices of singers, weighed down without refreshment of the breath, would never reach a perfect end without them, and so we have decided that, since it is clear that they are necessary, they will be arranged after the chapter on the modes, because it is through them that the differentiation of the species as well as their accord is more fully grasped.

Also just as a noun demands a verb so that speech may be perfect, so also the species of modes are arranged by means of the distinctions of the pauses for the perfection of melodies; and the chapter on the pauses is added to the preceding one especially to indicate this. Also note that a mode and a pause occur as correlatives, as has been shown above, where it was said: "If the mode is perfect, then the pause is perfect; if imperfect, then it is imperfect."* And thus it is clear why it should be arranged here.

And because we are dealing here with pauses, therefore let us see first what is a pause, and what is the reason for its invention. How many its distinctions are will be made clear below in the right place. First therefore we say: A pause is a division of sound made for the requisite quantity, or a pause is for the refreshment of tired breath, as punctuation is. The pause was invented so that it might state the distinctions of the modes as to their being perfect and imperfect, or for the refreshment of tired breath, or for the purpose of avoiding a harsh collision or discord of voices, or so that through it the different species of the modes might be in accord.

Now that these things have been briefly discussed, let us broach the division of the text. Therefore let this present reading be divided principally into two parts, in the first of which the author shows what he should deal with, and in the second it is accomplished. The first begins **Here I shall give the species of the pauses**, etc., the second **In twofold species**, etc. This second part is divided into two. In the first he deals with those things which contribute to the existence of this chapter, in the second with those which contribute to its proper existence. Thus the order is clear: The first part begins **In twofold species**, etc., the second **This man has decided**. Also the first of these parts is divided into two, in the first of which he divides the pause into single and composite, and in the second he continues regarding its perfection and imperfection. Therefore the first begins **In twofold species**, etc., and the second **When the pause holds**, etc. This second part is divided into two. In the first he deals with perfection and imperfection as regards pauses, in the second he shows how much space or spaces each one should contain. The first part begins **When the pause holds**, etc., the second **The semibreve pause**, etc. Also that part in which he divides the pauses into single and composite is divided into two parts, for in the first he deals with the division of the pauses, in the second he gives examples of them. The first begins **In twofold species**, etc., the second **The form of the singles**, etc. And thus the meaning and division of the leonine verses is clear. The text is clear by itself.

> **Here[1] I shall give the species[2] of the pauses and how much[3] these have.**
> 1 that is, in this chapter
> 2 that is, the distinctions
> 3 as to the quantity of units of time

Quamlibet[1] inde[2] metas,[3] si vis[4] hinc[5] ordine[6] metas.[7]
1 sive pausam
2 id est, postea
3 id est, colligas
4 O cantor
5 id est, ab illis
6 id est, regulariter
7 id est, divisiones seu differentias
Describit prosa pausam quis cernere glosa.[1]
1 unde superius: pausa est divisio soni facta in debita
quantitate
In bina[1] **specie discernitur**[2] **arte**[3] **sophiae.**[4]
1 id est, duplici
2 sive pausa
3 id est, secundum artem
4 id est, huius scientiae
Aut est composita[1] **vel simplex**[2] **pausa petita.**[3]
1 sive utputa duplata, triplata vel quadruplata
2 id est, sola
3 id est, posita vel inventa

    Simplex dicatur etc. Hic vult actor de simplicibus pausis regulam
ostendere generalem, (fol. 155) dicens, quod illa pausa simplex dicitur
et perfecta, secundum quando pausatur secundum quantitatem unius modi aut
alicuius speciei; per quod innuitur, quod pausa semper morem insequitur
sui modi.
    Simplicium etc. Ostenso superius quid sit pausa et quot sunt eius
species sive partes, hic vult actor recitare differentiam primi membri,
dicens, quod omnis pausa simplex aut est perfecta aut etiam imperfecta.
Perfecta dicitur illa, quando non transmutat modum propter sui adventum,
vel quando reddit talem modum a parte ante qualem a parte post.
    Tot spatiis nebit etc. Hic datur regula generalis de protractione
omnium pausationum, quae talis est: figura pausationis tot spatia
continet et etiam intervalla quot tempora in se dicitur continere,
secundum quod expresse continetur inferius supra textum.

    Quasi diceret: pausae modorum suorum ordinationem propriam
consecuntur:
Simplex[1] **dicatur quae iura modi comitatur.**
1 sive pausa
Simplicium[1] **forma**[2] **duplex**[3] **est quam dabo norma.**[4]
1 sive pausarum
2 id est, protractionis repraesentatio
3 scilicet perfecta aut imperfecta
4 id est, regulariter
Aut perfecta[1] **datur aut imperfecta**[2] **locatur.**
1 simplex pausa sive
2 propter sui modi imperfectionem sive
Regula est: pausa perfecta est atque simplex, quando reddit talem

----

28 actor hic recitare *cod.*   31 reddit [[alium]] talem *cod.*
49 reddat *pro* reddit *Sowa*

You may gather[3] any one[1] then,[2] if you want[4] from there[5] the boundaries[7] in order.[6]
1 pause
2 that is, afterwards
3 that is, you may collect
4 O cantor
5 that is, from them
6 that is, regularly
7 that is, the divisions or distinctions
The prose describes the pause you can see in the gloss.[1]
1 as it says above: a pause is a division of the sound made for the requisite quantity
In twofold[1] species it is recognized[2] by the art[3] of wisdom.[4]
1 that is, of two kinds
2 the pause
3 that is, according to the art
4 that is, of this science
The pause that is sought[3] is either composite[1] or single.[2]
1 for example, double, triple, or quadruple
2 that is, alone
3 that is, placed or invented

The single may be said, etc. Here the author wishes to give a general rule about single pauses, (fol. 155) saying that that pause is called single and perfect according to when the pause is made according to the quantity of one mode or some species; by which it is suggested that the pause always follows the custom of its mode.

The form of the singles, etc. Having shown above what a pause is and how many its species or parts are, here the author wishes to explain the distinction of the first portion, saying that every pause that is single is either perfect or imperfect. That one is said to be perfect, when it does not transform the mode as a result of its arrival, or when it makes the mode before it of the same kind as the mode after it.

The pause will entwine, etc. Here is given a general rule about the notation of all pauses, which is as follows: The figure of a pause contains as many spaces and intervals as it is said to contain in itself of units of time, according to what is expressly contained below over the text.

He means to say that pauses follow the proper arrangement of their modes:
The single[1] may be said to be that which accompanies the laws of its mode.
1 pause
The form[2] of the singles[1] is of two kinds,[3] which I shall give according to the pattern.[4]
1 the pauses
2 that is, the representation of their notation
3 that is to say perfect or imperfect
4 that is, regularly
It is either given as perfect[1] or positioned as imperfect.[2]
1 the single pause
2 on account of the imperfection of its mode
The rule is: A pause is perfect and single when it has the mode

modum a parte ante qualem post:

  Ante modum talem cum pausa tenet, sibi qualem
  Post,[1] haec perfecta fore dicitur undique lecta.[2]
  1 dat sive vel tenet
  2 eo quod non transmutat modum propter sui adventum

Alia regula de eadem: converte sic: simplex est pausa, si
penultima vox speciei praepositae

  Simplex est par ei penultima si speciei

fuerit par, id est aequalis, ei, similiter et dicitur esse perfecta:

  Praepositae fuerit vox, nec perfectio deerit.[1]
  1 id est, deficiet

Alia regula est de imperfectione pausarum, quae talis est: pausa est
imperfecta, si modus suus fuerit imperfectus:

  Imperfecta datur tunc quando modus variatur.

Ecce confirmat regulam praecedentem, dicens, quod pausa dispositionem
sequitur specierum:

  Pausa tenere forum vult semper iure modorum.

Hic datur doctrina generalis de notitia: pausa tot spatia continet
quot tempora comprehendit:

  Tot spatiis nebit quot tempora pausa tenebit.

  Semibrevis etc. Hic intendit actor de figuris pausationum
differentias specificare, quantitatem cuiuslibet ostendendo pariter et
figuram, unde in primis videndum est, quid sit figura pausationis et quot
sunt pausationum differentiae, et quae sit cognitio inter illas.

  Ad primum dicimus: figura pausationis est signum vel tractus circa
divisionem soni; tractus, dico, factus in debita quantitate sive
proportione. Pausationum vel tractuum differentiae sunt haec: quaedam
dicitur semibrevis, quaedam recta brevis, vel maior, quaedam longa minor,
vel maior, quaedam dicitur finis punctorum, quaedam divisio modorum,
quaedam divisio sillabarum, quaedam suspiratio. Et istas tres ultimas
actoritate prosae decrevimus hic adiungi.

  Incipiamus ergo a semibrevi, licet sit minus digna; duplex tamen ad
hoc ratio nos coegit, quarum una est quia imperfectum appetit perfici, et
sic maiori et velociori auxilio indiget quam perfectum. Item alia ratio
multofortius nos coegit, scilicet quod primo oscura vitia extirpemus, ne
fructum impediant exportatum. Superius audivistis, quomodo quidam, suae
opinionis imperitiam ignorantes, per singula capitula prosam artis
reprehendere praesumpserunt, istud siquidem capitulum per tractus
singulos pausationum penitus corrumpentes. Dicebant et enim pausam trium
temporum quinque lineas et quatuor spatia sustinere, pausam duorum
quatuor <lineas> et tria spatia, rectam brevem pausam tres lineas et duo
spatia, semibrevem maiorem et suspirium maius vocabant duas lineas et
unum spatium integrum, suspirium minus dimidium spatii, et sic prosae

----

9 ei pausae similiter *cod.* 28-31 *crux in marg.* 31 tercies *pro* tres
Sowa 35 maiore *pro* maiori *Sowa* velociore *pro* velociori *Sowa*
37 *linea in marg.* 42 tercia *pro* tria *Sowa* tercies *pro* tres *Sowa*
43 maiorem [[quidem]] et *cod.* 44 spatium *add. super scriptum*

before it of the same kind as it is after:

When the pause holds the same mode before,
As after,[1] this is said to be and is read everywhere as
perfect.[2]
1 as it gives or holds after
2 because it does not transform the mode on account of its
arrival

Another rule about the same: Interpret it thus: The pause is single
if the penultimate note of the species that is put before it

It is single if the penultimate note of the species
is even with, that is equal to, it; and similarly it is said to be
perfect:

That is put before it is even with it; and perfection will not be
lacking.[1]
1 that is, be missing

There is another rule about the imperfection of pauses, which is as
follows: The pause is imperfect if its mode is imperfect:

It is given as imperfect when the mode is varied.
Here he confirms the preceding rule, saying that the pause follows
the placement of the species:

The pause always wants to hold its position by the law of the
modes.
Here is given a general principle about the concept: A pause
contains as many spaces as it includes units of time:

The pause will entwine as many in the spaces as it will hold
units of time.

The semibreve pause, etc. Here the author intends to specify the
distinctions of the figures of the pauses, showing the quantity of each
one as well as its figure. And so first it should be seen what is the
figure of a pause and how many distinctions of pauses there are, and what
is the understanding of the difference between them.

First we say: The figure of a pause is a sign or a line that
concerns the division of the sound; a line, I say, made for the requisite
quantity or proportion. The distinctions of pauses or lines are these:
One is called a semibreve, one a correct breve, or a larger one, one a
smaller long, or a larger one, one is called the end of the written
notes, one the division of the modes, one the division of the syllables,
one a breath. And we have decided to add those last three here by the
authority of the prose.

Let us begin therefore with the semibreve, although it is less
worthy. Two reasons have forced us to do this, of which one is that
something that is imperfect seeks completion and thus needs greater and
faster help than something that is perfect. Also another reason has
forced us much more strongly, which is that we should first eradicate
faults of obscurity, lest they hinder the carrying away of the fruit of
knowledge. You have heard above how some people, unaware of the
ignorance of their view, have presumed to censure the prose treatise in
every single chapter, indeed completely corrupting that chapter on the
individual lines of pauses. For they said* that the pause of three units
of time takes up five lines and four spaces, a pause of two units four
lines and three spaces, a correct breve pause three lines and two spaces;
a larger semibreve and a larger breath they were calling two lines and
one whole space, a smaller breath half a space; and in this way they

sententiam et materiam in nichilum redigebant. Quorum opinioni nos
acquiescere non volentes eorum opinionem dicimus esse nullam.

    Cuius rei ratio sic clarescat: omnis semibrevis sive in figura
composita sive per se dicitur imperfecta; si ergo sit imperfecta,
quicquid loco ipsius repertum est dicetur similiter imperfectum. Sed
pausa semibrevis pro utraque saepius reperitur, ergo figurari tenebitur
imperfecta, quod concedimus. Item per dictum suum patet quod figurari
debeat imperfecta, ex quo dimidium spatii ei pro minore semibrevi
tribuunt figurando. Per hoc innuunt dimidium spatii imperfectionem
10 designare. Cuius conclusio est: si imperfectio per tale dimidium
designetur, perfectio per plenum spatium ostendetur, ex quo inter
perfectum et imperfectum nullum medium fit repertum, ergo nulla
semibrevium pausa plus quam dimidium spatii tenebitur possidere, ne
perfectionis beneficium surripere videatur.

    Item quod nihil sit dicere vel dictu, quod nulla differentia
assignari debeat inter tales quoad pausam, patet sic: semibreves non
differunt in forma nec per se positae nec cum aliis coadiunctae, ergo
neque pausae pro ipsis positae vel repertae, ad hoc ut signatum signum
proprium repraesentent. Si quis modo simili obiciat de brevibus minoribus
20 et maioribus, eo quod pausae pro eis positae deberent aequales similiter
figurari, dicimus, quod non est simile hinc et inde, quoniam istae sunt
perfectae et sub certa proportione temporum mensuratae, (fol. 155v) et
sic certas metas certitudinem temporis seu temporum designantes attingere
meruerunt; aliae vero, quia imperfectae sunt et sub proportione
imperfecti temporis constitutae, pausas indivisibiles retinebunt, certas
metas nullatenus attingentes.

    Item si eorum sententia vel opinio esset vera, quando dicunt pausam
semibrevem maiorem spatium continere, recta brevis pausa spatium et
dimidium utrobique importaret, cum in se semibrevem minorem et maiorem
30 proportionaliter repraesentet, sed iuxta dictum suum duo spatia
comprehendit, ergo sub tali opinione sibi ipsis possunt et debent
contrarii nuncupari. Ex quo concluditur eorum sententiam esse nullam,
immo penitus evitandam, cum alibi dicatur:

      Conveniet nulli qui secum dissidet ipse.

    Nos igitur, contra tales nolentes amplius garrulare, antecessorum
scripta sequimur approbata, dicentes semibrevem pausam tam minorem quam
maiorem medium spatii continere, vel circa medium fieri. Et sic
imperfectum dicimus quicquid certum terminum non attingit, sicut patet
per circulum, qui, si in aliqua parte sui frangatur vel etiam deleatur,
40 iam non erit perfectus, sed semicirculus vocabitur ac etiam imperfectus.
Qua de causa credimus quamlibet semibrevem pausam medium spatii vel circa
et nihil amplius possidere. Idem iudicium est de pausis reliquis
faciendum circumstantiis omnibus specialiter indagatis.

----

2 volentes [[per locum a minori]] eorum *cod.*   esse [[falsam vel]]
nullam *cod.*   3 rei *add. in marg.*   10 talem *pro* tale *Sowa*   15 dictu
[[et]] quod *cod.*   16 quoad pausam *add. super scriptum*   25 constitutae
[[indivisibiles]] pausas *cod.*   28 spatium *add. in marg.*
29 importaret [[cum]] cum *cod.*   33 dicatur *add. super scriptum*
dicitur *pro* dicatur *Sowa*

reduced the meaning and material of the prose to nothing. And not
wishing to acquiesce in their view, we say that their view is nothing.

And let the reason for this become clear as follows: Every
semibreve, whether in a composite figure or by itself, is said to be
imperfect; if therefore it is imperfect, whatever is found in place of it
will similarly be said to be imperfect. A semibreve pause is often found
instead of a semibreve, and therefore it will be held to be figured as
imperfect, which we concede. Also by their own saying it is clear that
it should be figured as imperfect, as a result of which they allot half a
space to it in figuring it when it is instead of a smaller semibreve.
And by this they suggest that half a space designates imperfection. And
the conclusion to this is that if imperfection is designated by this
half-space, then perfection will by shown by a full space, as a result of
which there is no middle ground between something perfect and something
imperfect, and therefore no semibreve pause will be held to possess more
than half a space, lest it seem to steal the benefit of perfection.

Also the fact that there is nothing to say or to be said about the
fact that no difference should be assigned between such things as regards
the pause is clear from the following: Semibreves do not differ in their
form either placed by themselves or joined with others, therefore neither
do pauses placed or found by themselves, in order that the proper sign
may represent what is signified. If anyone objects in a similar manner
about smaller and larger breves -- that pauses placed instead of them
should similarly be figured as equal -- we say that it is not a similar
thing in the one case and the other, since the latter are perfect and
measured under a fixed proportion of units of time, (fol. 155v) and thus
they deserve to reach fixed boundaries that designate a fixed amount of a
unit or units of time; but the others, because they are imperfect and
established under the proportion of an imperfect amount of time, will
keep indivisible pauses and never reach fixed boundaries.

Also if their opinion or view were true, when they say that the
larger semibreve pause contains a space, then the correct breve pause
would convey a space and a half on both sides, since it represents
proportionally in itself a smaller and a larger semibreve, but according
to their own saying it includes two spaces, therefore with this view they
can and should be termed contradictory to themselves. As a result of
which it is concluded that their view is nothing, or rather should be
completely avoided, since it is said elsewhere:

"Let him agree with nobody who disagrees with himself."*

We therefore, not wishing to prate any more against these people,
follow the approved writings of our forebears, saying that both the
smaller and the larger semibreve pause contain half of a space or about
half of a space.* And thus we say that anything is imperfect that does
not reach a fixed ending, as is shown by the circle, which, if it is
broken or erased in any part of itself, will no longer be perfect, but
will be called a semicircle and imperfect. And for this reason we
believe that any semibreve pause possesses half of a space or there-
abouts and nothing more. The same judgement should be made about the
rest of the pauses when all the circumstances have been specifically
investigated.

Exemplum omnium pausationum patet hic:

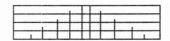

      Semibrevis[1] **pausa medium spatii**[2] **tenet, ausa**
      1 tam minor quam maior sive
      2 per quod imperfecta designatur sive
10   **Nil dare**[1] **plus credo**[2] **contra quosdam**[3] **tamen edo.**[4]
      1 id est, continere sive
      2 id est, assero vel spero
      3 novos artifices sive
      4 id est, dico
      Ecce brevi[1] **dabitur**[2] **spatium, nunc longa**[3] **potitur**
      1 sive pausae rectae brevi
      2 secundum nos sive
      3 tam minor quam maior
      Binis,[1] **vel ternis,**[2] **punctorum fine quaternis.**[3]
20   1 quo ad minorem
      2 quo ad maiorem
      3 sive longa pausa vel quaecumque sit illa

    Inque duas vere etc. converte sic: **que**, pro et, huiusmodi pausae
sive; **tenuere vere medium**, id est, metam aeque distantem; **in**, pro inter;
duas voces. Quasi diceret: ubicumque pausa inter duas voces reperitur,
debet distare aequaliter hinc et inde.

    Quidam tamen in suis artibus contrarium asserere sunt reperti, sic
dicentes: *quandocumque inter duas longas figuras suspirium non in medio*
30 *sed iuxta latus alicuius figurae ponitur, illa figura cuiuscumque tractus*
propinquior erit suspirium optinebit, utpote si tractus propinquior
figurae praecedenti extiterit, a parte finis eiusdem sumetur, si autem
propinquior figurae sussequenti extiterit, tunc a parte principii sumetur
eiusdem; et per hoc intelligendum est, quod nullus tractus inter duas
figuras medium tenere debet, sed iuxta illam a qua sumitur stare tenetur,
sicut patet in 'In seculum' etc., concludentes sic: *quoniam si medium*
optineret, tunc posset fieri ambiguitas utrum tempus sumeretur a
praecedenti figura vel a sussequenti etc.

    Nos siquidem opinionem talium quasi nullam aut puerilem sed potius
40 frivolam reputantes pausas quascumque inter duas voces vel figuras
positas distare facimus aequaliter hinc et inde, eo quod tanquam meta
sive divisio suum locum proprium, scilicet medium inter duo, possidet,
sic et istae suum locum proprium, id est medium inter duas figuras,
artificialiter possidebunt. Sicut videmus litteras in dictionibus ab
invicem distare aequaliter, licet a diversis sillabis dependeant,
similiter et voces seu figurae in eodem puncto positae, quamvis una ab
altera pluries sustrahatur.

3-6 *ex. in marg.*   14 id est [[ed]] dico *cod.*   27 decet *pro* debet *Sowa*
34 nullo *pro nullus cod.*

An example of all the pauses is given here:

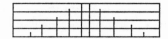

The semibreve[1] pause holds half of a space,[2] daring
1 both the smaller and the larger
2 by which the imperfect pause is designated
To give[1] nothing more, I believe[2] and relate,[4] contrary to the
views of certain people.[3]
1 that is, to contain
2 that is, I assert or hope
3 the new masters of the arts
4 that is, I say
Look, to the breve[1] will be given[2] a space, and now the long[3]
obtains
1 a pause of a correct breve
2 according to us
3 both the smaller and the larger
Two[1] or three,[2] and four at the end of the written notes.[3]
1 as regards the smaller
2 as regards the larger
3 whether it is a long pause or whatever it is

And within two notes, etc. Interpret thus: **And**, instead of: also
of this kind of pause; **indeed they have held the middle**, that is, a
boundary equally distant; **within**, instead of: between; **two notes**. He
means to say that whenever a pause is found between two notes, it should
be the same distance from both of them.

Nevertheless some are found to assert the contrary in their
treatises,* saying as follows: "Whenever a breath is placed between two
long figures, not in the middle but next to the side of one figure, that
figure whose line will be nearer will obtain the breath; for example if
the line stands nearer to the preceding figure, it will be taken from a
part of the end of that figure, but if it stands nearer to the following
figure then it will be taken from a part of the beginning of that figure.
And from this it should be understood that no line should be in the
middle between two figures but is considered to stand next to that one
from which it is taken, as is shown in 'In seculum'" etc. And they
conclude thus: ". . . since if it would obtain the middle, then there
could be ambiguity as to whether the time would be taken from the
preceding figure or from the following one," etc.

But we, indeed, judging the view of such people to be nothing, or
childish, or frivolous rather, make any pauses that are placed between
two notes or figures equally distant from both of them, because just as a
boundary or division possesses its own proper place, that is to say the
middle between two things, so these too will possess artificially their
own proper place, that is the middle between two figures. Just as we see
letters in words being equally distant from each other, although they may
be governed by different syllables, so also are notes or figures placed
on the same written note, although one may be several times removed from
the other.

Quod autem eorum opinio vel ratio deleri debeat in aeternum, patet
multiplici ratione. Una est et approbabilis, sicut modo supra tetigimus;
alia est, quoniam si propinquiores essent uni figurae quam alteri,
deformitatem propter inaequalitatem inducerent. Item si spatium esset
breve, sicut saepe contingit, nisi aeque distando ponerentur, propin-
quiorem forsitan macularent. Item si plures essent pausae, utputa duae
vel tres etc., et a diversis vocibus saepius resecatae seu etiam
dependentes, tunc una pausa propinquior voci a qua dependet ab alia pausa
prolongaretur, et etiam e converso. Quod ponere seu opinari fatuum est,
10 quoniam si esset verum, necesse esset aestimare, quanto deberet esse
propinquior uni quam alteri, quod nihil est aestimare. Item si hoc esset
verum, nulla pausatio esset perfecta propter finem punctorum, quod
falsum est, quoniam in omni modo perfecto est pausa perfecta, sicut
superius expressum est. Ideoque opinionem talium relinquentes approbato
usui consentimus.

Inque[1] duas vere voces[2] medium[3] tenuere.[4]
1 pro inter
2 id est, figuras
20   3 locum sive
4 id est, meruerunt tenere

Simplex duplatur etc. Facta superius mentione pausarum simplicium,
hic vult actor compositarum notitiam revelare, dicens, quod compositae ex
simplicibus componuntur, utputa a duabus vel a tribus vel pluribus sibi
invicem continue ordinatis, vel quando plures, utputa breves vel semibreves, alicui longae in diversis cantibus aequipollent, et sic per
unionem plurium compositae nuncupantur.

30   **Simplex[1] duplatur, triplatur, vel quadruplatur.[2]**
1 sive pausa
2 et hoc totum repertum est sive sub pari numero vel impari
Sic fit composita[1] ex simplicibus[2] redimita,[3]
1 inquam pausa
2 id est, per se positis
3 id est, adornata
Sive pari numero vel neve pari data vero.[1]
1 quo ad aequalitatem temporum in eis vel inaequalitatem

40   **Hic suspirorum** etc. Hic vult actor de suspiriis et modorum
divisionibus opinionem suam breviter recitare, dicens, quod compositores
artis musicae inter pausarum differentias addiderunt modorum divisionem
per tractulum obliquum factum, et hoc a parte inferiori, velud hic
protrahentes / / / . (fol. 156) Efficaciam tamen illius siluerunt,
innuentes per hoc quod signum solummodo vocaretur. De suspiriis hoc
dixerunt: *suspiratio est apparentia pausationis, et hoc est positum quia
suspiratio potest fieri cum tractu vel sine, et recte brevis minor vel*

----

14 opprobato *pro* approbato *Sowa*   24 quod [[illa]] compositae *cod.*
26 ordinatae *pro* ordinatis *cod.*   utputa [[br]] breves *cod.*   37 [[**Sive
par est numerus aut impar fit quoque verus**]] *cod.*   43 oblique *pro*
obliquum *Sowa*   inferiore *pro* inferiori *Sowa*

And the fact that their view or reason should be erased for eternity is clear for many reasons. And one of them is demonstrable, as we have just now touched on above; the other is that if the pauses were nearer to one figure than to the other, they would bring in a deformity on account of the inequality. Also if the space were short, as often happens if they are not placed at an equal distance, they might perhaps spoil the nearer one. Also if there were several pauses, for example two or three etc., and they were often cut from or dependent upon different notes, then one pause that is nearer the note on which it depends would be lengthened in comparison with the other pause, and also the reverse. And to place them this way or to think this is stupid, since, if it were true, it would be necessary to guess how much nearer it should be to one than to the other, which is to guess nonsense. Also, if this were true, no pause would be perfect at the end of the written notes, which is false, since in every perfect mode there is a perfect pause, as has been expressed above. Therefore, abandoning the view of such people, we agree with approved usage.

> **And within[1] two notes[2] indeed they have held[4] the middle.[3]**
> 1 instead of: between
> 2 that is, figures
> 3 place
> 4 that is, they have deserved to hold

The single is doubled, etc. Having made mention above of the single pauses, here the author wishes to reveal the concept of the composite ones, saying that the composite ones are made up from single ones, for example from two or three or more arranged continuously next to each other, or when several of them, for example breves or semibreves, are equipollent to some long in different melodies, and thus by means of the union of several of them they are termed composite.

> **The single[1] is doubled, tripled, or quadrupled.[2]**
> 1 pause
> 2 and all of this is found either in an even number or in an odd number
> **Thus the composite[1] occurs wreathed[3] from single ones,[2]**
> 1 pause, I say
> 2 that is, placed by themselves
> 3 that is, ornamented
> **Given indeed either with an even number or not with an even number.[1]**
> 1 as regards the equality or inequality of units of time in them

This man has decided, etc. Here the author wishes to explain his view briefly about breaths and the divisions of the modes, saying that composers in the art of music* have added to the distinctions of the pauses a division of the modes by means of a small line made obliquely in the lower part, notating it like this / / / . (fol. 156) But they have kept silent about the efficacy of this, suggesting in this way that it would only be called a sign. Of breaths they have spoken in this way:* "A breath is the appearance of a pause, and this is placed because a breath can occur with a line or without, and correctly a breath can be a

maior potest esse suspiratio. Nos equidem posteri, ipsos in quantum possumus imitantes, dicimus ista duo nunc pro quantitate unius temporis quo ad recreationem spirituum reperiri, nunc autem pro minori, et, secundum quod asserunt, pro maiori. Ne autem in ambiguum procedamus, illa de se nihil credimus importare, cum de suo esse nihil certum inferant vel securum. Et hac de causa cifrae comparavimus, quae, quamvis de se nihil significet, tamen significationis augmentum figuris aliis administrat, unde versus:

> *Nil cifra signat, sed dat signare sequenti.*

10

> **Hic[1] suspirorum metas[2] simul atque modorum[3]**
> 1 id est, iste venerabilis institutor
> 2 id est, divisiones vel differentias
> 3 id est, omnium
> **Addi[1] decrevit, qui prosae[2] carmina sevit.**
> 1 in numero aliarum pausationum sive
> 2 sive quam duximus exponendam
> **Proque brevi stabunt,[1] minus, aut plus,[2] nilve notabunt.[3]**
> 1 non de se sed causa recreationis spiritus fatigati

20

> 2 quam brevem
> 3 id est, signabunt

Hic recitat actor opinionem suam:

> **Signa manent vere nichil has nunc[1] credo valere.[2]**
> 1 id est, quandoque
> 2 id est, repraesentare quo ad pausam

Quasi diceret: sicut cifra nihil per se sed cum aliis significat, ita supradicta nihil quo est de se signant:

> **Sed tanquam ciffra sunt haec pausas tamen infra.**

Quidam dicebant *divisionem sillabarum* poni in numero pausationum;

30

quod non est ponere, quia nihil soni importat:

> **Sillabice vocis metam nil condere noscis.**

Hic excusat se actor satis sufficienter tractavisse de pausis:

> **Metro nolo dare de pausis plus tibi care.**

Modo restringit dictum suum, dicens, quod si ibi sit defectus, in glosulis ostendetur:

> **Cetera suplete, quid signet glosa indetae.**

----

7 se *add. super scriptum*   9 *dat add. in marg.*   11 *in marg.:* pro suspiriorum   14 *post* omnium *ras.*   23 **nunc** *add. super scriptum*

smaller or a larger breve." But we indeed, the next generation, imitat-
ing them as much as we can, say that those two are sometimes found in the
place of the quantity of one unit of time as regards the refreshment of
the breath, sometimes in the place of a smaller breve, and, according to
what they assert, in the place of a larger breve. But lest we proceed
into something ambiguous, we believe that they convey nothing by themselves, since they bring in nothing fixed or certain from their own
existence. And for this reason we have compared it to the cipher, which,
although it signifies nothing by itself, yet provides an increase in
significance for the other figures; whence the verse:

> "A cipher signifies nothing, but it gives significance to what
> follows."*

**This man[1] has decided that the boundaries[2] of the breaths and
also of the modes[3]**
1 that is, this revered establisher
2 that is, the divisions or distinctions
3 that is, of all of them
Should be added[1] -- he who sowed the poems for the prose.[2]
1 amongst the category of the other pauses
2 which we have thought it right to expound
**They will stand[1] in the place of a breve, and will note[3] less or
more[2] or nothing.**
1 not for themselves but for the purpose of refreshing a tired
breath
2 than a breve
3 that is, they will signify

Here the author explains his view:

> **The signs remain truly, but I believe that now[1] these boundaries
> are worth[2] nothing.**
> 1 that is, sometimes
> 2 that is, represent as regards the pause

He means to say that just as the cipher has no significance by itself
but only with other things, so those things mentioned above signify
nothing as regards themselves:

> **But nevertheless you pause below as if these things were
> ciphers.**

Some people said* that "the division of the syllables" should be
placed amongst the category of the pauses, but this is not to place
it at all because it conveys no sound:

> **You know that the boundary of the voice syllabically preserves
> nothing.**

Here the author excuses himself for not having dealt sufficiently
with the pauses:

> **I do not wish, dear one, to give you more in verse about the
> pauses.**

Now he restricts his saying, saying that if there is a lack there,
it will be shown in the glosses:

> **Supply the rest and let the gloss signify whatever is left out.**

\<Capitulum quartum\>

Sunt bene qui pangunt etc. In hoc loco vult actor agredi quartum
capitulum sui libri, in quo consonantiarum differentias specificat et
ostendit dissonantias evitando, et hoc est quia dissonantiae modulationem
cantuum impediunt et perturbant, et ideo de ipsis in cantu parum aut
nonquam fit mentio, ne confusio seu oscuritas generetur, propter quod
ipsas volumus evitare. Et hoc est quia in principio huius voluminis
promisimus evitare dubia et oscura, usitata et necessaria recitando; quae
igitur oscura et dubia scimus, postponimus, usitata et necessaria
recitantes, utilitati omnium compilando. Et est notandum, quod praedicta
10 capitula rationabiliter praecesserunt, quoniam sunt causae inventionis
istius, ex eo quod voces vel figurae per modorum seriem distributae
confuse et inutiliter proferrentur, nisi eis remedium aliquod adderetur,
per quod ordinatae discurrerent concordanter, quare necesse fuit tale
capitulum invenire, ei locum debitum assignando.

Consonantiarum igitur quaedam dicuntur concordantiae, quaedam
discordantiae. Concordantia dicitur esse, quando duae voces sub eodem
tempore proferuntur ita quod una secundum auditum potest compati cum
altera. Discordantia fieri dicitur e converso, id est, quando duae
voces in eodem tempore proferuntur ita quod una non potest compati cum
20 altera. Et nota quod huius discordantiae quasi infinitae sunt, tamen in
unicordo pro concordantiis seu convenientiis reputantur, in diversicordo
quidem positae propter levem transitum permittuntur vel ad hoc ut
concordantia tam sussequens quam praecedens melodior ac dulcior ratione
oppositi videatur. Concordantiarum vero triplex est modus, quia quaedam
sunt perfectae, quaedam mediae, quaedam siquidem imperfectae, sicut

----

3 dissonantiae [[ca]] modulationem *cod.* 8 proponimus *pro* postponimus
Sowa 10 capitula vel rationabiliter *cod.* 15 con[[cordan]]tiarum
cod., sonan *super scriptum* 17 una *add. super scriptum* 22 hoc *add.*
super scriptum

Chapter Four

There are certainly those who compose, etc. In this place the author
wishes to undertake the fourth chapter of his book, in which he specifies
and shows the distinctions of the consonances; avoiding the dissonances,
because dissonances hinder and disturb the musical sound of melodies, and
so little or no mention is made of them in melody, lest confusion or
obscurity be generated, and on this account we wish to avoid them. And
that is why at the beginning of this volume* we promised to avoid dubious
and obscure things, and recite useful and necessary things; and therefore
we reject those things that we know to be obscure and dubious, reciting
useful and necessary things, and bringing them together for the usefulness of everyone. And it should be noted that the previous chapters have
preceded this one with reason, since they are the cause of the creating
of this one, because notes or figures distributed through the sequence of
the modes would be performed in a confused and useless fashion unless
some remedy were added to them by which they might be arranged and flow
concordantly; and so it was necessary to create a chapter like this,
assigning it to its requisite place.

Of the consonances therefore some are called concords, some discords.
A concord is said to be when two notes are performed during the same unit
of time in such a way that according to one's hearing one is compatible
with the other. A discord is said to occur in the reverse way, that is
when two notes are performed at the same time in such a way that one is
not compatible with the other. And note that discords of this kind are
almost unlimited, yet they are judged to stand in a single sound in the
place of concords or accords, and indeed they are allowed to be placed in
a group of sounds for the purpose of an easy transition, or so that both
the following and the preceding concord might seem more melodious and
sweeter by contrast. But there are three modes of concords, because some
are perfect, some medial, some imperfect, as will be stated below over

inferius declarabitur supra textum. Et notandum est, quod huius
consonantiae possunt aliquando reperiri in eodem tempore et in eadem
voce, nunc autem in diversis temporibus ac vocibus, ut patebit.

Haec igitur praesens lectio in duas partes breviter dividatur, in
quarum prima facit actor de scematibus vocum, id est concordantiis,
mentionem, in secunda innuit dissonantias evitare. Ideo patet ordo:
prima incipit **Sunt bene qui pangunt** etc., secunda **Scismata** etc. Item
prima in duas: in prima ostendit modum scematis, in secunda illius
species manifestat. Prima incipit **Sunt bene** etc., secunda **Sex vult esse**
10 **sonis** etc. Haec secunda in duas: in prima ostendit sex esse
consonantias, in secunda procedit circa perfectionem et imperfectionem
earundem. Prima incipit **Sex vult esse sonis** etc., secunda **Perficitur**
primis etc. Et sic patet sententia et divisio leoninis.

> **Sunt bene qui**[1] **pangunt**[2] **cum voces scemata**[3] **tangunt.**
> 1 sive illi cantores
> 2 id est, modulationem cantuum continuant
> 3 id est, concordantias
> **Qui si discordent,**[1] **tunc voces scismata**[2] **mordent.**
20 1 id est, illi cantores
> 2 id est, discordantias

Sex vult esse sonis etc. Hic vult actor concordantiarum numerum ac
seriem recitare, dicens, quod sex sunt solummodo consonantiae adinventae,
quibus per cantus varios utimur, neque plures. Omnes autem alias
apellamus discordantias, eo quod sonos faciunt ab invicem discordantes
(fol. 156v) seu etiam discrepantes. Si quaeratur quare solummodo sex
concordantias habeamus et non plures, dicimus <quod> quemadmodum sex sunt
voces, ex quibus tota musica modulatur, sic sex sunt consonantiae vel
30 concordantiae, per quas cantuum variorum ad eundem finem tendentium
modulatio melicosa decenti serie fit sonora; vel quia in sonorum numero
sub eadem prolatione temporis seu temporum bipartito vel tripartito etc.
sex vocum genera solummodo sonorum aequipollentiam absque incursione
discrepantiae statuunt ad perfectionem totius melodiae.

Et ideo sex esse concordantias dicimus et non plures, quarum prior
est unisonus, secunda dyapason, tertia dyapente, quarta dyatessaron,
quinta ditonus, sexta et ultima semiditonus. Quidam vero ditonum et
semiditonum inter discordantias medias posuerunt, loco earum dyatessaron
cum dyapason et dyapente cum dyapason cum aliarum numero apponentes et
40 bis dyapason loco unisoni. Quod non est ponere quo ad numerum
antedictum, quoniam ibi est repetitio multiplicationis, secundum quod
inferius sequitur cum dicitur: *istae concordantiae possunt sumi in*
infinitum, unde textus **Scemata** etc. Sicut enim sex voces, ex quibus

----

2 aliquando *add. super scriptum*   19 **Qui**[[s]] *cod.*   25 autem
[[voces]] *alias cod.*   26 faciant *pro* faciunt *cod.*   31 in
[[consonantiarum]] numero *cod.,* sonorum *add. in marg.*   37 vero *add.*
super scriptum

the text. And it should be noted that consonances of this kind can sometimes be found in the same unit of time and on the same note, but sometimes in different units of time and on different notes, as will be shown.

Therefore let this present reading be divided briefly into two parts, in the first of which the author makes mention of the patterns of the notes, that is the concords, and in the second he suggests that the dissonances should be avoided. Therefore the order is clear: The first part begins **There are certainly those who compose**, etc., the second **The disunities**, etc. Also the first part is divided into two: in the first he shows the mode of a pattern, in the second he shows its species. The first begins **There are certainly those**, etc., the second **He wishes there to be six**, etc. This second part is divided into two: in the first he shows that there are six consonances, in the second he continues about their perfection and imperfection. The first begins **He wishes there to be six**, etc., the second **It is completed with the first**, etc. And thus the meaning and division of the leonine verses is clear.

> **There are certainly those[1] who compose[2] when the voices touch the patterns.[3]**
> 1 those cantors
> 2 that is, continue the sounding of melodies
> 3 that is, the concords
> **And if they are in discord,[1] then the notes take hold of disunities.[2]**
> 1 that is, those cantors
> 2 that is, discords

He wishes there to be six, etc. Here the author wishes to explain the number and sequence of the concords, saying that there are only six consonances devised which we use in different melodies, and no more. But all the others we call discords, because they make sounds that are discordant (fol. 156v) or discrepant with each other. If it is asked why we have only six concords and not more, we say that just as there are six notes from which the whole of music makes its sounds, so there are six consonances or concords by means of which the melodious sounding of various melodies that are aiming at the same ending occurs in sound in the proper sequence; or because in the bipartite or tripartite etc. category of sounds within the same performance of a unit of time or units of time there are only six genera of sounding notes that establish equipollence without the intrusion of discrepancy and for the perfection of all of melody.

And so we say that there are six concords and no more, of which the first is the unison, the second the dyapason, the third the dyapente, the fourth the dyatessaron, the fifth the ditone, and the sixth and last the semiditone. But some* have placed the ditone and semiditone among the medial discords, and in their place the dyatessaron with the dyapason, and the dyapente with the dyapason, placing them with the category of the others, and the double dyapason in place of the unison. But this is not putting them according to the aforementioned category, since that way involves the repetition of multiplication, according to what is discussed below,* when it says: "These concords can be continued to infinity;" whence the text **You can multiply the patterns**, etc. For just as the six notes from which music is made up are multiplied and repeated again

musica consistit, per mutationes varias multiplicatae iterum repetuntur, sic et istas concordantias per multiplicationem iterum repetitas supra totum et eidem reducibiles tanquam partes reperiri dicimus cum numero supradicto, sicut inferius ostendetur, nec per sustractionem earum minorari dicitur numerus antedictus. Quatenus autem ditonus et semiditonus in concordantiarum numero debeant collocari, patet per cantus musicos approbatos in quibus saepius sunt reperti, sicut patet in triplo de *Che sunt amoretes, Dex ou prai je trover,* et in multis aliis cantibus tam organis quam motellis, in quibus vel cantus incipiunt vel pausas
10 immediate praeambulas sussecuntur. Per quod patet, quod sunt concordantiae, eo quod a discordantia nonquam cantus aliquis inchoatur, nec post pausationem vel ante locum dicitur optinere.

Quid sit autem concordantia, superius est expressum. Concordantiarum igitur prima dicitur unisonus, id est aequisonantia vel unus sonus, et habet fieri quotienscumque duae voces a diversis locis seu temporibus et sub eadem prolatione vocis singulariter constitutae eundem sonum et in eodem signo proferunt hinc et inde. Secunda est dyapason, unde regula: quotienscumque quinque toni duobus semitoniis adhaerebunt, ibi dyapason non deerit, et fit in octava voce per litteram duplicatam, ut a G gravi
20 in g acutum, et sic de aliis, et dicitur a *dya,* quod est de, et *pason,* totum vel octo, quasi de spatio octo vocum constituta. Et nota quod quaelibet octava vox non facit dyapason, ut a H gravi in b rotundum acutum, et a b rotundo acuto in h quadratum superacutum, aut e converso. Tertia dicitur dyapente, unde regula: quotienscumque tres toni uni semitono adhaerebunt, ibi dyapente non deerit, et dicitur a *dya,* quod <est> de, et *pente,* quinque, quasi de quinque consistens, vel quia in quinta voce fit. Et nota, quod quaelibet quinta vox non facit dyapente, ut a H gravi in F gravem, et ab E gravi in b rotundum acutum, et sic de similibus, quoniam inter tales sunt duo toni et duo semitoni. Quarta
30 dicitur dyatessaron, unde regula: quotienscumque duo toni uni semitono adhaerebunt, ibi dyatessaron non deerit, et dicitur a *dya,* quod est de, et *tessara,* quatuor, quasi de quatuor vel in quarta voce consistens. Et nota, quod quaelibet quarta vox non facit dyatessaron, ut ab F gravi in h quadratum acutum, et sic de aliis, quoniam ibi est tritonus. Quinta dicitur ditonus, unde regula: ditonus est planum spatium duarum vocum duos tonos comprehendens, et dicitur a *dia,* quod est duo, et tonus. Sexta et ultima dicitur semiditonus, in se tonum et semitonum comprehendens.

Et sic patet in universo numerus concordantiarum. Tonus propter

----

2 reperetitas *pro* repetitas *cod.*   3 et sint idem *cod.*   idem *pro* eidem *cod.*   5 Quod *pro* Quatenus *Sowa*   8 Diex *pro* Dex *Sowa*   pourrai *pro* prai *Sowa*   10 sussecantur *pro* sussecuntur *cod.*   sint *pro* sunt *cod.* 14 vel quia unus *cod.,* quia *add. in marg.*   20 acutam *pro* acutum *cod.* 20 *ultimum* et *add. super scriptum*   22 octavi *pro* octava *cod.* 22-23 in b rotundo acuto *pro* in b rotundum acutum *cod.*   23 quadratum [[acu]] superacutum *cod.*   25 semitonio *pro* semitono *Sowa*   28 in b rotundo acuto *pro* in b rotundum acutum *cod.*   29 semitonia *pro* semitoni *Sowa*   35 est *add. super scriptum*   36 tonos *add. in marg.*   dicitur a *add. in marg.*   37 semitonium *pro* semitonum *Sowa*   38 concorcordantiarum *pro* concordantiarum *cod.*

through various mutations, so we say that these concords are found repeated again by means of multiplication above the whole, and are also reducible to it like parts of it together with the number mentioned above, as will be shown below, and the number mentioned above is not said to be diminished by subtracting them. But to what extent the ditone and the semiditone should be included in the number of concords is clear from the approved musical melodies in which they are often found, as is shown in the triplum of "Che sunt amoretes," "Dex ou prai je trover," and in many other melodies, both organa and motets, in which they either begin the melodies or follow immediately after the introductory pauses. And by this it is clear that they are concords, because a composition never begins from a discord, nor is said to obtain a place after or before a pause.

What a concord is has been expressed above. And the first of the concords is called the unison, that is an equal sound or one sound, and it occurs whenever two notes from different places or units of time, put together singly within the same performance of a note, produce the same sound from the same sign in both cases. The second is the dyapason; whence the rule: Whenever five tones will stick to two semitones, there a dyapason will not be lacking; and it occurs on the eighth note by means of a repeated letter, like from low G to high g, and so on for the others; and it is so-called from *dya,* which is from, and *pason,* the whole or eight, as it is made up from the space of eight notes. And note that some eight notes do not make a dyapason, for example from low H to high round b, and from high round b to very high square h, and the reverse. The third is called the dyapente; whence the rule: Whenever three tones will stick to one semitone, there a dyapente will not be lacking; and it is so-called from *dya,* which is from, and *pente,* five, as consisting of five, or because it occurs on the fifth note. And note that some five notes do not make a dyapente, like from low H to low F, and from low E to high round b, and so on for similar things, since between these notes there are two tones and two semitones. The fourth is called the dyatessaron; whence the rule: Whenever two tones will stick to one semitone, there a dyatessaron will not be lacking; and it is so-called from *dya,* which is from, and *tessara,* four, as from four or consisting in the fourth note. And note that some four notes do not make a dyatessaron, like from low F to high square h, and so on for the others, since there is a tritone there. The fifth is called the ditone; whence the rule: The ditone is an open space of two notes that includes two tones, and is so called from *dia* which is two, and *tonus.* The sixth and last is called the semiditone, which includes a tone and a semitone in itself.

And thus the number of concords is clear throughout. A tone, on

affinitatem concordantiarum, eo quod omnibus aliis sit originis
fundamentum, sic describitur: *tonus est legitima spatii quantitas inter
duas voces.* Aliter describitur sic: *tonus est quaedam percussio auris
indissoluta usque ad auditum.* Quomodo autem se habeant haec omnia etc.,
quae praetermittimus in proportionibus numerorum, relinquimus exponendum
philosophis de inventione totius musicae tractantibus, quia hic non licet
talia recitare.

Exemplum omnium concordantiarum patet hic:

Unisonus, dyapason, diapente, dyatessaron, ditonus, semiditonus

Perficitur primis etc. Hic innuit actor quod huius concordantiarum
quaedam dicuntur perfectae, scilicet unisonus et dyapason, aliae mediae,
scilicet dyapente et dyatessaron; aliae imperfectae tamen concordant,
scilicet ditonus et semiditonus, et hac de causa non possunt cantum
aliquem terminare.

Per hoc vult actor innuere sex esse consonantias huius artis
generales, quibus musica modulatur:

Sex vult esse sonis rata concordantia, ponis.
Unisonum[1] pungis dyapason,[2] postea iungis[3]
1 id est, aequisonantiam
2 id est, duplum, quod est de toto vel octo
3 id est, adiungis
Hiis[1] dyapente, sere[2] dyatessaron,[3] hinc[4] subiere
1 sive supradictis
2 id est, adiunge
3 quae quarta vox dicitur
4 id est, postea
Ditonus,[1] et semi,[2] volo ditonus[3] ob metra demi.[4]
1 id est, tertia vox
2 sive semiditonus
3 hanc sillabicam adiectionem vel quasi
4 id est, sustrahi
Perficitur[1] primis,[2] medians aliis,[3] caret immis.[4]
1 huius concordantia sive
2 duabus sive
3 scilicet dyapente et dya<tessaron>
4 scilicet ditono et semiditono

----

6 philophis *pro* philosophis *cod.*   28 **pungu** *pro* **pungis** *cod.*
43 concordia *pro* concordantia *Sowa*   45 *post* dya *ras.*

account of its relationship to the concords, because it is the foundation
of the origin to the others, is described in this way: "A tone is the
legitimate quantity of space between two notes."* It is described in
another way thus: "A tone is a certain striking of the ear that reaches
the hearing undissipated."* But how all these things occur etc., which
we omit in discussing the proportions of the numbers, we leave for the
philosophers who deal with the invention of the whole of music to
expound,* since we are not allowed to recite such things here.

An example of all the concords is given here:

Unisonus, dyapason, diapente, dyatessaron, ditonus, semiditonus

It is perfect with the first ones, etc. Here the author suggests
that of the concords of this kind some are called perfect, that is to say
the unison and the dypason, some are called medium, that is to say the
dyapente and the dyatessaron; but some are imperfect concords, that is to
say the ditone and the semiditone, and for this reason they can not
finish any composition.

Here the author wishes to suggest that there are six general
consonances of this art with which music sounds:
    **He wishes there to be six concords established in the sounds
    that you put.**
    You write the unison[1] and the dyapason,[2] and afterwards join[3]
    1 that is, an equal sound
    2 that is, double, which is from all or eight
    3 that is, you add
    To these[1] the dyapente; connect[2] the dyatessaron;[3] then[4] come
    1 those mentioned above
    2 that is, add
    3 which is called the fourth note
    4 that is, afterwards
    **The ditone,[1] and the semi-,[2] for I wish "ditone"[3] to be removed[4]
    because of the meter.**
    1 that is, the third note
    2 the semiditone
    3 the inclusion of these syllables or the appearance of it
    4 that is, taken away
    **It is perfect[1] with the first ones,[2] having the others[3] in the
    middle, and the last ones are lacking.[4]**
    1 a concord of this kind
    2 two
    3 that is to say the dyapente and the dyatessaron
    4 that is to say the ditone and the semiditone

Has[1] **teneat tantum, qui vult**[2] **bene fingere**[3] **cantum.**
1 sive concordantias supradictas
2 ille cantor
3 id est, componere

Scemata quis care etc. Hic vult actor innuere, quod perfectae
concordantiae et mediae (fol. 157) possunt sumi in infinitum per
iterationem multiplicationis, sicut voces in gamma per variationem
mutationis, quod sic patet: quicquid concordat cum toto, concordat cum
10 partibus; verbi gratia, primus sonus datus in concordantia supra primum,
ergo et secundus supra secundum. G dico, quia quicquid concordat secundo
g, ergo et primo, et non e converso. Probatio: quae aequalia sunt
eidem, sibi invicem sunt aequalia. Dyapente et dyatessaron secundum suas
species bene concordant secundo g, in quo consistit perfecta concordia,
ergo et primo, et non e converso, quia omne totum ponit suas partes, et
non e converso, quia totum <est> maius sua parte, non autem e converso.
Et sic patet quod supradictae concordantiae possunt multiplicari in
infinitum, eo quod quicquid cum dyapason concordat, cum suis partibus
inferioribus dicitur convenire.
20

Scemata[1] **quis care per cantus multiplicare,**
1 id est, concordantias, utputa dyatessaron cum dyapason vel
dyapente cum dyapason
Per hoc innuit actor quod supradictae concordantiae possunt sumi in
infinitum:
Nam totum munit quod scemate partibus unit.

Nam totum etc. converte sic: **nam** pro quia, quia **totum munit** illud;
scemate, id est, concordantia; **quod unit**, id est, adaequat; **partibus**,
30 suis suple.
Quasi diceret: totum, id est, secundus sonus vel dyapason, praemunit
primum sonum, supra quem datur in concordantia, scemate, id est,
concordantia, quem quidem primum sonum per concordantiam adaequat, suis
partibus, id est, dyapente et dyatessaron, quae sunt membra seu partes
ipsius totius, et sic dyapente cum dyapason vel dyatessaron cum dyapason
concordant et similiter bis dyapason et sic de aliis.
Cismata etc. Hic ostendit actor, quomodo permissum est et licentia-
tum ab actoribus primis, inter colores musicos sive concordantias
discordantias seminare, ad hoc ut concordantia quaelibet dulcior et
40 competentior habeatur.
Scema etc. converte sic: **que** pro sed vel pro quia; quia magistri
dicunt, id est, asserunt; **scema**, id est, concordantiam; **poni melos**, id
est, dulcius; post **cismata**, id est, discordantias inornatas.
Cismata etc. Hic excusat se actor, quare de dissonantiis in hoc
capitulo non voluit facere mentionem, dicens, quod cismata contumeliosa

----

9 mutatonis *pro* mutationis *cod.*   10 gratia [[quic]] primus *cod.*,
gratia qui primus *Sowa*   11 igitur *pro* ergo *Sowa*   quod *pro* quia *cod.*
dico quod *in marg.*   quicquid ergo concordat *cod.*   17 multiplicare *pro*
multiplicari *Sowa*   18-19 suis partibus inferioribus *add. in marg.*
44 excusat se se actor *cod.*

Let him hold these[1] only, who wishes[2] to contrive[3] a melody properly.
1 the concords mentioned above
2 that cantor
3 that is, to put together

You can multiply the patterns, etc. Here the author wishes to suggest that perfect and medial concords (fol. 157) can be produced up to infinity by the repetition of multiplication, just as notes can in the scale by the variation of mutation. And this is clear as follows: Whatever concords with the whole, concords with the parts; for example the first sound given in concord above the first, therefore also the second above the second. I mean the G, because whatever concords with the second g will also therefore concord with the first, and not the reverse. The proof: Those things which are equal to the same thing are equal to each other.* The dyapente and the dyatessaron according to their species concord properly with the second g, at which there exists a perfect concord, therefore they do also with the first, and not the reverse, because every whole thing assumes its parts and not the reverse, because a whole is better than a part, but not the reverse. And thus it is clear that the above-mentioned concords can be multiplied up to infinity, because whatever concords with a dyapason is said to accord with its lower parts.

> **You can multiply the patterns,[1] dear one, through the melodies,**
> 1 that is, the concords; for example the dyatessaron with the dyapason or the dyapente with the dyapason
>
> Here the author suggests that the above-mentioned concords can be produced up to infinity:
>
> **For the whole furnishes that which it unites in the parts by pattern.**

For the whole, etc. interpret thus: **For**, instead of: because; because **the whole furnishes** that; **by pattern**, that is, by concord; **which it unites**, that is, equals; **in the parts**, supply: its.

He means to say that the whole, that is, the second sound or dyapason, secures the first sound above which it is given in concord, by the pattern, that is, by concord, and indeed it equals this first sound by concord with its parts, that is, the dyapente and dyatessaron, which are portions or parts of the whole, and thus the dyapente concords with the dyapason or the dyatessaron with the dyapason and similarly with the double dyapason and so on for the others.

The first cantors, etc. Here the author shows how it is allowed and licensed by the first authors to scatter discords amongst the rhetorical colors or concords of music, so that each concord might appear as sweeter and more suitable.

They say that the pattern, etc. interpret thus: **and**, instead of: but; or instead of: because; because the masters **say**, that is, assert; **the pattern**, that is, the concord; **harmoniousness should be put**, that is, more sweetly; after the **disunities**, that is, discords that are not ornamented.

The first cantors, etc. Here the author excuses himself, because he did not wish to make mention of dissonances in this chapter, saying that

sunt et discrepantia.   Nam voces ab invicem discordantes offendunt
animam, in sensu particulari, utputa in aure, chacephaton generantes, et
sic auditum impediunt et perturbant.   Et licet utile esset de ipsis
facere mentionem, ad hoc ut cognita facilius vitarentur, vel ad hoc ut
cognitio unius oppositi per alterum perfectius sciri posset, eo quod unum
non potest complete sciri nisi per alterum, tamen quia de ipsis nullus
cantus efficitur quo est de se, licet saepius apponantur, ideo ipsa
praetermittimus, exponentes scemata e quibus cantus omnis sumpsit
exordium et in quibus solummodo terminatur.

10

       Cismata[1] cantores nunc[2] subiunxere priores.
       1 id est, discordantias
       2 id est, quandoque; et hoc ante perfectam concordantiam vel
       post sed raro
Hic subiungit rationem, quare discordantiae cum concordantiis
seminantur:
       Scema melosque soni dicunt post cismata poni.
Hic excusat se actor, quare de discordantiis in metro noluit facere
mentionem,

20

       Cismata quae recolo mala per metra pandere nolo.
dicens:
       Sunt metra[1] pacifica, quis[2] cismata[3] sunt inimica.[4]
       1 id est, carmina metrice compilata
       2 id est, quibus
       3 id est, discordantiae
       4 id est, nociva
       Nec[1] magis hiis[2] metris petit ars[3] sinit haec arimetris.[4]
       1 pro et non
       2 sive discordantiis

30

       3 id est, praesens introductio
       4 id est, philosophis de proportione tractantibus numerorum

----

2 chachephaton *pro* chacephaton *Sowa*   3 ac *pro* et *Sowa*   22 **subinimica**
pro **sunt inimica** *Sowa*   28 pro et et non *cod*.

disunities are annoying and discrepant. For notes that are discordant
with each other offend the mind, generating a cacophony for one particular sense, for example for the ear, and thus they hinder and disturb
the hearing. And although it would be useful to make mention of them,
so that once known they could more easily be avoided, or so that the
understanding of one opposite thing could be more perfectly known by
means of the other -- because one can not be completely known except
by means of the other -- yet because no melody is made up of them by
themselves, although they are often added to it, therefore we leave them
out, expounding the patterns from which every melody has taken its
beginning and at which alone it ends.

>**The first cantors have now[2] added disunities.[1]**
>1 that is, discords
>2 that is, sometimes; and this is before a perfect concord, and
>rarely after

Here he adds a reason why discords are scattered with concords:

>**They say that the pattern and harmoniousness of the sound should
>be put after the disunities.**

Here the author excuses himself for not wishing to make mention of
discords in the verse,

>**The disunities, which I consider bad, I do not wish to explain
>through the verses.**

saying:

>**Verses[1] are peaceful, and disunities[3] are hostile[4] to them.[2]**
>1 that is, poems put together in verse
>2 that is, to these verses
>3 that is, discords
>4 that is, harmful

>**Nor does[1] the treatise[3] attempt more in verse with these[2] but
>leaves these things to the arithmeticians.[4]**
>1 instead of: and it does not
>2 discords
>3 that is, the present introduction
>4 that is, the philosophers who deal with the proportion of
>numbers

\<Capitulum quintum\>

\<Pars prima\>

Unit discantus etc. Terminatis capitulis antedictis, per quae
praeparatio et consumatio omnium cantuum designatur, in hoc loco vult
actor agredi quintum capitulum sui libri, in quo de discantu faciet
mentionem, qui est genus et vinculum ad omnium cantuum genera principale
vel radicale, nam in eo omnium cantuum genera continentur, et ad eum sunt
generaliter reducenda. Et notandum est, quod ratione duplici ordinari
debuit post praedicta. Prima igitur ratio est, quia est genus generale
continens universaliter supradicta, unde cum contenta uno modo sint causa
inventionis continentium, sicut patet de *vino et dolio,* licet alio
respectu continentia quo est de se contentis maneant fundamentum, tamen
quia praedicta capitula sub isto contenta sunt causa quare istud oportuit
inveniri, ideoque sicut causa ante cantum sic praeambula capitula ante
istud. Item istud est iunctura, mediante qua praedicta ad invicem
conveniunt, et a quo firmiter vinciuntur; et quia vinculum posterius est
eis quae ab eodem vinculo vinciuntur, ideo decrevimus praesens capitulum
ceteris praecedentibus apponendum.

Videamus igitur in primis, quid sit discantus et quot sunt eius
species sive membra. Ad primum dicimus, quod discantus est aliquorum
cantuum diversorum concordantia secundum modum et aequipollentiam sui
aequipollentis, et sunt tot species sicut et in modo a parte aequipollentis, qui dicitur secundus cantus, quo ad partem tenoris, qui
dicitur primus cantus; et sciendum est, quod utriusque sex species sunt
repertae, sicut dictum fuit superius in capitulo sex modorum.

Et notandum est, quod a parte primi cantus tria sunt consideranda,
scilicet sonus et ordinatio et modus. Sonus hic sumitur pro musica,

----

1 *lit. maj. deest*   2 purpuratio *pro* praeparatio *Sowa*   12 invenire *pro*
inveniri *cod.*   13 iunctum *pro* iunctura *Sowa*   quo *pro* qua *cod.*
19 concordia *pro* concordantia *Sowa*   21 cantus [[qui dicitur s]] quo *cod.*

270

Chapter Five

Part One

Discant unites, etc. Having finished the above chapters, by means of which the preparation and consummation of all melodies is designated, in this place the author wishes to undertake the fifth chapter of his book, in which he will make mention of discant, which is a principal or basic genus and bond for the genera of all compositions; for in it the genera of all compositions are contained and to it they must generally be reduced. And it should be noted that it is for two reasons that it should be positioned after what has been said before. And the first reason is that it is a general genus containing universally the things that have been said above, whence, since in one way the things that are contained are the cause for the invention of the things that contain them, as is clear from "vino et dolio," -- although in another respect the things that contain them as regards themselves remain the foundation of the things that are contained -- yet, because the chapters that have gone before, that are contained in the category of this one, are the cause that this one had to be invented, therefore, just as the cause comes before the melody, so the introductory chapters came before this one. Also this one is the juncture by the help of which the chapters that have gone before are in accord with each other and by which they are firmly bound; and because the bond comes after those things which are bound by the same bond, therefore we have decided that the present chapter should be added to the rest that have gone before.

Let us first see therefore what discant is and how many species or portions it has. First we say that discant is the concord of some disparate melodies according to mode and the equipollence of its equipollent part, and it has as many species as there are in the modes with respect to the equipollent part, which is called the second melody, and as regards the tenor, which is called the first melody. And it should be known that for each of them six species are found, as has been said above in the chapter on the six modes.

And it should be noted that with respect to the first melody three things should be considered, that is to say sound, arrangement, and mode.

ordinatio pro numero punctorum ante pausam, modus pro quantitate brevium
et longarum; similiter a parte secundi sunt ista consideranda. Et
notandum est, quod primus et secundus et omnes alii cantus in tribus ad
minus sunt considerandi similes, scilicet in ordinatione, (fol. 157v)
numero et concordantia, saepius et in modo: in ordinatione, ut sit longa
contra longam et sic de aliis, vel aliquod aliud aequipollens; in numero,
ut tot sint puncti a parte primi quot a parte secundi, vel aequipollens
istis, aut etiam e converso. In modo et in ordinatione sunt idem, nisi
in hoc, quod ordinatio ad omnes modorum convenientias et aequipollentias
se extendit, modus solummodo ad se ipsum. In concordantia, ut in debito
modo primus concordet secundo et tertio vel quarto, si ibi sint, vel e
converso. Nota tamen, quod perfectae concordantiae et mediae sunt inter
primum et alios specialiter apponendae, quippe cum primus det aliis
originem ac illis maneat fundamentum. Unde regula est super hoc
specialiter attributa, quae talis est: *omne illud quod fit in pari debet*
concordari omni illi quod fit in impari, sive sit in primo sive in
secundo sive in tertio et sic de aliis. Sed sumuntur hic quandoque duo
puncti vel tres pro uno vel loco unius, quorum unus ponitur in
concordantia, sive sit primus sive unus aliorum, propter colorem musicae.

Haec igitur praesens lectio in duas partes breviter dividatur, in
quarum prima agit actor de discantu generaliter, in secunda de quadam
eius specie, quae copula nuncupatur. Prima incipit **Unit discantus** etc.,
secunda **Copula cantores** etc. Item prima in duas: in prima agit de
discantu sub vera musica comprehenso, in secunda ostendit quod ad huius
compositionem necesse est saepius introducere falsam musicam sive fictam.
Ideo patet ordo: prima pars incipit **Unit discantus** etc., secunda **Utilis**
est multum. Et sic patet sententia et divisio leoninis.

       Unit[1] **discantus**[2] **varios per scemata**[3] **cantus**[4]
       1 id est, aequat
       2 id est, organum generale
       3 id est, concordantias
       4 id est, modulos
       More modi dantis[1] **vel scilicet aequiperantis.**[2]
       1 id est, secundum tenorem, qui alios cantus dat
       2 id est, secundum morem secundi, tertii vel quarti, qui
       aequiperantur primo
       Haec[1] **modus, ac ordo, numerus**[2] **sic, scemaque cordo.**[3]
       1 quae hic exprimuntur sive
       2 sunt nota certa discantus
       3 id est, iungo

----

1 pausationem *pro* pausam *Sowa*   4 consideranda *pro* considerandi *Sowa*
5 et in concordantia *Sowa*   8 autem *pro* aut *Sowa*   ordine *pro*
ordinatione *Sowa*   9 ordo *pro* ordinatio *cod.*   13 primum et et alios
cod.   15 decet *pro* debet *Sowa*

Sound is used here for music, arrangement for the number of written notes before a pause, mode for the quantity of breves and longs. Similarly with respect to the second melody these things should be considered. And it should be noted that the first melody and the second and all the other melodies should be considered as similar in three things at least, that is to say in arrangement, (fol. 157v) number, and concord; and often also in mode: in arrangement, so that there is a long against a long, and so on for the others, or something else equipollent; in number, so that there are as many written notes with respect to the first melody as there are with respect to the second, or something equipollent to these, or the reverse. In mode and in arrangement are the same, except in this way, that arrangement extends itself to all the accords and equipollences of the modes, but mode only to itself. In concord, so that in the requisite mode the first melody concords with the second, and the third or the fourth if they are there, or the reverse. But note that perfect and medial concords should be placed specifically between the first melody and the others, since the first gives the origin to the others and remains the foundation to them. Whence there is a rule that is specifically laid out on this topic, which is as follows:* "Everything that occurs in an even position must concord with everything that occurs in an odd position, whether it is in the first melody or the second or the third and so on for the others. But sometimes two or three written notes are used here instead of one or in the place of one, and one of them is placed in concord, whether it is the first or one of the others, on account of the rhetorical color of the music."

Therefore let this present reading be divided briefly into two parts, in the first of which the author deals with discant in general, in the second with a certain species of it, which is termed copula. The first begins **Discant unites**, etc., the second **Copula makes cantors**, etc. Also the first part is divided into two: in the first he deals with discant included under true music, in the second he shows that for putting discant together it is often necessary to introduce false or contrived music. Therefore the order is clear: the first part begins **Discant unites**, etc., the second **Non-truthful music**. And thus the meaning and division of the leonine verses is clear.

> **Discant[2] unites[1] different melodies[4] through patterns[3]**
> 1 that is, equalizes
> 2 that is, organum in general
> 3 that is, concords
> 4 that is, musical lines
> **In the fashion of the mode of the giving melody,[1] or, that is to say, of the equivalent one.[2]**
> 1 that is, according to the tenor, which gives the other melodies
> 2 that is, according to the fashion of the second, third, or fourth melody, which are equivalent to the first
> **These things[1] -- mode and order, number[2] and pattern, -- I tie together.[3]**
> 1 which are expressed here
> 2 or the fixed notes of the discant
> 3 that is, I join

Nota[1] **manent certa discantus**[2] **arte reperta.**
1 id est, signa manifesta
2 id est, diversorum cantuum
Sive par est numerus, aut impar[1] **fit quoque verus.**
1 in tali ordinatione sive, et hoc dupliciter, aut quo ad
punctorum numerum aut etiam specierum
Hic subiungitur ratio, quomodo numerus potest esse aut par aut impar:
Nam duo nunc puncti, pro quodam sunt ibi puncti.
Scemate tunc primus manet aut alium reperimus.

10

Utilis est multum etc. Hic vult exprimere quod non solum vera musica
sufficit ad discantum, immo nonquam discantus sciri perfecte poterit vel
componi, nisi falsa musica, id est ficta, ad compositionem ipsius manum
porrexerit ad vitricem. Et nota, quod eius inventio fuit necessitas in
hac arte, et hoc est, quia sine ipsa in diversis cantibus perfectam
concordantiarum notitiam habere nullatenus poteramus, secundum rectam et
veram in eis habitudinem proportionis. Hanc igitur, si necesse sit,
saepius eligamus, sine qua nullus ad perfectionem cantuum diversorum
poterit laudabiliter pervenire.

20   Et nota, quod quandoque per h quadratum in signo non proprio positum
designatur, et alicubi per b molle. Et fit inter h mi et c fa ut ratione
descensus in secundo cantu vel aliis, nonquam autem in primo, et inter f
et g tam in gravibus quam acutis et tunc per h quadratum dicitur figurari. Fit et enim quandoque sed raro inter G et a vel d et e, tam in
gravibus quam acutis, et tunc per b molle dicitur reperiri.

Si quaeratur, quid sit falsa musica sive ficta, dicimus, quod falsa
musica est variatio vocum necessaria de tono in semitonium vel e converso
per falsam mutationem sive fictam. Alii sic describunt: falsa musica
est illud, quod est imponibile in aliquo propassu, et fit <in> cantu
30 organico ad melodiam faciendam. Littera per se patet.

Utilis[1] **est multum non verax**[2] **musica, cultum**[3]
1 id est, necessaria
2 id est, per falsam mutationem ficta
3 ecce ratio quare fuit inventa
Cantus[1] **ostendit, et nunc bona scemata**[2] **prendit.**[3]
1 alicuius, utputa dupli vel tripli vel quadrupli etc.
2 id est, bonas concordantias et perfectas
3 id est, comprendit

----

7 subiungit rationem *pro* subiungitur ratio *Sowa*   9 *add. in marg.*
17 portionis *pro* proportionis *cod.*   fuerit *pro* sit *cod.*   21 mi *add.*
super scriptum   fa ut *add. super scriptum*   27 est *add. super*
scriptum   necessaria *add. super scriptum*   29 impossibile *pro*
imponibile *Sowa*   <in> *suppl. Sowa*

The notes[1] **remain fixed that are found in the art of discant.**[2]
1 that is, signs that are clear
2 that is, of disparate melodies
Whether the number is even or odd,[1] **it is also true.**
1 in this kind of arrangement and in two ways: either as regards the number of notes or the number of species
Here the reason is added as to how the number can be either even or odd:
For sometimes two written notes are written there instead of a certain one.
Then the first remains in the pattern or we find another one.

Non-truthful music, etc. Here he wishes to express the fact that not only true music suffices for discant, but rather never could discant be perfectly known or put together unless false music, that is, contrived music, held out its hand as to a stepchild for the putting together of it. And note that its invention was a necessity in this art, and this is because without it we were not able in any way to have a perfect knowledge of the concords in disparate melodies, according to a correct and true condition of proportion in them. Let us choose this often therefore, if it is necessary, since without it nobody can reach the perfection of disparate melodies in a praiseworthy fashion.

And note that sometimes it is designated by a square h placed at a sign that is not proper, and at other places by a soft b. And it occurs between h mi and c fa ut by reason of a descent in the second melody or the others, but never in the first, and between both low and high f and g, and then it is said to be figured by a square h. And it also occurs sometimes but rarely between g and a, or d and e, both high and low, and then it is said to be found through soft b.

If it is asked what false or contrived music is, we say that false music is the necessary variation of notes from a tone to a semitone or the reverse by a false or contrived mutation. Others describe it thus:*
False music is that which can be imposed in a certain situation, and it occurs in organal melody to make a musical sound. The text is clear by itself.

Non-truthful[2] **music is very useful,**[1] **and shows the refinement**[3]
1 that is, necessary
2 that is, contrived through false mutation
3 this is the reason why it was invented
Of the melody,[1] **and now takes**[3] **good patterns.**[2]
1 of any one, for example the duplum or triplum or quadruplum etc.
2 that is, good and perfect concords
3 that is, includes

<Pars secunda>

Copula cantores etc. Facta superius mentione de organo in generali
prout est genus ad omnes cantuum species generale seu etiam radicale, et
illud a nobis et aliis discantus specialiter apellatur, in hoc loco de
quadam ipsius specie sive membro, quae copula dicitur, vult actor
propositum declarare, dicens, quod vix aut nonquam sine copula perfecta
discantus cognitio poterit perhiberi, eo quod in suo genere discantum
reddit melicum et placentem, licet in hoc suae rectitudinis nil amittat.

Et est notandum, quod copula est illud medium, quod inter discantum
et organum speciale dicitur reperiri, unum ab altero per hoc subtiliter
10   dividendo. Unde copula est id, quod profertur recto modo aequipollentiae
universo. Alio modo dicitur sic: copula est id ubique, qu<o fit>
multitudo punctorum simul iunctorum per suos tractus, et hoc sub specie
primi modi et sub recta serie figurarum, sicut patet in *Alleluya* de
Posui tam in triplo cantu quam secundo, et hoc secundum dispositionem
discantus; nunc autem secundum dispositionem organi specialis, sicut
patet in duplo de *Iudea et Ierusalem*. Punctus, prout hic sumitur, est
illud, ubi fit multitudo actuum alicui punctorum termino singulariter
attributa. Nota tamen quod vox, figura, sonus, punctus, actus idem sunt;
in hoc tamen differunt, quod figura et punctus saepius pluralitatem
20   repraesentant, alia vero non. Quare autem hic ponitur illud membrum
patet, eo quod adiacet (fol. 158) capitulo praecedenti tanquam pars suo
toto.

Litteram igitur breviter sic expone: **Copula**, id est, talis species
discantus; **facit cantores dociles**, id est, habiles ad doctrinam
memoriter retinendam; **et meliores**, id est, meliori modo se habentes et
etiam firmiori.

Copula figmentum etc. Hic vult actor assignare differentiam inter
copulam et discantum, dicens, quod copula delicatiori modo et subtiliori
voce quam discantus praecipue provulgatur, licet in figuris et rectitud-
30   ine temporum sint eadem. Et ex hoc resultat, quod inter discantum et
organum speciale sit copula mediatrix. Comitatur namque cum discantu in
figuris et in recta proportione temporum et mensura, tamen organo
speciali in prolatione vocum melicoso sonitu redimita. Littera per se
patet.

Copula[1] cantores dociles[2] facit et meliores.
1 id est, talis cantuum species sive modulatio
2 id est, clericos subtiliores
Qua[1] sine discantus[2] perfecte non dabo[3] cantus.
40   1 sive copula
2 id est, organi generalis quo ad summam perfectionem
3 id est, dare potero

----

1 organo [[super]] in *cod.*   6 eo *add. super scriptum*   7 *inter* nil *et*
amittat *ras.*   9 subtiliter per hoc *Sowa*   11 qu<o fit> *scripsi*; quod
cod.; quod <fit> *Sowa*   22 toti *pro* toto *cod.*   28 delicatiore *pro*
delicatiori *Sowa*   subtiliore *pro* subtiliori *Sowa*

                            Part Two

     Copula makes cantors, etc. Having made mention above of organum in
general, inasmuch as it is a general or even a basic genus for all
species of melodies, and it is specifically called discant by us and by
others, in this place the author wishes to state a proposition about a
certain species or portion of it, which is called copula, saying that
scarcely or never can a perfect understanding of discant be presented
without copula, because in its genus it makes discant melodious and
pleasing, although by so doing it loses nothing of its correctness.
     And it should be noted that copula is that medial thing which is said
to be found between discant and special organum, by this means subtly
dividing one from the other. Whence copula is that which is performed
with the correct mode of equipollence throughout. It is described in
another way thus: Copula is that everywhere in which there occurs a
number of written notes joined together by their lines, and this is in
the species of the first mode and with a correct sequence of figures, as
is shown in the "Alleluia" of "Posui" both in the third melody and in
the second, and this is according to the disposition of discant; but
sometimes it is according to the disposition of special organum, as is
shown in the duplum of "Iudea et Ierusalem." A written section as it is
used here is that where there occurs a number of actual written notes
specifically attributed to some ending of the written notes. But note
that note, figure, sound, written note, and actual written note are the
same; but they differ in this, that figure and written note often
represent plurality, but the others do not. However the reason why that
portion is placed here is clear: It is because it comes close to (fol.
158) the preceding chapter as a part to its whole.
     Therefore expound the text briefly as follows: **Copula**, that is, this
species of discant; **makes cantors docile**, that is, clever at retaining a
principle in their memories; **and better**, that is, bearing themselves in a
better and stronger way.
     The copula bears, etc. Here the author wishes to assign the
difference between copula and discant, saying that copula is especially
promulgated in a more delicate way and a more subtle voice than discant,
although they are the same in the figures and the correctness of the
units of time. And from this it results that between discant and special
organum copula is the mediator. For it is a companion with discant in
the figures and in the correct proportion of units of time and in
measure, yet with special organum in the performance of the notes, which
is wreathed with a melodious sound. The text is clear by itself.

          Copula[1] makes cantors docile[2] and better.
          1 that is, this species or sounding of melodies
          2 that is, clerics more subtle
          **And without it[1] I shall not give[3] perfectly the melodies of
          discant.[2]**
          1 copula
          2 that is, of organum in general as regards the height of
          perfection
          3 that is, be able to give

Hic ostendit actor quid sit copula:
> **Unio punctorum**[1] **fit copula multa suorum,**
> 1 ante pausationem sive, quia ibi debent esse plures figurae
> **Quos**[1] **serit, et punctus**[2] **in se multos tenet actus.**[3]
> 1 sive punctos
> 2 sive illius copulae
> 3 continet in se multas sonorum proportiones
> **Copula**[1] **figmentum vocum**[2] **gerit, idque**[3] **retentum**
> 1 id est, quoddam prolationis scema
> 2 id est, figurarum
> 3 figmentum sive
> **Est sub mensura**[1] **discantus, subque figura.**[2]
> 1 id est, sub recta et aequali proportione temporum
> 2 id est, quo ad dispositionem propriam figurarum

Hic vult actor per hoc concludere, quod copula est medium inter discantum et organum:
> **Sic est discantus comes organici quoque cantus.**

Hic ostendit actor modum quorundam notatorum seu magistrorum sic copulam protrahentes:
> **Vox prior e ternis tractum det ut hic** ⌐ **fore cernis.**

Ecce recitat, quod solus usus a pluribus introductus facit inde notitiam manifestam:
> **Nosse suum vere dat saepius usus habere.**

----
15 per hoc concludere per hoc *cod*.

Here the author shows what copula is:
>**Much union of its written notes[1] is a copula,**

1 before a pause, because there must be many figures there
>**And these[1] it connects, and the written section[2] holds in itself many actual written notes.[3]**

1 the written notes
2 of that copula
3 contains in itself many proportions of sounds
>**The copula[1] bears the representation of the notes,[2] and that[3] is held back**

1 that is, a certain pattern of performance
2 that is, of the figures
3 the formation
>**Under the measure[1] of discant, and with its figure.[2]**

1 that is, with the correct and equal proportion of units of time
2 that is, as regards the proper disposition of the figures
Here the author wishes to conclude with this, that copula is the medial thing between discant and organum:
>**Thus it is the companion of discant and also of organal melody.**

Here the author shows the way of certain notators or masters who notate the copula in this way:
>**Let the first note out of the three have a line, as you can**

>**see here** **.**

Here he explains the fact that only usage introduced by many people makes the concept of it clear:
>**Frequent usage allows us to have the knowledge of it truly.**

\<Capitulum sextum\>

Nobis organica etc. Declarato superius capitulo de discantu, quod
est genus ad omnem cantuum speciem se extendens, in hoc siquidem capitulo
organi specialis, quod et duplex dicitur, proponit actor pro posse suo
modum et seriem declarare. Et nota, quod doctrina capituli praecedentis
ad omne genus cantuum se extendit, in quibus recta mensurae proportio sit
reperta, quare illud capitulum dicimus generale. Doctrina enim istius ad
quandam cantuum specialem differentiam solummodo se restringit, et ideo
dicimus istud speciale. Ex hoc igitur patet ordinatio partis praeambulae
ad sequentem, eo quod speciale derogat generali, vel aliter patet sic:
10 in praecedenti capitulo fecit actor mentionem breviter de discantu, qui
sub certa diminutione temporum et etiam quantitate nec non et exigentia
regulari per districtum terminum coartatur. In hoc autem capitulo de
speciali organo, quod et duplex dicitur, vult actor facere mentionem,
quod si per se positum sit repertum, more suo gradiens, regularum metas
sub certa figurarum ac temporum serie distributas transcendere aut
interrumpere non veretur, ex quo resultat irregularitas subtiliter
intuenti. Cum ergo praecedens capitulum per certas regulas coartetur,
istud siquidem earum rectitudini saepius sit repugnans. Sicut enim
regulare ante irregulare, sic praecedens capitulum ordinari dicitur ante
20 istud.

Notandum quod organum dicitur multipliciter, aut per se, aut cum
alio. Cum alio superius generaliter est expressum; hic igitur per se et
specialiter exponatur. Organum igitur per se aut specialiter sumptum
dicitur esse, quicquid profertur secundum aliquem modum tamen non rectum.
Sed tamen modus non sumitur hic ille per quem discantus currit vel
profertur, quia talis procedit regulariter. Non rectus dicitur ad
differentiam alicuius recti, quia longae et breves in recto sumuntur

----

3 *inter* quod *et* et *ras*.   14 more suo suo gradiens *cod*.   23 autem *pro*
aut *Sowa*   25 tamen [[rectus]] modus *cod.*, tamen rectus modus *Sowa*

Chapter Six

To us the special organal voice, etc. Having stated above in the
chapter on discant that it is a genus that extends itself to every
species of melody, in this chapter the author proposes to state as best
he can the mode and sequence of special organum, which is also called
double organum. And note that the principle of the preceding chapter
extends itself to every genus of melody in which the correct proportion
of measure is found, and that is why we call that chapter general. For
the principle of this one restricts itself to a certain special distinction of melody only, and therefore we call this one special. Therefore
from this the arrangement of the introductory part to what follows is
clear, because the special gives way to the general. Or it is clear in
another way as follows: In the preceding chapter the author made mention
briefly of discant, which, with a fixed diminution and quantity and also
regular requirement of units of time, is confined by a strict limit. But
in this chapter the author wishes to make mention of special organum,
which is also called double organum, which, if it is found placed by
itself, moving in its own fashion, is not afraid to transcend or break
through the boundaries of the rules, which are distributed under a fixed
sequence of figures and units of time, from which results a certain
irregularity to him who is paying close attention. Since therefore the
preceding chapter is confined by fixed rules, this one indeed often
rejects their correctness. For just as regular comes before irregular,
so the preceding chapter is said to be arranged before this one.

It should be noted that organum is named in many ways: either by
itself, or with another. Organum with another has been elucidated
generally above; here therefore let organum by itself or special organum
be expounded. Therefore organum by itself or used specially is said to
be whatever is performed according to some mode that is not a correct
one. But mode is not used here as the one by which discant runs or is
performed, because such a one proceeds regularly. One that is not
correct is so called to distinguish it from a correct one, because the
longs and breves in the correct one are used in the requisite way and not

debito modo et principaliter. Cum alio dicitur, quicquid profertur
per aliquam rectam mensuram, ut dictum est superius, scilicet cum
aequipollente, cui se tenet vel habet in universo usque ad finem alicuius
puncti, ubi se conveniunt secundum rectam concordantiam et perfectam.

Et scias, quod ista species inter cetera cantuum genera sonorum
modulos purpurat et insignit; nam per eam quaeque vocum sonoritas
instrumentis sive naturalibus sive artificialibus concordata est
reducibilis ad numerum rectae vocis. Ideoque istam speciem sive illud
capitulum ad consummationem huius opusculi decrevimus reservandum.

10   Haec siquidem praesens lectio in duas partes breviter dividatur, in
quarum prima ostendit actor de quo debet agere, in secunda exequitur.
Prima pars incipit **Nobis organica**, secunda **Nunc per se dabitur** etc.
Prima remanet indivisa, sed secunda in duas dividitur, in quarum prima
distinguit de organo specialiter, in secunda de cognitione illius dat
doctrinam. Et quia prius est totum per species sive partes cognoscere
quam ad cognitionem partium accedere, eo quod totum ponit suas partes et
non e converso, ideo patet ordo. Prima pars incipit **Nunc per se dabitur**
etc., secunda **Vox penultima** etc. Item prima istarum in duas dividitur.
In prima distinguit de organo, specialitatem ipsius per sequentem regulam
20   ostendendo, in secunda ipsius convenientiam cum alio manifestat. Ideo
patet ordo: prima pars incipit **Nunc per se dabitur** etc., (fol. 158v)
secunda **More modi graditur** etc. Item prima in duas: in prima procedit
generaliter circa variam dispositionem ipsius, in secunda specialiter
practicam illius manifestat. Prima pars incipit **Nunc per se dabitur**
etc., secunda **More modique dati** etc. Et sic patet sententia et divisio
leoninis.

Allicit haec animos etc. Hic vult actor ostendere quod organum
speciale sive duplex prae ceteris optinet dominii dignitatem. Nam si in
suo genere prout decet lucide proferatur dulci voce et laudabiliter
30   concordante, omnia cantuum genera superat et excludit delicata dulcedine
melodiae. Hinc est quare pellicit animos auditorum, mimos et alios
artifices per suum artificium modulos exercentes superat et devincit,
quia sine consideratione ipsius non possent tantam sonorum dulcedinem
exercere, vel promere resonando, eo quod primo et principaliter
consideratur in mente quam proferatur in actu. Et sic per prolationem
organi naturalis sonorum modulatio variata secundum modum aut non modum
ad instrumenta sonora perducitur resonanda, quare dicimus vocem cassam et
omissam ad rectam vocem esse reducibilem et ipsi penitus deservire. Per
quod patet omnem sonum artificiali instrumento fictum esse reducibilem ad
40   organum naturale quo ad punctorum numerum et mensuram, licet impedimentum
linguae saepius hoc offendat.

----

3 equipollentia *pro* aequipollente *Sowa*   cuius *pro* cui *cod.*
15 cognoscere *add. in marg.*   22 **graditur** *add. super scriptum*
33 tantam [[vocum]] dulcedinem *cod.*, sonorum *in marg.*

incidentally. Organum with another is said to be whatever is performed
by means of some correct measure, as has been said above, that is to say
with its equipollent part, to which it holds itself or occurs throughout,
up to the end of some written section, where they accord with each other
according to a correct and perfect concord.

And you should know that this species among the rest of the genera of
melodies embellishes and adorns the musical occurrences of sounds; for by
means of it any sonority of notes concording on either natural or
artificial instruments is reducible to the category of the correct note.
Therefore we have decided that this species or this chapter should be
kept for the consummation of this little work.

Indeed let this present reading be divided briefly into two parts, in
the first of which the author shows what he should deal with, in the
second he describes it. The first part begins **To us the special organal
voice**, the second **Sometimes it will be given**, etc. The first remains
undivided, but the second is divided into two parts, in the first of
which he makes a distinction regarding organum in its special sense, and
in the second he gives a principle about the understanding of it. And
because one should first understand the whole by means of its species or
parts before broaching the understanding of the parts, because the whole
establishes its parts and not the reverse, therefore the order is clear.
The first part begins **Sometimes it will be given**, etc., the second **The
penultimate note**, etc. Also the first of these is divided into two. In
the first he makes a distinction about organum, showing its special
nature by means of a rule that follows, in the second he displays its
accord with another. Therefore the order is clear: The first part
begins **Sometimes it will be given**, etc., (fol. 158v) the second **It moves
in the manner of a correct mode**, etc. Also the first part is divided
into two. In the first he proceeds generally about the different
disposition of it, in the second he specially displays the practice of
it. The first part begins **Sometimes it will be given**, etc., the second
And it moves in the manner of the given mode, etc. And thus the meaning
and division of the leonine verses is clear.

It entices minds, etc. Here the author wishes to show that special
or double organum obtains the dignity of pre-eminence over the others.
For if in its genus, as is fitting, it is performed clearly, with a voice
that is sweet and concordant in a praiseworthy fashion, it surpasses and
shuts out all genera of melodies with the delightful sweetness of its
musical sound. That is why it attracts the minds of its listeners, and
overcomes and conquers musicians and other masters of the arts who employ
musical sounds by their own skill, because without a consideration of it
they would not be able to employ such sweetness of sounds, or produce
them in sound, because firstly and not incidentally it is considered in
the mind rather than performed in actuality. And thus by means of the
performance of natural organum the production of sounds that is varied
according to a mode or not a mode is brought to sound on sounding
instruments, and so we say that a voice that is empty or one that is left
out is reducible to a correct voice and completely subject to it. By
which it is clear that every sound that is contrived on an artificial
instrument is reducible to natural organum as regards the number and
measure of written notes, although the hindrance of the tongue often
prevents this.

Nobis[1] organica specialis vox[2] fit amica.[3]
1 cantoribus
2 id est, organum speciale, quod et duplex organum appellatur
3 id est, amicabilis
Organa dupla[1] serit quorum[2] modulos[3] sibi quaerit.[4]
1 id est, organum duplex vel speciale
2 sive organorum
3 id est, cantus vel concordantias
4 id est, acquirit

10   Allicit[1] haec animos, superat[2] modulamine[3] mimos,[4]
1 id est, quadam dulcedine attrahit
2 id est, excellit
3 id est, per dulcem concordantiam
4 id est, ioculatores
Si bene[1] pandatur[2] ac dulci[3] voce regatur.
1 id est, sicut debet
2 id est, manifestetur, nota
3 id est, concordante vel melicosa
Instrumentorum[1] cleat[2] huic[3] vox cassa sonorum,

20   1 sive artificialium
2 id est, firmat
3 sive organicae voci naturaliter prolatae ad differentiam non
cassae
Qua sine[1] perfecta[2] nequit haec[3] fore, nec bene secta.[4]
1 sive naturali voce
2 id est, perfecte sonans
3 id est, illa quae est cassa
4 id est, nec prout decet divisa

30   **Nunc per se dabitur** etc. Hic dicit actor, quod organum speciale
dupliciter sumitur vel consideratur, scilicet aut per se aut cum alio.
Si per se, regularum artis deviat a praeceptis, nam per varias
concordantias distributum rectae mensurae seu regularis habitudinem
negligit dulcedine melodiae. Hinc est quia rectum modum spernere voluit,
alium, qui non rectus dicitur, appetendo, et hoc innuitur per textus
seriem manifeste, cum dicitur **More modique dati** etc.

Nunc per se dabitur[1] nunc cum reliquo[2] reperitur.
1 sive organum speciale, et hoc supra burdonem in tenore
40   2 sive cum discantu
Cum per se[1] tantum vult iure[2] suo dare cantum.
1 id est, quotiens per se ponitur supra burdonem tenoris
2 id est, tunc relicta mensura stricta vult melice se proferri

----
10 **hoc** *pro* **haec** *Sowa*   16 decet *pro* debet *Sowa*

To us[1] the special organal voice[2] is a friend.[3]
1 who are cantors
2 that is, special organum, which is also called double organum
3 that is, friendly
It connects double organa[1] whose[2] musical sounds[3] it seeks[4] for itself.
1 that is, double or special organum
2 those of the organa
3 that is, melodies or concords
4 that is, acquires
It entices[1] minds, and surpasses[2] musicians[4] with its euphony,[3]
1 that is, attracts them by a certain sweetness
2 that is, prevails over
3 that is, by its sweet concord
4 that is, jongleurs
If it is well[1] displayed[2] and ruled by a sweet[3] voice.
1 that is, as it should be
2 that is, demonstrated; take note
3 that is, concordant or melodious
The empty voice of sounding instruments[1] benefits[2] this one,[3]
1 artificial ones
2 that is, strengthens
3 the organal voice that is produced naturally, according to the distinction that it is not empty
And without it[1] this one[3] could not be perfect,[2] nor well sectioned.[4]
1 the natural voice
2 that is, sounding perfectly
3 that is, the one that is empty
4 that is, nor divided as it should be

Sometimes it will be given, etc. Here the author says that special organum is used or considered in two ways, that is to say either by itself or with another. If it is by itself, it deviates from the precepts of the rules of the art, for, distributed by means of various concords, it neglects the condition of correct or regular measure by the sweetness of its musical sound. This is why it wanted to reject the correct mode, seeking another which is called not correct; and this is suggested clearly through the sequence of the text, when it says **And it moves in the manner of the given mode**, etc.

Sometimes it will be given by itself,[1] sometimes it is found with the other.[2]
1 special organum, and this is above the drone in the tenor
2 with discant
When by itself,[1] it only wishes to give its melody by its own law.[2]
1 that is, whenever it is placed by itself above the drone of the tenor
2 that is, then it abandons strict measure and wishes to be performed melodiously

Et nota, quod licet rectam relinquat mensuram, cum habet modum et
mensuram in se:
>   **More modique dati graditur non rectificati,**
>   **Nam sonus[1] aptatur[2] per scemata[3] voxque vagatur[4]**
>   1 id est, ordinatio vocum
>   2 id est, politur
>   3 id est, per varias concordantias
>   4 id est, vagare cernitur propter dulcedinem melodiae, sicut
>   [tropus ?] in sui revolutione

10
>   **Nunc ibi prolixe,[1] cito[2] nunc, scemate vix e[3]**
>   1 id est, cum multa mora
>   2 hoc est celeriter descendendo
>   3 modo subiungit rationem quare prolixe profertur
>   **Tollitur,[1] inde modum rectum negat, hoc quoque nodum[2]**
>   1 id est, sustrahitur
>   2 modo subiungit causam, quare relinquit rectum modum et rectam
>   dispositionem figurarum
>   **Saepe ligaturae rectae[1] fugit, et sine iure.[2]**
>   1 id est, secundum quod se habet in discantu, ubi recte

20
>   proportionatur unaquaeque figura
>   2 id est, contra regulas artis

   More modi graditur etc. Ostenso superius qualiter organum speciale
sive duplex per se positum reperitur, in hoc loco vult actor ostendere
quomodo et qualiter cum alio copulatur, dicens quod quotienscumque cum
alio organo fit repertum, coartatur habitudine regulari, et discantus
modum et ordinem induit proportionaliter in omnibus et importat.
   Vox penultima etc. In fine sui capituli vult actor quandam regulam
inserere generalem, quae ad cognitionem totius capituli dicitur oportuna

30 quo ad voces plenius et perfectius discernendas, quae talis: *organum
speciale cognoscitur per penultimam, per concordantiam, per figuram.*
Alia insequitur regula, quod *quicquid invenitur ante longam pausationem,
dicitur esse longum.* Tertia et ultima est, quod *quicquid figuratur
longum secundum modum organi ante perfectam concordantiam, dicitur esse
longum.* Littera per se patet.

>   (fol. 159) **More modi graditur recti quandoque potitur**
>   **Atque ligaturis semper rectisque figuris,**
>   **Et tunc artatur et cum reliquo sociatur.**

40
>   **Vox penultima dat, vel consonantia cedat**
>   **Atque figura, notas tria dant simul haec tibi notas.**
>   **Norma docet quaedam quod longum tutius edam.**
>   **Quod sequitur pausa longans sint scemata causa.**

----
9 cantus *pro* [tropus ?] *Sowa*   40 **cumque sonantia** *cod.,* **consonantia**
Sowa   41 **hoc** *pro* **haec** *Sowa*   43 **longas** *pro* **longans** *Sowa*

And note that although it abandons correct measure, yet it has mode
and measure in itself:

> **And it moves in the manner of the given mode that is not the**
> **correctly-made one,**
> **For the sound[1] is made suitable[2] by means of the patterns,[3] and**
> **the voice wanders[4]**
> 1 that is, the arrangement of the notes
> 2 that is, is refined
> 3 that is, by means of various concords
> 4 that is, is perceived to wander on account of the sweetness of
> the musical sound, as a trope does in its unwinding
> **Sometimes broadly[1] there, sometimes swiftly,[2] and scarcely from**
> **the pattern[3]**
> 1 that is, with much delay
> 2 this is descending quickly
> 3 now he adds a reason why it is performed broadly
> **Is removed;[1] then it denies the correct mode, and also this**
> **knot[2]**
> 1 that is, is taken away
> 2 now he adds the cause for its abandoning the correct mode and
> the correct disposition of the figures
> **Of the correct ligature[1] it often flees, without the law.[2]**
> 1 that is, according to the way it occurs in discant, where each
> figure is correctly proportioned
> 2 that is, against the rules of the art

It moves in the manner of a correct mode, etc. Having shown above
how special or double organum is found placed by itself, in this place
the author wishes to show how and in what way it is joined with another,
saying that whenever it is found with another organum, it is confined by
the regular condition and takes on and conveys the mode and order of
discant proportionally in all things.

The penultimate note, etc. At the end of his chapter the author
wishes to insert a certain rule which is said to be suitable for the
understanding of the whole chapter, as regards determining the notes more
fully and more perfectly, which is this: "Special organum is understood
by its penultimate, by concord, and by figure." Another rule follows,
that "whatever is found before a long pause is said to be long." The
third and last rule is that "whatever is figured long according to the
mode of organum before a perfect concord is said to be long." The text
is clear by itself.

> **(fol. 159) It moves in the fashion of a correct mode sometimes**
> **and possesses**
> **Ligatures always and correct figures,**
> **And then it is restricted, and joined with the other.**
> **The penultimate note occurs or may yield to the consonance**
> **And the figure; these three things together give the notes, you**
> **note to yourself.**
> **A certain precept teaches that I may more safely utter something**
> **long.**
> **Let the patterns be the reason that a long pause follows.**

Quod perit hiis poscunt hoc longum scemata, noscunt
Hoc bene psallentes, hanc artem sponte legentes.

   Musa frui requie etc. Huius libelli materia sub quadam metrorum
serie compilata, cuius confectio actorem proprium multis vigiliis et
studii exercitio praegravatum reddidit atque fessum, ideoque fine sui
operis imminente proponit animum a curis et laboribus revocare, sociorum
vel auditorum begnivolentiam quam adoptat humiliter requirendo, ad hoc ut
sui opusculi sarcina praegravatus, quam ob utilitatem plurium optinuit,
10 eorum gratiam et consensum habere iugiter mereatur.
   Laudo deum patrem etc. Actor iste sui operis consummationem
percipiens imminere, laboris studio iam cessante, laudes exibere nititur
omnium creatori, commemorationem faciens beatae et gloriosae semperque
virginis Mariae, nec non et omnium sanctorum consortium adiungendo,
favore quorum et auxilio mediante quod incepit dubius et incertus securus
existimat fine laudabili complevisse.

      Musa frui requie, pete, gaude fine laborum.
      Pande benignorum cuivis secreta sophiae.
20   **Laudo deum patrem, cum sanctis confero matrem,**
      Quis mea complevi compendia, floribus aevi.˙

   Quis mea etc. converte sic: **quis**, id est, ad laudem et reverentiam
quorum omnium; vel **quis**, id est, auxilio quorum; vel **quis**, id est,
commemorationem quorum, quia per doctrinam huius libelli poterunt in
ecclesiis Dei decentius et solemnius in commemorationum modulis venerari;
vel **quis**, id est, quibus mediantibus; **complevi**, id est, compilavi vel
perfeci; **mea compendia**, id est, mea carmina breviter et utiliter
compilata; **floribus aevi**, id est, in ferventi flosculo iuventutis vel
30 aetatis virilis.

      Hic metra de prosa qui finxit luce iocosa,
      Vivat in aeternum regem laudando supernum.
      Amen.
      Anno millesimoque ducentesimo quoque nono
      Post decies septem, cartam prosae fore neptem
      Decrevi festo Clementis carmine praesto.

      Sit decus huic musae praesens velut ore Medusae
40   **Hostes contrivit, sic scriba suos ubi vivit.**
      Amen.

----

1 **pariter** *pro* **perit** *Sowa*   10 mereretur *pro* mereatur *Sowa*
27 **quis** *sine sublinea in cod.*   27-28 vel [[complevi]] perfeci *cod.*

> They know that it gives way to these, and the patterns demand
> that this be long,
> Those who chant this well, and read this treatise of their own
> accord.

O Muse, enjoy your rest, etc. Since the material of this little book
has now been compiled in a certain sequence of verses, the putting
together of which has made its own author weighed down and tired with
many sleepless nights and the pursuit of hard work, therefore, as the end
of his work is near at hand, he proposes to restore his soul from its
cares and labors, humbly asking for the benevolence of his colleagues and
hearers, which he strives for, so that, weighed down by the burden of his
little work, which he has obtained for the usefulness of many, he may
deserve to have both their favor and their acceptance.

I praise God the Father, etc. This author, seeing that the
consummation of his work is at hand, and since the hard work of his labor
is now ceasing, strives to confer praises on the Creator of all things,
commemorating the blessed and glorious and ever-virginal Mary, as well
as including the community of all the saints, by whose favor and with
whose aid that which he began in doubt and uncertainty he safely
considers he has brought to a praiseworthy conclusion.

> O Muse, enjoy your rest,* seek and rejoice in the end of your
> labors.
> Extend the mysteries of your wisdom to any of the well-disposed.
> I praise God the Father, and include the Mother and the saints.
> For whom I have completed my brief introductions, in the flower
> of my age.

For whom I have completed, etc. interpret thus: **For whom,** that is,
for the praise and reverence of all of them; or, **For whom,** that is, by
whose help; or **For whom,** that is, for their commemoration, because by
means of the principle of this little book they will be able to be
venerated in the churches of God more properly and more solemnly in the
musical sounds of their commemorations; or **For whom,** that is, by whose
help; **I have completed,** that is, I have brought together or finished; **my
brief introductions,** that is, my poems brought together briefly and
usefully; **in the flower of my age,** that is, in the shining flower of
youth or manhood.

> He who contrived verses about the prose in a pleasant light,
> Let him live for eternity praising the King on high.
> Amen.
> In the twelve hundred and ninth year
> After seventy, I have decided that these pages should serve as a
>   granddaughter to the prose
> On the feast of St. Clement with this poem.
>
> May there be present glory to this Muse, and as with the face of
> Medusa
> He destroyed his enemies, so may the scribe destroy his where he
> lives.
> Amen.

PARALLEL READINGS

(These are correlated with the main text by page and line reference.
Readings follow the cited editions and are arranged in chronological
order.)

PROLOGUE

Page 64:

3-10   Cf. Lambertus (ed. Reaney/Gilles P *1*, 1): Quoniam circa
artem musicam necessaria qu*a*edam ad utilitatem cantantium tractare
proponimus, necesse est . . .
    Cf. Franco (ed. Reaney/Gilles *Prologus* 3-4): Quoniam cum
videremus multos tam novos quam antiquos in artibus suis de
mensurabili musica multa bona dicere, et e contrario in multis et
maxime in accidentibus ipsius scienti*a*e deficere et errare . . .

7-8   Cf. Lambertus (ed. Reaney/Gilles IV *5*, 8-9): Verumptamen
quidam in artibus suis referunt, perfectam figuram se habere per
ultra mensuram; et quosdam etiam modos, sicut primum et quartum esse
per ultra mensurabiles, id est non rectam mensuram habentes, quod
falsum est; quia si verum esset, tunc posset fieri cantus naturalis
de omnibus imperfectis, quoniam imperfectam dicunt esse perfectam.

19   Cf. Cato, *Disticha*, III, 7 (ed. Nève, 29):
Alterius dictum aut factum ne carpseris umquam,
Exemplo simili ne te derideat alter.

21   Cf. Horace, *Epistles,* I, 2, 35-36 (ed. Klingner, 245):
                          . . . si non
Intendes animum studiis et rebus honestis,
Invidia vel amore vigil torquebere.
    Cf. Horace, *Epistles,* II, 1, 76-82 (ed. Klingner, 279-80):
Indignor quicquam *reprehendi,* non quia crasse
Compositum illepideve putetur, sed quia nuper,
Nec veniam antiquis, sed honorem et praemia posci.
Recte necne crocum floresque perambulet Attae

291

(Page 64:)

Fabula si dubitem, clament periisse pudorem
Cuncti paene patres, ea cum *reprehendere* coner,
Quae gravis Aesopus, quae doctus Roscius egit.
(My italics.)

Cf. *Proverbia Sententiaeque Latinitatis Medii Aevi* (ed. Walther, no. 28342a):

Si commissorum discussor eris propriorum,
Non alienorum *reprehensor* eris vitiorum.
(My italics.)

25 Cf. Lambertus (ed. Reaney/Gilles I *7*, 1): Partes autem ipsius alias habet theorica, alias pratica.

Page 66:

1-2 Cf. *Proverbia Sententiaeque Latinitatis Medii Aevi* (ed. Walther, no. 14823):

Metra iuvant animos, comprehendunt plurima paucis,
Pristina commemorant; satis sunt hec tria legenti.

3-4 Cf. Lambertus (ed. Reaney/Gilles I *1*, 1): In principio autem huius scientiae scire opinamur quid sit musica . . .

6-7 Cf. Boethius, *De institutione musica* (ed. Friedlein 187, 20-22): Et prima quidem mundana est, secunda vero humana, tertia, quae in quibusdam constituta est instrumentis.

Cf. Lambertus (ed. Reaney/Gilles I *2*, 1): Sed haec dividitur, quia alia instrumentalis, alia humana.

7-18 Cf. Boethius, *De institutione musica* (ed. Friedlein 187, 23 - 189, 12).

12-20 Cf. Capella (ed. Eyssenhardt IX, 930): . . . quae rhythmicis et melicis astructionibus continetur . . .

Cf. Cassiodorus, *Institutiones* II, v, 5 (ed. Mynors 144): Musicae partes sunt tres: armonica - rithmica - metrica. Armonica est scientia musica quae decernit in sonis acutum et gravem. Rithmica est quae requirit incursionem verborum, utrum bene sonus an male cohaereat. Metrica est quae mensuram diversorum metrorum probabili ratione cognoscit, ut verbi gratia heroicon, iambicon, heleiacon, et cetera.

Cf. Isidore of Seville, *Etymologiae*, (ed. Lindsay III, xviii, 3-9): Musicae partes sunt tres, id est, harmonica, rythmica, metrica. Harmonica est, quae decernit in sonis acutum et gravem. Rythmica est, quae requirit incursionem verborum, utrum bene sonus an male cohaereat. Metrica est, quae mensuram diversorum metrorum probabili ratione cognoscit, ut verbi gratia heroicon, iambicon, elegiacon, et cetera.

Cf. Isidore of Seville, *Etymologiae* (ed. Lindsay I, xxxix, 9):

(Page 66:)

A rebus quae scribuntur, ut heroicum, elegiacum, bucolicum.
  Cf. Lambertus (ed. Reaney/Gilles I *2*, 4-8): Et etiam dividitur,
quia alia harmonica, alia rithmica, alia metrica. Harmonica vero
est illa quae discernit inter sonos gravem et acutum. Vel
harmonica est illa quae consistit in numeris dupliciter et
mensuris: una localis secundum proportionem sonorum et vocum,
alia temporalis secundum proportionem longarum breviumque
figurarum. Et est idem harmonica, quod discretio modulationis et
veraciter canendi scientia, et facilis ad perfectionem canendi
via, plurimumque vocum per dissimilium proportionalis
consonantia, et scientia de numero relato ad sonum. Rithmica
vero, est illa quae in scansione verborum requirit, utrum bene
vel male cohaereant dictiones: quod cantando utendum est, tanquam
legendo. Metrica vero est illa quae mensura diversorum metrorum
ostendit probabili ratione, ut patet in heroico, iambico et
elegio metro.

21-25 Cf. Capella (ed. Eyssenhardt IX, 930): . . . officium meum
est bene modulandi sollertia . . .
  Cf. Cassiodorus, *Institutiones* II, v, 4 (ed. Mynors 144): . . .
musica scientia est disciplina quae de numeris loquitur . . .
  Cf. Lambertus (ed. Reaney/Gilles I *2*, 6): Et est idem
harmonica, quod discretio modulationis et veraciter canendi
scientia, et facilis ad perfectionem canendi via, plurimumque vocum
per dissimilium proportionalis consonantia, et scientia de numero
relato ad sonum.

25-34 Cf. Johannes Afflighemensis (ed. van Waesberghe III, 9):
Alii musicam quasi modusicam a modulatione, alii quasi moysicam ab
aqua, quae *moys* dicitur, appellatam opinantur.

35-39 Cf. Cassiodorus, *Institutiones* II, v, 1 (ed. Mynors 142- 3): Nam
Musae ipsae appellatae sunt *apo tu maso,* id est a quaerendo, quod
per ipsas, sicut antiqui voluerunt, vis carminum et vocis modulatio
quaereretur.
  Cf. Isidore of Seville, *Etymologiae* (ed. Lindsay III, xv, 19-23):
Musica est peritia modulationis sono cantuque consistens. Et dicta
Musica per derivationem a Musis. Musae autem appellatae *apo tou
masai,* id est a quaerendo, quod per eas, sicut antiqui voluerunt, vis
carminum et vocis modulatio quaereretur.
  Cf. Johannes Afflighemensis (ed. van Waesberghe III, 1): Dicitur
autem musica, ut quidam volunt, a musa, quae est instrumentum quoddam
musicae decenter satis et ioconde clangens.
  Cf. Lambertus (ed. Reaney/Gilles I *5*, 1): Genus vero huius
scientiae est peritia modulationis harmonicae . . .
  Cf. Lambertus (ed. Reaney/Gilles I 4, 1): Musica enim dicitur a
Musis quae, secundum fabulam, dicuntur filiae Jovis.

39-42 Cf. *Biblia Sacra, Genesis* iv, 21: et nomen fratris eius Iubal
ipse fuit pater canentium cithara et organo.
  Cf. Boethius, *De institutione musica* (ed. Friedlein 197-198.)
  Cf. Cassiodorus, *Institutiones* II, v, 1 (ed. Mynors 142):

(Page 66:)

> Gaudentius quidam, de musica scribens, Pythagoram dicit huius rei
> invenisse primordia ex malleorum sonitu et cordarum extensione
> percussa.
>> Cf. Isidore of Seville, *Etymologiae* (ed. Lindsay III, xvi, 1-4):
> Moyses dicit repertorem musicae artis fuisse Tubal, qui fuit de
> stirpe Cain ante diluvium. Graeci vero Pythagoram dicunt huius
> artis invenisse primordia ex malleorum sonitu et cordarum
> extensione percussa.
>> Cf. Guido of Arezzo (ed. van Waesberghe XX, 4-8).
>> Cf. Johannes Afflighemensis (ed. van Waesberghe III, 12-18).
>> Cf. Lambertus (ed. Reaney/Gilles I *11*, 1-2): Moyses dicit
> repertorem artis *musicae* fuisse *Jubal* qui fuit de stirpe Cayn ante
> diluvium. Graeci vero *Pythagoram* dicunt huius artis primordia
> invenisse.

46-47   Cf. Boethius, *De divisione* (ed. Pozzi, 107): Quam magnos
         studiosis afferat fructus scientia dividendi quamque apud peripateti-
         cam disciplinam semper haec fuerit in honore notitia, docet . . .

Page 68:

25-26   Cf. Lambertus (ed. Reaney/Gilles I *7*, 1): Partes autem ipsius
         alias habet theorica, alias pratica.

Page 70:

10-11   Cf. *Analecta hymnica* LIV, 188:
         Nulla salus est in domo,
         Nisi cruce munit homo
         Superliminaria.

14-15   Cf. *Proverbia Sententiaeque Latinitatis Medii Aevi* (ed. Walther,
         no. 3827):
         Crux vestimenti dat premia nulla ferenti,
         Hoc animo senti, nisi sit prius insita menti.

19-20   Cf. Johannes de Garlandia (ed. Reimer I, 1): Habito de ipsa
         plana musica, quae immensurabilis dicitur, nunc est praesens
         intentio de ipsa mensurabili, quae organum quantum ad nos
         appellatur, prout organum generaliter dicitur ad omnem mensurabilem
         musicam.
            Cf. Franco (ed. Reaney/Gilles I, 7): Dividitur autem
         mensurabilis musica in mensurabilem simpliciter et partim.

25-26   Cf. Johannes de Garlandia (ed. Reimer I, 3): Sciendum est ergo,
         quod ipsius organi generaliter accepti tres sunt species, scilicet

(Page 70:)

      discantus, copula et organum, de quibus dicendum est per ordinem.

26-28   Cf. Johannes de Garlandia (ed. Reimer I, 2): Unde organum et
    est species totius mensurabilis musicae et est genus diversimode
    tamen, prout dictum est superius.
        Cf. Franco (ed. Reaney/Gilles I, 10-12): Et sciendum quod
    organum dupliciter sumitur, proprie et communiter. Est enim organum
    proprie sumptum organum duplum, quod purum organum appellatur.
    Communiter vero dicitur organum quilibet cantus ecclesiasticus
    tempore mensuratus.

28-30   Cf. Lambertus (ed. Reaney/Gilles IV 2, 1): Primo igitur
    sciendum est quod tria tantummodo sunt genera per quae tota
    mensurabilis musica discurrit, scilicet discantus, hoketus et
    organum.

Page 74:

14-15   Cf. Ovid, *Metamorphoses* I, 568-746 (ed. Van Proosdij, 24-30.)

Page 76:

10-11   Cf. Boethius, *De institutione arithmetica* (ed. Friedlein 89,
    19-22): . . . constat punctum ipsum . . . cum et longitudinis et
    latitudinis et profunditatis expers sit . . .

13-15   Cf. Cassiodorus, *Institutiones* II, v, 9 (ed. Mynors 149): Caelum
    ipsum, sicut supra memoravimus, dicitur sub armoniae dulcedine
    revolvi . . .
        Cf. Isidore of Seville, *Etymologiae* (ed. Lindsay III, xvii,
    14-17): Itaque sine Musica nulla disciplina potest esse perfecta,
    nihil enim sine illa. Nam et ipse mundus quadam harmonia sonorum
    fertur esse conpositus, et caelum ipsud sub harmoniae modulatione
    revolvi.
        Cf. Isidore of Seville, *Etymologiae* (ed. Lindsay III, xix,
    10-12): Ad omnem autem sonum, quae materies cantilenarum est,
    triformem constat esse naturam.
        Cf. Lambertus (ed. Reaney/Gilles IV, 4, 7-8): Et ideo non
    immerito ad summam refertur trinitatem, quia res quaelibet naturalis
    ad similitudinem divinae naturae ex tribus constare invenitur. In
    vocibus et sonis, et rebus omnibus trina tantum consistit
    consonantia, scilicet dyatessaron, dyapente et dyapason.

Page 78:

16   Cf. Ovid *Remedia Amoris* 364 (ed. Henderson 13):
          Qui volet, impugnent unus et alter opus.

Page 80:

41-42   Cf. Boethius, *Philosophiae Consolatio* IV, ii, 36 (ed. Rapisarda
         130): Est enim, quod ordinem retinet servatque naturam; quod
         vero ab hac deficit, esse etiam, quod in sua natura situm est,
         derelinquit.
             Cf. Lambertus (ed. Reaney/Gilles IV *1*, 1): Cum secundum quod
         dicit Boetius nichil est quod non retinet ordinem, servatque naturam
         summopere in cunctis actibus humanis, ordo considerari debet ne
         quod actum est nichil esse per dictum Boetii perfectum ordinis
         arguatur.

Page 82:

15-17   Cf. Franco (ed. Reaney/Gilles II, 2): Discantus sic dividitur:
         . . . alius copulatus qui copula nuncupatur . . .

26   Cf. Lambertus (ed. Reaney/Gilles IV *1*, 4): . . . ac etiam
         orthographiam cognoscere et conservare et regulariter eam describere
         . . .

29-31   Cf. Elias Salamon (ed. Gerbert III, 18a): Quid est littera?
         Minima pars vocis compositae, quae scribi non potest, ideo subiectum
         puncti appellatur.

30   Cf. Johannes Afflighemensis (ed. van Waesberghe II, 4): Sed
         sicut grammatica, dialectica et ceterae artes, si non essent
         conscriptae ac per praecepta elucidatae, incertae haberentur et
         confusae, ita et haec.

CHAPTER ONE, Part One

Page 86:

4-7   Cf. Lambertus (ed. Reaney/Gilles IV *2*, 3): Unde notandum est,
         quod tres generalissimae sunt species per quas omnes modi, id est

(Page 86:)

> omnis cantus, in quo consistit maneries, dinoscuntur et
> discernuntur, ac etiam moderantur, scilicet figura, tempus et
> mensura.

11-16   Cf. Lambertus (ed. Reaney/Gilles IV *2*, 4-5): . . . ideo primo de
repraesentatione formaque figurarum tam de simplicibus quam de
compositis, quot tempora quaelibet figura pro sua parte continet in
se . . . et quomodo per huius figuras denotetur longitudo seu
brevitas cantus.

13-16   Cf. Johannes de Garlandia (ed. Reimer II, 1): Sequitur de
repraesentatione figurarum sive notularum, videlicet quomodo per
huiusmodi figuras denotetur longitudo vel brevitas.

17-19   Cf. Johannes de Garlandia (ed. Reimer II, 2): Unde figura
est repraesentatio soni secundum suum modum.
Cf. Lambertus (ed. Reaney/Gilles IV *3*, 1): Unde figura est
repraesentatio soni secundum suum modum, et secundum aequipollentiam
sui aequipollentis . . .
Cf. Franco (ed. Reaney/Gilles IV, 1): Figura est repraesentatio
vocis in aliquo modorum ordinatae . . .

Page 88:

1-3   Cf. Johannes de Garlandia (ed. Reimer II, 3): Et sciendum,
quod huiusmodi figurae aliquando ponuntur sine littera, aliquando cum
littera; sine littera ut in caudis vel conductis, cum littera ut in
motellis.
Cf. Lambertus (ed. Reaney/Gilles IV *3*, 2): Sed huius figurae
aliquando ponuntur cum littera, aliquando sine; cum littera vero ut
in motellis et similibus, sine littera ut in neumis conductorum et
similibus.
Cf. Franco (ed. Reaney/Gilles XI, 21-25): Discantus autem aut
fit cum littera, aut sine et cum littera. Si cum littera, hoc est
dupliciter: cum eadem vel cum diversis. Cum eadem littera fit
discantus in cantilenis, rondellis, et cantu aliquo ecclesiastico.
Cum diversis litteris fit discantus, ut in motetis qui habent triplum
vel tenorem, quia tenor cuidam litterae aequipollet. Cum littera et
sine fit discantus in conductis, et discantu aliquo ecclesiastico qui
improprie organum appellatur.
Cf. Anonymous IV (ed. Reckow 45, 16-18): Et notandum, quod
quaedam figurae accipiuntur sine litera et quaedam cum litera.

3-13   Cf. Johannes de Garlandia (ed. Reimer II, 4-9): Inter
figuras, quae sunt sine littera et cum littera, talis datur
differentia, quoniam ille, [*recte* illae] quae sunt sine littera,
debent, prout possunt, amplius ad invicem ligari. Sed huiusmodi
proprietas aliquando amittitur propter litteram huiusmodi figuris
associatam. Sed huiusmodi figurarum tam litterae societarum quam non

(Page 88:)

societarum dantur divisiones sequentes ac etiam regulae. Prima
divisio est haec: figurarum quaedam ligantur ad invicem, quaedam
non. Figura ligata est, ubicumque fit multitudo punctorum simul
iunctorum per suos tractus. Figura non ligata est, ubicumque non
fit multitudo punctorum etc. . . .
    Cf. Lambertus (ed. Reaney/Gilles IV 3, 3-5): Inter enim figuras
quae sunt cum littera, vel sine, talis datur differentia, quoniam
illae quae sunt sine littera debent prout possunt amplius ad invicem
ligari. Sed huius proprietas aliquando omittitur propter litteram
his figuris associatam. Et huius figurarum proprietas tam litterae
sociatarum quam non dantur divisiones ac etiam regulae sequentes.
    Cf. Franco (ed. Reaney/Gilles IV, 2): Figurarum aliae simplices,
aliae compositae.
    Cf. Franco (ed. Reaney/Gilles VII, 2): Ligatura est coniunctio
figurarum simplicium per tractus debitos ordinata.
    Cf. Anonymous IV (ed. Reckow 45, 18-19): Sine litera
coniunguntur in quantum possunt vel poterunt; cum litera quandoque
sic, quandoque non.

Page 90:

14-16   Cf. Franco (ed. Reaney/Gilles IV, 4): Simplicium tres sunt
    species, scilicet longa, brevis et semibrevis.

22-23   Cf. Johannes de Garlandia (ed. Reimer II, 12): Unde sequitur
    regula: omnis figura simplex portans tractum magis a parte dextra
    quam a sinistra semper significat longitudinem.
    Cf. Anonymous VII (ed. Coussemaker 379b): Figura continens in se
duo tempora, proprietas sua est quod habeat tractum a parte dextra,
et talis tractus dicitur signum longitudinis sue.

36-37   Cf. Lambertus (ed. Reaney/Gilles IV 3, 7): Quarum igitur prima
    super omnes fons est et origo ipsius scientiae atque finis, quae
    perfecta longa merito vocatur . . .

Page 92:

2-3   Cf. Johannes de Garlandia (ed. Reimer III, 9): . . . quia plica
    nihil aliud est quam signum dividens sonum in sono diverso.
    Cf. Lambertus (ed. Reaney/Gilles IV 8, 3): Unde notandum
quod plica nichil aliud est quam signum dividens sonum in sono
diverso . . .

9-12   Cf. Johannes de Garlandia (ed. Reimer II, 15): Plica longa
    dicitur illa, quae habet duplicem tractum, scilicet a parte dextra
    longiorem quam a sinistra, et est duplex, ascendendo et descendendo.

(Page 92:)

      Cf. Anonymous VII (ed. Reaney *8*, 13): Proprietas plicarum longarum tam ascendendo quam descendendo est quod habeant tractum longiorem a dextra quam a sinistra.

      Cf. Anonymous IV (ed. Reckow 44, 4-9): Iterato est et alia longa, quae significat duo tempora vel tria, ut supradictum est, quae dicitur plica ascendens vel descendens secundum quod aliqui dicunt. Et est illa, si fuerit ascendens, quae portat tractum ascendendo vel aliter cum duplici tractu ascendendo in dextera et sinistra; sed tractus in dextera, si fuerit longior, longitudinem significat . . .

22-26   Cf. Lambertus (ed. Reaney/Gilles IV *8*, 11): Ascendendo autem duos habet diversos, unum in dextera parte ascendendo significans plicam, alium in sinistra parte ascendendo significans brevitatem, ut hic [▌].

Page 94:

9-10   Cf. Johannes de Garlandia (ed. Reimer II, 18): Omnis figura brevis sumitur sine tractu praeter plicam, quae accipitur cum duplici tractu vel uno propter divisionem soni.

Page 98:

38-42   Cf. Lambertus (ed. Reaney/Gilles IV *3*, 6): Quapropter ad omnia discernenda prolata scire debemus quod sex tantummodo figurae sunt adinventae; quarum binae et binae semper sunt affines, etiam in forma et quantitate consimiles, sed in potestate, arte, regula differunt et natura.

Page 102:

30-31   Cf. Johannes de Garlandia (ed. Reimer I, 22): Ad quod dicendum, quod unum solum tempus, prout hic sumitur, est illud, in quo recta brevis habet fieri in tali tempore, quod fit indivisibile.

      Cf. Lambertus (ed. Reaney/Gilles IV *14*, 1-2): Quoniam fieri posset quaestio quid sit tempus, ad quod respondendum est quod tempus, ut hic sumitur, est quaedam proportio iusta in qua recta brevis habet fieri in tali videlicet proportione, quod possit dividi in duas partes non aequales vel in tres tantummodo aequales et indivisibiles, ita quod vox non alterius in tempore discretionem habere possit.

      Cf. Franco (ed. Reaney/Gilles V, 12): Unum tempus appellatur

(Page 102:)

illud quod est minimum in plenitudine vocis.

31-33   Cf. Johannes de Garlandia (ed. Reimer I, 20):   Recta vero brevis
est, quae unum solum tempus continet.
         Cf. Anonymous VII (ed. Reaney *1*, 6):   Recta brevis est illa quae
continet in se unum.
         Cf. Lambertus (ed. Reaney/Gilles IV *3*, 10):   Tertia recta
brevis dicitur, ab eo quod unum rectum et integrum continet in se
tempus . . .
         Cf. Franco (ed. Reaney/Gilles V, 10):   Recta brevis est quae unum
solum tempus continet . . .
         Cf. Anonymous IV (ed. Reckow 23, 7-8):   Brevis simplex est, quae
continet unum tempus in statu supradicto.

33-34   Cf. Johannes de Garlandia (ed. Reimer I, 23):   Sed huiusmodi
tempus habet fieri tripliciter: aliquando enim per rectam vocem,
aliquando per vocem cassam, aliquando per vocem amissam.
         Cf. Lambertus (ed. Reaney/Gilles IV *14*, 3):   Unde sciendum est
quod tempus habet fieri tripliciter: aliquando enim voce recta,
aliquando cassa, aliquando omissa.
         Cf. Franco (ed. Reaney/Gilles I, 5):   Tempus est mensura tam
vocis prolatae quam eius contrarii, scilicet vocis amissae, quae
pausa communiter appellatur.

41-44   Cf. Lambertus (ed. Reaney/Gilles IV *3*, 12):   Quinta
semibrevis maior dicitur, et hoc a semis, sema, semum quod est
imperfectum, et brevis quasi imperfecta brevis.
         Cf. Lambertus (ed. Reaney/Gilles IIIa *4*, A3):   Et dicitur
semitonium a semus, -ma, -mum, quod est imperfectum, et tonus, quasi
imperfectus tonus.

Page 104:

1-5   Cf. Lambertus (ed. Reaney/Gilles IV *3*, 7-8):   . . . nam a
perfectione trinae aequalitatis nomen habere sumpsit, eo quod sub
certa dimensione longitudinis unius per vocis accentum in mora trium
temporum aequaliter proportionata manet.   Seipsamque in novem partes
diminuendo dupliciter partiens . . .

6-7   Cf. Lambertus (ed. Reaney/Gilles IV *3*, 9):   . . . eo quod nisi
duo tempora continet in se, affinitatem forma et proprietate
perfectae figurae tenens . . .

8-10   Cf. Lambertus (ed. Reaney/Gilles IV *5*, 7):   Unde si quaerat
aliquis utrum posset fieri modus sive cantus naturalis de omnibus
imperfectis sicut fit de omnibus perfectis, responsio cum probatione
quod non, cum puras imperfectas nemo pronuntiare possit.

Page 106:

11-13   Cf. Lambertus (ed. Reaney/Gilles IV 5, 7): Unde si quaerat
aliquis utrum posset fieri modus sive cantus naturalis de omnibus
imperfectis sicut fit de omnibus perfectis, responsio cum probatione
quod non, cum puras imperfectas nemo pronuntiare possit.

Page 108:

18-22   Cf. Lambertus (ed. Reaney/Gilles IV 6, 2-3): Praeterea
notandum est quod perfecta figura in uno corpore quandoque duplicari
videtur . . . nisi quod ne in compositione sive ordinatione tenoris
plana musica frangatur . . .
        Cf. Franco (ed. Reaney/Gilles IV, 13): Duplex longa sic formata
duas longas significat, quae idcirco in uno corpore duplicatur, ne
series plani cantus sumpti in tenoribus disrumpatur.

24-25   Cf. Johannes de Garlandia (ed. Reimer II, 14): Duplex longa
est illa, quando latitudo transit longitudinem.
        Cf. Anonymous VII (ed. Reaney 8, 5): Figura continens in se sex
tempora sive duas longas debet esse latior quam sit longa cum cauda.
        Cf. Lambertus (ed. Reaney/Gilles IV 6, 2): . . . perfecta figura
. . . cuius latitudo transit longitudinem . . .
        Cf. Anonymous IV (ed. Reckow 44, 10-14): Iterato est et alia
longa, quae dicitur duplex longa, quae significat duplicem longam sex
temporum vel quinque ad minus. Et est illa, quae est nimis
protracta, ut videtur quasi essent duae longae vel tres in uno
quadrangulo iacentes cum tractu uno in parte destra [*sic*]
descendente.

Page 112:

1-6   Cf. Johannes de Garlandia (ed. Reimer II, 21-23): Figurarum
simul ligatarum quaedam dicitur ascendendo, quaedam descendendo.
Figura descendendo dicitur esse illa, quando secundus punctus
ligaturae inferior est primo. Ascendendo dicitur esse, quando
secundus punctus altior est primo.
        Cf. Anonymous VII (ed. Reaney 9, 3-5): Notandum quod quaedam
ligantur ascendendo, quaedam descendendo. Illa ligatura dicitur
ascendere cuius secundus punctus altior est quam primus. Illa
ligatura dicitur descendere cuius secundus punctus inferior est quam
sit primus.
        Cf. Franco (ed. Reaney/Gilles VII, 3-5): Ligaturarum alia
ascendens, alia descendens. Ascendens est illa cuius secundus
punctus altior est primo . . . Descendens vero est cuius primus
punctus altior est secundo . . .
        Cf. Anonymous IV (ed. Reckow 47, 7-10): Quae quidem reductio

(Page 112:)

> quandoque contingit, quando soni ponuntur in eodem sono, quoniam omnis ligatura dicitur ascendendo vel descendendo, ut superius dictum est. Sed quae sunt in eodem sono, non sunt ascendendo vel descendendo.

2-3   Cf. Johannes de Garlandia (ed. Reimer VI, 5-6): Item omnes voces, quae accipiuntur in eodem sono, non possunt ligari vel facere figuram compositam, quia omnis figura composita vel ligata dicitur ascendendo vel descendendo. Et quaecumque sunt in eodem sono, non sunt ascendendo vel descendendo, ergo ex his non fit ligatura, id est figura ligata.
> Cf. Anonymous IV (ed. Reckow 27, 22-23): . . . si fuerint in eodem sono, non coniunguntur actuali coniunctione penes materiam, sed subintelliguntur coniungi.
> Cf. Anonymous IV (ed. Reckow 47, 9-12): Sed quae sunt in eodem sono, non sunt ascendendo vel descendendo. Ergo ex ipsis non fit ligatura materialis, sed per reductionem longarum et brevium solo intellectu iuxta aequipollentiam bene ligantur.

7-8   Cf. Johannes de Garlandia (ed. Reimer II, 30): A parte finis etiam quatuor sunt species, quia quaedam dicitur cum plica, quaedam sine plica, quaedam perfecta circa finem, quaedam imperfecta circa finem.
> Cf. Franco (ed. Reaney/Gilles VII, 7): A parte autem finis: alia cum perfectione, alia sine.

34-35   Cf. Johannes de Garlandia (ed. Reimer VI, 1): Sed sciendum, quod numquam debet poni aliqua figura sine proprietate, ubi potest poni cum proprietate.
> Cf. Anonymous IV (ed. Reckow 52, 16-19): Est quaedam alia regula ad oppositum, quod nil debetis notare sine proprietate, quod potestis <notare> cum proprietate, et nil debemus facere sine perfectione, quod facere possumus cum perfectione.

Page 116:

8   Cf. Johannes de Garlandia (ed. Reimer III, 2): Omnis figura ligata cum proprietate posita et perfecta paenultima dicitur esse brevis et ultima longa.
> Cf. Anonymous VII (ed. Reaney 9, 12): . . . de tribus ligatis, ultima nota valet unam longam, et prima est longa et altera brevis.
> Cf. Anonymous IV (ed. Reckow 45, 23-25): . . . omnis figura ligata cum proprietate et perfectione sic est intelligenda: paenultima eius brevis est, ultima vero longa . . .

CHAPTER ONE, Part Two

Page 120:

33-37   Cf. Johannes de Garlandia (ed. Reimer II, 25): A parte principii quatuor sunt species, quia quaedam dicitur cum proprietate, id est cum proprietate propria, quaedam sine proprietate, quaedam per oppositum cum proprietate, quaedam sine opposito cum proprietate.
    Cf. Franco (ed. Reaney/Gilles VII, 6): Item ligaturarum alia cum proprietate, alia sine, alia cum opposita proprietate.
    Cf. Anonymous IV (ed. Reckow 45, 13-16): Figurarum simul ligatarum quaedam dicuntur cum proprietate propria a parte sui principii, quaedam sine proprietate, quaedam cum opposita proprietate etc. . . .

Page 122:

26-28   Cf. Johannes de Garlandia (ed. Reimer II, 27): Ascendendo proprietas est, ut nullum habeat tractum.
    Cf. Anonymous VII (ed. Coussemaker 380b): Proprietas ligature duarum ascendendo est quod ullum [*sic*] habeat tractum.
    Cf. Franco (ed. Reaney/Gilles VII, 19): Item omnis figura ascendens cum proprietate dicitur, si careat omni tractu . . .
    Cf. Anonymous IV (ed. Reckow 43, 2-4): . . . et si fuerit ascendens, et primus non habeat tractum suo modo, cum proprietate dicitur.

30-35   Cf. Johannes de Garlandia (ed. Reimer II, 26): Unde regula: omnis figurae descendendo proprietas est, ut primus punctus habeat tractum a latere sinistro.
    Cf. Anonymous VII (ed. Coussemaker I, 380b): Proprietas ligature trium descendendo est quod habeat tractum a parte sinistra.
    Cf. Franco (ed. Reaney/Gilles VII, 17): Omnis ligatura descendens tractum habens a primo punctu descendentem a parte sinistra, cum proprietate dicitur . . .
    Cf. Anonymous IV (ed. Reckow 43, 1-2): Unde regula: omnis figura descendens in principio, si primus punctus habeat tractum in sinistra parte, cum proprietate dicitur . . .

40-41   Cf. Johannes de Garlandia (ed. Reimer III, 2): Omnis figura ligata cum proprietate posita et perfecta paenultima dicitur esse brevis et ultima longa.
    Cf. Anonymous VII (ed. Reaney 9, 12): . . . de tribus ligatis, ultima nota valet unam longam, et prima est longa et altera brevis.
    Cf. Anonymous IV (ed. Reckow 45, 23-25): . . . omnis figura ligata cum proprietate et perfectione sic est intelligenda: paenultima eius brevis est, ultima vero longa . . .

Page 124:

40-41   Cf. Johannes de Garlandia (ed. Reimer VI, 8): Item omnis
    figura ligata ultra tres suo proprio modo reducitur ad tres per
    aequipollentiam.
        Cf. Anonymous VII (ed. Reaney *9*, 12): Et sciendum quod omnis
    ligatura excedens tres ligatas debet reduci ad tres ligatas.
        Cf. Anonymous IV (ed. Reckow 48, 4-5): Et notandum est, quod
    omnis ligatura ultra tres ad tres ligatas eiusdem speciei reducitur
    vel debet reduci, hoc est, quod omnis ligatura ultra tres cum
    proprietate et perfectione ad tres ligatas cum proprietate et
    perfectione reducitur quoad longitudinem et brevitatem earundem . . .

Page 126:

19-20   Cf. Johannes de Garlandia (ed. Reimer III, 3): Si sint ibi
    praecedentes vel praecedens, omnes ponuntur pro longa.
        Cf. Anonymous IV (ed. Reckow 45, 25-26): . . . praecedens vel
    praecedentes, si fuerint, pro longa habentur vel habeantur.

28-29   Cf. Lambertus (ed. Reaney/Gilles IV *12*, 3-4): . . . si in
    fronte primae figurae quinariae ligaturae proprietas extiterit . . .
    duae primae semibreves sunt inequales . . .

33-36   Cf. Johannes de Garlandia (ed. Reimer VI, 8): Item omnis
    figura ligata ultra tres suo proprio modo reducitur ad tres per
    aequipollentiam.

42-44   Cf. Johannes de Garlandia (ed. Reimer VI, 9): Item . . . duae
    ligatae sequentes reducuntur ad tres ligatas per aequipollentiam, et
    hoc est secundum propriam proprietatem . . .

Page 128:

19-20   Cf. Johannes de Garlandia (ed. Reimer VI, 1): Sed sciendum,
    quod numquam debet poni aliqua figura sine proprietate, ubi potest
    poni cum proprietate.
        Cf. Anonymous IV (ed. Reckow 52, 16-19): Est quaedam alia regula
    ad oppositum, quod nil debetis notare sine proprietate, quod potestis
    <notare> cum proprietate, et nil debemus facere sine perfectione,
    quod facere possumus cum perfectione.

Page 132:

38-41   Cf. Johannes de Garlandia (ed. Reimer II, 28):   Ascendendo
    sine proprietate, ut habeat tractum, descendendo, ut non habeat.

Page 134:

8-9   Cf. Johannes de Garlandia (ed. Reimer VI, 2):   Alia regula,
    quod numquam ponatur simplex vel non ligata, ubi potest poni ligata
    vel composita.
        Cf. Anonymous IV (ed. Reckow 52, 15-16):   . . . regula est
    quaedam apud tales: nil debemus disiungere, quod iungere possumus.

Page 142:

10-11   Cf. Johannes de Garlandia (ed. Reimer VI, 1):   Sed sciendum,
    quod numquam debet poni aliqua figura sine proprietate, ubi potest
    poni cum proprietate.
        Cf. Anonymous IV (ed. Reckow 52, 16-19):   Est quaedam alia regula
    ad oppositum, quod nil debetis notare sine proprietate, quod potestis
    <notare> cum proprietate, et nil debemus facere sine perfectione,
    quod facere possumus cum perfectione.

23-28   Cf. Johannes de Garlandia (ed. Reimer II, 29):   Ascendendo
    vel descendendo dicitur per oppositum cum proprietate, ut primus
    punctus habeat tractum ascendendo a latere sinistro . . .
        Cf. Franco (ed. Reaney/Gilles VII, 21):   Item omnis ligatura tam
    ascendens quam descendens, tractum gerens a primo puncto ascendentem,
    cum opposita proprietate dicitur . . .

Page 144:

12-15   Cf. Lambertus (ed. Reaney/Gilles IV 9, 19):   Prima autem
    minor semibrevis dicitur, secunda maior, vel e converso, quia ambae
    nisi solo tempore mensurantur, nisi quod aliquando pro altera brevi
    ponantur; tunc enim duo tempora compleantur.
        Cf. Lambertus (ed.Reaney/Gilles IV 7, 3-6):   Seipsamque [rectam
    brevem] in duas diminuit partes non aequales vel in tres tantummodo
    aequales et indivisibiles.   Quarum prima pars duarum semibrevis minor
    appellatur, secunda vero maior, et e converso . . . Et sic binarius
    non aequalis seu ternarius aequalis semibrevium figurarum semper ad
    rectam brevem aequipollere debet . . . vel ad alteram brevem . . .

Page 146:

31-34   Cf. Anonymous IV (ed. Reckow 23, 7-11): Brevis simplex est,
quae continet unum tempus in statu supradicto . . . quod potest
frangi . . . in duobus, in tribus vel quatuor <ad> plus in voce
humana . . .

Page 148:

4-5   Cf. Lambertus (ed. Reaney/Gilles IV *9*, 19): Prima autem
minor semibrevis dicitur, secunda maior, vel e converso, quia ambae
nisi solo tempore mensurantur . . .

17   Cf. Lambertus (ed. Reaney/Gilles IIIa *14*, 4): . . . statim
offendit animam et generatur in sensu particulari, utpote in aure,
dissonantia quae cacophonia appellatur; a cacos, quod est malum, et
phonos, quod est sonus, quasi malus sonus.

Page 150:

29-30   Cf. Johannes de Garlandia (ed. Reimer XIII, 11): Longae
et breves in organo tali modo dinoscuntur, scilicet per
<concordantiam>, per figuram, per paenultimam.

30-32   Cf. Johannes de Garlandia (ed. Reimer XIII, 4): Organum per se
dicitur id esse, quidquid profertur secundum aliquem modum non
rectum, sed non rectum.

Page 152:

17-18   Cf. Johannes de Garlandia (ed. Reimer VI, 1): Sed sciendum,
quod numquam debet poni aliqua figura sine proprietate, ubi potest
poni cum proprietate.
         Cf. Anonymous IV (ed. Reckow 52, 16-19): Est quaedam alia regula
ad oppositum, quod nil debetis notare sine proprietate, quod potestis
<notare> cum proprietate, et nil debemus facere sine perfectione,
quod facere possumus cum perfectione.

26-29   Cf. Johannes de Garlandia (ed. Reimer II, 36): Perfecta
ascendendo est illa, quando ultimus punctus stat perpendiculariter
supra paenultimam.
         Cf. Franco (ed. Reaney/Gilles VII, 22): Omnis ligatura ultimum
punctum recte gerens supra penultimum est perfecta . . .
         Cf. Anonymous IV (ed. Reckow 43, 4-6): Perfectio figurae in fine

(Page 152:)

>   dinoscitur: si ascendat in fine, et ultimus recte se habeat
>   iacendo supra paenultimam, perfectionem eius denotat . . .

Page 154:

10-15   Cf. Johannes de Garlandia (ed. Reimer II, 37): Imperfecta
     est, quando stat obliquo modo.
          Cf. Franco (ed. Reaney/Gilles VII, 23): Imperfecta autem
     redditur ligatura duobus modis: . . . secundo vero si duo ultima
     puncta ligaturae in uno corpore obliquo ascendente commiscentur . . .

25-28   Cf. Franco (ed. Reaney/Gilles VIII, 3): Plicatur enim
     ligatura perfecta dupliciter, ascendendo et descendendo.
          Cf. Franco (ed. Reaney/Gilles VIII, 2): Quid autem sit plica
     dictum est prius in capitulo de simplicibus figuris.

Page 158:

1-2   Cf. Johannes de Garlandia (ed. Reimer II, 31): Cum plica
     dicitur esse illa, quando ultimus punctus portat tractum a parte
     dextra, et hoc est dupliciter, aut ascendendo aut descendendo.

Page 178:

39-40   Cf. Johannes de Garlandia (ed. Reimer VI, 1): Sed sciendum,
     quod numquam debet poni aliqua figura sine proprietate, ubi potest
     poni cum proprietate.
          Cf. Anonymous IV (ed. Reckow 52, 16-19): Est quaedam alia regula
     ad oppositum, quod nil debetis notare sine proprietate, quod potestis
     <notare> cum proprietate, et nil debemus facere sine perfectione,
     quod facere possumus cum perfectione.

Page 182:

14-16   Cf. Johannes de Garlandia (ed. Reimer VI, 2): Alia regula,
     quod numquam ponatur simplex vel non ligata, ubi potest poni ligata
     vel composita.
          Cf. Anonymous IV (ed. Reckow 52, 15-16): . . . regula est
     quaedam apud tales: nil debemus disiungere, quod iungere possumus.

(Page 182:)

27-30   Cf. Johannes de Garlandia (ee. Reimer VI, 7): Item omnis
figura non ligata debet reduci ad figuram compositam per
aequipollentiam.

35-36   Cf. Johannes de Garlandia (ed. Reimer VI, 2): Alia regula,
quod numquam ponatur simplex vel non ligata, ubi potest poni ligata
vel composita.
        Cf. Anonymous IV (ed. Reckow 52, 15-16): . . . regula est
quaedam apud tales: nil debemus disiungere, quod iungere possumus.

CHAPTER TWO

Page 184:

13-15   Cf. Lambertus (ed. Reaney/Gilles IV *1*, 4): . . . ac
etiam orthographiam cognoscere et conservare et regulariter eam
describere . . .
        Cf. Elias Salamon (ed. Gerbert III, 18a): Quid est littera?
Minima pars vocis compositae, quae scribi non potest, ideo subiectum
puncti appellatur.

20-25   Cf. Johannes de Garlandia (ed. Reimer I,5): Sed quia in
huiusmodi discantu consistit maneries sive modus, in primis videndum
est, quid sit modus sive maneries, et de speciebus ipsius modi sive
maneriei et gratia huiusmodi maneriei ac specierum eius plura alia
videbimus.
        Cf. Lambertus (ed. Reaney/Gilles IV *16*, 1-2): Cum superius
declaratum sit de omni genere figurarum et de temporibus et mensura,
ac etiam de plicis, et in huius consistit modus seu maneries, et
modus consistat in sonorum modulatione et vocum discretione. Nunc
autem videndum est quid sit modus et quot sint, et qualiter a
principali figura omnes modi constare videntur.
        Cf. Franco (ed. Reaney/Gilles II, 3): Sed quia quilibet
discantus per modos procedit, idcirco primo de modis et consequenter
de eorum signis, scilicet de figuris, est tractandum.

26-27   Cf. Johannes de Garlandia (ed. Reimer I, 6): Maneries eius
appellatur, quidquid mensuratione temporis, videlicet per longas vel
per breves, concurrit.
        Cf. Anonymous VII (ed. Coussemaker I, 378a): Modus in musica est
debita mensuratio temporis, scilicet per longas et breves; vel
aliter: modus est quidquid currit per debitam mensuram longarum
notarum et brevium.
        Cf. Lambertus (ed. Reaney/Gilles IV *16*, 3): Modus autem seu
maneries, ut hic sumitur, est quidquid per debitam mensuram

(Page 184:)

  temporalem longarum breviumque figurarum et semibrevium
transcurrit.
    Cf. Anonymous IV (ed. Reckow 22, 7-9): . . . modus vel maneries
vel temporis consideratio est cognitio longitudinis et brevitatis
meli sonique.

27-29 Cf. Lambertus (ed. Reaney/Gilles IIIb *1*, 3): . . . quoniam
  modus dicitur discretio modulationis a moderando, eo quod omnis
  cantus regularis ecclesiasticus et quaelibet res naturalis per modum
  seu per modos regulariter discernitur ac moderatur . . .

Page 186:

14-15 Cf. Anonymous VII (ed. Reaney *2*, 2): Primus modus
  appellatur primus quia levior est omnibus aliis . . .

Page 188:

44-46 Cf. Johannes de Garlandia (ed. Reimer I, 17): Recta mensura
  appellatur, quidquid per rectam mensuram rectae longae vel rectae
  brevis profertur.

Page 192:

7-20 Cf. Lambertus (ed. Reaney/Gilles P *2*, 2): Nam sicut in arbore
  una natura virtutem multarum vegetativam propaginum complantavit,
  sic in homine ratio ex unius *scientia* scientiam rerum multarum
  docuit invenire.
    Cf. Lambertus (ed. Reaney/Gilles P *4*, 2): Nam qui vineam
plantare vel unam arbusculam inserere vel unum asinum *onerare*
cognoverit, sicut in uno ita in omnibus facere, vel melius, non
dubitabit.

Page 194:

40-42 Cf. Johannes de Garlandia (ed. Reimer I, 32): Modus
  perfectus dicitur esse, quandocumque ita est, quod aliquis modus
  desinit per talem quantitatem vel per talem modum sicut per illam,
  qua incipit.
    Cf. Lambertus (ed. Reaney/Gilles IV *16*, 7): Perfectus vero est

(Page 194:)

   ille qui habet fieri et finire recto moderamine et per talem
   quantitatem, numerum et maneriem, sicut per qualem incipit.
       Cf. Anonymous IV (ed. Reckow 23, 22-23): Modorum . . . Perfectus
   dicitur, quando terminatur per eandem quantitatem, qua incipit.

Page 196:

1-2   Cf. Johannes de Garlandia (ed. Reimer I, 34): Omnis modus
         dicitur imperfectus, quandocumque ita est, quod aliquis modus desinit
         per aliam quantitatem quam per illam, qua incipit . . .
             Cf. Anonymous IV (ed. Reckow 23, 23-24): Imperfectus vero
         dicitur, quando per aliam terminatur quam per illam, in qua incipit.

7-11   Cf. Johannes de Garlandia (ed. Reimer I, 10): Prima enim
         procedit ex una longa et altera brevi et altera longa, et sic usque
         in infinitum.

19-21   Cf. Anonymous VII (ed. Reaney 5, 4-5): Aequipollentia enim
         intelligenda est in omnibus modis. Aequipollentia dico ut, si non
         sequatur post unam longam duae breves per ordinem, accipiatur illud
         quod loco duarum brevium invenitur . . .
             Cf. Franco (ed. Reaney/Gilles XIII, 8): Et notandum quod in
         omnibus istis observanda est aequipollentia in temporibus . . .

29-31   Cf. Johannes de Garlandia (ed. Reimer I, 29): Prima vero
         talis est: longa ante longam valet longam et brevem.
             Cf. Anonymous VII (ed. Reaney 3, 1): In isto primo modo sex
         dantur regulae, quarum prima est: longa ante longam valet longam et
         brevem.
             Cf. Lambertus (ed. Reaney/Gilles IV 4, 14): Eius autem regula
         talis est et natura, quod quandocunque *longa perfecta* reperta est
         ante longam semper tria tempora tenet . . .
             Cf. Franco (ed. Reaney/Gilles V, 3): Si autem longam longa
         sequatur, tunc prima longa sub uno accentu tribus temporibus
         mensuratur et perfecta longa nuncupatur . . .

32-33   Cf. Johannes de Garlandia (ed. Reimer VII, 9): Unde regula:
         Omnis pausatio simplex debet esse aequalis paenultimae modi
         praecedentis.
             Cf. Anonymous VII (ed. Reaney 3, 2): Secunda regula est: tanta
         est pausa, quanta est penultima.

45-46   Cf. Boethius, *Philosophiae Consolatio* IV, ii, 36 (ed. Rapisarda
         130): Est enim, quod ordinem retinet servatque naturam; quod vero ab
         hac deficit, esse etiam, quod in sua natura situm est, derelinquit.
             Cf. Anonymous VII (ed. Reaney 3, 3-4): . . . quod in omnibus
         modis ordo debet teneri. Quilibet enim modus habet suum ordinem.
             Cf. Lambertus (ed. Reaney/Gilles IV 1, 1): Cum secundum quod
         dicit Boetius nichil est quod non retinet ordinem, servatque naturam

(Page 196:)

> summopere in cunctis actibus humanis, ordo considerari debet ne quod
> actum est nichil esse per dictum Boetii perfectum ordinis arguatur.

Page 198:

1-3   Cf. Johannes de Garlandia (ed. Reimer IV, 2): Unde prima regula
primi modi dicitur esse tres ligatae ad invicem in principio et in
posterum cum duabus et duabus ligatis etc., et hoc totum cum
proprietate et perfectione . . .
    Cf. Anonymous IV (ed. Reckow 51, 16-18): Primus modus formalis
capituli primi sic per puncta materialia proprie figuratur: tres
ligatae cum proprietate et perfectione, postmodum duae ligatae cum
proprietate et perfectione . . .

Page 200:

11-13   Cf. Johannes de Garlandia (ed. Reimer XI, 13): Unde
regula: omne, quod fit impari, debet concordari omni illi, quod fit
in impari . . .

23-26   Cf. Johannes de Garlandia (ed. Reimer I, 10-11): Prima enim
procedit ex una longa et altera brevi et altera longa, et sic usque
in infinitum. Secunda autem e converso, videlicet ex una brevi et
altera longa et altera brevi.
    Cf. Anonymous IV (ed. Reckow 22, 9-11): Primus constat ex longa
brevi, longa brevi, longa brevi etc. Secundus constat ex brevi
longa, brevi longa, brevi longa etc.

29-35   Cf. Johannes de Garlandia (ed. Reimer IV, 4): Secundi modi
prima regula sumitur ita: duae et duae cum proprietate etc. et tres
in fine sine proprietate et <perfectae> . . .
    Cf. Anonymous IV (ed. Reckow 51, 30-31): Principium secundi
<modi> sic figuratur: duae, duae, duae etc. cum proprietate et
perfectione et tres in fine sine proprietate et cum perfectione.

Page 204:

25-26   Cf. Johannes de Garlandia (ed. Reimer I, 12): Tertia ex una
longa et duabus brevibus et altera longa.
    Cf. Anonymous IV (ed. Reckow 22, 11-12): Tertius constat ex
longa et duabus brevibus, longa et duabus brevibus etc.

Page 208:

1   Cf. Johannes de Garlandia (ed. Reimer VIII, 3):   Pausationum vel
            tractuum . . . quaedam divisio modorum . . .

22-24   Cf. Johannes de Garlandia (ed. Reimer I, 14):   Quinta ex omnibus
            longis.
                    Cf. Anonymous IV (ed. Reckow 22, 13-14):   Quintus ex longa,
            longa, longa etc.

Page 210:

18-20   Cf. Johannes de Garlandia (ed. Reimer I, 15):   Sexta ex omnibus
            brevibus.
                    Cf. Anonymous IV (ed. Reckow 22, 14):   Sextus ex brevi, brevi,
            brevi etc.

31-34   Cf. Johannes de Garlandia (ed. Reimer IV, 10-11):   Sextus
            sumitur hoc modo . . . Alia regula de eodem . . . scilicet quatuor
            ligatae cum proprietate et postea tres et tres et tres cum
            proprietate etc. . . .
                    Cf. Anonymous IV (ed. Reckow 56, 11-13):   . . . quidam posuerunt
            quatuor ligatas in principio sine tractu et postmodum tres ligatas,
            tres, tres semper cum proprietate et perfectione.   Et per istam
            figurationem intelligebant sextum modum.

Page 212:

25-30   Cf. Lambertus (ed. Reaney/Gilles IV *16*, 4-5):   Unde notandum,
            quod ad similitudinem naturalium instrumentorum novem modos esse
            dicimus adinventos.   Ad quorum cognitionem discernendam et multorum
            etiam errorem distruendum, tres liberaliores excipiuntur: scilicet
            primus, quartus et septimus.

32-33   Cf. Lambertus (ed. Reaney/Gilles IV *16*, 9):   Primus modus
            dicitur qui tantum componitur perfectis figuris . . .

35-36   Cf. Lambertus (ed. Reaney/Gilles IV *16*, 33):
            Octavus inaequalibus
            binis semibrevibus
            semper potietur:

37   Cf. Lambertus (ed. Reaney/Gilles IV *16*, 35):
            Nonus semibrevibus
            tribus et aequalibus
            sic perficietur:

(Page 212:)

43-45   Cf. Lambertus (ed. Reaney/Gilles IV *16*, 37): Notandum autem
   quod nullus aut raro cantus aliquis perfectus sive motellus ex istis
   duobus ultimis invenitur, propter difficultatem semibrevitatis.
        Cf. Lambertus (ed. Reaney/Gilles IV *16*, 9): Primus modus dicitur
   qui tantum componitur perfectis figuris . . .
        Cf. Lambertus (ed. Reaney/Gilles IV *5*, 7): Unde si quaerat
   aliquis, utrum posset fieri modus sive cantus naturalis de omnibus
   imperfectis sicut fit de omnibus perfectis, responsio cum probatione
   quod non, . . .

Page 216:

14-20   Cf. Anonymous VII (ed. Reaney 7, 7-8): Notandum est quod
   motellus, cuiuscunque modi sit, debet iudicari de eodem modo de quo
   est tenor. Et ratio est quia tenor est fundamentum motelli et
   dignior pars, et a digniori et nobiliori debet res denominari.

23-29   Cf. Johannes de Garlandia (ed. Reimer XI, 16-31): Et notandum,
   quod sunt tres species discantus: aut rectus modus contra rectum,
   aut modus per ultra mensuram contra modum per ultra mensuram, aut
   rectus contra per ultra mensuram. Rectus ad rectum sumitur
   dupliciter: aut eodem ordine, aut ordine converso. Rectus ad rectum
   eodem ordine sumitur dupliciter: aut aliquis rectus ad se ipsum aut
   ad reliquum. Ad se ipsum hoc est tripliciter: aut primus contra
   primum, aut secundus contra secundum, aut sextus contra sextum.
   Rectus ad reliquum sumitur dupliciter: aut primus contra sextum, aut
   secundus contra sextum.
        Cf. Anonymous IV (ed. Reckow 76, 7-20): Et notandum est, quod
   discantus cum tenore multas et plures considerationes habet. Una
   est, quando in discantu et in tenore fuerit modus rectus, id est, cum
   fuerit ex utraque parte modus secundum longitudinem rectarum longarum
   et rectarum brevium, et sic dicitur rectus ad rectum. Est et alius
   modus, qui dicitur habundans supra rectam mensuram rectae
   longitudinis et rectae brevitatis, et dicitur contra ultra mensuram,
   vel potest dici modus obliquus transumptive, et sic obliquus ad
   obliquum. Tertius modus de utroque supradictorum. Rectus ad rectum
   multiplex est: aut primus cum primo vel contra primum, vel secundus
   contra secundum, aut sextus contra sextum. Alio modo a diverso ad
   diversum ut primus contra secundum, primus contra sextum et
   secundus ad sextum cum subversionibus illorum . . .

29-33   Cf. Johannes de Garlandia (ed. Reimer XI, 87): Rectus modus ad
   modum per ultra mensuram dicitur dupliciter: aut eodem ordine, aut
   ordine converso.

33-38   Cf. Johannes de Garlandia (ed. Reimer XI, 55-64): Modus per
   ultra mensuram ad <modum per ultra mensuram> sumitur dupliciter: aut
   eodem ordine, aut ordine converso. Eodem ordine sumitur dupliciter:
   aut ad se ipsum aut ad reliquum. Ad se ipsum dicitur tripliciter:

(Page 216:)

> aut tertius ad se ipsum, aut quartus ad se ipsum, aut quintus ad
> se ipsum. Modus per ultra mensuram ad reliquum in eodem ordine
> dicitur dupliciter: aut tertius ad quintum, aut quartus ad
> quintum.
>
> Cf. Anonymous IV (ed. Reckow 76, 17-33): Sunt quidam alii modi
> ultra rectam mensuram se habentes, quamvis aliquam participationem
> habeant cum praedictis etc. Et sunt tertius, quartus et quintus. Et
> dicimus, quod fit triplici modo ut de aliis: ad idem ut tertius
> contra tertium, quartus contra quartum, quintus contra quintum; ad
> diversum sic: tertius contra quartum, tertius contra quintum,
> quartus contra tertium, quartus contra quintum, quintus contra
> tertium, quintus contra quartum.

38-42   Cf. Johannes de Garlandia (ed. Reimer XI, 98-100): Impar contra
imparem dicitur dupliciter: aut primus tertio in tantum quod primus
aequipollet debito ordine sexto et sextus tertio mediante secundo, et
ita sumitur primus tertio, sed non proprie sed per reductionem
dicitur, aut primus quinto. Primus tertio dicitur dupliciter: aut
primus loco primi et tertius secundi, aut tertius loco primi et
primus secundo.

> Cf. Anonymous IV (ed. Reckow 76, 34 - 77, 2): Rectus contra
> ultra mensuram vel obliquum multis modis: primus contra tertium,
> primus contra quartum, primus contra quintum; aliter: secundus
> contra tertium vel quartum vel quintum, sextus contra tertium vel
> quartum vel quintum.

Page 220:

3-6   Cf. Johannes de Garlandia (ed. Reimer XI, 10): In modo, ut sit
longa contra longam vel breves aequipollentes longae.

23-25   Cf. Anonymous IV (ed. Reckow 61, 8-9): . . . qui sciunt
reducere vel facere mutando de uno modo alium . . .

Page 222:

9-12   Cf. Franco (ed. Reaney/Gilles XI, 36): Notandum quod tam in
discantu quam in triplicibus etc. inspicienda est aequipollentia in
perfectionibus longarum, brevium et semibrevium . . .

Page 224:

8-17   Cf. Lambertus (ed. Reaney/Gilles IV *17*, 1):   Cum dictum sit
    superius de diversitate multiplicium figurarum, et de modis et multis
    aliis praecedentibus, nunc autem dicendum est de quadam armonia
    resecata quae, quantum ad nos, hokettus vulgariter appellatur.

18-19   Cf. Isidore of Seville, *Etymologiae,* (ed. Lindsay III, xx, 4-5):
    Harmonica est modulatio vocis et concordantia plurimorum sonorum, vel
    coaptatio.

Page 230:

19-21   Cf. Anonymous IV (ed. Reckow 61, 8-9):   . . . qui sciunt
    reducere vel facere mutando de uno modo alium ut illi, qui dicunt
    secundum modum de quinto . . .

Page 236:

35-37   Cf. Franco (ed. Reaney/Gilles V, 21):   De semibrevibus autem et
    brevibus idem est iudicium in regulis prius dictis.

CHAPTER THREE

Page 244:

9-10   Cf. Johannes de Garlandia (ed. Reimer VII, 10):   Si autem
    modus ante pausationem sit perfectus, et pausatio dicitur perfecta,
    si vero sit imperfectus, et pausatio erit imperfecta.
        Cf. Anonymous IV (ed. Reckow 58, 29 - 59, 3):   Unde regula: si
    modus sit perfectus ante vel imperfectus, et post inceperit, sicut
    ante terminaverit, pausatio erit perfecta; et si distinguitur a modo
    ante dicto et post, sic erit <im>perfecta et contraria eisdem in situ
    longarum et brevium eiusdem.

12-13   Cf. Johannes de Garlandia (ed. Reimer VII, 1-2):   Sequitur
    de pausationibus.   Unde primo videndum est, quid sit pausatio.

14-16   Cf. Johannes de Garlandia (ed. Reimer VII, 3):   Pausatio est
    dimissio soni facta in debita quantitate.
        Cf. Anonymous IV (ed. Reckow 57, 9-11):   . . . pausatio est quies

(Page 244:)

vel dimissio soni in debita quantitate temporis vel temporum longae
vel brevis alicuius modi modorum sex supradictorum.
    Cf. Franco (ed. Reaney/Gilles IX, 2): Pausa est obmissio vocis
rectae in debita quantitate alicuius modi facta.

Page 246:

23-25   Cf. Johannes de Garlandia (ed. Reimer VII, 5): Pausatio simplex
    dicitur, quando pausatur secundum quantitatem unius alicuius modi
    sive maneriei.
        Cf. Anonymous IV (ed. Reckow 57, 13-14): Simplex modus
    pausationis est, quando fit pausatio ad quantitatem unius longae vel
    brevis alicuius modi supradictorum.

29-31   Cf. Johannes de Garlandia (ed. Reimer VII, 6-7): Simplicium
    quaedam dicitur perfecta, quaedam imperfecta. Perfecta dicitur illa,
    quae non transmutat modum propter sui adventum, sed aequalem
    praecedenti, quando advenit, repraesentat, vel quando reddit talem
    modum post sicut et ante.
        Cf. Anonymous IV (ed. Reckow 57, 21-23): Unde regula: omnis
    pausatio primi modi vel secundi etc., si reddiderit talem modum post
    se sicut ante, perfecta dicitur vel perfecta debet dici.

32-35   Cf. Johannes de Garlandia (ed. Reimer VIII, 4-5): Recta
    brevis [pausatio] est tractus respiciens longitudinem secundum
    latitudinem unius spatii. Longa est tractus respiciens longitudinem
    duorum spatiorum vel plurium.
        Cf. Anonymous IV (ed. Reckow 60, 20-25): Simplex pausatio vel
    tractus materialis <fit> secundum distantiam latitudinis unius spatii
    et est unius temporis tantum. Quod si fuerit tractus longus secundum
    distantiam ab aliqua regula in tertiam vel duorum spatiorum, duorum
    temporum erit; si fuerit longus ab aliqua regula in quartam vel iuxta
    similitudinem longitudinis eiusdem, trium temporum erit.

Page 248:

26-32   Cf. Johannes de Garlandia (ed. Reimer VIII, 2-3): Unde
    figura pausationis est signum vel tractus significans dimissionem
    soni factam in debita quantitate. Pausationum vel tractuum quaedam
    dicitur recta brevis, quaedam longa, quaedam finis punctorum, quaedam
    divisio modorum, quaedam divisio sillabarum, quaedam suspiratio.
        Cf. Franco (ed. Reaney/Gilles IX, 3): Pausationum sex sunt
    species . . . et finis punctorum.

40-44   Cf. Lambertus (ed. Reaney/Gilles IV *14*, 9-13): Quarum prima
    perfecta pausa vocatur, continens in longitudinem quinque lineas, a

(Page 248:)

> summo usque deorsum, habens omnem potestatem, regulam et naturam,
> quam habet perfecta figura. Secunda vero pausula imperfecta
> nominatur, quae summitatem continet quatuor linearum, habens
> potestatem imperfectae figure, et illius quae vocatur altera
> brevis. Tertia vero suspirium breve nuncupatur, continens
> summitatem trium linearum, et ponitur pro brevi recta. Quarta
> est semisuspirium maius, continens summitatem duarum, et ponitur
> pro semibrevi maiore. Quinta est semisuspirium minus quod inter
> duas lineas medium tenet, et ponitur pro semibrevi minore, quod
> est indivisibile.

Page 252:

29-38   Cf. Lambertus (ed. Reaney/Gilles IV *17*, 5-8): Quandocunque
inter duas longas figuras suspirium non in medio, sed iuxta latus
alicuius figurae positum invenitur, illa figura cuius tractus
propinquior erit, suspirium obtinet. Ut pote si tractus propinquior
figurae praecedentis extiterit, a parte finis eiusdem sumetur; si
autem propinquior figurae subsequentis extiterit, tunc a parte
principii sumetur eiusdem . . .
>   Et per hoc intelligendum est quod nullus tractus inter duas
> figuras medium tenere debet, sed iuxta illam a qua sumitur stare
> tenetur, ut patet in IN SECULUM, et in eiusdem tertia conversione
> secundi modi. Quoniam si medium teneret, tunc fieri posset
> ambiguitas utrum tempus sumeretur a praecedenti figura vel a
> subsequenti.

44-47   Cf. Capella (ed. Eyssenhardt IX, 969): Dividitur sane
numerus in oratione per syllabas, in modulatione per arsin ac thesin,
in gestu figuris determinatis schematisque conpletur.

Page 254:

30-31   Cf. Johannes de Garlandia (ed. Reimer VII, 13): Pausatio
composita vel duplex dicitur, quando simplex duplatur vel triplatur
vel quadruplatur etc.
>   Cf. Anonymous IV (ed. Reckow 58, 18-19): Duplex pausatio est,
> quando simplex, sive fuerit longa vel brevis, duplatur vel triplatur
> vel quadruplatur etc. . . . .

40-44   Cf. Johannes de Garlandia (ed. Reimer VIII, 7): Divisio modorum,
cum tractus obliquo modo positus, et hoc in inferiori parte et minor
apparet recta brevi.

Page 254, 46-
Page 256:

1   Cf. Johannes de Garlandia (ed. Reimer VIII, 9): Suspiratio
est apparentia pausationis sine existentia, et hoc est propositum,
quia suspiratio potest fieri cum tractu vel sine, et maior <vel>
minor rectae brevis potest esse suspiratio.
         Cf. Anonymous IV (ed. Reckow 61, 13): Est et alia pausatio, quae
videtur esse pausatio et non est, et vocatur suspirium.

29   Cf. Johannes de Garlandia (ed. Reimer VIII, 3): Pausationum
vel tractuum . . . quaedam divisio sillabarum . . .

                              CHAPTER FOUR

Page 258:

15-20   Cf. Johannes de Garlandia (ed. Reimer IX, 2):
Consonantiarum quaedam dicuntur concordantiae, quaedam discordantiae.
Concordantia dicitur esse, quando duae voces iunguntur in eodem
tempore, ita quod una vox potest compati cum alia secundum auditum.
Discordantia dicitur contrario modo.
         Cf. Johannes de Garlandia (ed. Reimer IX, 25): Discordantia
dicitur esse, quando duae voces iunguntur in eodem tempore, ita quod
secundum auditum una vox non potest compati cum alia.
         Cf. Lambertus (ed. Reaney/Gilles IIIa *14*, 1-3): Istarum autem
specierum quaedam sunt concordantes, quaedam discordantes, quaedam
magis, quaedam minus. Concordantia vero dicitur esse, quando duae
voces in eodem tempore compatiuntur, ita quod una cum alia secundum
auditum suavem reddat melodiam: tunc est consonantia. Discordantia
vero per oppositum dicitur . . . scilicet quandocumque voces in
eodem tempore iunguntur, ita quod secundum auditum una cum alia non
compatitur, tunc est dissonantia.
         Cf. Franco (ed. Reaney/Gilles XI, 3-4): Concordantia dicitur
esse quando duae voces vel plures in uno tempore prolatae se compati
possunt secundum auditum. Discordantia vero e contrario dicitur,
scilicet quando duae voces sic conjunguntur quod discordant
secundum auditum.

24-25   Cf. Johannes de Garlandia (ed. Reimer IX, 5):
Concordantiarum triplex est modus, quia quaedam sunt perfectae,
quaedam imperfectae, quaedam mediae.
         Cf. Franco (ed. Reaney/Gilles XI, 5): Concordantiarum tres sunt
species, scilicet perfecta, imperfecta et media.
         Cf. Anonymous IV (ed. Reckow 85, 32-33): . . . istae sex
dicuntur primae concordantiae, et dicuntur perfectae et imperfectae
<et> mediae . . .

Page 260:

1-3   Cf. Johannes de Garlandia (ed. Reimer IX, 1):   Sequitur de
    consonantiis in eodem tempore.
        Cf. Franco (ed. Reaney/Gilles XI, 2):   Sed quia discantus
    quilibet per consonantias regulatur, videndum est de consonantiis et
    dissonantiis factis in eodem tempore et in diversis vocibus.

28-31   Cf. Lambertus (ed. Reaney/Gilles IIIa *14*, 9):   Sciendum est
    autem quod sicut sex sunt voces quibus tota musica conformatur, ita
    et sex tantummodo sunt concordantiae quarum tres primae genera sunt
    generalissima omnium concordantiarum . . .

35-37   Cf. Guido of Arezzo (ed. van Waesberghe IV, 12):   Habes
    itaque sex vocum consonantias, id est tonum, semitonium, ditonum,
    semiditonum, diatessaron et diapente.
        Cf. Johannes de Garlandia (ed. Reimer IX, 12):   Sic apparet, quod
    sex sunt species concordantiae, scilicet unisonus, diapason,
    diapente, diatesseron, ditonus, semiditonus.

37-40   Cf. Lambertus (ed. Reaney/Gilles IIIa *14*, 7-10):   Mediae vero
    sunt ditonus et semiditonium . . . omnium concordantiarum.   . . .
    Prima scilicet est dyatessaron, secunda dyapente, tertia dyapason,
    quarta dyatessaron cum dyapason, quinta dyapente cum dyapason, sexta
    bis dyapason.

Page 262:

5-12   Cf. Anonymous IV (ed. Reckow 77, 28 - 78, 1):   . . . vel
semiditono ditono <pro concordantiis imperfectis>, quamvis ditonus et
semiditonus apud aliquos non sic reputantur.

13-38   Cf. Capella (ed. Eyssenhardt IX, 932-934).
        Cf. Cassiodorus (ed. Mynors II, 7).
        Cf. Guido of Arezzo (ed. van Waesberghe VI, 6-11).
        Cf. Lambertus (ed. Reaney/Gilles IIIa *5*, 1 - *13*, 5).
        Cf. Anonymous IV (ed. Reckow 69, 5-14).
        Cf. Anonymous II (ed. Coussemaker 308a-309a).

Page 264:

2-4   Cf. Capella (ed. Eyssenhardt IX, 930):   Verum tonus est
    spatium cum legitima quantitate . . .
        Cf. Lambertus (ed. Reaney/Gilles IIIa *3*, 1-2):   Tonus autem
    est perfectum spatium duarum vocum, duo semitonia continens non
    aequalia.   Est enim tonus quaedam percussio aeris indissoluta usque
    ad auditum . . .

(Page 264:)

19-23   Cf. Johannes de Garlandia (ed. Reimer IX, 6-10): Perfecta
dicitur esse illa, quando duae voces iunguntur in eodem tempore, ita
quod secundum auditum una vox non percipitur ab alia propter
concordantiam, et unisonantia dicitur aut aequisonantia, ut in
unisono et diapason. Imperfecta dicitur, quando duae voces iunguntur
in eodem tempore, ita quod una vox ex toto percipitur ab alia
secundum auditum, et hoc dico secundum concordantiam, et sunt duae
species, scilicet ditonus et semiditonus. Media dicitur esse illa,
quando duae voces iunguntur in eodem tempore, quod nec dicitur
perfecta vel imperfecta, sec partim convenit cum perfecta et partim
cum imperfecta, et duae sunt species, scilicet diapente et
diatesseron.

Cf. Anonymous VII (ed. Reaney *11*, 23): Notandum est quod
unisonus et dyapason sunt consonantiae perfectae, dytonus et
semidytonus sunt inperfectae, dyatessaron et dyapente dicuntur
mediae.

Cf. Franco (ed. Reaney/Gilles XI, 6-11): Perfectae concordantiae
dicuntur quando plures voces conjunguntur, ita quod una ab alia vix
percipitur differre propter concordantiam. Et tales sunt duae,
scilicet unisonus et dyapason . . . Imperfectae dicuntur quando duae
voces multum differre percipiuntur ab auditu, non tamen discordant.
Et sunt duae, scilicet ditonus et semiditonus . . . Mediae vero
concordantiae dicuntur quando duae voces conjunguntur, meliorem
concordantiam habentes quam praedictae, non tamen ut perfectae.
Et sunt duae, scilicet diapente et diatessaron . . .

Cf. Anonymous IV (ed. Reckow 77, 25-28): . . . et hoc secundum
concordantiam unisoni vel diapason pro concordantia vel concordantiis
perfectis vel diatesseron diapente pro concordantiis mediis vel
semiditono ditono <pro condordantiis imperfectis> . . .

Page 266:

6-19   Cf. Johannes de Garlandia (ed. Reimer IX, 14-20): Et sciendum,
quod supradictae concordantiae possunt sumi in infinitum. Probatio:
sit primus sonus datus supra primum G, secundus sonus supra secundum
g, quod dicitur unisonus vel aequisonantia, quod idem est. Dico,
quod quidquid concordat secundo g et primo. Probatio: quae
aequalia sunt eidem sibi invicem sunt aequalia. Sed diapente bene
concordat secundum suam speciem secundo g, ergo et primo et non e
converso, quia si illud quod minus videtur inesse, inest et illud
quod magis et non e converso. Et omne totum ponit suas partes et non
e converso, quia omne totum est maius sua parte et non e converso.

Cf. Franco (ed. Reaney/Gilles XI, 18): Et nota quod tam
concordantiae quam discordantiae possunt sumi in infinitum, ut
diapente cum dyapason, dyatessaron cum dyapason . . .

12-13   Cf. Boethius, *Geometria* (ed. Friedlein 378, 1-2): Cum
spacia et intervalla eidem sunt aequalia, et sibi invicem sunt
aequalia.

(Page 266:)

37-40   Cf. Johannes de Garlandia (ed. Reimer XI, 14-15): Sed duo
puncti sumentur hic pro uno, et aliquando unus eorum ponitur in
concordantia propter colorem musicae, sit primus, sit secundus. Et
hoc bene permittitur et licentiatur ab auctoribus primis et invenitur
in organo in pluribus locis et praecipue in motellis etc.
   Cf. Franco (ed. Reaney/Gilles XI, 30): Deinde prosequendo
per consonantias, commiscendo quandoque discordantias in locis
debitis . . .
   Cf. Anonymous IV (ed. Reckow 78, 5-7): Sunt quidam boni
organistae et factores cantuum, qui non regulariter iuxta
considerationem praedictam ponunt discordantias loco concordantiae
vel concordantiarum . . .
   Cf. Anonymous II (ed. Coussemaker I, 311b): Componitur autem
discantus ex consonantiis principaliter et ex dissonantiis
incidentaliter, ut discantus sit per se pulchrior et ut per ipsas
magis consonantiis delectemur.

Page 268:

11-14   Cf. Johannes de Garlandia (ed. Reimer X, 18): Sciendum est,
quod omnis discordantia ante perfectam concordantiam sive mediam
aequipollet concordantiae mediae, et hoc proprie sumitur ante
unisonum vel diapason.
   Cf. Franco (ed. Reaney/Gilles XI, 20): Item sciendum est quod
omnis imperfecta discordantia immediate ante concordantiam bene
concordat.

CHAPTER FIVE, Part One

Page 270:

18-20   Cf. Johannes de Garlandia (ed. Reimer XI, 3): Unde
discantus est aliquorum diversorum cantuum [con]sonantia secundum
modum et secundum aequipollentis sui aequipollentiam per
concordantiam.
   Cf. Lambertus (ed. Reaney/Gilles IV *2*, 2): Discantus vero est
aliquorum diversorum generum cantus duarum vocum sive trium in quo
trina tantummodo consonantia . . .
   Cf. Franco (ed. Reaney/Gilles II, 1): Discantus est aliquorum
diversorum cantuum consonantia . . .
   Cf. Anonymous IV (ed. Reckow 74, 2-3): Discantus est aliquorum
diversorum cantuum concordantia.
   Cf. Anonymous II (ed. Coussemaker I, 311b): Discantus est

(Page 270:)

aliquorum diversorum cantuum consonantia secundum modum et secundum
equipolentiam.

20-23   Cf. Johannes de Garlandia (ed. Reimer XI, 4-5): Et sunt tot
species sicut et in modo a parte aequipollentis, qui dicitur secundus
cantus, quot a parte tenoris, qui dicitur primus cantus. Et sunt sex
species, ut dicitur etc.
          Cf. Anonymous IV (ed. Reckow 74, 3-8): Et oportet, quod ad minus
sint ibi duae voces concordantes ad invicem secundum quod dicam, et
hoc est secundum considerationem habitudinis illorum ad invicem, quod
fit multiplici modo tam ex parte <dis>cantus quam ex parte tenoris.
Cantus vel tenor est primus cantus primo procreatus vel factus.
Discantus est secundo procreatus vel factus supra tenorem
concordatus.

Page 270, 24-
Page 272:

12   Cf. Johannes de Garlandia (ed. Reimer XI, 6-12): Et
sciendum est, quod a parte primi tria sunt consideranda, scilicet
sonus, ordinatio et modus. Sonus sumitur hic pro musica, ordinatio
sumitur pro numero punctorum ante pausationem, modus sumitur pro
quantitate brevium vel longarum. Et similiter a parte secundi ista
supradicta, scilicet sonus, ordinatio et modus, sunt consideranda.
Et sciendum, quod primus et secundus in tribus simul et semel sunt
considerandi, scilicet in modo, in numero, in concordantia. In
modo, ut sit longa contra longam vel breves aequipollentes
longae. In numero, ut tot sint puncti secundum aequipollentiam a
parte secundi quot a parte primi vel e converso. In
concordantia, ut debito modo primus bene concordet secundo et e
converso.
          Cf. Anonymous IV (ed. Reckow 74, 21-22): Et notandum est, quod
tria semper habere debetis in memoria: sonum vel proportionem,
concordantiam et tempus et quantum temporis.

14-19   Cf. Johannes de Garlandia (ed. Reimer XI, 13-14): Unde
regula: omne, quod fit impari, debet concordari omni illi, quod fit
in impari, si sit in primo vel secundo, et hoc in primo modo sive
secundo vel tertio. Sed duo puncti sumentur hic pro uno, et
aliquando unus eorum ponitur in concordantia propter colorem musicae,
sit primus, sit secundus.

20-22   Cf. Franco (ed. Reaney/Gilles II, 2): Discantus sic
dividitur: . . . alius copulatus qui copula nuncupatur . . .

Page 274:

11-19   Cf. Lambertus (ed. Reaney/Gilles IIIa 4, B1-2): Nunc autem
     oritur quaestio quid vel quae sit necessitas in musica regulari de
     falsa musica, seu de falsa mutatione, cum enim nullum regulare debeat
     accipere falsum, sed potius verum. Ad hoc dicendum est quod mutatio
     sive falsa musica non est inutilis, immo necessaria propter
     consonantiam bonam inveniendam.

CHAPTER FIVE, Part Two

Page 276:

4   Cf. Franco (ed. Reaney/Gilles II, 2): Discantus sic dividitur:
     . . . alius copulatus qui copula nuncupatur . . .

5-6   Cf. Johannes de Garlandia (ed. Reimer XII, 1): Dicto de
     discantu dicendum est de copula, quae multum valet ad discantum,
     quia discantus numquam perfecte scitur nisi mediante copula.

8-10   Cf. Johannes de Garlandia (ed. Reimer XII, 2): Unde copula
     dicitur esse id, quod est inter discantum et organum.
        Cf. Anonymous IV (ed. Reckow 83, 11-14): Tertia diversitas est
     cum eodem tenore, sed in duplo et triplo per modum extraneum se
     habet, ut prima <nota> esset nimis longa et <secunda> nimis brevis,
     et ut videatur participare temporaliter inter discantum et organum;
     et neque est discantus neque organum.

10-12 Cf. Johannes de Garlandia (ed. Reimer XII, 3): Alio modo
     dicitur copula: copula est id, quod profertur recto modo
     aequipollente unisono. Alio modo dicitur: copula est id, ubicumque
     fit multitudo punctorum.

12-15 Cf. Anonymous IV (ed. Reckow 84, 16-17): . . . ut patet in
     Alleluia Posui adiutorium, quoniam ibi ponatur loco copulae sub tali
     forma . . . Et iste modus dicitur primus irregularis, et bene
     competit organo puro.

16-18 Cf. Johannes de Garlandia (ed. Reimer XII, 5): Punctus, ut
     hic sumitur, est, ubicumque fit multitudo tractuum.

18-20 Cf. Anonymous IV (ed. Reckow 40, 28 - 41, 2): Puncta
     supradicta dicuntur apud quosdam notae, quare unus punctus nota
     vocatur; apud aliquos figurae vocantur, quare nota figura potest
     dici; apud aliquos simplices soni dicuntur, et sic materiali signo
     pro formali intelligitur etc.

CHAPTER SIX

Page 280, 21-
Page 282:

1   Cf. Johannes de Garlandia (ed. Reimer XIII, 1-6): Organum
         dicitur multipliciter: generaliter et specialiter. De organo
         generaliter dictum est superius; nunc autem dicendum est de ipso in
         speciali. Organum in speciali dicitur dupliciter: aut per se aut
         cum alio. Organum per se dicitur id esse, quidquid profertur
         secundum aliquem modum non rectum, sed non rectum. Rectus modus
         sumitur hic ille, per quem discantus profertur. Non rectus dicitur
         ad differentiam alicuius rectae, <quia> longae et breves rectae
         sumuntur debito modo primo et principaliter.

1-4   Cf. Johannes de Garlandia (ed. Reimer XIII, 8-9): Organum
         autem <cum alio> dicitur, quidquid profertur per <aliquam> rectam
         mensuram, ut dictum est superius. Et eius aequipollentia tantum se
         tenet in unisono usque ad finem alicuius puncti, ut secum convenit
         secundum aliquam concordantiam.

Page 284:

38-40   Cf. Johannes de Garlandia (ed. Reimer XIII, 3): Organum in
         speciali dicitur dupliciter: aut per se aut cum alio.
             Cf. Franco (ed. Reaney/Gilles XIV, 2): Sciendum quod organum
         purum haberi non potest, nisi supra tenorem ubi sola nota est in
         unisono, ita quod, quando tenor accipit plures notas simul,
         statim est discantus . . .

Page 286:

1-2   Cf. Franco (ed. Reaney/Gilles XIV, 1): Organum proprie
         sumptum est cantus non in omni parte sua mensuratus.
             Cf. Anonymous IV (ed. Reckow 82, 24-25): Et videtur esse modus
         irregulativus quoad modos supradictos ipsius discantus, quamvis in se
         sit regularis.

30-31   Cf. Johannes de Garlandia (ed. Reimer XIII, 11): Longae et
         breves in organo tali modo dinoscuntur, scilicet per <concordantiam>,
         per figuram, per paenultimam.
             Cf. Franco (ed. Reaney/Gilles XIV, 3): Ipsius organi longae et
         breves tribus regulis cognoscuntur.
             Cf. Anonymous IV (ed. Reckow 86, 13-14): In puro autem organo
         multiplici via et modo longae et breves cognoscuntur.

(Page 286:)

32-35   Cf. Johannes de Garlandia (ed. Reimer XIII, 14): Alia
    regula: quidquid accipitur ante longam pausationem vel ante
    perfectam concordantiam dicitur esse longum.
        Cf. Johannes de Garlandia (ed. Reimer XIII, 13): Alia regula:
    quidquid figuratur longum secundum organa ante pausationem vel loco
    <concordantiae> dicitur longum.
        Cf. Franco (ed. Reaney/Gilles XIV, 6): Tertia regula est:
    quidquid accipitur immediate ante pausationem quae finis punctorum
    dicitur, est longum, quia omnis penultima longa est.
        Cf. Anonymous IV (ed. Reckow 86, 19-21): Item omnis punctus
    paenultimus ante longam pausationem sicut in fine puncti vel
    clausulae est longus.

Page 288:

18 and 32   Cf. Ovid, *Tristia* II, 354 (ed. Owen):
        Vita verecunda est, Musa iocosa mea.

NOTES TO
THE TRANSLATION

(Notes are tied to the translation by means of an asterisk in the English text. Here page and line reference are given, and, for ease of reference, a short quotation from the text.)

PROLOGUE

Page 65:

Some people. The author is referring to the treatise of Lambertus. This does not become evident until later, when Lambertus is mentioned by name:
> **Infatuated with his new treatise, Lambertus is now caught.**
> (Prologue 75)

For the majority of the treatise our author retains the general reference, either in the singular ("someone"), or, as here, in the plural ("some people"). The actual wording of this lengthy and florid introduction, however, is immediately and deliberately reminiscent of the beginning of the treatise of Lambertus. Franco also appears to have had one or both of these passages in mind as he wrote his prologue. (See Introduction, p. 8, and Parallel Readings, p. 291.)

the prose work. The work in question is clearly the music treatise of Johannes de Garlandia, attacked by Lambertus and strongly defended by our author.

the best summary of this science. That Garlandia's little work was highly regarded is clear from the number of references to it and imitations of it in later thirteenth-century theory. Nowhere else, however, is its exact stature stated in clearer terms.

"Never carp . . . " This quotation is the beginning of one of the Distichs attributed to Cato the Elder (Book III, No.7, ed. Nève p.29):
> Never carp at any one else's word or deed,
> Lest he mock you for the same thing.
Marcus Porcius Cato "Censorius," 234-149 B.C., was one of the great traditional moralists of the Republic, although the *Disticha* dates from Imperial times. This book became steadily more popular from the seventh

(Page 65:)

century onwards, until by the twelfth century it was considered a standard elementary text. (See R. R. Bolgar, *The Classical Heritage*, pp. 124, 197, 423.)

"If the censurer . . . " This appears to be a conflation of two passages in Horace. In the second Epistle of Book I, addressed to Lollius Maximus, Horace suggests that a perusal of Homer will serve as an effective course in moral philosophy:

> . . . if you do not
> Bend your mind to study and honorable things,
> You will be kept awake and tormented by envy or lust.
> (*Epistles*, I, 2, 35-36 [ed. Klingner, 245])

The word *reprehensor* perhaps reflects the author's recollection of a different passage on criticism, that in the opening Epistle of Horace's second book, addressed to Augustus:

> I am annoyed that any work should be censured,
> Not because it is crude or inelegant,
> But because it is recent;
> And also that pardon is not asked for the ancients,
> But honor and rewards.
> If I wondered whether a play of Atta could still stand
> Amidst all the saffron and flowers,
> Almost all the old folk would cry out that
> Shame was dead.
> And the same if I tried to censure the plays
> Of stern Aesop or learned Roscius.
> (*Epistles*, II, 1, 76-82 [ed. Klingner, 279-80])

It is also possible that the author had in mind the remarkable rhyming couplet given in Walther (no. 28342a [see Parallel Readings, p. 292]) which more accurately reflects the current context:

> If you examine your own sins,
> You won't censure others'.

Page 67:

". . . in few words." Many of these common maxims and proverbs do not have a single obvious source. A large number, however, have been collected together in the helpful series *Carmina Medii Aevi Posterioris Latina* (Göttingen, 1963-). See also Koehler, Margalits, and Werner. The alliteration is particularly noteworthy in the Latin formulation of this widely held sentiment. (See Parallel Readings, p. 292.)

instrumental music. Cf. Boethius, *De institutione musica* I, ii (ed. Friedlein 187, 20-22. The following sentences are a very brief summary of the remainder of Boethius' chapter.

the number of sounds. For the sources of all of these definitions see the Parallel Readings, p. 293.

'sicox,' wind. None of these words is Greek, as the author appears to believe. Indeed *moys* may in fact be derived from an old Egyptian

(Page 67:)

hieroglyphic. The etymology was probably introduced into Latin with the translation of the *Antiquities* of Josephus in the sixth century, and its association with music seems to have begun in the ninth century with Johannes Scotus Erigena. It quickly became adopted as one of the standard derivations and appears in Remigius of Auxerre, Johannes Afflighemensis, Jerome of Moravia, and Marchettus, among many others. See Noel Swerdlow, "'Musica Dicitur A Moys, Quod Est Aqua'," *Journal of the American Musicological Society* XX (1967): 3-9. For an historical sketch of definitions of music, see Heinrich Hüschen, "Musik," in *MGG*, vol. 9 (Kassel, 1961), especially pp. 971-980.

". . . the striking of stretched strings." Cf. Isidore of Seville, *Etymologiae* (ed. Lindsay III, xv, 19-23 and xvi, 1-4).

Page 71:

"Furnishes himself with a cross." This is the beginning of the tenth verse of the sequence *Laudes crucis attollamus* for the Feast of the Exaltation of the Holy Cross by Adam of St. Victor. The meter of the Latin fragment betrays its late origin, and this sequence in particular was popular in Paris, both at the Abbey and at the Cathedral. (See Margot Fassler, "Who Was Adam of St. Victor? The Evidence of the Sequence Manuscripts," *Journal of the American Musicological Society* XXXVII [1984]: 246, 255-256.)

" . . . inculcated in his mind." Another common maxim. The same sentiment is conveyed by a single verse *sententia:*
   Crux in mantellis non est purgatio pellis.
   (You won't save your skin with a cross on your coat.)
(*Proverbia Sententiaeque Latinitatis Medii Aevi* [ed. Walther], no. 3824.)

in place of the copula. Compare Johannes de Garlandia (ed. Reimer I, 3): "It should be known therefore that of organum in its generic sense there are three species, that is to say discant, copula, and organum . . ." and Lambertus (ed. Reaney/Gilles, IV 2, 1): "First therefore it should be known that there are only three genera through which the whole of measurable music runs, that is to say discant, hocket, and organum."

Page 75:

The story of Argus is well known. The mythological monster Argus appears in many ancient sources including the *Prometheus Bound* of Aeschylus and Apollodorus Mythographus. The version of the story best known to the Middle Ages was that of Ovid's *Metamorphoses* (I, 568-746), where the monster with a hundred eyes is appointed by Juno to guard Io, the beautiful nymph whom Jupiter had ravished and turned into a heifer in order to disguise her indentity from his jealous wife. Taking pity on Io's misfortune, Jupiter sends Mercury to kill Argus by lulling all his

(Page 75:)

eyes to sleep with his pipes. (This is the occasion for one of Ovid's brief stories within a story, describing the invention of the reed-pipes.) Argus is killed and Io finally freed.

Page 77:

eloquence marked with a cross. Several small square crosses are in fact marked in the margins of the manuscript.   (These are indicated in the *apparatus criticus.*) Out of twelve, eight occur in the first chapter.

Page 79:

"Let whoever wishes attack." This is the beginning of a line from the *Remedia Amoris* of Ovid (*Remedia Amoris* 364, ed. Henderson 13), in which the poet scorns the rare individual who might attack his work. "Let this one or that, if they wish, assail my work."

Page 81:

" . . . and retain its nature." This line is from *The Consolation of Philosophy* of Boethius (IV, ii, 36 [ed. Rapisarda 130]), in which Philosophy argues that good men are strong and evil men weak. It is quoted in the treatise of Lambertus (ed. Reaney/Gilles IV *1*, 1).

Page 83:

six chapters. The present edition follows this division precisely, according to the arrangement given by the author in the following paragraph.

CHAPTER ONE, Part One

Page 87:

the smallest unit. See Prologue 83.

two or more. This is not a very satisfactory definition of a central term and concept, though its meaning becomes clear through the course of the treatise. In this the author follows Johannes de Garlandia, who introduces the term towards the beginning of his first chapter (ed. Reimer I, 4), but without explanation.

in the right place. See Chap.Iii 135; Chap.Iii 183.

Page 93:

Some people.   See Lambertus (ed. Reaney/Gilles IV *8*, 11).

Page 95:

made clear above.   See Chap.Ii 93.

Page 97:

" . . . *subtle and deep.*"   No source has been found for this line, which may have been composed as a clever condensation of the surrounding word-play by the author himself.

Page 99:

certain people.   The culprit does *not* appear to be Lambertus this time, since the Lambertus treatise describes the imperfect long as "having an affinity in form and propriety with the perfect figure."   (ed. Reaney/Gilles IV *3*, 9.)

Page 101:

the rule somewhere.   See Chap.Ii 103.

some people asserting.   The following concept does not occur in the Lambertus treatise.

" . . . *and that is larger.*"   No source has been found either for this or the following maxim.

Page 103:

" . . . *the number of sounds.*"   See Prologue 67.

Page 105:

some people in their treatises.   See Lambertus (ed. Reaney/Gilles IV *3*, 7-8).

affinity in form and propriety with the larger long.   See Lambertus (ed. Reaney/Gilles IV *3*, 9).

imperfect figures by themselves.   See Lambertus (ed. Reaney/Gilles IV *5*, 7).

general in all places.   See Johannes de Garlandia (ed. Reimer I, 29); Lambertus (ed. Reaney/Gilles IV 4, 14); Anonymous VII (ed. Coussemaker I,

(Page 105:)

378b); Franco (ed. Reaney/Gilles V 3); and Chap.II 197.

Perceive those. See Chap.II 199.

Page 107:

from their remark. See Lambertus (ed. Reaney/Gilles IV 5, 7).

Page 109:

And some have said. See Lambertus (ed. Reaney/Gilles IV 3, 12).

Page 113:

in the treatise. See Johannes de Garlandia (ed. Reimer VI, 1), and Chap.Iii 129, Chap.Iii 143; Chap.Iii 153; Chap. Iii 179.

and elsewhere. See Chap. II 187; Chap II 215.

Page 117:

the rule of the treatise. See Johannes de Garlandia (ed. Reimer III, 2); and cf. Anonymous IV (ed. Reckow 45, 23-25); Anonymous VII (ed. Coussemaker I, 381a); and Chap. Iii 123.

CHAPTER ONE, Part Two

Page 125:

". . . *with two confirmations.*" No source has been found for this maxim.

Page 127:

Certain people. See Lambertus (ed. Reaney/Gilles IV 12, 3).

always unequal semibreves. See Lambertus (ed. Reaney/Gilles IV 12, 4).

units of time that they have. See Johannes de Garlandia (ed. Reimer VI, 8).

figured with proper propriety. See Johannes de Garlandia (ed. Reimer VI, 9).

Page 129:

laid out elsewhere. See Johannes de Garlandia (ed. Reimer VI, 1); and
Chap.Iii 113; Chap.Iii 143; Chap.Iii 153; Chap.Iii 179.

Page 133:

Placed in front. These last two verses were written in the lower margin
of the folio, but would appear to belong in this location. Space was
left for interlinear glosses, but none were added.

some people. See Lambertus (ed. Reaney/Gilles IV *9*).

Page 135:

the treatise says elsewhere. See Johannes de Garlandia (ed. Reimer
VI, 2).

Page 137:

figuring it in this manner. See Lambertus (ed. Reaney/Gilles IV *10*).

as is shown here. See Lambertus (ed. Reaney/Gilles IV *10*).

Page 139:

some people say. Not in Lambertus, but see Johannes de Garlandia (ed.
Reimer VI, 8).

stated this clearly above. See Chap.Iii 125.

Page 141:

four units of time separately. Not in Lambertus.

Page 143:

the treatise teaches. See Johannes de Garlandia (ed. Reimer VI, 1).

some people. See Lambertus (ed. Reaney/Gilles IV *10*).

Page 145:

some are not afraid to assert. See Lambertus (ed. Reaney/Gilles IV
9, 19).

as has been said above. See Chap.Iii 137.

Page 149:

some people say. See Lambertus (ed. Reaney/Gilles IV *9*, 19).

And Master Lambertus says. See Lambertus (ed. Reaney/Gilles IV *9*, 19).

as some people assert. See Lambertus (ed. Reaney/Gilles IV *7*, 6).

Page 159:

the plica can be arranged in two ways. The material in the following
two paragraphs on ascending and descending plicas is covered twice
(though in slightly different form) in the manuscript: by the last part
of the second gathering and the beginning of the third. Duplicated
material is given in Appendix I.

Page 163:

Certain new writers. See Lambertus (ed. Reaney/Gilles IV *10*).

Page 167:

Nevertheless some people. See Lambertus (ed. Reaney/Gilles IV *9*, 19).

Page 173:

the view of certain people. Not in Lambertus.

Page 179:

elsewhere in the treatise. See Johannes de Garlandia (ed. Reimer VI,
1); and Chap.Ii 113; Chap. Iii 129; Chap.Iii 143; Chap.Iii 153.

CHAPTER TWO

Page 185:

these represent its orthography. Cf. Prologue 83.

Page 187:

by means of one. Cf. Chap.Ii 113; ChapII 215.

" . . . *as it relates to sound.*" Cf. Prologue 67.

(Page 187:)

can be termed authentic. This appropriation of terms from the melodic modes appears to be original with this author. It was perhaps suggested by the Lambertus *musica plana* treatise, which contains a discussion of the melodic modes (see Reaney/Gilles IIIb *1*, 40), including the term "collateral."

Page 191:

The word in the verse is *brios*: perhaps this word is related to *bria* (= *mensura*). The *Mittellateinisches Wörterbuch* gives the present treatise as the only source for the word. Cf. also Chap.II 205.

Page 197:

it is said elsewhere. See Boethius, *The Consolation of Philosophy* (IV, ii, 36 [ed. Rapisarda 130]). Cf. Prologue 81; and Lambertus (ed. Reaney/Gilles IV *1*, 1).

Page 213:

in their chapter on the modes. See Lambertus (ed. Reaney/Gilles IV *16*).

" . . . first, fourth, and seventh." See Lambertus (ed. Reaney/Gilles IV *16*, 5).

according to the binary number. See Lambertus (ed. Reaney/Gilles IV *16*, 33).

three equal semibreves. See Lambertus (ed. Reaney/Gilles IV *16*, 35).

by means of a perfect mode. Not in Lambertus in precisely this formulation, but cf. Lambertus (ed. Reaney/Gilles IV *16*, 7 and 37).

by means of perfect figures or notes. See Lambertus (ed. Reaney/Gilles IV *5*, 7).

Page 215:

by means of one. Cf. Chap.Ii 113; Chap.II 187.

music of the universe or music of man. Cf. Boethius, *De institutione musica* (ed. Friedlein 187, 23 - 189, 12); and Prologue 67.

Page 217:

this kind of ordering of the melodies. Not in Lambertus.

Page 219:

so on with the other modes. Not in Lambertus.

Henricus de Daubuef. See Introduction, pp. 38-43.

" . . . its customs and hearth." The verses are a variant of a common
formulation: "Tot sunt . . . quot . . . " ("There are as many . . . as
there are . . . "). See, for example, the couplet from Basel,
Universitätsbibliothek A XI 67, folio 219 *verso* (quoted in Jakob Werner,
Lateinische Sprichwörter und Sinnsprüche des Mittelalters, no. 34):
> Tot sunt doctores, quot verno tempore flores;
> Tot sunt errores, quot habet natura colores.
> (There are as many doctors as there are flowers in spring,
> There are as many errors as there are colors in nature.)

Page 221:

as the prose treatise says. Cf. Johannes de Garlandia (ed. Reimer
XI, 10).

Page 225:

as Isidore says. See Isidore of Seville, *Etymologiae,* (ed. Lindsay III,
xx, 4-5).

CHAPTER THREE

Page 245:

" . . . then it is imperfect." See Chap.II 197; Chap.II 213.

Page 249:

For they said. See Lambertus (ed. Reaney/Gilles IV *14,* 9-13).

Page 251:

" . . . who disagrees with himself. " No source has been found for
this maxim.

half of a space. Not in Garlandia.

Page 253:

in their treatises.   See Lambertus a(ed. Reaney/Gilles IV *17*, 5-8).

Page 255:

composers in the art of music.   Cf. Johannes de Garlandia (ed. Reimer VIII, 7).

they have spoken in this way.   See Johannes de Garlandia (ed. Reimer VIII, 9).

Page 257:

" . . . *to what follows.*"   Cf. Anon. algor. Salem: "To these figures is added this zero, which is called a cipher, and has no significance besides its place."

Some people said.   See Johannes de Garlandia (ed. Reimer VIII, 3).

CHAPTER FOUR

Page 259:

at the beginning of this volume.   See Prologue 71; Prologue 73.

Page 261:

But some.   See Lambertus (ed. Reaney/Gilles IIIa *14*, 7-10).

discussed below.   See Chap.IV 267.

Page 265:

" . . . *between two notes.*"   Cf. Capella (ed. Eyssenhardt VIII, 930).

" . . . *reaches the hearing undissipated.*"   Cf. Lambertus (ed. Reaney/Gilles IIIa *3*, 2).

to expound.   Cf. Prologue 67.

Page 267:

equal to each other.   Cf. Boethius, *Geometria* (ed. Friedlein 378, 1-2).

CHAPTER FIVE, Part One

Page 273:

which is as follows.   Cf. Johannes de Garlandia (ed. Reimer XI, 13-14).

Page 275:

Others describe it thus.   Not in Lambertus.

CHAPTER SIX

Page 289:

O Muse, enjoy your rest.   There is a faint but distinct echo in the Latin of these verses of the famous defence of Ovid to his critics (*Tristia* II, 354 [ed. Owen]):
             "My muse may be wanton, but my life is virtuous."

APPENDIX I

Material Duplicated by Gatherings 1 and 2
of the Manuscript

.....(fol. 146) in qua potest dupliciter ordinari, ascendendo videlicet et descendendo. Et nota, quod si plica tangat aliquem punctum ascendentem in fine alicuius figurae, semper tales faciet imperfectos quoad formam solummodo et non quoad effectum, sive plica ascendat sive descendat. Qualiter autem ipsos imperfectos faciat, patet hic

, et sic in omnibus figuris, in quibus ultimus punctus altior est paenultimo, debet plica dupliciter ordinari. Exemplum qualiter plica debet ordinari in omnibus figuris perfectis, in quibus ultimus punctus inferior est paenultimo, patet hic, et hoc dupliciter,

aut ascendendo aut descendendo, et sic de omnibus aliis. Exemplum plicae in omnibus figuris compositis et imperfectis, in quibus potest dupliciter ordinari, tam ascendendo scilicet quam descendendo,

patet hic, et sic de omnibus aliis imperfectis figuris exemplificandum est dupliciter. Littera per se patet.

----

8 decet *pro* debet *Sowa*   9 decet *pro* debet *Sowa*   12 aliis [[in quibus]] exemplum *cod*.   14 potest *add. super scriptum*   17 est *add*. *super scriptum*

338

.....(fol. 146) in which it can be arranged in two ways, that is
ascending and descending. And note that if the plica touches any
ascending written note at the end of any figure, it will always make such
notes imperfect, as to their form only and not as to their effect,
whether the plica ascends or descends. And how it makes them imperfect

is clear here ◢ ◥ ◢ ◣ ◣ , and in this way in all figures in which
the last written note is higher than the penultimate the plica should be
arranged in two ways. An example of how the plica should be arranged in
all perfect figures in which the last note is lower than the penultimate
is given here, and this occurs in two ways, either ascending or

descending ◣ ◣ ◣ ◣ , and in this way for all the others. An example
of the plica in all composite and imperfect figures in which it can be
arranged in two ways, that is to say both ascending and descending, is

given here ◩ ◩ ◥ ◣ ◪ ◣ ◣ ◢ ◢ , and it should be exemplified in
this way in both ways for all the other imperfect figures. The text is
clear by itself.

APPENDIX II

Historical Records and Documents Relating to
Lambertus and Henricus Tuebuef

(These are presented here unedited, except for some punctuation and
capitalization and the expansion of abbreviations. All dates are given
in new style.)

Sources of the documents transcribed below are abbreviated as
follows:

AN, LL 76:	Paris, Archives Nationales, LL 76.
AN, LL 77:	Paris, Archives Nationales, LL 77.
AN, LL 81:	Paris, Archives Nationales, LL 81.
AN, S 6213:	Paris, Archives Nationales, S 6213.
Arsenal, 1064:	Paris, Bibliothèque de l'Arsenal, 1064.
BN, latin 5185 CC:	Paris, Bibliothèque Nationale, latin 5185 CC.
BN, latin 5526:	Paris, Bibliothèque Nationale, latin 5526.
BN, latin 14673:	Paris, Bibliothèque Nationale, latin 14673.
Chartularium:	*Chartularium Universitatis Parisiensis.* Ed. Denifle and Chatelain. 4 vols. Paris, 1891-1899. Reprint, 1964.
Dubois:	Dubois, Gérard. *Historia ecclesie parisiensis.* 2 vols. Paris, 1690-1710.
Glorieux:	Glorieux, Palémon. *Aux Origines de la Sorbonne.* 2 vols. Etudes de philosophie médiévale LIV. Paris, 1965.

Guérard: *Cartulaire de l'église Notre-Dame*.   Ed.
                      M. Guérard.   4 vols.   Collection des
                      cartulaires de France IV-VII.   In
                      *Collection de documents inédits sur
                      l'histoire de France*.   Series 1.   Paris,
                      1850.

Molinier: Molinier, Auguste (ed.).   *Obituaires de
                      la province de Sens*.   Recueil des
                      historiens de la France.   Obituaires.
                      4 vols. Paris, 1902-1923.

DOCUMENT 1 [April 8, 1270]
    Universis presentes litteras inspecturis, officialis parisiensis
salutem in Domino. Notum facimus quod coram Stephano de <?>docino et
Roberto de Turonis clericis nostris iuratis ad hoc a nobis specialiter
destinatis, quibus fidem adhibemus, constitutus **magister Lambertus
decanus ecclesie Senogiensis**, infirmus corpore sanus tamen mente ut prima
facie apparebat, voluit coram predictis clericis quod omnia que in suo
testamento existente apud Senogias in archa sua ad pedem lecti sui
continentur et scripta sunt, sint firma et stabilia prout in eodem
testamento sunt constituta, excepto quod de dicto testamento revocavit et
amovit ac detraxit clausulam totaliter ubi fit mencio quod ipse Lambertus
legabat in subsidium terre sancte et ad opus ecclesie Senogiensis
residuum bonorum suorum; et addidit predicto testamento ea que inferius
continentur, videlicet quod legavit domicelle Marie moranti in hospicio
suo sexaginta solidos paris., item magistro Laurencio qui fuit suus
capellanus, quadriginta solidos. Item nepotibus et neptibus suis
nominatis in dicto testamento omnes culcitras et omnia lintheamina et
alia utensilia domus sue. Item pauperibus magistris scolaribus
commorantibus in vico magistri Roberti de Sorbona, canonici parisiensis,
apud Parisius, epistolas Pauli glosatas cum duobus ewangelistis Johanne
videlicet et Luca, et residuum omnium bonorum suorum in quibuscumque
rebus et locis consistat. Et ad ea que dictus magister Parisius
facienda, petenda et exequenda, magistrum Robertum de Sorbona, canonicum
parisiensem, suum constituit executorem. Hec autem acta sunt coram
predictis clericis nostris quibus fidem adhibemus prout nobis una voce
retulerunt. In cuius rei testimonium et ad relationem ipsorum, sigillum
curie parisiensis litteris presentibus duximus apponendum.
    Datum anno Domini M°CC°lx° nono, die martis ante Pascha.

[AN, S 6213, no. 36; Glorieux, vol. 2, no. 278 (pp. 324-325)]

DOCUMENT 2 [January 1249]
    Universis presentes litteras inspecturis, L. decanus totumque
capitulum Parisiense, salutem in Domino . . . Nos, ecclesie nostre
evidenti utilitate pensata, ac volentes eiusdem ecclesie indempnitati in
posterum providere, tam presentis indulgencie auctoritate quam nostra,

die ad hoc secundum ecclesie nostre consuetudinem assignata, domibus
claustri nostri pensiones inferius annotatas duximus imponendas; quas,
cedentibus vel decedentibus canonicis qui nunc eas obtinent, successores
eorum qui ipsas domos obtinebunt, capitulo persolvent annuatim, secundum
formam inferius annotatam. Imposuimus domibus Odonis de Sancto Dyonisio
pensionem XIIII libr.; domibus Johannis de Lachi sex libr.; domibus
Odonis archidiaconi pensionem XII libr.; domibus Transmundi XVI libr.;
domibus Nevelonis Silvanectensis XII libr.; domibus Auberti de Nemosio XV
libr.; domibus decani XII libr.; domibus Othoboni XII libr.; domibus
Nicholai de Campania VII libr.; domibus Stephani Cardinalis decem libr.;
domibus Remundi Episcopi VIII libr.; domibus Petri Pape VIII libras;
domibus Remundi de Claro Monte novem libr.; domibus Petri de Boissiaco
decem libras; domibus Petri Juvenis VII libr.; domibus Henrici
succentoris novem libr.; . . . domibus **Henrici Tuebuef** c sol.; domibus
Hugonis de Caprosia septem libr.; domibus Adenulfi VII libr.; domibus
Milonis de Corbolio centum sol.; domibus Radulfi de Chevriaco centum
sol.; domibus Johannis archidiaconi VIII libr. Medietas autem harum
pensionum solvent annuatim, infra purificationem beate Marie, alia
medietas infra ascensionem Domini. Facta est autem imposicio predictarum
pensionum suprascriptis domibus, salvis antiquis oneribus alias dictis
domibus impositis, solvendis a possessoribus earumdem terminis consuetis.
. . . Ad hec, ad tollendum discordias que super vacantibus domibus inter
canonicos nasci consueverunt, ac ad providendum canonicis deservientibus,
ut habeant domos in claustro in quibus capita reclinent, statuimus ut in
ipsis domibus, quando vacabunt, obtinendis, antiquiores canonici, dummodo
resideant et residere credantur, aliis preferantur. Actum in capitulo
nostro anno Domini MCCXLVIII, mense januario.

[AN, LL 81; Guérard, vol. 2, pp. 413-415]

DOCUMENT 3 [April 1249]
    Frater Radulfus, quondam abbas ecclesie Sancti Victoris, **magistri**
Raymundus et **Henricus dicti Tuebuef, canonici Parisienses**, executores
testamenti bonae memoriae Guillelmi quondam Parisiensis Episcopi etc.
Cum idem Dominus Episcopus dum viveret praecepisset statui suum
anniversarium in Ecclesia Parisiensi super decima de Maciaco movente de
conquestu suo proprio et etiam nobis iniunxisset expresse ut ad hoc
Capitulo Parisiensi certam assignaremus portionem; nos, habito post
mortem eiusdem Domini Episcopi super hoc diligenti tractatu ordinavimus,
assignamus et volumus ut Capitulum Parisiense ex nunc in perpetuum
percipiat annuatim infra festum Beati Martini hyemense super decima
praedicta de Maciaco tres modios ybernagii eiusdem decimae ad mensuram
Parisiensem ad opus anniversarii dicti Domini Episcopi die jovis ante
Paschae floridum annis singulis perpetuo celebrandi etc. quae omnia
Capitulum acceptavit. . . . Actum anno Domini MCCXL° nono, mense aprili.

[AN, LL 81, f. 142; Dubois, vol. 2, pp. 372-373; Guérard, vol. 2, p. 87]

DOCUMENT 4 [September 13, 1249]
    Anno Domini M°CC°XL° nono, die lune post nativitatem beate Virginis,
fecit Ansellus miles, dominus Turnomii, homagium ligium venerabili patri
Galtero, Parisiensi episcopo, de castro et castellania de Turnomio et

omnibus pertinenciis dictorum castri et castellanie, et tam de omnibus
hiis que ipse tenebat et possidebat, quam de omnibus hiis que alii
quicumque tenebant et possidebant in castro et castellania supradictis,
salvo iure sive porcione de qua non fecit idem dominus homagium, quam
frater eius habebat, si quam iam habebat . . . Ad dictum autem homagium
admisit ipsum Ansellum dominus Parisiensis, et ipsum investavit de eodem
per anulum aureum, in camera ipsius episcopi apud Sanctum Victorem,
presentibus et videntibus fratre Johanne de Monte Mirabili, ordinis
predicatorum, magistro Natali, canonico et officiali Parisiensi; **Henrico
dicto Tuebuef, canonico Parisiensi**; Simone de Cociniaco, Roberto de Villa
Baart, militibus; magistris Roberto, canonico Cameracensi, Petro de
Crameillis, Nicolao Metensi; Simone, thesaurario de Braio; Renodo,
cambellano domini Parisiensis; Johanne, clerico domini episcopi, et
Johanne Alemant, canonico Pruvinensi, et pluribus aliis.

[BN, latin 5526; Guérard, vol. 1, pp. 158-159]

DOCUMENT 5 [December 30, 1261]
    Henricus de Serbonio, parisiensis canonicus, ad firmam quatuor
annorum, pro octoginta libris Turonensibus annuatim solvendis,
praeposituram Roseti a capitulo accipit. . . . Datum anno Domini
millesimo ducentesimo sexagesimo primo, die veneris post nativitatem
Domini.

[AN, LL 81; Guérard, vol. 2, p. 283]

DOCUMENT 6 [February 18, 1264]
    Universis presentes litteras inspecturis officialis curie Parisiensis
salutem in Domino. Notum facimus quod coram nobis constitutus Johannes
dictus de Atrio de Roseto de omnibus accionibus contencionibus
controversus arreragiis querelis debitis forestis habitis inter ipsum et
capitulum Parisiensem **dominum Henricum dictum Tuebuef, prepositum de
Roseto, canonicum Parisiensem**, et que dictum capitulum et **Henricus** ab
ipso terre predictorum posset petere usque in diem hodiernum, compromisit
in predictum capitulum Parisiensem et se voluntati eorum totaliter
subiecit, coram nobis promittens fide in manu nostra prestita corporali,
idem Johannes quod ipse inviolabiter observabit quicquid dictum
capitulum alte et basse super premissis duxerit ordinandum, et quantum ad
hoc se supposuit iurisdiccioni curie nostre quocumque maneat vel existat,
volens et concedens quod in ipsum possimus ex iis preferre sentenciam, si
contra predicta venire in parte presumeret vel in toto. Datum anno
Domini M^{o}CC^{o}LX°iij^o die martis ante Cathedram Sancti Petri.

[AN, LL 76, p. 327; Guérard, vol. 2, p. 278]

DOCUMENT 7 [March 1, 1269]
    Universis presentes litteras inspecturis, ego **Henricus de Serbona,
canonicus Parisiensis**, salutem in Domino. Universitati vestre notum
facio, quod ego a venerabilibus viris decano et capitulo Parisiensi
preposituram suam de Roseto recepi ad firmam, usque ad sex annos
continuos, a crastino nativitatis Domini instantis continue computandos,

cum omnibus pertinenciis et rebus, quas Milo de Breolio, miles,
percipiebat, quando dictam preposituram tenebat, et sub eisdem eciam
condicionibus,sub quibus eam tunc temporis tenebat; hoc addito, quod ego
Henricus omnia forismaritagia ad preposituram pertinencia procurabo,
levabo et habebo, ita quod terciam partem dictorum forismaritagiorum
ponam in melioracionem et reedificacionem domus capituli de Roseto. Et
habebo omne ius quod habent et habere possunt, usque ad dictum terminum,
in hominibus commorantibus in castalaniis de Columbario, de Cantumerula
et de Sezannya, qui dicuntur homines de corpore ecclesie Parisiensis;
addito eciam, quod ego **Henricus**, in refectione et reparacione halarum de
Roseto, quadraginta libras Turonenses ponere teneor et plus, si necesse
fuerit, ut eas taliter reparatas de coopertura scilicet et aliis, usque
ad dictum terminum, in statu competenti teneor retinere, pro
quaterviginti libris Turonensibus, solvendibus dicto capitulo annis
singulis de dictis sex annis, medietate videlicet infra octavas beati
Johannis Baptiste, et alia medietate infra octavas beati Andree. Et
promiserunt dicti decanus et capitulum etc. Datum anno Domini millesimo
ducentesimo sexagesimo VIII°, die veneris ante Letere Jerusalem.

[AN, LL 81; Guérard, vol. 2, p. 284]

DOCUMENT 8 [February 1272]
    Universis presentes litteras inspecturis, officialis curie reverendi
patris domini Ancheri, cardinalis, archidyaconi Parisiensis, salutem in
Domino. Notum facimus quod, coram nobis, in capitulo Parisiensis
ecclesie, capitulo more solito congregato, constituti, Ogerus, gener
decani, Johannes forbitor, Guillermus regratarius, Dyonisius, filius
Johannis Guerini, et Johannes de Atrio, de Roseto, Robertus de Brouil,
Petrus Chocart, Symon Randon et Johannes de Prato, de Venula, asseruerunt
quod inter ipsos et alios homines de Roseto et de parrochia de Venula, ex
una parte, et dictos decanum et capitulum Parisiense, ex altera,
discordie materia vertebatur, super eo quod dicti decanus et capitulum
dicunt et asserunt, ipsos homines de Roseto et de parrochia Venule
teneri ad custodiam incarceratorum et incarcerandorum, apud Rosetum, per
prepositum aut per mandatum decani et capituli predictorum; item, super
eo quod dicti decanus et capitulum petebant ab eisdem hominibus, quod
ipsi emendarent hoc quod, ad petitionem **domini Henrici dicti Tuebuef,
canonici Parisiensis, prepositi** dicti loci et vices eorum gerentis
ibidem, noluerunt custodire duos captos et incarceratos in carcere
eorumdem decani et capituli, videlicet quemdam pro raptu, et alium pro
fractione ville nocturna; qui incarcerati, propter defectum custodie,
evaserunt. Qui Ogerus, Johannes forbitor, Guillermus, Dyonisius et
Johannes de Atrio, pro se et pro aliis hominibus de Roseto, exceptis
nobilibus, clericis et quibusdam quos dicebant burgenses regis, pro
quibus cavere noluerunt, voluerunt et expresse concenserunt, pro se et
heredibus suis, coram nobis in dicto capitulo existentibus, quod
venerabiles viri Gaufridus decanus et Garnerus, archidiaconus ecclesie
Parisiensis, quos capitulum ad hoc nominaverunt et deputaverunt, dictis
caventibus pro se et aliis predictis consentientibus et ratum habentibus,
tam de possessione et usus dicte custodie quam de proprietate et iure
ipsorum decani et capituli, super eadem custodia de plano cognoscant et
inquirant. Et primo super usu et possessione dicte custodie; ita quod,
si contingat ipsos decanum et archidyaconum vel alterum ipsorum aliquo

casu ad hoc vacare seu interesse non posse, quod dictum capitulum alium
vel alios de ipso capitulo, loco ipsorum amborum vel illius qui interesse
non posset, ponere et subrogare poterit; et facta ab ipsis inquisitione
et cognitione huiusmodi super usu et possessione ac proprietate et iure
dictorum decani et capituli, super predictis ordinent, pronuntient et
statuant, prout voluerint et viderint esse faciundum. Et promiserunt
dicti caventes, fide in manu nostra prestita corporali et sub penis
predictis, quilibet in solidum, quod contra premissa non venient ullo
iure, et quod facient et procurabunt ab aliis hominibus predictis omnia
et singula antedicta, ac statutum et ordinationem illorum qui a dicto
capitulo sunt vel erunt ad premissa deputati, tenere et inviolabiter
observare; et quod contra premissa non venient ullo iure; et se, quantum
ad hec, dicti caventes iuridictioni nostre curie subiecerunt. Datum anno
Domini millesimo ducentesimo LXX primo, mense februario.

[AN, LL 81; Guérard, vol. 2, pp. 141-143]

DOCUMENT 9 [April 13, 1278]
    Universis presentes litteras inspecturis, officialis curie
Parisiensis, salutem in Domino. Notum facimus quod, in nostra presencia
constitutus, Symon de Vallibus, armiger, recognovit in iure, coram nobis,
quod ipse venatus fuerat in garannia, que dicitur Bois en Lais,
venerabilium virorum decani et capituli Parisiensis. Asseruit eciam in
iure, coram nobis, quod nullum ius venandi habebat in dicta garanna.
Asseruit eciam quod hoc emendavit in capitulo Parisiensi, in manu decani,
nomine suo et capituli Parisiensis, et quod de emenda et super expensas
quas dicti decanus et capitulum fecerunt, in citando et in procurando
eum excommunicari auctoritate decani Sancti Clodoaodi, occasione
premissorum, stabit voluntati et ordinacioni venerabilium virorum domini
Gervasii de Clinocampo et **Henrici Tuebuef, canonicorum Parisiensium**.
Iuravit autem, etc. Datum anno Domini millesimo ducentesimo septuagesimo
septimo, die mercurii ante Pascha.

[AN, LL 81; Guérard, vol. 2, p. 285]

DOCUMENT 10 [April 4, 1279]
    Universis presentes littera inspecturis, officialis curie
Parisiensis, salutem in Domino. Notum facimus quod, in nostra presencia
constitutus, **dominus Henricus, dictus Tuebuef, canonicus Parisiensis**,
asseruit in iure, coram nobis, se emisse a Johanne dicto Cachant, nepote
Andree, maioris de Civilliaco, et Basilia dicta Maiorissa, eius uxore,
medietatem cuiusdam molendini dicti Toillon, quod est situm in valle de
Sulciaco, medietatem cuiusdam salceye, medietatem cuiusdam pascui, quod
est iuxta dictum molendinum, onerata in undecim solidis Parisiensibus
annui census, et medietatem cuiusdam prati, quod est prope dictum
molendinum, ad tres denarios Parisienses census annui, et medietatem
cuiusdam domus, site iuxta dictum molendinum, oneratam in uno obolo
Turonensi census annui; que omnia sita sunt in territorio de Sulciaco, in
censiva et dominio venerabilium virorum decani et capituli Parisiensis,
prout in litteris curie Parisiensis super hoc confectis plenius
continetur. Que omnia, prout superius sunt expressa, recognovit in iure,
coram nobis, se dedisse ex nunc et in perpetuum concessisse dictis decano

et capitulo et ecclesie Parisiensi; promittens dictus **Henricus**, fide in
manu nostra prestita corporali, quod contra donationem et concessionem
predictas quoquo iure communi vel speciali, per se vel per alium, non
veniet in futurum, nec venire procurabit. In cuius rei testimonium, ad
petitionem dicti **Henrici**, presentes litteras sigillo Parisiensis curie
fecimus sigillari. Datum anno Domini MCCLXXIX°, die martis post Pascha.

[AN, LL 76, p. 229; AN, LL 81, f. 230; Guérard, vol. 2, p. 193; cf. AN,
LL 81, f. 229]

DOCUMENT 11 [March 19, 1283]
    Anno etc. **Henricus Tuebuef Canonicus Parisiensis** emendavit in pleno
capitulo in manu Garneri archidiaconi praesedentis in capitulo factum
sive iniuriam seu etiam vilaniam quam fecerat Aegidio Vigili in claustro
parisiensi tam pro dicto capitulo quam pro dicto Aegidio et juravit quod
stabit voluntati et ordini capituli alte et basse.
    Die sabbato in crastino eidem **Henrico** assignata in Capitulo ad
judicandum de emenda et ad taxandum eandem congragatis in Capitulo et
vocatis per domos canonicis . . . et condemnaverunt dictum **Henricum** in
centum marchas pro emenda. Supposita tamen ab omnibus gratia super
remissione alicuius quantitatis huius emendae facienda eidem et postmodum
vocato eidem **Henrico**, succentor, qui dicta die praeerat in Capitulo vice
omnium et communi assensu omnium iniunxit eidem **Henrico** quod pro iniuria
quam fecerat Capitulo verberando communem servientem eorum et pro iniuria
illata eidem servienti et pro fractione libertatis claustri solveret
centum marchas infra Pascha cui sententiae acquievit.

[AN, LL 81, f. 238-239]

DOCUMENT 12 [March 26, 1286]
    Anno etc. martis post Laetare. Capitulum Parisiense concessit
Henrico Tuebuef, canonico Parisiensi, sepulturam suam in Ecclesia
Parisiensi post mortem suam.

[AN, LL 81, f. 242]

DOCUMENT 13 [April 9, 1286]
    In nomine Domini, amen. Universis presentes litteras inspecturis,
capitulum Parisiense salutem in Domino. Severitatis aut clemencie gloria
non est in iudiciis affectanda, set, perpenso iudicio in delictis
perpetratis sunt pene, prout res expostulat, statuende. Ea propter, cum
nobis, capitulo Parisiensi, fuisset ex parte venerande Universitatis
Parisiensis expositum quoddam homicidium in personam cuiusdam scolaris
Parisiensis perpetratum in paraviso vel prope, et quosdam alios excessus
perpetratos fuisse die veneris ante brandones; et quod quidam clerici de
choro nostro, videlicet Thomassimus Coillete, Johannes Boiliave et
Colinus Martelli, presentes interfuerant, operam, consilium, et auxilium
dederant in predicto facinore perpetrando: fuimus ex parte Universitatis
postea requisiti, quod super premissis exhiberemus mature iusticie
complementum. Nos autem requisitioni predicte benigniter inclinati,
veram dilectionem et affectionem quam habemus erga dictam Universitatem

servare merito cupientes, **magistros** Johannem de Bertencuria, Dudonem et **Henricum dictum Tuebuef, canonicos nostros in capitulo**, deputavimus ad inquirendum super premissis plenariam veritatem. Predicti vero canonici vice nostra et mandato processerunt ad inquirendum veritatem, peritis in utroque iure presentibus, diligenter. Et de consilio eorumdem fecerunt predictos Thomassinum, Johannem et Colinum iurare, tactis sacrosanctis Evangeliis, quod super premissis dicerent veritatem. Verum, quia per confessiones eorumdem non potuit constare de veritate facti, testes fuerunt producti super premissis et eadem tangentibus, et diligenter per doctos concanonicos examinati. Tandem depositionibus testium in capitulo publicatis et diligenter examinatis, mandavimus pro clericis supra dictis. Et ipsi presentes in capitulo a nobis interrogati utrum ratam et gratam haberent inquestam predictam, et utrum vellent stare ordinacioni nostre super premissis, responderunt quod sic. Et hoc iuramento proprio firmaverunt. Verum quia per depositiones testium predictorum non potuimus eosdem invenire adeo culpabiles, quod de iure condempnare possemus ipsos ad penam homicidii sustinendam, licet in quibusdam aliis inventi fuerint excessisse: nos, deliberacione super premissis habita diligenti, adhibita sollempnitate que in talibus fieri consuevit, de consilio peritorum per nostram diffinitivam sententiam ordinamus et statuimus in hunc modum, videlicet, dictos Thomassinum et Johannem ex nunc beneficio quod habent in ecclesia nostra Parisiensi, scilicet denariis matutinalibus et choro nostro Parisiensi, imperpetuum privantes; item, quod a die qua exibunt de carcere nostro, iter arripiant ad Romanam curiam propter sue absolutionis beneficium impetrandum; item, quod a die predicta extra dyocesim et civitatem Parisiensem moram contrahent per triennium, nullatenus reversuri donec dictum triennium sit elapsum. Dictum vero Colinum Martelli ex nunc privamus imperpetuum choro nostro; item, quod a die qua exibit de carcere nostro, accedet ad sedem apostolicam, sue absolutionis beneficium petiturus; item, quod a die predicta extra dyocesim et civitatem Parisiensem moram contrahet continue per triennium, et quod antea non redebit, nisi veneranda Universitas predicta velit eidem super reversu ad civitatem et dyocesim facere gratiam specialem. Et ad hoc predictos Thomassinum, Johannem et Colinum in scriptis per nostram diffinitivam sententiam condempnamus. Datum et actum in capitulo Parisiensi, anno Domini M°CC° octogesimo quinto, die martis post Ramos Palmarum.

[Chartularium, no. 534]

DOCUMENT 14 [June 11]
     III ID. JUNII. De domo Sancte Marie, obierunt Gacho et Erfredus, subdiaconi.
     De domo Sancte Marie, obiit **Herricus Tuebuef, subdiaconus**; qui dedit ecclesie Parisiensi medietatem cuiusdam molendini, quod vocatur Tooeillum, apud Suciacum, in censiva capituli Parisiensis. Capitulum vero constituit fieri quolibet anno in quo proventus predicte medietatis molendini debent distribui[t] canonicis et maiori altari [servi] servientibus in vigilia et in missa et matricularii laici duodecim denarios habebit.
     Alia autem medietas molendini empta fuit pro anniversario Gaufridi de Barro, cardinalis. Honera autem et census dicti molendini plenius continentur in anniversario predicti Gaufridi, quod fit XIX kalendas

septembris. Et super istis omnibus habentur littere sigillate sigillo
officialis Parisiensis.

[BN, latin 5185 CC, f. 213; Guérard, vol. 4, pp. 77-78; Molinier, vol. 1,
part 1, pp. 137-138]

DOCUMENT 15 [May 27]
     VI Kal. Anniv. domni Heimerici, sancte Romane ecclesie dyaconi
cardinalis et cancellarii, qui cenobium istud speciali amore diligens,
dedit nobis plurimorum sanctorum reliquias, thecis argenteis honorifice
conditas, et in cultu altaris casulas et pallia aliaque diversi generis
ornamenta.
     Item anniv. soll. domni Johannis, Lexoviensis episcopi.
     Item anniv. Johannis de Cathena et patris eius et Chambaldi, pro
cuius anima dedit nobis prebendam unam in ecclesia Montisleterici . . .
     Item anniv. **domni Henrici, dicti Tubuef, canonici Parisiensis**, de
cuius beneficio habuimus XX libr. turon.

[BN, latin 14673; Molinier, vol. 1, part 1, p. 561]

DOCUMENT 16 [June 9]
     <Anniv.> **Henrici Tuebeuf**; Dudonis de Lauduno . . .

[Arsenal, 1064; Molinier, vol. 1, part 1, p. 218]

DOCUMENT 17 [December 12]
     Pridie idus. Ob. Maria Merceria, que dedit nobis partem suam de
omnibus que habebant inter se et maritum suum.
     Ob. Petrus dictus li Ourliers.
     Item obiit Robertus de Urcheyo, clericus quondam **domini Henrici
dicti Tuebuef**, qui dedit nobis decem libras positas in augmentacione
novem arpentorum terre site in finagio de Bauchisiaco, quam emimus a
liberis defuncti Gerardi de Paleya, militis, proppe molendinum Gerardi de
Plesseto, armigeri.

[Molinier, vol. 1, part 2, p. 966]

APPENDIX III

Index of Compositions Cited or Quoted in the Treatise

Compositions are listed in alphabetical order according to the orthography that appears in the treatise. Page and line references from the edition are given, as well as a brief extract from the passage in which the composition is mentioned. Manuscripts inventoried are those in which the composition appears in the version which is cited or quoted in the treatise (three-part motet, organum setting etc.). Manuscripts in which other versions of the piece appear are given on a new line after the indication Cf. If different forms of citation are used for the same composition, these are listed separately, but the reader is referred to a main entry for the manuscript inventory.

The following sigla are used:

ArsA: Paris, Bibliothèque de l'Arsenal, 135.

ArsB: Paris, Bibliothèque de l'Arsenal, 3517-3518.

Ba: Bamberg, Staatliche Bibliothek, Lit. 115.

BN 11266: Paris, Bibliothèque Nationale, lat. 11266 .

Boul: Boulogne-sur-Mer, Bibliothèque Municipale, 148.

Ca: Cambrai, Bibliothèque Municipale, A 410.

Cl: Paris, Bibliothèque Nationale, nouv. acq. fr. 13521.

F: Florence, Biblioteca Mediceo-Laurenziana, Plut. 29.1.

F18:   Florence, Biblioteca Nazionale, Banco Rari 18.

Fauv: Paris, Bibliothèque Nationale, fr. 146.

Hu: Burgos, Monasterio de las Huelgas.

LoB: London, British Library, Egerton 274.

LoC: London, British Library, Add. 30091.

LoD: London, British Library, Add. 27630.

Ma: Madrid, Biblioteca Nacional, 20486.

Mo: Montpellier, Faculté de Médecine, H 196.

MüA: Munich, Bayerische Staatsbibliothek, Mus. 4775.

MüB: Munich, Bayerische Staatsbibliothek, Musikfragment E III, 230-231.

Tu: Turin, Biblioteca Reale, Vari 42.

V: Rome, Biblioteca Vaticana, Reg. lat. 1490.

W1:   Wolfenbüttel, Herzog August-Bibliothek, Helmstedt 628.

W2:   Wolfenbüttel, Herzog August-Bibliothek, Helmstedt 1099.

Worc: Worcester, Cathedral Library, Add. 68.

Alleluya (= Res nova/Virgo decus castitatis/Alleluya)
   (*Cap*.II 196, 22: "Exemplum primae speciei sine littera patet
      hic . . .")

   Mo, 96v; Ba, 59v; Hu, 105; Ars B I, 2; Ars B II, 118; Boul, 92.
   Cf. Lo C, 5v; Boul, 92.

Alleluya Hic Martius (= Alleluya Hic Martinus)
   (*Cap*.Iii 142, 33: ". . . et hoc praecipue reperitur in *Alleluya* de
      Hic Martius.")

   F, 134; W2, 79v; Rome, Biblioteca Apostolica Vaticana, Ottob. lat.
      3025 ("Vatican Organum Treatise"), 49.
   Cf. Paris, Bibliothèque Nationale, lat. 1337, 272v.

Alleluya Posui (= Alleluya Posui Adiutorium)
   (*Cap*.Vii 276, 13-14 ". . . sicut patet in *Alleluya* de *Posui* tam in
      triplo cantu quam secundo . . ."

   F, 36; Mo, 16.

Amen (from Ave Maria)
>   (*Cap*.II 226, 32: "Exemplum earundem irregulariter positarum
>   sine tenore saepius et confuse patet in hoc exemplo de *Ave
>   Maria* . . . ")

>   See *Ave Maria*.

Ave Maria
>   (*Cap*.II 226, 32: "Exemplum earundem irregulariter positarum
>   sine tenore saepius et confuse patet in hoc exemplo de *Ave
>   Maria* . . . ")
>   (*Cap*.II 228, 29: "Hic vult actor ostendere qualiter huius
>   semibreves . . . positae sunt confuse . . . ut in *Ave
>   Maria* hoquetato.")

>   Not found.

Ave Regina (= Ave Regina/Alma redemptoris/Alma)
>   (*Cap*.II 206, 27: "Propter superhabundantiam litterae, sicut patet
>   hic . . . ")

>   Mo, 323v; Ba, 3v; Hu, 113v.

Che sunt amor<es?> (= Diex ou porrai je/Che sont amouretes/Omnes)
>   (*Cap*.II 200, 42: "Exemplum illius speciei cum littera patet
>   hic . . . ")

>   See *Dex ou prai je trover* and see also *Omnes* (1).

Chorus innocentium/In Bethleem/Veritatem (= Chorus innocencium/In
>   bethleem/In bethleem)
>   (*Cap*.II 238, 12: "Exemplum qualiter . . . conversio regulariter
>   reperitur . . . ")

>   Ba, 24v.
>   Cf. W1, 44v; Ma, 125; F, 382; W2, 163; Ca, 130; Cl, 382; BN
>   11266, 39v.

Cum gaudio (from Amor vincens/Marie preconio/Aptatur)
>   (*Cap*.Iii 162, 33: "Exemplum illius binariae, quam sola brevis

sequitur . . . cum littera tam ascendendo quam descendendo patet
hic . . . ")

Mo, 321v; Ba, 36v; Hu, 116v; F18, 144v; BN 11266, 37.
Cf. Ars A, 291; Lo D, 61.

Dex ele ma tot motur emble (?= Deus ele m'a tolu)
    (*Cap*.II 206, 43: "Longa vero praecedens tria tempora continebit, et
        debet signari per tractulum, qui vocatur divisio modorum, sicut
        patet hic . . .")

Not found. See Ludwig, vol. 2, p. 137 (No. 1157).
Cf. Lambertus (ed. Reaney/Gilles IV *5*, 20).

Dex ou prai je trover (= Diex ou porrai je/Che sont amouretes/Omnes)
    (*Cap*.IV 262, 8: "Quatenus autem ditonus et semiditonus in
        concordantiarum numero debeant collocari, patet . . . in triplo
        de *Che sunt amoretes, Dex ou prai je trover*, et in multis aliis
        cantibus . . . ")

Mo, 326v; Ba, 12; Tu, 30v; V, 114v.
Cf. Ca, 131.
See also *Che sunt amor<es?>* and *Omnes* (1).

Domine, Domine, rex gloriae
    (*Cap*.Iii 182, 5: "Ecce ostendit, qualiter supra litteram divisive
        scandere ab aliquibus sunt repertae . . . ")

Not found.
Cf. Lambertus (ed. Reaney/Gilles IV *16*, 35).

Douche amiete (= Ma jolivete/Douche amiete/V...)
    (*Cap*.II 210, 18: "Hic accedit actor ad notitiam sextae speciei, quae
        ex omnibus rectis brevibus seminatur . . . cum littera, sicut
        patet hic . . . ")

Mo, 224v.

Im bethlehem
In Bethleem
    (*Cap*.II 208, 30: "Et nota, quod duplex longa ob defectum
        planae musicae, aut propter colorem eiusdem ibi saepius
        reperitur . . .")
    (*Cap*.II 210, 11: "**Nunc duplo constat *In Bethleem* tibi monstrat.**")

W1, 44v; Ma, 125; F, 382; W2, 163.
Cf. Ba, 24v.
See also *Chorus innocentium/In Bethleem/Veritatem.*

In omni fratre tuo (= Mout me fu grief/In omni fratre tuo/In seculum)
    (*Cap*.Iii 166, 25: "Si autem haec quaternaria figura . . . bis per
        oppositum figuretur, sicut patet in hoc exemplo de *In omni fratre
        tuo* . . .")

    Mo, 66v; Ba, 27; Cl, 376.
    Cf. Lo B, 54v; Lo C, 4v; Boul, 92; Hu, 96.

In seculum (1) (= In seculum breve)
    (*Cap*.II 226, 17: "Exemplum qualiter huius semibreves in brevi modo
        debent artificialiter hoquetari patet hic . . . ")
    (*Cap*.II 252, 36: " . . . *nullus tractus inter duas figuras
        medium tenere debet, sed iuxta illum a qua sumitur stare
        tenetur* . . . ")

    Ba, 64.
    Cf. Mo, 3. Cf. Lambertus (ed. Reaney/Gilles IV *17*, 7).

In seculum (2) (= In seculum longum)
    (*Cap*.II 230, 35: "Exemplum quomodo et qualiter huius longae et
        breves in longo modo debent regulariter ordinari vel hoquetari
        patet hic . . . ")

    Ba, 63v.
    Cf. Mo, 1v; Ma, 122v.

Iudea et Ierusalem
    (*Cap*.Vii 276, 16: " . . . copula est id ubique, qu<o fit> multitudo
        punctorum simul iunctorum per suos tractus, et hoc sub specie
        primi modi et sub recta serie figurarum . . . nunc autem secundum
        dispositionem organi specialis . . . ")

    W1, 13; F, 65; W2, 47.

[*Mane prima*] (= Conditio/O natio/[Mane prima])
    (*Cap*.II 204, 25: "Haec autem [tertia] species est, quae procedit ex
        una longa et duabus brevibus et altera longa, tam sine littera
        quam cum littera. Sine littera ut hic . . . ")

    See *O natio* and see also *O natio/Conditio/Mane prima.*

Manere (1) (= Au douz tans/Biau dous amis/M[ane]re
    (*Cap*.II 208, 22: "Actor dicit, quod quinta species, quae
        ultramensurabilis est, ex omnibus longis undique perlustratur,
        ut patet hic . . . ")

    Mo, 163v; Ba, 9v; Tu, 7v.

Manere (2)
    (*Cap*.II 226, 45: "Exemplum qualiter huius semibreves supra tenorem
        primi modi regulariter hoquetantur patet hic . . . ")
    (*Cap*.II 228, 28: "Hic vult actor ostendere qualiter huius semibreves
        per cantus varios et praecipue per hoquetos positae sunt confuse
        . . . ")
    (*Cap*.II 228, 35: "Si [hoquetatio] sit perfecta, tunc ex sola parte
        resecatio fit reperta, sicut patet in hoc exemplo . . . ")

    Not found as hocket.

O natio (= Conditio/O natio/[Mane prima])
    (*Cap*.II 204, 25: "Haec autem [tertia] species est, quae procedit ex
        una longa et duabus brevibus et altera longa, tam sine littera
        quam cum littera. Cum littera sic . . . ")

    Mo, 87v; Ba, 49v; Darmstadt, Hessische Landesbibliothek, 3317, 7;
        Fauv, 11v; Lo D, p. 108.
    Cf. Worc, bv.
    See also [*Mane prima*] and *O natio/Conditio/Mane prima*.

O natio/Conditio/Mane prima (= Conditio/O natio/Mane prima)
    (*Cap*.II 236, 45: "Exemplum qualiter brevis modus in sextam
    speciem conversus . . . per conversionem simplicem extorquetur
    patet . . . ")

    See *O natio* and see also [*Mane prima*].

Omnes (1)
    (*Cap*.Ii 110, 11: **"Hanc tamen asconde velud hic sub lege secundae."**)
    (*Cap*.II 200, 36: "Exemplum qualiter disponitur figura binaria ante
        ternariam patet hic . . . ")
    (*Cap*.II 202, 39: **"Saepe duas ternis velut hic praecedere cernis."**)

    See *Dex ou prai je trover* and see also *Che sunt amor<es?>*.

Omnes (2) (= Ut celesti/Cum sit natus/Omnes)
    (*Cap*.II 202, 1: "Exemplum qualiter ternaria per se posita reperitur
       patet hic . . . ")

    Ba, 11v.
    Cf. Mo, 235v.

Par une matinee (= Par une matinee/Melli[s] stilla maris/Domine)
    (*Cap*.II 236, 43-44: " . . . nisi semibrevium superfluitas
       propter superhabundantiam litterae alicubi hoc excludat,
       sicut patet . . . ")

    Mo, 72v; Cl, 374v.
    Cf. Mo, 355v.

Plorans clama (from Chorus innocencium/In bethleem/In bethleem)
    (*Cap*.Iii 162, 41: "Exemplum ternariae eiusdem generis . . . cum
       littera patet hic . . . ")

    See *Chorus innocentium/In Bethleem/Veritatem.*

Portare
    (*Cap*.II 232, 1: "Hic dat actor doctrinam, quod non semper
       supradictae voces tam longae quam breves et semibreves
       regulariter ordinantur. Exemplum qualiter a regula deviant
       antedicta patet hic . . . ")

    Not found as hocket.

Poure socors (= Poure secors/Gaude chorus/Angelus)
    (*Cap*.II 224, 37: "Si supra tenorem sit talis resecatio ordinata, hoc
       erit sine littera, nisi aliquando eveniat in motellis, sicut
       patet . . . ")

    Mo, 71v; Ba, 19v; Cl, 390.
    Cf. Ars B II, 117v; Hu, 87.

Pro patribus
    (*Cap*.II 234, 10: "Et hoc praecipue et expresse per tertiam speciem
       hoquetatam, dicens, quod in ea et in aliis speciebus perfectis
       sit longarum et brevium hoquetatio pro voluntate ordinata, sicut
       patet hic . . . ")

    Not found as hocket.

Virgo decus castitas (= Res nova/Virgo decus castitatis/Alleluya)
   (*Cap*.II 196, 7:   "Hic intendit actor primae speciei notitiam
        breviter declarare, dicens, quod prima species est illa quae
        a recta longa incipit et recta brevi et longa, et sic usque
        in infinitum potentialiter . . . . Cum littera sicut patet
        hic . . .")

   See *Alleluya*.

Vox in rama (from Chorus innocencium/In bethleem/In bethleem)
   (*Cap*.Iii 162, 24:   "Exemplum illius binariae figurae, quae trium
        temporum aequippollentiam repraesentat . . . Cum littera . . .
        patet hic . . . ")

   See *Chorus innocentium/In Bethleem/Veritatem*.

BIBLIOGRAPHY

A. MANUSCRIPTS

(Manuscripts listed in Appendix II and III are not included here)

Erfurt. Wissenschaftliche Bibliothek der Stadt. Ca 8° 94.

Milan. Biblioteca Ambrosiana. D5.

Munich. Bayerische Staatsbibliothek. Cbm. Cat. 13.

Munich. Bayerische Staatsbibliothek. Cbm. Cat. 3.

Munich. Bayerische Staatsbibliothek. Cbm C. 14. C1-4.

Munich. Bayerische Staatsbibliothek. Clm 11348.

Munich. Bayerische Staatsbibliothek. Clm 14523.

Munich. Bayerische Staatsbibliothek. Clm 14397.

Munich. Bayerische Staatsbibliothek. Clm 14675.

Munich. Haupt-Staats-Archiv. Reg. St. Emmeram. Lit. 19½.

New York. Columbia University. X 88 Ar 512.

Paris. Bibliothèque Nationale. Fonds latin 16069.

Paris. Bibliothèque Nationale. Fonds latin 8422.

Rome. Biblioteca Apostolica Vaticana. Regin. lat. 1146.

B. MEDIEVAL AND CLASSICAL SOURCES

Alan of Lille. *De Planctu Naturae*. Ed. J. P. Migne. Patrologia Latina
    CCX. Paris, 1855.

Alexander of Hales. *Summa Theologiae*. Ed. Klumper. 4 vols.
    Quaracchi, 1924-1948.

Alexander of Villedieu. *Doctrinale*. Ed. Dietrich Reichling. *Das
    Doctrinale des Alexander de Villa-Dei*. Monumenta Germaniae
    Paedagogica, Schulordnungen, Schulbücher und pädagogische
    Miscellaneen XII. Berlin, 1893.

"Annotatio manuscriptorum librorum Bibliothecae Monasterii S.
    Emmerami Ratisbonae." See Munich, Bayerische Staatsbibliothek,   Cbm
    Cat. 3, folios 54-61v.

[Anonymous II.] [*Tractatus De Discantu*.] Ed. Coussemaker.
    Scriptorum de musica medii aevi nova series I, pp. 303-319. Paris,
    1864.

[Anonymous IV.] [*De Musica*.] Ed. Fritz Reckow. *Der Musiktraktat
    des Anonymus 4*. 2 vols. Beihefte zum Archiv für Musikwissenschaft
    IV-V. Wiesbaden, 1967.

[Anonymous VII.] [*De Musica Libellus*] Ed. Coussemaker.
    Scriptorum de musica medii aevi nova series I, pp. 378-383. Paris,
    1864.
    Ed. Gilbert Reaney. Corpus Scriptorum de Musica XXXVI. Forthcoming.

[Aristoteles Latinus.] *Categoriae vel Praedicamenta*. Ed. Lorenzo
    Minio-Paluello. Aristoteles Latinus I, 1-5. Bruges, 1961.

Bernard Silvestris. *Cosmographia*. Ed. Peter Dronke. Textus
    minores LIII. Leiden, 1978.

Boethius, Anicius Manlius Severinus. *De Institutione Arithmetica*. Ed.
    Friedlein. *Anicii Manlii Torquati Severini Boetii De
    Institutione Arithmetica Libri Duo, De Institutione Musica Libri
    Quinque, Accedit Geometria Quae Fertur Boetii*. Leipzig, 1867.
    Reprint: Frankfurt, 1966.

------. *De Divisione*. Ed. Lorenzo Pozzi. *Trattato sulla divisione*.
    Padua, 1969.

------. *De Institutione Musica*. Ed. Friedlein. *Anicii Manlii
    Torquati Severini Boetii De Institutione Arithmetica Libri Duo, De
    Institutione Musica Libri Quinque, Accedit Geometria Quae Fertur
    Boetii*. Leipzig, 1867. Reprint: Frankfurt, 1966.

-----. *Geometria*. Ed. Friedlein. *Anicii Manlii Torquati Severini Boetii De Institutione Arithmetica Libri Duo, De Institutione Musica Libri Quinque, Accedit Geometria Quae Fertur Boetii*. Leipzig, 1867. Reprint: Frankfurt, 1966.

-----. *Philosophiae Consolatio*. Ed. Emanuele Rapisarda. Catania, 1961.

Capella, Martianus. *De Nuptiis Philologiae et Mercurii*. Ed. F. Eyssenhardt. *Martianus Capella*. Leipzig, 1866.

Cassiodorus [Flavius Magnus Aurelius Cassiodorus, Senator]. *Institutiones*. Ed. R. A. B. Mynors. *Cassiodori Senatoris Institutiones*. Oxford, 1937.

Cato [Marcus Porcius Cato 'Censorius'] (attrib.). *Disticha*. Ed. Joseph Nève. *Catonis Disticha*. Liège, 1926.

Eberhard of Béthune. *Graecismus*. Ed. Johann Wrobel. Corpus grammaticorum medii aevi I. Breslau, 1887.

Elias Salamon. *Scientia Artis Musicae*. Ed. M. Gerbert. *Scriptores ecclesiastici de musica sacra* III, pp. 16-64. St. Blasien, 1784.

Franco of Cologne. *Ars Cantus Mensurabilis*. Ed. Gilbert Reaney and André Gilles. *Franconis de Colonia Ars Cantus Mensurabilis*. Corpus Scriptorum de Musica XVIII. [n. p.], 1974.

Geoffrey of Vinsauf. *Poetria Nova*. Ed. Edmond Faral, *Les arts poétiques*. Trans. Margaret Nims, *Poetria Nova of Geoffrey of Vinsauf*. Toronto, 1967.

Gervase of Melkley. *Ars Versificaria*. Ed. Hans-Jürgen Grabner. "Ars Poetica." In *Forschungen zur Romanischen Philologie* XVII. Münster, 1965.

Guido of Arezzo. *Micrologus*. Ed. van Waesberghe. *Guidonis Aretini Micrologus*. Corpus Scriptorum de Musica IV. n.p., 1955.

Horace [Quintus Horatius Flaccus]. *Ars Poetica*. Ed. James Kirkland. Boston, 1901.

-----. *Epistulae*. Ed. Frideric Klingner. *Q. Horati Flacci Opera*. Leipzig, 1959.

Isidore of Seville. *Etymologiae*. Ed. W. M. Lindsay. *Isidori Hispalensis Episcopi Etymologiarum sive Originum Libri XX*. Oxford, 1911.

Jacques de Liège. *Speculum Musicae*. Ed. Roger Bragard. *Jacobi Leodiensis Speculum Musicae*. Corpus Scriptorum de Musica III. [n. p.], 1973.

Johannes Afflighemensis. *De Musica.* Ed. van Waesberghe. *Johannis Affligemensis De Musica cum Tonario.* Corpus Scriptorum de Musica I. Rome, 1950.

Johannes de Garlandia. *De Mensurabili Musica.* Ed. Erich Reimer, *Johannes de Garlandia: De mensurabili Musica: Kritische Edition mit Kommentar und Interpretation der Notationslehre.* 2 vols. Beihefte zum Archiv für Musikwissenschaft X-XI. Wiesbaden, 1972.

John of Salisbury. *Metalogicon.* Ed. C. C. J. Webb. Oxford, 1929.

Lambertus. [*De Musica.*] Ed. Coussemaker. *Scriptorum de musica medii aevi nova series* I, pp. 251-281. Paris, 1864. Ed. André Gilles and Gilbert Reaney. Corpus Scriptorum de Musica. Forthcoming.

"Liberia ecclesiae sancti Emmerammi Ratisbonensis." See Munich, Bayerische Staatsbibliothek, Clm 14397, folios 14-19v.

Matthew of Vendôme. *Ars Versificatoria.* Ed. Edmond Faral. *Les arts poétiques du XIIe et du XIIIe siècle.* Paris, 1924. Reprint: 1971. Trans. Roger Parr. *Matthew of Vendôme: Ars Versificatoria (The Art of the Versemaker).* Mediaeval Philosophical Texts in Translation XXII. Milwaukee, 1981.

[Menger, Dionysius.] "Registrum sive Inventarium librorum bibliothecae monasterii Sancti Emmerammi episcopi et martyris." See Munich, Bayerische Staatsbibliothek, Clm 14675.

Ovid [Publius Ovidius Naso]. *Metamorphoses.* Ed. Van Proosdij. *P. Ovidii Nasonis Metamorphoseon Libri I-XV.* Leiden, 1959.

-----. *Remedia Amoris.* Ed. A. A. R. Henderson. *P. Ovidi Nasonis Remedia Amoris.* Edinburgh, 1979.

-----. *Tristia.* Ed. S. G. Owen. *Ovidi Nasonis Tristium Liber II.* Oxford, 1915.

Philippe de Vitry. *Ars Nova.* Ed. Reaney, Gilles, and Maillard. *Philippi de Vitriaco Ars Nova.* Corpus Scriptorum de Musica VIII. [n. p.], 1964.

Thomas Aquinas. *Summa Theologica.* In *Opera Omnia.* Rome, 1882-.

C. MODERN STUDIES AND REFERENCE WORKS

Allgemeine deutsche Biographie. 56 vols. Leipzig, 1875-1912.

Analecta hymnica medii aevi. Ed. Blume and Dreves. 55 vols. Leipzig, 1886-1922.

Anderson, Gordon. "Magister Lambertus and Nine Rhythmic Modes." *Acta Musicologica* XLV (1973): 57-73.

-----. "The Notation of the Bamberg and Las Huelgas Manuscripts." *Musica Disciplina* XXXII (1978): 19-67.

Anspach, August Eduard. *Las Etimologías en la tradición manuscrita medieval.* León, 1966.

Baldwin, John. *Masters, Princes, and Merchants: The Social Views of Peter the Chanter and His Circle.* 2 vols. Princeton, 1970.

Baltzer, Rebecca. "Lambertus." In *The New Grove Dictionary of Music and Musicians,* vol. 10. London, 1980.

Becker, Gustav. *Catalogi bibliothecarum antiqui.* Bonn, 1885.

Beer, Ellen. "Parisian Book Illustrations at the Time of Louis IX (King and Saint) in the Last Quarter of the 13th Century." *Zur Kunstgeschichte* XLIV (1981): 62-91.

Bernhard, Michael. *Wortkonkordanz zu Anicius Manlius Severinus Boethius De Institutione Musica.* Bayerische Akademie der Wissenschaften, Veröffentlichungen der Musikhistorischen Kommission IV. Munich, 1979.

Bernt, Günter. *Das lateinische Epigramm in Übergang von der Spätantike zum frühen Mittelalter.* Münchener Beiträge zur Mediävistik und Renaissance-Forschung II. Munich, 1968.

Bezzel, Irmgard. *Bayerische Staatsbibliothek München: Bibliotheksführer: Geschichte und Bestände.* Munich, 1967.

Bischoff, Bernhard. *Literarisches und künstlerisches Leben in St. Emmeram (Regensburg) während des frühen und hohen Mittelalters.* Studien und Mitteilungen zur Geschichte des Benediktiner-Ordens und seiner Zweige LI. Munich, 1933.

-----. "Studien zur Geschichte des Klosters St. Emmeram im Spätmittelalter (1324-1525)." In *Mittelalterliche Studien: Ausgewählte Aufsätze zur Schriftkunde und Literaturgeschichte,* vol. 2. Stuttgart, 1967.

-----. *Die südostdeutschen Schreibschulen und Bibliotheken in der Karolingerzeit.* 2 vols. *Die Bayrischen Diözesen.* Leipzig, 1940. Reprint: Wiesbaden, 1960. *Die vorwiegend Österreichischen Diözesen.* Wiesbaden, 1980.

Bolgar, R. R. *The Classical Heritage and Its Beneficiaries.* Cambridge, 1954.

Bonnard, Fourier. *Histoire de l'abbaye royale et de l'ordre des chanoines réguliers de St. Victor de Paris.* 2 vols. Paris, 1904-1908.

Branner, Robert. *Manuscript Painting in Paris During the Reign of Saint Louis: A Study of Styles*. Berkeley, 1977.

Buhle, Edward. *Die musikalischen Instrumente in den Miniaturen des frühen Mittelalters: Ein Beitrag zur Geschichte der Musikinstrumente*. Vol. 1: *Die Blasinstrumente*. Leipzig, 1903.

Catalogus codicum manu scriptorum Bibliothecae Regiae Monacensis. Munich, 1856-.

Chartularium Universitatis Parisiensis. Ed. Denifle and Chatelain. 4 vols. Paris, 1891. Reprint, 1964.

Cheney, C. R. (ed.). *Handbook of Dates for Students of English History*. Royal Historical Society Guides and Handbooks IV. London, 1955.

Coussemaker, Charles Edmond Henri de. *Scriptorum de musica medii aevi nova series*. 4 vols. Paris, 1864-1876.

Curtius, Ernst Robert. *European Literature and the Latin Middle Ages*. Trans. Willard Trask. Bollingen Series XXXVI. New York, 1953.

Du Cange, Charles (ed.). *Glossarium Mediae et Infimae Latinitatis*. 7 vols. Paris, 1840-50.

Erdmann, Carl. "Leonitas: Zur mittelalterlichen Lehre von Kursus, Rhythmus und Reim." In *'Corona Quernea': Festgabe Karl Strecker zum 80. Geburtstage dargebracht*. Leipzig, 1941.

Faral, Edmond. *Les arts poétiques du XIIe et du XIIIe siècle*. Paris, 1924. Reprint, 1971.

Fassler, Margot. "Who Was Adam of St. Victor? The Evidence of the Sequence Manuscripts." *Journal of the American Musicological Society* XXXVII (1984): 233-269.

Friedlein, Gottfried (ed.). *Anicii Manlii Torquati Severini Boetii De Institutione Arithmetica Libri Duo, De Institutione Musica Libri Quinque, Accedit Geometria Quae Fertur Boetii*. Leipzig, 1867. Reprint: Frankfurt, 1966.

Frobenius, Wolf. "Zur Datierung von Francos Ars Cantus Mensurabilis." *Archiv für Musikwissenschaft* XXVII (1970): 122-127.

General Rules for the Editions of Corpus Scriptorum de Musica. Rome, 1950.

Gerbert, Martin (ed.). *Scriptores ecclesiastici de musica sacra*. 3 vols. St. Blasien, 1784.

Glauche, Günter. *Schullektüre im Mittelalter: Entstehung und Wandlungen des Lektürekanons bis 1200 nach den Quellen dargestellt.* Münchener Beiträge zur Mediävistik und Renaissance-Forschung V. Munich, 1970.

Glorieux, Palémon. *Aux Origines de la Sorbonne.* 2 vols. Etudes de philosophie médiévale LIV. Paris, 1965.

------. *La Faculté des arts et ses maîtres au xiiie siècle.* Etudes de philosophie médiévale LIX. Paris, 1971.

A Glossary of Later Latin to 600 A. D. Ed. Alexander Souter. Rev. ed. Oxford, 1964.

Grabner, Hans-Jürgen. "Ars Poetica." In *Forschungen zur Romanischen Philologie* XVII. Münster, 1965.

Guérard, M. (ed.). *Cartulaire de l'église Notre-Dame de Paris.* 4 vols. Collection des cartulaires de France IV-VII. *Collection de documents inédits sur l'histoire de France.* Series 1. Paris, 1850.

Gümpel, Karl-Werner. *Die Musiktraktate Conrads von Zabern.* Akademie der Wissenschaften und der Literatur, Abhandlungen der Geistes- und Sozialwissenschaftlichen Klasse, 1956 No. 4. Wiesbaden, 1956.

Haar, James. "Roger Caperon and Ramos de Pareia." *Acta Musicologica* XLI (1969): 26-36.

Hauke, Hermann. *Katalog der lateinischen Handschriften der Bayerischen Staatsbibliothek München: Clm 28111-28254.* Catalogus codicum manu scriptorum Bibliothecae Monacensis, IV, 7. Wiesbaden, 1986.

Hemmerle, Josef. *Die Benediktinerklöster in Bayern.* Germania Benedictina, vol. 2. Augsburg, 1970.

Hughes, Andrew. "Franco of Cologne." In *The New Grove Dictionary of Music and Musicians,* vol. 6. London, 1980.

Huglo, Michel. "De Francon de Cologne à Jacques de Liège." *Revue belge de musicologie* XXXIV (1980): 44-60.

------. "Les 'libelli' de tropes et les premiers tropaires-prosaires." In *"Pax et Sapientia": In Memoriam Gordon A. Anderson.* Stockholm, 1986.

------. "Recherches sur la personne et l'oeuvre de Francon." Forthcoming.

------. *Les tonaires: Inventaire, analyse, comparaison.* Publications de la Société française de musicologie III, 2. Paris, 1971.

Hüschen, Heinrich. "Musik." In *Die Musik in Geschichte und Gegenwart,* vol. 9. Kassel, 1961.

Ineichen-Eder, Christine. *Mittelalterliche Bibliothekskataloge Deutchlands und der Schweiz IV, 2: Bistümer Passau und Regensburg.* Munich, 1977.

Jan, Karl von (ed.). *Musici Scriptores Graeci.* Leipzig, 1895.

Kennedy's Revised Latin Primer. London, 1962.

Klemm, Elisabeth. *Die romanischen Handschriften der Bayerischen Staatsbibliothek: Katalog der illuminierte Handschriften der Bayerischen Staatsbibliothek in München.* 4 vols. Wiesbaden, 1980-.

Klingner, Frideric (ed.). *Q. Horati Flacci Opera.* Leipzig, 1959.

Klopsch, Paul. *Einführung in die mittellateinische Verslehre.* Darmstadt, 1972.

Kneale, William and Martha. *The Development of Logic.* Oxford, 1962.

Koehler, Friedrich. *Ehstländische Klosterlektüre.* Tellinn, 1892.

Kottje, Raymund. "Klosterbibliotheken und monastische Kultur in der zweiten Hälfte des 11. Jahrhunderts." *Zeitschrift für Kirchengeschichte* LXXX (1969): 145-162.

[Kraus, Johann Baptist.] *Bibliotheca principalis ecclesiae et monasterii ord. S. Benedicti ad S. Emmeramum Epis. et Martyr.* 4 vols. Regensburg, 1748.

Kretzmann, Kenny, and Pinborg, (eds.). *The Cambridge History of Later Medieval Philisophy from the Rediscovery of Aristotle to the Disintegration of Scholasticism 1100-1600.* Cambridge, 1982.

Lambert, Bernard, O.S.B. *Bibliotheca Hieronymiana manuscripta: La Tradition manuscrite des oeuvres de St. Jérôme.* 7 vols. Instrumenta Patristica IV, 1a-4b. Steenbrugge, 1964-1972.

Lebeuf, Jean. *Histoire de la ville et de tout le diocèse de Paris.* Paris, 1755-58. Reprint, 1883.

Lexicon Latinitatis Medii Aevi. Ed. Albert Blaise. Turnholt, 1975.

Lipphardt, Walther. "Notation." In *Die Musik in Geschichte und Gegenwart,* vol. 9. Kassel, 1961.

Manuscripts of Polyphonic Music: 11th - Early 14th Century. Ed. Gilbert Reaney. Répertoire international des sources musicales B/IV/1. Munich, 1966.

Margalits, Eduard. *Florilegium Proverbiorum Universae Latinitatis: Proverbia, Proverbiales, Sententiae, Gnomaeque Classicae, Mediae et Infimae Latinitatis.* Budapest, 1895.

Masi, Michael. "Manuscripts Containing the 'De Musica' of Boethius."
    Manuscripta XV (1971): 89-95.

Mediae Latinitatis Lexicon Minus. Ed. J. F. Niermeyer. Leiden, 1976.

Meyer, Wilhelm. "Radewins Gedicht über Theophilus und die Arten der
    gereimten Hexameter," in *Gesammelte Abhandlungen zur
    mittellateinischen Rythmik* I. Berlin, 1905.

Mittellateinisches Wörterbuch bis zum ausgehenden 13. Jahrhundert.
    Munich, 1967-.

Molinier, Auguste (ed.). *Obituaires de la province de Sens*. Recueil
    des historiens de la France. Obituaires. 4 vols. Paris, 1902-1923.

Musik in Bayern. 2 vols. Tutzing, 1972.

Neue deutsche Biographie. Berlin, 1953-.

Nims, Margaret. *Poetria Nova of Geoffrey of Vinsauf*. Toronto, 1967.

Norberg, Dag. *Introduction à l'étude de la versification latine*
    Stockholmiensia V. Uppsala, 1958.

Novum Glossarium Mediae Latinitatis Ab Anno DCCC Usque Ad Annum MCC.
    Copenhagen, 1957-.

Owen, S. G. (ed.). *P. Ovidi Nasonis Tristium Liber Secundus*.
    Amsterdam, 1967.

Pächt, Otto. *Illuminated Manuscripts in the Bodleian Library Schools*.
    Oxford, 1966. *Italian School*. Oxford, 1970. *British, Irish and
    Icelandic Schools*. Oxford, 1973.

Panofsky, Erwin. *Gothic Architecture and Scholasticism*. Latrobe,
    Pennsylvania, 1951. Reprint: New York, 1957.

Parkes, Malcolm. "The Influence of the Concepts of *Ordinatio* and
    Learning and Literature: Essays Presented to Richard William Hunt.
    Oxford, 1976.

Parr, Roger. *Matthew of Vendôme: Ars Versificatoria (The Art of the
    Versemaker)*. Mediaeval Philosophical Texts in Translation XXII.
    Milwaukee, 1981.

Patrologia Latina. Ed. J. P. Migne. 221 vols. Paris, 1844-

Piendl, Max. "Fontes monasterii S. Emmerami Ratisbonensis: Bau- und
    kunstgeschichtliche Quellen." In *Quellen und Forschungen zur
    Geschichte des ehemaligen Reichstiftes St. Emmeram in Regensburg*.
    Thurn und Taxis-Studien I (1961): 79.

Piltz, Anders. *The World of Medieval Learning*. Trans. David Jones.
    Totowa, 1981.

Raby, F. J. E. *A History of Christian-Latin Poetry from the
    Beginnings to the Close of the Middle Ages.* 2nd. ed. Oxford, 1953.

Rasch, Rudolf. *Iohannes de Garlandia en de Ontwikkeling van de
    voor-Franconische Notatie.* Musicological Studies XX. Brooklyn,
    1969.

Rashdall, Hastings. *The Universities of Europe in the Middle Ages.*
    Ed. Powicke and Emden. 3 vols. Oxford, 1936.

Reaney, Gilles, and Maillard (eds.). *Philippi de Vitriaco Ars Nova.*
    Corpus Scriptorum de Musica VIII. [n. p.], 1964.

Reaney and Gilles (eds.). *Franconis de Colonia Ars Cantus Mensurabilis.*
    Corpus Scriptorum de Musica XVIII. [n. p.], 1974.

Reckow, Fritz. *Der Musiktraktat des Anonymus 4.* 2 vols. Beihefte
    zum Archiv für Musikwissenschaft IV-V. Wiesbaden, 1967.

------. "Proprietas und Perfectio; zur Geschichte des Rhythmus, seiner
    Aufzeichnung und Terminologie im 13. Jahrhundert." *Acta Musicologica*
    XXXIX (1967): 115-143.

Reimer, Erich. *Johannes de Garlandia: De mensurabili Musica:
    Kritische Edition mit Kommentar und Interpretation der
    Notationslehre.* 2 vols. Beihefte zum Archiv für Musikwissenschaft
    X-XI. Wiesbaden, 1972.

Revised Medieval Latin Word-List. Ed. R. E. Latham. London, 1965.
    Reprint, 1973.

Sachs, Klaus-Jürgen. *Der Contrapunctus im 14. und 15. Jahrhundert:
    Untersuchungen zum Terminus, zur Lehre und zu den Quellen.* Beihefte
    zum Archiv für Musikwissenschaft XIII. Wiesbaden, 1974.

Sanders, Ernest. "Sources, MS, V, 2: Early Motet." In *The New Grove
    Dictionary of Music and Musicians*, vol. 17. London, 1980.

Sanftl, Colomann. "Catalogus veterum codicum manuscriptorum ad S.
    Emmeram Ratisbonae." See Munich, Bayerische Staatsbibliothek, Cbm
    C. 14, C1-4.

Schlötterer, Reinhold. "Münchener Musikhandschriften." In *Die Musik
    in Geschichte und Gegenwart*, vol. 9. Kassel, 1961.

Schmid, Hans. *Die musiktheoretischen Handschriften der Benediktiner-
    Abtei Tegernsee: Ein Beitrag zur Erfassung und Sichtung der
    musiktheoretischen Hinterlassenschaft des Mittelalters.* Ph. D.
    dissertation, Ludwigs-Maximilians-Universität, Munich, 1951.

Seebass, Tilman. *Musikdarstellung und Psalterillustration im früheren
    Mittelalter: Studien ausgehend von einer Ikonologie der Handschrift
    Paris Bibliothèque nationale fonds latin 1118.* 2 vols. Bern, 1973.

Silano, Giulio. "Glossators." In *Dictionary of the Middle Ages*, vol. 5. New York, 1985.

Sowa, Heinrich. *Ein anonymer glossierter Mensuraltraktat 1279.* Königsberger Studien zur Musikwissenschaft IX. Kassel, 1930.

Stahl, William Harris. *Martianus Capella and the Seven Liberal Arts.* 2 vols. Records of Civilization: Sources and Studies LXXXIV. New York and London, 1971.

Steger, Hugo. *Philologia musica: Sprachzeichen, Bild und Sache im literarisch-musikalischen Leben des Mittelalters: Lire, Harfe, Rotte und Fidel.* Münstersche Mittelalter-Schriften II. Munich, 1971.

Stump, Eleonore. *Boethius's De Topicis Differentiis.* Ithaca and London, 1978.

Swarzenski, Georg. *Die Regensburger Buchmalerei des X. und XI. Jahrhunderts: Studien zur Geschichte der deutschen Malerei des frühen Mittelalters.* Denkmäler der süddeutschen Malerei des frühen Mittelalters I. Stuttgart, 1969.

Swerdlow, Noel. "'Musica Dicitur A Moys, Quod Est Aqua'." *Journal of the American Musicological Society* XX (1967): 3-9.

The Theory of Music: Manuscripts from the Carolingian Era up to c. 1500 in the Federal Republic of Germany. Ed. Michel Huglo and Christian Meyer. Répertoire international des sources musicales B/III/3. Munich, 1986.

Thesaurus Linguae Latinae. Leipzig, 1900-.

Thorndike, Lynn. *University Records and Life in the Middle Ages.* Records of Civilization: Sources and Studies XXXVIII. New York, 1944.

Ursprung, Otto. *Die katholische Kirchenmusik.* Handbuch der Musikwissenschaft, Lieferung 74, vol. 9. Potsdam, [1931].

van Waesberghe, Joseph (ed.). *Guidonis Aretini Micrologus.* Corpus Scriptorum de Musica IV. n.p., 1955.

------. *Johannis Affligemensis De Musica cum Tonario.* Corpus Scriptorum de Musica I. Rome, 1950.

Walther, Hans. *Proverbia Sententiaeque Latinitatis Medii Aevi: lateinische Sprichwörter und Sentenzen des Mittelalters in alphabetischer Anordnung.* Carmina Medii Aevi Posterioris Latina II-. Göttingen, 1963-.

Wattenbach, Wilhelm. *Deutschlands Geschichtsquellen im Mittelalter: Die Zeit der Sachsen und Salier.* 3 vols. Darmstadt, 1967-71.

Werner, Jakob. *Lateinische Sprichwörter und Sinnsprüche des Mittelalters aus Handschriften gesammelt.* 2nd. rev. ed. Heidelberg, 1966.

West, Martin. *Textual Criticism and Editorial Technique Applicable to Greek and Latin Texts.* Stuttgart, 1973.

Wiesend, Reinhard. *Die Notierungen der Musikbeispiele in den Münchner Guido-Handschriften.* Magister-Prüfung, Ludwigs-Maximilians-Universität, Munich, 1971.

Willis, James. *Latin Textual Criticism.* Illinois Studies in Language and Literature LXI. Urbana, 1972.

Wright, Craig. "Leoninus, Poet and Musician." *Journal of the American Musicological Society* XXXIX (1986): 1-35.

Yudkin, Jeremy. "Notre Dame Theory: A Study of Terminology, Including a New Translation of the Music Treatise of Anonymous IV." Ph. D. dissertation, Stanford University, 1982.

-----. "The Anonymous of St. Emmeram and Anonymous IV on the *Copula.*" *The Musical Quarterly* LXX (1984): 1-22.

-----. "The Influence of Aristotle on French University Music Texts." In proceedings of the conference "Musical Theory and Its Sources: Antiquity and the Middle Ages." Forthcoming.

-----. "The Rhythm of Organum Purum." *The Journal of Musicology* II (1983): 355-376.

-----. *The Music Treatise of Anonymous IV: A New Translation.* Musicological Studies and Documents XLI. Neuhausen- Stuttgart, 1985.

Ziolkowski, Jan. *Alan of Lille's Grammar of Sex: The Meaning of Grammar to a Twelfth-Century Intellectual.* Speculum Anniversary Monographs X. Cambridge, Massachusetts, 1985.

[Zirngibl, Roman.] "Catalogus manuscriptorum bibliothecae monasterii S. Emmerami." See Munich, Bayerische Staatsbibliothek, Cbm. Cat. 13.

INDEX
VERBORUM ATQUE NOMINUM

148:33,36,39; 160:13,25; 162:24; 166:
12,31; 174:11; 180:36; 220:1,3,8,13,26,
31,33,40; 222:9,10,11,13,25; 224:10,12;
226:4,10; 232:35,40; 234:38; 236:3,6,
24,36; 238:14; 260:33; 270:19; 272:9;
276:10
aequip(p)ollentialiter 166:33; 168:37
aequip(p)ollere 130:12,26; 132:15; 142:
10; 146:45; 156:9; 162:21; 166:20; 168:
29; 242:8; 254:27
aequisonantia 262:14; 264:29
aequivalere 132:14
aequivocatio 140:5
aequivoce 96:19
aequivocus 86:19; 98:44
aequus 126:32
aestimare 254:10,11
aetas 288:30
aeternus 254:1; 288:33
aevum 288:21,29
affectus 150:31
affinitas 76:6,25; 104:7; 110:10; 264:1
agere 68:9,10,12; 72:2; 82:9,16; 88:17,
19,34; 100:14; 118:16,17,20,23,25,29,
31,34,35,41; 120:4,5; 154:42; 184:21;
188:21; 194:5,11,17,24,27,34; 220:13,
16,19,23,31; 244:12,22,24,30,34; 272:
21,23; 282:11
ag(g)redi 78:36; 86:3; 184:4; 192:47;
258:1; 270:3
alienus 216:13
alimentum 74:11; 192:11
ala 76:37; 78:1
allicere 68:13; 282:27; 284:10
altercare 138:19
altercatio 138:28; 214:24
alternare 232:1,29
alternatio 230:34; 232:40; 234:35
altrinsecatio 224:33,39; 228:34; 242:2
altus 70:16; 96:19,21,25,30,34,37,39;
98:21,21,23; 112:4; 120:26; 136:14;
154:32; 222:31
ambiguitas 252:37
ambiguus 256:4
ampliatio 104:40
angere 160:5
anima 66:11; 268:2
animus 66:1; 70:14; 80:10; 192:14; 282:
27,31; 284:10; 288:7
annus 288:35
antecedere 68:3
antecessor 64:10; 70:30; 74:34; 94:34;
132:44; 186:9; 250:35
anterior 136:44; 150:1; 156:23,24
antesupremus 140:33
anthonomasice 224:16
antiquus 66:38
ap(p)arere 94:21; 100:17; 122:12; 134:29;
158:4; 186:19
aperte 74:42; 232:17
apertus 160:26
apetibilis 134:24
apositio 224:41
apotumasion 66:37
apparentia 254:46
ap(p)ellare 90:30; 94:36,39; 98:44; 102:
2,8,9,12; 104:41; 106:4; 186:25,29,37,
42; 204:16,20; 214:22; 260:26; 276:3;
284:3; 98:44
ap(p)etere 68:18; 76:11,32; 248:34;
284:35
ap(p)onere 64:7; 68:12; 90:34; 92:16;

92:19; 96:46; 98:45; 100:22; 100:43;
118:37; 150:3; 160:45; 170:41; 172:32;
174:27; 184:20; 188:24; 190:42; 222:41;
260:39; 268:7; 270:16; 272:13
appositio 234:36
ap(p)rehendere 134:21,22; 156:19
approbabilis 64:13; 254:2
ap(p)robare 64:22; 72:38; 74:5; 92:28,36;
94:19; 130:27; 150:20; 160:28; 204:23;
230:4; 250:36; 254:14; 262:7
ap(p)ropriatio 98:37; 102:13
aptare 286:4
aptus 76:5; 182:17
aqua 66:25,26,29,30,33; 66:30; 96:28;
224:23
arbitrari 146:36; 148:24
arbor 192:7,8
arguere 82:3; 100:32; 106:14; 122:2,12;
144:17; 164:12
argumentum 144:35
Argus 74:4,14,15,20,23,28
arimetrus 268:27
armariolum 224:24
armonia 66:9; 76:14; 96:18; 224:17,18;
234:39
armonicus 150:34
arrogantia 72:6
ars 64:1,2,4,11,13; 66:39,41; 68:33,35;
70:18,36; 74:1,3,5,38,41; 76:22; 82:14,
26; 84:12; 86:9,14,23; 90:8; 94:5; 96:
2,7; 98:39; 100:5; 102:29; 104:1,26;
106:9; 110:33; 112:34,48; 114:25; 116:
7,10; 126:32; 132:2,43; 134:2,8,18,27;
136:3,32,33; 138:33; 142:8,10; 144:12;
146:20,30; 148:26; 158:27; 160:19,22,
37; 162:7; 164:1,9,21,35; 166:24,36;
170:13; 178:39; 180:21; 182:17,22,40;
184:12,30; 186:4,7,47 188:15,19; 190:
44; 192:12; 194:13; 198:17; 202:9,35;
204:5; 206:10; 212:23,26,34; 214:30,36;
230:1; 234:42; 236:15,19; 246:12,15;
248:38; 252:28; 254:42; 264:25; 268:27;
274:1,15; 284:32; 286:21; 288:2
artare 186:3; 286:39
artifex 68:40; 252:13; 282:32
artificialis 66:17; 282:7,39; 284:20
artificialiter 94:29; 98:6; 102:36; 128:
17; 134:16; 136:28; 160:3,24; 162:9,20;
164:23; 186:18; 188:12; 198:19; 212:20;
220:25; 226:12,18; 242:3; 252:44
artificiose 184:22
artificium 114:25; 164:4; 282:32
ascensus 92:32,34,35,37; 120:20,23; 122:
29; 142:30; 148:45;152:34,34,35,37,39,
43,44,45; 154:1,26; 160:36
ascondere 110:11
asilus 152:4
asserere 64:8; 66:29; 92:24; 98:10; 100:
20; 104:8; 106:10; 144:10,12; 148:33;
164:31; 190:19; 198:38; 214:32; 252:12,
28; 256:4; 266:42
assidue 208:38; 210:10
assignare 86:1,3; 100:6,8,9,11,12,13,21;
102:2; 104:13; 118:7; 124:54; 128:45;
134:3; 142:21; 152:23; 154:18; 156:33;
158:39; 168:26; 172:38,39,42; 174:1,3,
8,9; 182:14; 226:7; 250:16; 258:14;
276:27
assimulare 196:37,39
associare 88:7; 130:42; 178:29
atestare 66:20
attingere 198:28; 244:2; 250:23,26;38

14; 224:8; 228:15; 256:33; 266:6,21;
cassus 102:34,35; 282:37; 284:19,23,27;
cathena 66:9
Catho 64:18
cauda 88:2; 90:25,32; 92:17,41,43; 96:
35,36; 98:45; 100:7,9; 122:36; 158:29;
160:47; 170:39,40,41; 172:21,32,34;
174:6,7,16,19,21; 176:1,3,26,42,43;
178:22,24
causa 78:35,37; 86:7; 92:18,28; 96:30;
102:1,12; 108:14; 112:42; 128:23,25;
144:22,22; 146:1,1,2,4,13,25; 150:27;
154:32; 156:2,28; 184:10; 200:4; 204:
22; 208:42; 216:21; 222:4; 226:8; 244:
13; 250:41; 256:6,19; 258:10; 264:22;
270:8,11,12; 286:16,43
causare 136:33; 144:33,39,42,45; 146:11,
12; 154:47
causator 146:30
Caym 66:40
cedere 78:28; 154:5; 162:7; 176:13;
286:40
celeriter 286:12
cellula 74:44
censere 154:16
cernere 104:28; 114:21; 116:18,32; 120:
33; 122:25; 130:1,19; 132:14; 134:22;
136:12; 150:26; 178:18; 180:38; 188:10;
194:36; 198:32; 202:39; 212:1,19; 234:
18; 246:9; 278:20; 286:8
certitudo 250:23
certus 70:22; 86:8; 98:18; 104:3; 106:35;
128:47; 178:37; 184:16; 188:44; 190:33;
196:42,43,44; 226:4,6; 242:7; 250:22,
23,25,38; 256:5; 272:40; 274:1; 280:
11,15,17
cessare 78:10; 288:12
chacephaton 268:2
c(h)oma 96:35,38; 98:21
chorus 110:6
cif(f)ra 256:6,9,26,28
circulum 250:39
circumdare 176:25,35,41; 178:15
circumstantia 178:28; 250:43
cisma 266:37,43,44,45; 268:11,17,20,22
clarescare 250:3
clausa 242:10; 222:35
cleare 284:19
clemens 288:37
clericus 64:2; 74:33; 192:4,22,39;
276:38;
clerus 80:19
coadiungere 80:1; 104:29; 130:3; 146:12;
158:27; 172:34; 178:32; 180:29; 250:17
coaptatio 224:19
coartare 280:12,17; 286:26
cogere 128:23,24,31; 148:38; 248:34,36
cognitio 102:17,26; 110:45; 118:14; 162:
16; 194:3; 212:28; 220:14; 224:15; 236:
8,17; 242:7; 248:25; 268:5; 276:6; 282:
14,16; 286:29
cognoscere 78:45; 88:26; 92:7; 102:13;
132:26; 150:29; 160:13; 164:13,16; 170:
12; 174:4; 182:32; 194:31; 202:15; 224:
21,25; 268:4; 282:15; 286:31
cohaerere 216:13
collateralis 186:30
colligare 88:6; 94:31; 116:16; 134:39;
170:30; 246:4
collisio 244:18
collocare 160:26; 168:3; 262:6
colloquare 80:30

color 68:27; 74:26; 76:1,6,21,28; 108:40;
170:36; 206:26,34; 208:31; 222:16; 266:
38; 272:19
columpna 188:4
comes 278:17
comitare 246:39; 276:31
commemoratio 76:4; 288:13,25; 288:26
commendabilis 64:15; 74:37; 76:33; 190:
45; 192:12
commendare 66:43; 74:44; 76:29; 236:39
commodus 64:14; 76:5; 78:45
communis 72:36; 80:20; 96:3; 100:40; 132:
30,33; 162:8; 186:14
communiter 100:38; 146:17; 150:20; 216:6;
224:25
comparare 96:31; 168:37; 256:6
comparatio 106:20
compati 78:40; 80:16; 258:17,19
compellere 212:25
compendium 192:44; 288:21,28
compendiose 74:42
competens 108:40; 114:24; 124:29; 142:21;
154:39,46; 178:38; 216:14; 266:40
compilare 64:2,27; 68:24,26; 74:42,43;
78:45; 104:11,14; 116:21; 124:6; 182:32;
184:31; 190:44; 214:12; 222:33; 258:9;
268:23; 288:5,27,29
complere 144:15; 166:40; 180:18; 268:6;
288:16,21,27;
complexio 66:8
componere 74:1; 106:18; 164:23; 170:31;
184:22,29; 212:31,32; 214:1,10,16,22;
216:10; 218:1,13,22; 224:22; 234:35,42;
236:2,13,16; 238:31; 254:25; 266:4;
274:13
compositio 86:8; 92:43; 162:5; 164:26;
182:17,19; 72:25; 274:13;
compositor 72:22; 254:41
compositus 64:4; 66:17; 82:8,10; 84:5,8;
86:23,24; 88:21,42; 90:12,21; 92:44; 98:
16; 106:7; 110:44; 112:1,3; 118:24,34;
120:6,8,22,33,40,42;134:4,5,6,9,10,30,
36,37,38; 136:33; 140:15; 142:41; 144:
33,40; 154:4,18,20,21,31,38; 156:21;
158:26,28,30,40,46; 164:17,35; 166:17;
168:42; 170:4,38; 172:7; 174:2; 176:15;
178:18; 182:11,21,23,30,32,36,38,40,45,
46; 184:2; 186:47; 188:2,11;
194:11,12,13,14; 196:10; 198:1,22; 212:
5,41; 214:38; 216:22; 224:42,43; 228:31;
236:40; 238:39; 244:27,33; 246:17; 250:
4; 254:24,28,33
compre(he)ndere 66:1; 96:33; 108:23; 112:
41; 160:24; 174:40; 190:2; 216:44; 248:
19; 250:31; 262:36,38; 272:24;72:15;
274:39
computare 196:5
concedere 80:40,41; 94:28; 104:10; 106:
13; 128:17,30; 130:7; 136:15,16; 144:
26,35; 160:27; 164:21,25; 196:36; 198:
34; 214:13; 250:7
concludere 74:32; 104:12; 146:5; 168:40;
186:31; 250:32; 252:36; 278:15
conclusio 250:10
concordanter 258:13
concordantia 86:21; 96:29,36; 150:30;
258:15,16,21,23,24; 260:5,18,23,28,30,
35,42;262:2,6,10,13,39;264:1,8,19,27,
43; 266:2,7,10,17,22,24,29,32,33,38,39,
42; 268:13,15; 270:19; 272:5,10,12,19,
32; 274:16,38; 282:4; 284:8,13,33; 286:
7,31,34

JEREMY YUDKIN is a professor of music in the School for the Arts at Boston University. He has written numerous papers and articles on aspects of medieval music theory. His books include translations of the treatise of Anonymous IV and the chapter on music in the sixteenth-century schoolbook known as Paedagogus. His latest book is *Music in Medieval Europe*.